W9-BLI-914

TRUMPOCALYPSE

TRUMPOCALYPSE

THE END-TIMES PRESIDENT, A BATTLE AGAINST THE GLOBALIST ELITE, AND THE COUNTDOWN TO ARMAGEDDON

Part II in The Babylon Code Series

PAUL McGUIRE AND TROY ANDERSON

FaithWords

NEW YORK   NASHVILLE

Copyright © 2018 by Paul McGuire, PhD, and Troy Anderson

Cover design by Bruce Gore | Gore Studio, Inc. Cover copyright © 2018 by Hachette Book Group, Inc.

Hachette Book Group supports the right to free expression and the value of copyright. The purpose of copyright is to encourage writers and artists to produce the creative works that enrich our culture.

The scanning, uploading, and distribution of this book without permission is a theft of the authors' intellectual property. If you would like permission to use material from the book (other than for review purposes), please contact permissions@hbgusa.com. Thank you for your support of the authors' rights.

FaithWords
Hachette Book Group
1290 Avenue of the Americas, New York, NY 10104
faithwords.com
twitter.com/faithwords

First Edition: January 2018

FaithWords is a division of Hachette Book Group, Inc. The FaithWords name and logo are trademarks of Hachette Book Group, Inc.

The publisher is not responsible for websites (or their content) that are not owned by the publisher.

The Hachette Speakers Bureau provides a wide range of authors for speaking events. To find out more, go to www.hachettespeakersbureau.com or call (866) 376-6591.

Paul McGuire, PhD, and Troy Anderson are represented by Alive Literary Agency, 7680 Goddard Street, Suite 200, Colorado Springs, CO 80920, www.aliveliterary.com.

Scripture quotations marked (KJV) are taken from the King James Version of the Bible.

Scripture quotations marked (NKJV) are taken from the New King James Version®. Copyright © 1982 by Thomas Nelson, Inc. Used by permission. All rights reserved.

Scripture quotations marked (NIV) are taken from the Holy Bible, New International Version. Copyright © 1973, 1978, 1984, 2011 by Biblica, Inc. Used by permission of Zondervan. All rights reserved worldwide. (www.zondervan.com)

Scripture quotations marked (MEV) from *The Modern English Version*. Copyright © 2014 by Military Bible Association. Used by permission.

Scripture quotations marked (ESV) from *The Holy Bible, English Standard Version. ESV ® Permanent Text Edition® (2016)*. Copyright © 2001 by Crossway Bibles, a publishing ministry of Good News Publishers. Used by permission.

Scriptures noted (NASB) are taken from the New American Standard Bible®, copyright © 1960, 1962, 1963, 1968, 1972, 1975, 1977, 1995 by The Lockman Foundation. Used by permission.

Library of Congress Control Number: 2017956473

ISBNs: 978-1-4789-9359-9 (hardcover), 978-1-4789-9361-2 (ebook)

Printed in the United States of America

LSC-C

10 9 8 7 6 5 4

We dedicate Trumpocalypse *to every person who chose not to go along with "the program" or "business as usual." This book is dedicated to all those who chose to obey their consciences before God and stand up and do what was and is right. We dedicate this book to all those heroes who demonstrated quiet courage when no one was looking and to all those who demonstrated courage in plain sight, because both are needed.*

Contents

Contents

PART III: NINEVEH MOMENT

TRUMPOCALYPSE

Introduction

The God Factor

Did God show up? In watching the news after the election, the secular media keep asking "How did this happen?" "What went wrong?" "How did we miss this?" Some are in shock. Political pundits are stunned. Many thought the Trump/Pence ticket didn't have a chance. None of them understand the God-factor.

—FRANKLIN GRAHAM, PRESIDENT OF THE
BILLY GRAHAM EVANGELISTIC ASSOCIATION[1]

It's the riveting prophetic mystery of the unprecedented times we find ourselves in.

On November 8, 2016—a date political theorist Noam Chomsky believes "might turn out to be one of the most important in human history"—Americans elected Donald John Trump as the forty-fifth president of the United States, sending shock waves around the world.[2]

The stunning victory of "the chaos candidate" not only confounded the predictions of pundits and pollsters but also created an eschatological mind-twister for students of the Apocalypse who are convinced the world is on the fast track to the end of human civilization.[3]

Many are now asking: Will President Trump guide America and the free world through a series of major crises as the biblical end-time narrative unfolds, as many people with prophetic gifts are predicting, or will he trigger the "Trumpocalypse"—the media meme for concerns that Trump's presidency will result in World War III and nuclear Armageddon?

Since his thunderbolt election, Trump's presidency has ignited end-time mania among Christians, Jews, Muslims, New Age adherents, and others curious as to how his presidency may fit into an increasingly mystifying prophetic puzzle, and whether the controversial and bombastic billionaire could paradoxically be a "John the Baptist" figure who will help usher in the "Messiah" and ultimately the Second Coming.[4]

"There have been at least a dozen Jewish rabbis who have said the Messiah is on Earth now, he's been identified, and he's soon going to make himself known," noted Thomas R. Horn, a bestselling prophecy author and chief executive officer of SkyWatchTV. "They called on Trump and [Russian president Vladimir] Putin to use their power to rebuild the Temple and reinstitute Temple service. I'm not saying that they think Trump is the Messiah. What I think is that most of the rabbis think he's John the Baptist and the Messiah is about to appear. He's the forerunner."[5]

The months leading up to the historic election were marked by a proliferation of prophecies about the "end-times president"—ranging from French seer Nostradamus's purported prediction that the election of a "shameless, audacious bawler" would lead to the end of the world to business consultant Lance Wallnau's belief that God raised Trump up to serve as a "wrecking ball to the spirit of political correctness" and as a "wild card that messes up the elite globalists' insider game."[6]

Throughout the 2016 presidential race, the world became intensely fascinated with the prophecies involving Trump and former U.S. secretary of state Hillary Clinton and how a series of seemingly unrelated events—the populist uprising against the globalist elite and an explosion in occult phenomena—align with what prophecy scholars believe is a convergence in end-time markers.

When the *Economist*—a prestigious magazine famed for its annual predictions—published "The World in 2017" cover article featuring eight tarot cards, including a Judgment card with Trump seated atop the world, wrapped in an American flag and holding instruments of royal coronation, the oracular cryptogram of Trump's presidency became what is arguably the paramount question of our time.[7]

"[*The Economist*] also happens to be owned by the Rothschild family and has a knack for touching on Illuminist pictures, hints, and outright disclosures guaranteed to make conspiracy theorists do a double-take," explained S. Douglas Woodward, an Oracle and Microsoft executive and prophecy expert. "This year it has truly outdone itself. (By the way in 1988 the magazine predicted on its cover that in 2018 there would be a one-world government with a global currency and singular economic system. That is sure to pique any Bible prophecy buff's interest.)"[8]

In *Trumpocalypse*, the sequel to our bestselling globalism exposé, *The Babylon Code: Solving the Bible's Greatest End-Times Mystery*, we've uncovered exclusive and explosive information about the prophetic significance of Trump's presidency and what it means for America's future, the world's future, and your future. In these pages, we'll explore:

- The enigmatic prophecies and "biblical codes" involving Trump.
- The hidden link to unfolding end-time events and the "unraveling."
- The revolution against the globalist elite that began with Brexit and culminated with Trump's election.
- "The coming crash" and global economic "reset" announced by International Monetary Fund officials.
- The occult elite's secret plan for humanity and campaign of mass deception.
- A high-level plot to assassinate the president.
- Why Trump and millions of "deplorables" are fighting to stop the hidden agenda of the Establishment—now largely controlling both

political parties—that is making the "1 percent" even richer while working- and middle-class people watch their incomes and net worths flatline or plummet.

- The president's enigmatic link to plans to rebuild the Third Temple in Jerusalem and broker the Israeli-Palestinian peace deal.

Featuring over fifty exclusive interviews with highly respected geopolitical, economic, and military affairs experts; prominent faith leaders; and biblical scholars, *Trumpocalypse* reveals the results of a two-and-a-half-year journalistic investigation that unearthed answers to the questions many have about Trump's presidency and its nexus to unfolding prophetic events; the dangers of globalization; the impact the economic "reset" will have on your finances and life; the initial rollout of microchip implants for workers worldwide; stunning revelations about the Illuminati's secret plans for humanity; a series of catastrophic, world-altering crises that many believe Trump will face during his time in office; and whether Trump could paradoxically help usher in the great, end-times revival amid the prophesied "shaking" that will radically change all our lives.

We'll also address the concerns of critics who believe Trump could be a "Manchurian candidate" that the globalist elite have "deviously put up"—with or without his knowledge—to help make a "giant stride in the direction of a 'New World Order' in which America will be reduced to a mere satrapy in a grandiose scheme of totalitarian 'global governance'" preceded by a debt-fueled economic implosion that will make the Great Depression seem like a period of prosperity.[9]

Trumpocalypse or Reprieve?

Our investigation comes amid a global debate about Trump's presidency and the fate of humanity. Before and after the election, the media and progressives expressed concerns about what they coined the "Trumpocalypse," while faith leaders and conservatives described Trump's presidency as a "reprieve" or the "Nineveh Moment" foreseen by world-renowned evangelist Billy Graham.[10]

The *Urban Dictionary* defined "Trumpocalypse" as the "catastrophic destruction or damage of civilization following the election of Donald Trump." The "Trumpocalypse" meme and Twitter hashtag captured the zeitgeist of the world regarding Trump's election, an event the *New York Times* described as a "stunning repudiation of the Establishment."[11]

Amid headlines in the *Washington Post* such as "The Horsemen of the Trumpocalypse," former President Barack Obama and others expressed alarm at handing the "nuclear codes" over to a neophyte politician whose personality—as profiled in the *Atlantic*—is marked by "sky-high extroversion combined with off-the-chart low agreeableness" and anger at his "emotional core." "How can you trust him with the nuclear codes?" Obama said at a rally in Durham, North Carolina, shortly before the election. "You can't do it."[12]

Chomsky went further, arguing that the Republican Party—now in control of the presidency and both the House and Senate—has become the "most dangerous organization in world history" and is "dedicated to racing as rapidly as possible to destruction of organized human life… Similar observations held for the other huge issue concerning human survival; the threat of nuclear destruction, which has been looming over our heads for seventy years and is now increasing."[13]

Frank von Hippel, a nuclear physicist and professor of public and international affairs emeritus at Princeton University, believes the "irresponsibility, ignorance, and impulsiveness" of Trump create an increased danger of a nuclear conflagration over the next decade that could result in "a chance of a third of us blowing up the world."[14]

Near the end of Trump's first week in office, the Bulletin of the Atomic Scientists voted to move the hands of the Doomsday Clock to two and a half minutes to midnight—the closest the clock has been to midnight since 1953 when the first hydrogen bomb was tested. The scientists said world leaders have failed to come to grips with humanity's most pressing existential threats: nuclear weapons and climate change. "As we marked the seventieth anniversary of the Doomsday Clock, this year's clock deliberations felt more urgent than usual...as trusted sources of information came under attack, fake news was on the rise, and words were used by a president-elect of the United States in cavalier and often reckless ways to address the twin threats of nuclear weapons and climate change," opined the organization's executive director, Rachel Bronson.[15]

As we noted in *The Babylon Code*, a growing number of physicists, mathematicians, computer scientists, economists, biologists, and philosophers at Oxford, Cambridge, MIT, and the University of California, Berkeley believe the world needs to start thinking seriously about the threat of human extinction. Oxford University's Future of Humanity Institute releases annual reports addressing "one of the most important issues of our age—global catastrophic risk." The reports explore the threat of nuclear war, a global pandemic, catastrophic climate change, and even a "global totalitarian state." A nuclear conflict is considered one of the top threats.[16]

In dozens of interviews for *Trumpocalypse*, faith leaders and prophecy scholars said they believe the world is in the final countdown to the Apocalypse. They believe the world is facing unparalleled dangers, including the highest risk of nuclear conflict since the Cold War. As evidence, they cite the recent nuclear showdown between Trump and North Korean leader Kim Jong-un, who made repeated threats to reduce the United States to "ashes"—generating global headlines and angst and reigniting fears of a Third World War. In September 2017, Trump said at the United Nations that unless Kim Jong-un backs down, "We will have no choice than to totally destroy North Korea."[17]

But rather than focusing on Trump's seemingly unpredictable

personality, many view his election—perhaps one of the greatest political feats in modern history—as a divine reprieve. "The surprise election of Donald Trump offers hope to stop, reverse, and overturn many of these developments [the redefinition of marriage, war on religious freedom, and deterioration of America's relationship with Israel]," explained Rabbi Jonathan Cahn, the *New York Times* bestselling author who was named by *Charisma* magazine as one of the top forty spiritual leaders of the last forty years. "Thus, it can provide a major window for the gospel and revival."[18]

In the time leading up to the election, Franklin Graham learned that hundreds of thousands of Christians were praying for America: "This year they came out to every state capitol to pray for this election and for the future of America. Prayer groups were started. Families prayed. Churches prayed. Then Christians went to the polls, and God showed up. While the media scratches their heads, and tries to understand how this happened, I believe that God's hand intervened [on election night] to stop the godless, atheistic progressive agenda from taking control of our country."[19]

In recent decades, and largely during the Obama administration, many Americans watched with dismay as their nation—one the Pilgrims dedicated to God in the Mayflower Compact four centuries ago—underwent a radical and malevolent transformation.

Many trace the beginning of this downward slide to the 1962 U.S. Supreme Court decision removing prayer from schools, followed by the 1973 decision legalizing abortion. In the ensuing decades, as millions of babies died on the altars of lust and selfish convenience, God was largely jettisoned from most spheres of influence—government, media, entertainment, education, and business. Meanwhile, as wickedness took its toll, the national debt soared and Christians, whose biblical views weren't welcome in an increasingly secular and occult-enmeshed society, experienced soft persecution while America spiraled downward toward darkness. Then, near the end of Obama's second term, the Supreme Court legalized same-sex marriage, and Obama celebrated by lighting up the White House in rainbow colors.

"The election [of Trump] was a complete repudiation of Barack Obama: his fantasy world of political correctness, the politicization of the Justice Department and the IRS, an out-of-control EPA, his neutering of the military, his nonsupport of the police and his fixation on things like transgender bathrooms," *New York Times* columnist Maureen Dowd, quoting her brother, wrote in her column shortly after Thanksgiving of 2016. "Since he became president, his party has lost sixty-three House seats, ten Senate seats and fourteen governorships. The country has signaled strongly in the last two midterms that they were not happy. The Dems' answer was to give them more of the same from a person they did not like or trust. Preaching—and pandering—with a message of inclusion, the Democrats have instead become a party where incivility and bad manners are taken for granted, rudeness is routine, religion is mocked and there is absolutely no respect for a differing opinion."[20]

A New "Golden Age"?

While some faith leaders view Trump's election as a "reprieve"—perhaps a temporary pause in God's prophetic time clock—the *Washington Post* observed that conservatives saw it as new "golden age for Republicans on Capitol Hill." "President-elect Donald Trump's stunning victory has delivered to GOP congressional leaders the gift they dreamed of even if they never quite believed it was within reach: A Republican president to sign Republican bills passed by a uniformly Republican Congress." As the results were posted on election night, Trump said it was "time to bind the wounds," that he would be a "president for all Americans," and that "the forgotten people" of the country would be "forgotten no longer." In the wake of the election, conservatives and faith leaders pointed out that he would appoint one and perhaps more conservative justices to the Supreme Court—reshaping the nation's highest court for decades to come. In early 2017, the U.S. Senate approved Trump's first nominee to the high court, federal judge Neil Gorsuch, to replace Justice Antonin Scalia.[21]

Trump's election brought a wave of optimism to conservative America and was described as "the greatest miracle in the history of U.S. politics." Prior to the election, Americans were deeply pessimistic about the future, with economic experts predicting a historic stock market crash and economic downturn if Trump won. Instead, Trump's election was followed by a stock market rally with the dollar once again becoming the strongest currency in the world—hitting its highest level since March 2003. A Bloomberg poll found that "in some cases Americans are the most hopeful they have been in more than a decade." Meanwhile, the percentage of Americans who said they believe the United States would experience "continuous good times" in the immediate future rose to 46 percent.[22]

Jan Markell, founder of Olive Tree Ministries and host of the nationally syndicated *Understanding the Times* radio show, wrote an intriguing article, "So Is the Rapture Now on Hold?" "Are happy days here again?" Markell asked rhetorically. "I am sensing that even Rapture-watching believers, some anyway, now think that event is delayed while America returns to prosperity. Thanks to the 2016 election results, we may now return to the role of international leader. A report [following the presidential election] said that in the wake of Brexit and Donald Trump, the European Union may fall apart. Have prophecy watchers been proven wrong? Neither of these fit into the presumed 'agenda.'"[23]

The Prophesied "Unraveling"

Despite initial euphoria among Christians and conservatives, Trump's election doesn't mean the world's colossal problems—unparalleled levels of national, corporate, and consumer debt exceeding $217 trillion globally; widespread government corruption; the growing threat of a catastrophic war, to name a few—have somehow magically disappeared.[24]

A strange and perplexing chaos is enveloping the planet, what some are calling the "unraveling," with the strong potential to bring about major crises—ranging from global financial cataclysm to nuclear war to a potential peace deal that could engulf the Middle East in conflict. President Trump will likely face these and other critical developments during his time in office.

The all-important factor in these scenarios is the leadership, decisions, and policies of the Trump administration. Most liberals and progressives fear Trump is emotionally unstable, impulsive, arrogant, narcissistic, and almost fascist-like in his political beliefs. They are afraid he will overreact and order the launch of nuclear missiles into enemy territories in a crisis—provoking a nuclear exchange that escalates into World War III.

Since Trump's election, politicians, celebrities, and others have expressed concerns that he will abuse his power as president and become a dictator in the style of Adolf Hitler. They are concerned he will gain control of the Christian, conservative, and alt-right media; conduct Joseph McCarthy–like communist witch hunts; and use the populist movement to radically transform America into a military fascist police state. "Democracy is now in crisis," billionaire investor George Soros, a major funder of the Democratic Party, wrote in his *Project Syndicate* column. "Even the U.S., the world's leading democracy, elected a con artist and would-be dictator as its president." Meanwhile, many Americans—especially members of the LGBT community, minorities, and youth—are worried that Trump is the champion of angry, white, working- and middle-class Americans, especially "angry white men" who desire payback.[25]

The question is this: Is President Trump really this budding right-wing dictator who is dangerously impulsive and would press the button in a fit of rage and launch World War III? Or despite his bombastic style and flame-throwing rhetoric, is Trump—a highly successful entrepreneur who built a global business empire—a strategic thinker who carefully considers the consequences of his decisions and actions and is highly pragmatic versus ideological?

In this book, we'll delve into little-known and previously unrevealed details about Trump's life that will give us an indication of what we can expect: *Trumpocalypse* or "Reprieve."

Eight Signs of Coming Mega-Disruption

Trump's presidency comes at a time of mega-disruption in America—a nation that is deeply divided and was on the verge of civil unrest following the election and inauguration protests when Madonna mused about "blowing up the White House." Trump's rise to power also comes at a time of growing geopolitical and economic instability worldwide. The political, military, financial, and prophetic experts interviewed for *Trumpocalypse* foresee a myriad of threats that will likely impact all our lives in unprecedented ways.[26] This is a list of eight of the most critical and potentially dangerous ones:

1. **The high probability of a military or terrorist attack**, including an electromagnetic pulse (EMP) or weapon of mass destruction attack, on the United States far greater in magnitude than the terrorist attacks of September 11, 2001. Sid Roth, host of the popular television show *It's Supernatural!*, says he believes Trump will guide America through an unparalleled crisis during his time in office. "What I believe is that somewhere in his serving time America will bump into a crisis that no one can solve," Roth says. "What it is, I don't know. It could be a nuclear invasion. But there will be something horrific that is going to happen

while he's in the White House." Before the election, many Christian leaders prophesied that God had raised up Trump to lead the nation through a time of crisis.[27]

2. **A series of high-profile attacks**, including cyber attacks, against major American institutions such as the stock market, government, military, utility companies, and banking and financial institutions.

3. **A military conflict involving North Korea, Russia, Iran, Syria, and China**, along with the United States, its Indo-Asia-Pacific allies, NATO, European nations, and Israel. A serious conflict, or even a thermonuclear war, could erupt between North Korea and America, in the region of Ukraine, Syria, and Russia, or in the Middle East. This could result in catastrophic destruction and loss of life, crash the global economy, and destabilize the world's geopolitical balance. A July 2017 NBC News/Survey Monkey National Security Poll found that 76 percent of Americans are worried the United States will become involved in a major war over the next four years. That's up 10 percent from February 2017. Americans believe North Korea poses the greatest immediate danger (41 percent) compared to ISIS (28 percent) and Russia (18 percent).[28]

4. **A worldwide economic crisis** involving the crash of the dollar and a multitrillion-dollar derivatives blowout. In preparation for a possible "crackup of civilization" involving an American financial collapse, revolt against the elite, or a Super-EMP attack, wealthy Americans from Silicon Valley to New York are buying property in New Zealand. Foreigners bought over 1,400 square miles of property in New Zealand in the first ten months of 2016, a fourfold increase over the same period in the prior year. In the seven days following Trump's election, 13,401 Americans registered with New Zealand's immigration authorities as a first

step toward seeking residency—seventeen times the normal rate. In an extensive article in the *New Yorker* called "Doomsday Prep for the Super-Rich," the cofounder of Reddit, a news aggregation site, estimated that over half of Silicon Valley insiders are prepping for doomsday and many view New Zealand as a "utopia" to ride out the Apocalypse. The article cited a *National Geographic* survey that found 40 percent of Americans believe stockpiling supplies or building a bomb shelter is a wiser investment today than a 401(k) plan.[29]

5. **A series of environmental crises or catastrophic disasters** such as the eruption of massive earthquakes or volcanoes along the Ring of Fire in the Pacific Rim that stretches twenty-five thousand miles in a horseshoe shape from New Zealand to Japan, over to Alaska, and down to California and South America. New research found a mega-quake of magnitude 8.3 could unzip all at once along the entire eight-hundred-mile San Andreas Fault in California, unleashing an "alarming scenario of destruction." Meanwhile, volcanoes Turrialba in Costa Rica, Pavlof in Alaska, Campi Flegrei in Italy, Sakurajima in Japan, and Popocatepetl in Mexico, among others, are reawakening—setting off "alarm among the scientist community that warns about a chain of imminent eruptions." If the Yellowstone supervolcano erupts, which scientists are increasingly concerned about, it would spew vast quantities of sulfur dioxide and other gases into the atmosphere, leading to climate cooling that could last up to a decade and cause widespread crop losses and famine.[30]

6. **A civil war in America** beginning with riots, demonstrations, and violent confrontations between police and demonstrators and escalating into race wars and warfare between liberal and conservative parts of the nation, along with warfare between population centers composed of different ethnic and racial groups.

7. **The rebuilding of the Jewish Temple** and the possibility of an Israeli-Palestinian peace agreement. Trump is interested in brokering a peace treaty between Israel and Palestine—describing it as "the ultimate deal." His son-in-law and senior adviser, Jared Kushner, who is from an Orthodox Jewish family and was named by *Time* as one of its one hundred most influential people, is working to negotiate the deal. Trump, a real estate mogul and developer, could play a key role in rebuilding the Third Temple in Jerusalem. A few days after the election, the nascent Sanhedrin sent a letter to Putin and Trump asking them to join forces and act as "modern-day Cyrus figures" in rebuilding the Jewish Temple. If Trump successfully closes the deal to rebuild the Temple—after all, he's the author of *The Art of the Deal*—the potential exists for a temporal peace between Israel and its neighbors. If this happens, it could be a fulfillment of 1 Thessalonians 5:3, which says, "While people are saying, 'Peace and safety,' destruction will come on them suddenly, as labor pains on a pregnant woman, and they will not escape." From a prophetic perspective, this biblical verse is a warning that could involve the Antichrist and the seven-year Tribulation period. A temporal time of peace and safety during the first half of the Tribulation, the Bible says, would be followed by intense persecution of the Jews, unparalleled global disasters, famine, and war that would wipe out three-quarters of all life on the earth—culminating in the Battle of Armageddon and the second coming of Christ. This wouldn't mean that Trump is the Antichrist, but it could mean that he, as with any powerful world leader, especially an American president, could be used by powerful, secretive forces without knowing it.[31]

8. **Tensions between Israel, militant Muslim nations, and the Palestinians** could erupt at any time, and Trump's efforts could

easily backfire if he is too ambitious with a potential peace agreement. The treaty could fall apart and create a new Middle Eastern conflict. The traditional location of the ancient Jewish temples is in the Temple Mount area where the Muslim Dome of the Rock shrine is located. Tampering with the Dome of the Rock could easily ignite the Third World War.

Historic Impact on the American Psyche

Trump's presidential campaign and election have had a historic impact on the American psyche. His enormous force of charisma and personality, along with his economic, political, and spiritual beliefs, has resulted in a seismic shift in the consciousness of America.

The very fact that Trump won the election against such formidable opposition—including attacks by the media, the Republican elite and their political dynasties like the Bush family, powerful globalists, multinational corporations, tech giants, Hollywood celebrities, and other influential players—is unprecedented in American politics.

Many experts, including political prognosticators and media, were bollixed by what happened. From the beginning, they seemed to view it as a given that Clinton would win the election until the final hours on election night when Trump won in the Electoral College.

Trump emerged victorious despite the endless attacks, including the media's collusion with Clinton and the Democratic Party, as revealed by the anti-secrecy website WikiLeaks. During the campaign, WikiLeaks revealed that several prominent media figures were working closely with the Clinton campaign and that cable news employees shared questions with Clinton in advance of televised town hall events and debates.[32]

But instead of admitting they were wrong, the media continued to deny and obfuscate. Even after the election, they created a series of stunning falsehoods based on Hitler's theory of the "big lie," accusing the alternative media, including Matt Drudge—founder of the popular Drudge Report—of acting as Russian agents or unknowingly passing on Russian propaganda.[33] The claim was ridiculous, and honest members of the media, along with most Americans, saw through the hype of "fake news."

Near the end of the campaign, a Gallup survey found that America's trust and confidence in the mass media "to report the news fully, accurately and fairly" had dropped to its lowest level in Gallup polling history. Only 32 percent of Americans said they had a great deal or a fair amount of trust in the media, down from a high of 72 percent in 1976 in the wake of widely lauded examples of investigative journalism involving the Watergate scandal and Vietnam. Meanwhile, Republicans who said they trust the media plummeted to 14 percent, down from 32 percent only a year earlier. Another survey using data gathered by the Media Insight Project, a partnership between the Associated Press–NORC Center for Public Affairs Research and the American Press Institute, found only 6 percent of people have a "great deal of confidence" in the press.[34]

Speaking of this poll, Woodward says, "There is a general sentiment amongst most of the middle class that the mainstream media is in fact in the tank with the globalists, with the elite, with the Establishment. People are getting this notion that there is a mind control project in America and the mind control project is essentially not to tell us the truth about what is really going on, but to feed us lies."[35]

A subsequent NPR/PBS poll released in the summer of 2017 found more Americans trust the White House than the mainstream media. Of those surveyed, 37 percent said they trust the Trump administration, compared to 30 percent for the media and 29 percent for Congress. More than half (56 percent) of Democrats expressed faith in the media, but only 9 percent of Republicans did.[36]

Taking on the Establishment

For decades, millions of evangelical Christians have been the targets of religious harassment and discrimination by the media, Hollywood, government, and the public educational system. While just about every other group in America has enjoyed special privileges and protections, Bible-believing Christians have been openly attacked, mocked, and forced by the government, law enforcement, and employers to do things that violate their faith. Many have been subjected to shaming, "hate speech hysteria," loss of employment, and other negative experiences due to their Christian beliefs.[37]

One of the most significant aspects of Trump's presidential campaign is that he challenged the failing Establishment with ideas based on ones developed at our nation's founding—first by the Pilgrims and later by our Founding Fathers. These revolutionary heroes carefully crafted the U.S. Bill of Rights to protect Americans—at the time from British tyranny—from the very types of abuses taking place today. These concepts—as outlined in the Declaration of Independence that "all men are created equal, that they are endowed by their Creator with certain unalienable Rights"—are the foundation of the American experiment. America traces its origins to the religious separatists, the Pilgrims, who fled persecution from England on the Mayflower in 1620 in search of religious freedom in the New World. This is one of the reasons why Trump's campaign slogan "Make America Great Again" deeply resonated in the hearts and minds of average Americans.

Trump's astonishing rise to power came at the right time for many people. He's an outsider who never held political office and a successful businessman who had to produce actual results in the real world, not just play political games. He was free to speak candidly about the true state of our political system and government—one that is far more corrupt and ineffective than most people realized. Trump shined a light into the darkness. When he walked onstage during the debates, it was obvious this was not the same old, same old everyone was used to. Trump's body language, facial expressions, and tough-guy remarks from his upbringing in Queens, New York, lit the stages and the American people on fire. But most of all, Trump made it obvious that the system was incompetent, crooked, and rigged.

In one of his most memorable speeches shortly before the election, Trump said the "Clinton machine" had directed a worldwide network that rigged the economy against the working class.

> It's a global power structure that is responsible for the economic decisions that have robbed our working class, stripped our country of its wealth and put that money into the pockets of a handful of large corporations and political entities... The Clinton machine is at the center of this power structure. We've seen this firsthand in the WikiLeaks documents, in which Hillary Clinton meets in secret with international banks to plot the destruction of U.S. sovereignty to enrich these global financial powers, her special interest friends, and her donors... This is a struggle for the survival of our nation... Our great civilization, here in America and across the civilized world, has come upon a moment of reckoning. We've seen it in the United Kingdom, where they voted to liberate themselves from global government and global trade deals, and global immigration deals that have destroyed many of those nations. But the central base of world political power is right here in America, and it is our corrupt political Establishment that is the greatest power behind the efforts at radical globalization and the disenfranchisement of working people.[38]

When Trump spoke, the light bulbs turned on in the heads of millions of Americans. They understood why after the last six decades of

Democrat vs. Republican politics that nothing had changed for the better and why countless millions of Americans were out of work as their jobs had been moved overseas, along with seventy thousand manufacturing plants relocated to China, Mexico, and other nations.[39]

Finally, the American people understood what they had always suspected: that the elite in both parties had secretly worked together to bamboozle them and enrich the people they were really working for—the globalist elite, multinational corporations, special interest groups, and big donors. The North American Free Trade Agreement (NAFTA), General Agreement on Tariffs and Trade (GATT), and Central America Free Trade Agreement (CAFTA) treaties, along with the proposed North American Union—one of ten regional unions proposed by the United Nations—were sold to the American people by prominent politicians as big job creators that would fuel an economic boom in America and globally.

But people aren't stupid. They suspected that the "1 percent," which Trump and his family, ironically, are a part of, would get rich beyond their wildest dreams, thanks to these trade treaties. They also knew that the American working and middle class of all racial and ethnic groups would become poorer because of this, and that's exactly what happened to many people who lost their jobs, homes, and families. During the race, Trump blew the lid off the way the system really works. "Our politicians have aggressively pursued a policy of globalization—moving our jobs, our wealth, and our factories to Mexico and overseas," Trump said. "Globalization has made the financial elite who donate to politicians very wealthy. But it has left millions of our workers with nothing but poverty and heartache."[40]

As Trump continued to educate the American people about the economic stacked deck, people began to see the evidence that much of what the government was in the business of doing was completely ineffective, incompetent, or directly harmful.

As Trump pointed out, the government and the politicians simply made one lousy deal after another—allowing nations such as China to cheat America repeatedly. Despite the military invasions of Iraq and Afghanistan—the most expensive wars in U.S. history, costing an estimated $4 trillion to $6 trillion—the threat of terrorism is greater than ever, and now the world has ISIS and other terrorist groups to contend with. Meanwhile, our borders were left wide open, allowing known criminals and military-age males from militant Muslim nations into our country with little vetting. This isn't just Obama's fault. The policies of previous administrations, both Republican and Democrat, have contributed to this mess too.[41]

In the wake of all this disorder and calamity, Trump, given his ability to connect with ordinary people, inspired millions of Americans to feel real hope, and to feel that there is a possibility that they can once again experience the American dream.

The Revolution Is Viral

What Trump has done with his campaign and election is to inspire a major shift in consciousness among millions of Americans. They no longer feel alone or that they are being suppressed and told to shut up or be sent home. They don't fear that they will be fined, arrested, or sent to jail for simply exercising their constitutional liberties. A new optimism, boldness, hope, and courage have invigorated the land. Who Trump is and what he stands for are contagious, and they have spread virally across America despite the continual deception, attacks, shaming, and labeling of Trump supporters as "deplorables" or consumers of Russian propaganda.

This buoyancy and fresh vision for America have also infused evangelical Christians with a new spirit. After years of having to hang their heads low just to survive, they witnessed a living example of one man who was brave, compassionate, and positive and had the guts to take on the most powerful political forces on earth. Trump demonstrated to millions of evangelical Christians that even if it seems you're outnumbered you can peacefully, intelligently, and positively push back. In the power of the Holy Spirit, you can stand up for your God and what you believe in.

On a consistent basis now, the more honest cable television networks are featuring reports of intelligent and highly educated Christians pushing back against the suppression of their constitutional rights of freedom of speech and religion. For the first time in many decades, a new Christian movement, what Franklin Graham calls the "Christian revolution," has begun. Christian students on college and high school campuses are standing up for their faith in positive, intelligent, peaceful, and yet bold ways. Ordinary workingmen and women are rising in this new spiritual revolution and are no longer allowing people and groups to harm their businesses or churches for simply expressing or adhering to their faith.[42]

Out of this Christian revolution, countless souls will be saved because God's people are no longer afraid to proclaim the gospel and lead people into a saving knowledge of Jesus Christ. This Christian revolution could be the beginning of a mighty biblical awakening—one that started mysteriously with a string of prophecies beginning a decade ago and culminated with the election of an enigmatic figure who became seventy years, seven months, and seven days old on his first full day in the White House—January 21, 2017.[43]

Curiously, the number seven—the most significant biblical number, infused with prophetic mysteries by the universe's infinite mathematician—envelops Trump's life and may point toward some type of destiny involving Israel.

Trump was born on June 14, 1945, seven hundred days before Israel became a nation. Israel was seventy-seven days old, seven hundred and seventy-seven days after Trump was born. Israel's seventieth birthday will arrive seven hundred days after Trump's seventieth birthday. Trump won the election on Israeli prime minister Benjamin Netanyahu's seventh year, seventh month, and seventh day in office. In addition to being seventy years, seven months, and seven days old on his first full day in office, this occurred during year 5777 on the Hebrew calendar.

Strange coincidences involving sevens also surround Vice President Mike Pence. He took office at age fifty-seven. The last minute of his fifty-seventh year took place one minute before the fiftieth anniversary of Jerusalem on June 7, 2017. Is it possible that Trump and Pence both have "special destinies ahead of them"? Michael Snyder, founder of *The Economic Collapse Blog*, asked in an article exploring this phenomenon.[44]

On a stirring inauguration day, as if on divine cue, Trump, a Presbyterian, placed his hand on two Bibles—one given to him by his mother just before his ninth birthday and another used by Abraham Lincoln in 1861—and took the oath of office. Then, as he approached the podium to deliver his inaugural address, it began to rain in a nation long beset by drought.

"Mr. President, in the Bible rain is a sign of God's blessing, and it started to rain, Mr. President, when you came to the platform," Franklin Graham said in his inaugural prayer. "And it's my prayer that God will bless you, your family, your administration, and may he bless America."[45]

Discover Your Destiny in the "Christian Revolution"

Trump's presidency comes amid a sense that a massive spiritual oppression has been lifted off America. Before the election, many Americans realized they were in a battle for the soul and survival of their country. They prayed, got involved, and voted and—against what seemed insurmountable odds—watched as Trump was elected in one of the biggest political upsets in history.

"I said to one of my friends that we dodged the bullet," says Jim Garlow, pastor at Skyline Church in San Diego and a member of Trump's evangelical advisory board. "He responded back to me: 'We dodged a nuclear warhead.' We were in the throes of complete destruction. If Hillary would have been elected and served eight years...there would have been pastors facing fines and perhaps even imprisonment for standing for the truth in Scripture...We had [in Trump's election] a miraculous intervention comparable to the crossing of the Red Sea."[46]

Yet the battle has only begun. Prophecy experts believe a phased unraveling of America and the world is under way that will lead to what the elite call the global economic "reset" and the rollout of microchip implants for people worldwide. At the same time, many faith leaders believe the greatest spiritual awakening ever will occur amid the coming "shaking."[47]

Trump, despite his imperfections, may paradoxically pave the way for this spiritual rejuvenation followed by the greatest event in history—the second coming of Christ.

We believe God has raised up Trump to fight the globalist elites and their plan to unleash the New World Order on humanity. We need to stand with and pray for our president, live righteous lives, and seek the Lord's guidance. As long as we do that, Trump will not be defeated by the dark forces aligned against him, and we believe God will break the New World Order, at least temporarily, because Jesus Christ is Lord.[48]

Throughout American history, great leaders from George Washington to Abraham Lincoln to Ronald Reagan have understood that a fierce battle is waging in the invisible realm. We are all called to fight in this spiritual war. But to prepare we must put on the "full armor of God" (Eph. 6:11 NIV) and gain a solid understanding of what is truly going on behind the scenes in our world and the sheer magnitude of the diabolical forces we're up against. Hosea 4:6 says, "My people are destroyed for lack of knowledge" (MEV). The apostle Paul warned us not to be ignorant of Satan's "devices" (2 Cor. 2:11). James told us to submit to God, resist the devil, and "he will flee from you" (James 4:7 MEV).

God is not finished with America, and he is using Trump to help fulfill its prophetic destiny to take the good news to the ends of the earth for one final, end-times revival. We need to blow the shofar—the biblical trumpet heralding the beginning of battle—loud and clear because Trump is standing with Israel in defiance of the powerful forces aligned against the apple of God's eye (Zech. 2:8).

Many have a sense of urgency and want to do their part in this "Christian revolution." It's time for a paradigm shift. By all indicators, the world is on the fast track to the fulfillment of major end-of-the-age events. But that doesn't mean God simply wants us to ride out the prophetic superstorm until we're supernaturally whisked off to heaven.

Dozens of faith leaders and prophecy experts interviewed for *Trumpocalypse* agree that we're in the season preceding events during the end of days. This is even more reason to get out of our comfort zones, stand up to the New World Order, and do our part in the end-times harvest many believe will usher over "one billion souls" into God's kingdom.[49]

Jesus told us, "Occupy until I come" (Luke 19:13 KJV). Deuteronomy 20:4 says, "For the Lord your God is the one who goes with you to fight for you against your enemies to give you victory" (NIV).

Perhaps you'd like to know how God might use your talents and skills during this momentous time in history. Join us and discover how to fulfill your destiny in what famed evangelist Billy Graham and others are calling the world's "Nineveh Moment."

Part I

THE TRUMPOCALYPSE

Chapter One

Trumpocalypse Now

There should be no fear. We are protected and we will always be protected. We will be protected by the great men and women of our military and law enforcement. And most importantly, we will be protected by God.

—PRESIDENT DONALD J. TRUMP, INAUGURAL SPEECH[1]

Trump's provocative posturing and unpredictability is now inspiring a fresh wave of panic on the left. Those who spoke with Vocativ have envisioned scenarios that could lead to military coups led by loyalists of the president-elect and internment camps packed with political opponents, bloody social unrest and an all-out civil or nuclear war. Sound bonkers? Perhaps. But, for many, so was the prospect of a President Trump.

—SHANE DIXON KAVANAUGH, VOCATIV

Trumpocalypse Now Scenario: It's a minute until midnight, and an aide to President Trump awakens him with the spine-chilling news no president wants to hear—NATO is reporting a potential nuclear detonation near the Ukraine border where forty thousand NATO troops were sent in response to Russia's intensifying aggression in the region.

Intelligence reports suggested Russia has been considering the use of tactical nuclear weapons to force NATO out of the area. Though still groggy, Trump recalls that Russian president Putin's military doctrine calls for the use of tactical nukes in the event NATO moves to annex Ukraine, and that Putin recently ordered a 50 percent increase in nuclear training drills of his Strategic Missile Troops.[2]

But Trump hasn't had the best relationship with the intelligence community, and he's not completely confident in the integrity of information—a problem dating back to intelligence reports regarding Russian hacking of the presidential election.

A classified message comes in from an intelligence agency. As he reads, his phone begins to beep, a knock comes upon the door, and he hears a familiar voice tense with extreme urgency saying, "Mr. President." The military aide with the nuclear "football" that allows him to order a nuclear strike comes into the room. The nuclear launch suitcase contains the equipment and decision-making papers to order a nuclear response. This includes a black book with a menu of strike options, a three-by-five-inch card with authentication codes to confirm presidential identity, a list of secure bunkers where he can take shelter, and instructions for the Emergency Alert System.[3]

Seconds later, Trump is speaking to several aides about satellite photos revealing that Russia has eight tactical nuke launchers not far from NATO troops in Ukraine. Trump's advisers have previously informed him that Eastern Europe is the most likely place where a crisis could escalate to the nuclear level, mostly because the United States has guaranteed the security of the former Soviet republics in the area since the Cold War.[4]

Trump's generals and the intelligence officials need more information before recommending a course of action. They haven't been able to reach Putin, who is vacationing at a remote mountain lake. Is this a show of force and a bluff to force NATO to withdraw shortly before an attack? Trump decides it's a show of force, but not a bluff, and if there is not some kind of withdrawal of forces, that Russia will launch its tactical nukes. If NATO fires on Russian troops or territories, Trump believes Russia will strike back harder with the expectation that NATO will quickly move out of the area.

But Trump also knows that numerous generals and intelligence heads have long been waiting for an opportunity to engage Russia militarily, and any actions by the United States that could be perceived as either weak or overly aggressive could ignite a regional thermonuclear war that could easily escalate into Armageddon.

Time ticks away and passionate, heated arguments erupt among his top advisers. As Trump assesses the situation, he ponders recent actions by the EU and the global community to punish Putin for defying requests to quit making confrontational statements and temper Russia's military buildup. Trump believes if he could get Putin on the phone privately, he could work this out. But he has been told by some of his advisers that Kremlin hard-liners deliberately planned for this to occur while Putin was out of reach so they could force a military confrontation. They don't believe the United States or the EU has the stomach for a nuclear conflict and will retreat. In short, Trump and his advisers conclude the hard-liners are running the show, and attempts at negotiation would be useless.

Trump orders everyone out of the room except for two of his closest generals and the aide with the nuclear football. He asks his generals whether a counterattack will force the Russian hard-liners to retreat or if that would escalate the conflict into a regional thermonuclear war. As the clock ticks, there is still no confirmation from NATO regarding the nuclear strike near the Ukraine border.

Trump is faced with the most daunting decision of his presidency— one that literally could decide the fate of humanity. As they await further information, Trump is deep in thought about some Bible prophecy passages he read in a book that pastors gave him during the election.

The verses spoke of the end times, the seven trumpet judgments, and how before those judgments, the prophet Ezekiel predicted a major war would break out involving Russia. Then following those judgments would come the Battle of Armageddon—the last, great world war of history. In a moment of private soul searching, Trump asks himself, *Am I about to push the button for the Apocalypse?*

Presidents of the Apocalypse

In all of humankind's war-riddled history, leaders never possessed the power to destroy the planet until recently. Since President Harry S. Truman ordered the first atomic bomb dropped on Hiroshima on August 6, 1945, all subsequent presidents from Dwight D. Eisenhower to Trump have been acutely aware of this power and have known of biblical prophecies regarding the end of days. Of these presidents, though, not all believed these prophecies would come true as the Bible predicts. George H. W. Bush thought the Apocalypse could be avoided with the establishment of the New World Order, as did Bill Clinton and Barack Obama. Obama believed the world could build a global community in which peace would prevail through organizations such as the United Nations. On the other hand, Ronald Reagan became a strong believer in Bible prophecy after he read Hal Lindsey's *The Late Great Planet Earth*. Reagan was so impacted by this book and the Bible that he began preparing the military for the Apocalypse. "Sometimes, I wonder if we are destined to witness Armageddon," Reagan wrote in his diary in 1981.[5] Many people around him thought he took the prophecies too seriously and that he might inadvertently usher in Armageddon.

Likewise, many people have questioned whether Trump might be too impulsive and, unable to restrain himself, push the nuclear button. Frank von Hippel says, "Part of the psychology for decades after the end of the Cold War was that [nuclear war] is crazy. [World leaders] wouldn't be so crazy as to launch nuclear weapons. I think that presumption is declining because Putin talks so much about having nuclear weapons, and now we have somebody in the White House who...you really can't discount anything he might do."[6]

Seth Baum, executive director of the Global Catastrophic Risk Institute, agrees that Trump's "impulsive, combative behavior" combined with difficult geopolitical challenges suggest the probability of nuclear war is "unusually high" now.[7] Among millennials, Jennifer Lawrence, who starred in the *Hunger Games* film series, told *Entertainment Weekly* before the election that she feared a real apocalypse if Trump became president: "My view on the election is cut-and-dried: If Donald Trump is president of the United States, it will be the end of the world."[8]

However, David Horowitz, a noted conservative commentator and *New York Times* bestselling author, disputes the contention by von Hippel, Obama, Clinton, Chomsky, Baum, and others that Trump is so mercurial and impulsive that he poses an existential threat to humanity. "I would be more concerned about Hillary [Clinton] who was the chief inspirer of Obama's aggression in Libya," Horowitz says. "[Obama] overthrew the government of Libya and created a base for Al Qaeda and ISIS. They made Libya into a failed state. They're reckless. The Democrats start wars."[9]

Clinton's election strategy involved claims that Trump couldn't be trusted with the nation's nuclear forces—a political tactic reminiscent of a similar one Democratic president Lyndon B. Johnson used against Republican Arizona senator Barry Goldwater in the 1964 presidential election. "The Democrats are shameless and totally unscrupulous when it comes to flinging accusations at their opponents," Horowitz says. "Why would Trump spend his life building and constructing [a business empire]? Wars are incredibly destructive. A nuclear war is even more so. The idea that he can't control himself is absurd...why would he want to destroy all that?"[10]

John Hogue, the quintessential scholar of the sixteenth-century

French seer Nostradamus, agrees with Horowitz's assessment. "Similarly, people thought that Ronald Reagan was going to destroy the world, that he was going to be too polarizing of an agent in America—and I felt then what I feel now about Trump—that the whole quality of the loose cannon [aspect about him] actually is going to put pressure on world leaders to be more sober and cautious and careful like they were in the 1980s [when Reagan gave his 'evil empire' speech about the former Soviet Union]."[11]

In this book we'll present a psychological and spiritual profile of Trump from a cross section of experts to determine if the concerns about what the media and progressives have coined the "Trumpocalypse" are legitimate. But one thing is certain regardless of who occupies the White House: The world has never been a more dangerous place.

Most Prophetic and Dangerous Time in History

Terrorist attacks are sweeping Europe and threaten the United States. The rise of ISIS and its desire to obtain nuclear and other weapons of mass destruction is an ever-present danger. "There are over twenty different training camps—that is, what is known to the FBI—across America," says Michael Youssef, host of the international *Leading the Way* television program, megachurch pastor, and author of *The Barbarians Are Here*. "By the same token, there are militants underground who are basically plotting the next attack, and they've got people trained. They are not leaving anything to chance."[12]

Meanwhile, the world economy is teetering, and the disparity between the financial elite—the "1 percent"—and everyone else is threatening to tear apart the one-world order conceived by the globalist elites. An Oxfam study found that eight men, from Bill Gates to Michael Bloomberg, have amassed personal wealth equivalent to that of 3.6 billion people who make up the poorest half of humanity. "Such dramatic inequality is trapping millions in poverty, fracturing our societies, and poisoning our politics," observed Paul O'Brien, Oxfam America's vice president for policy and campaigns. The report—noting the richest 1 percent now possess the same wealth as the other 99 percent—found the gap between the rich and poor is far greater than previously estimated. It detailed how big business and the super-rich are fueling the inequality crisis by dodging taxes, driving down wages, and using their power to influence politics. Public anger over inequality has triggered political shock waves throughout the world, as seen with the election of Trump and the Brexit vote in the United Kingdom. "Americans want the political establishment to wake up to the way elites and special interests have rigged the system to enrich themselves at the expense of everyone else," O'Brien stated.[13]

Added to the fears caused by widening wealth inequalities are the destructive effects of food shortages, famine, droughts, the possibility of a cataclysmic asteroid strike, and the persistent threat of disastrous climate change. At the Starmus science festival in Trondheim, Norway, astrophysicist Stephen Hawking said it's only a matter of time before the world is decimated by a large asteroid strike or wiped out by overpopulation and climate change. "I am convinced that humans need to leave earth," Hawking told festival attendees. "We have given our planet the disastrous gift of climate change, rising temperatures, the reducing of polar ice caps, deforestation and decimation of animal species...[An asteroid strike] is not science fiction. It is guaranteed by the laws of physics and probability."[14]

Meanwhile, growing civil unrest, including thousands of people threatening to assassinate Trump on Twitter, comedian Kathy Griffin's video holding up Trump's fake bloody head, and, actor Johnny Depp's remark about the "last time an actor assassinated a president," has raised the possibility of political and race wars in the United States. America has never been more divided along racial, ethnic, and religious lines. A

Gallup poll found a record 77 percent of Americans perceive the nation as divided on its most important values. Moreover, the world is experiencing rising unemployment, a situation that will only worsen as artificial intelligence and robots eventually replace human jobs in many fields. In 2015, global unemployment stood at 197 million—27 million higher than the pre–Great Recession level in 2007.[15]

Further, a 2017 survey by the American Bible Society found that Americans are increasingly concerned about the nation's morality, or lack thereof. The annual State of the Bible survey found that 81 percent of Americans say morals are declining—a 5 percent increase from 2016. While political, ethical, and moral controversies abound and many see the nation's moral fabric decaying, "Those who are opening up the Word of God are discovering it to be a guide to help make sense of life and a source of eternal hope," said Roy Peterson, president and CEO of the American Bible Society.[16]

Finally, potential wars and nuclear conflicts are simmering around the world in Ukraine, Syria, Iraq, Iran, North Korea, the Pacific Rim, and Israel. A 2015 Brookings Institution poll found that 79 percent of evangelical Christians believe violence in the Middle East is a sign that the end times are "nearer." The poll found that 81 percent of evangelicals believe Christ will return but are unsure when it will happen. A total of 73 percent say world events will turn against Israel as the world gets closer to the Rapture (the belief that Christians will be supernaturally removed from Earth to join Christ in eternity).[17]

In an exclusive interview before his death in July 2016 at age ninety, Tim LaHaye, *New York Times* bestselling coauthor of the Left Behind series, said, "Actually, we have many more signs of the coming end of this world than any generation before us. Israel being drawn back into the Holy Land, according to Jesus' prophecy in the Olivet Discourse... Thrilling reports from the Wycliffe Bible translators, the thousands of other evangelistic mission ministries, plus the tens of thousands of evangelistic-minded churches that support them, give us just cause for believing we could be living in the last days just before the Rapture."[18]

Ron Rhodes, president of Reasoning from the Scriptures Ministries and the author of *The End Times in Chronological Order*, notes that 27 percent of the Bible is prophetic. He says Bible prophecy has become increasingly popular as people have watched an alignment of biblical predictions and world events in recent decades—everything from the rebirth of Israel in 1948 to religious apostasy to the rise of globalism. He explains that many Christians are now interested in prophecy due to what he calls "the convergence factor." To have one, two, or three prophecies coming to pass today would indicate the Second Coming is drawing near. "But when you have multiple prophecies converging at the same time, that is very significant." Rhodes notes that one of the key factors indicating convergence "is that the Muslim nations are aligning against Israel. The Bible predicts that the Muslim nations will attack Israel in conjunction with Russia." Rhodes says that so many prophecies converging in our day indicates "that we are living in the end times."[19]

The Enigma of God's Flawed Leaders

President Trump walks onto the world stage at a time of unprecedented global chaos. The Bible teaches that God "deposes kings and raises up others" (Dan. 2:21 NIV). This means that every political leader and head of state has been placed in his or her position by God either for judgment or for the good of the people. This does not mean that God desires or wants to put men like Adolf Hitler into positions of power. However, God has given mankind free will, and when a nation overwhelmingly chooses to elect a man like Hitler, he allows the people to have what they want.

Like every other president, Trump was placed in office by God. He has come to power in one of the most biblically prophetic times in human history. The Bible reveals that when God uses a man or a woman for his purposes, rarely is that person chosen because he or she is perfect.

This concept was reflected by Rabbi Jonathan Bernis, television host, author, and president and CEO of Jewish Voice Ministries International. Although Trump did not fit his picture of a president and he had many issues with him, he said, "But maybe it takes this kind of person to bring the change needed to turn this country around. I have a great expectation that God is doing something supernatural here through Donald Trump, and it would never have been something that I would have expected, but I think my consternation has shifted to hope. Israel has always been a key issue, and Donald Trump is a much better option for Israel than Hillary Clinton would have been. Donald Trump understands clearly the threat that Iran poses…Iran is the greatest threat that Israel faces in the world, and I think Israel has a true partner now with the Trump administration in standing against Iran."[20]

Throughout biblical history, God raised up flawed and imperfect leaders, and often those who did not even claim to be followers of his ways. Take the case of Cyrus the Great. Cyrus was the magnanimous sixth-century BC king of Persia who established the largest empire the world had yet known. He liberated the Jews held captive in the Babylonian Empire and helped them build the Second Temple. From Abraham to the apostle Paul, God worked through biblical figures despite their flaws and weaknesses. For example, Noah, the hero of the Flood, got drunk and naked. Moses, Israel's great liberator and lawgiver, secretly killed a man and retreated into self-imposed exile. King David was a murderer, liar, and adulterer, but he was the only man in the Bible whom God called "a man after his own heart" (1 Sam. 13:14 KJV). King Solomon was revered for his great wisdom and wealth, the book of Proverbs, and building Solomon's Temple, yet he had "seven hundred wives of royal birth and three hundred concubines" who "led him astray" (1 Kings 11:3 NIV). The apostle Peter, whom Jesus described as the "rock" upon which he would build his church, yielded to fear when Jesus was arrested and denied three times that he even knew his master (Luke 22:54–62).

Similarly, many American presidents have been broken leaders too. President Kennedy consorted with numerous mistresses, including Hollywood actress Marilyn Monroe. He often took illicit drugs because of the severe pain he endured from colitis, prostatitis, osteoporosis, and Addison's disease. Yet to this day Kennedy is considered one of our most honored presidents.[21]

Thomas Jefferson fathered children by one of his slaves. Grover Cleveland fathered an illegitimate child. Abraham Lincoln suffered from severe depression, or "melancholy." Harry S. Truman, who made the decision to drop atomic bombs on Japan to end World War II, had a terrible temper and at times exploded at his critics—especially critics of his family. Franklin D. Roosevelt had a mistress. Of course, the sexual escapades of Bill Clinton are well-known.[22]

Mysteries and Enigmas of Trump's Presidency

As we explore the secrets of Trump's presidency, we will examine the many complexities great leaders often have. We may well be at the point when major prophetic events begin to unfold, and Trump will play a key role as president in making decisions for our nation and world.

Does Trump have a deep-seated Messiah complex, or is it possible that whatever his imperfections and flaws, he is being used by God in far more mysterious ways than we realize? Are there ancient and contemporary prophecies that speak of the role of Trump and America in the last days? Do some of these prophecies foretell cataclysmic events in the not-too-distant future? Or do they point toward a more hopeful immediate future for America and the world? Perhaps, as many faith leaders believe, the choice is ours.

As the North Korean nuclear showdown raised fears of nuclear devastation in Asia, America, and other parts of the world, Franklin Graham observed that the world is slipping further and further away from God: "Jesus said, 'Because of the increase of wickedness, the love of most will grow cold'—and we're witnessing that all around us. Even people I talk to who aren't Christians recognize it and say the changes they see in the world are not good and are very concerning."

During the Presidential Inaugural Prayer Breakfast, Rabbi Jonathan Cahn—the senior rabbi at the nation's largest messianic congregation, the Beth Israel Worship Center in Wayne, New Jersey—told the audience that in world history only two civilizations came into existence on the "solitary foundation stone of God's calling and purposes." The first was Israel, and the second was America. "America was to be a city on a hill, a holy commonwealth," Cahn told the crowd. "Its first governments were established in the name of Jesus and for the glory of God...And as [American colonial governor John] Winthrop had prophesied, God had commanded a blessing. America would become the most blessed, the most powerful, and the most prosperous nation the world had ever seen, a praise and glory in the earth."[23]

Cahn went on to explain that just as Israel did in biblical times, America too turned away from God, ruled him out of its culture and government, and banned him from its public squares. In filling this void, America has "brought in idols of carnality and gain, and gods of materialism and licentiousness. We have replaced the eternal standards of righteousness for a new morality of immorality...What we once knew to be sin, we now call good, and what we once knew to be right, we now call intolerant and dangerous...If John Winthrop could return now, he would find his city on the hill darkened and progressing to judgment. For no nation can wage war against the God of its blessings and expect those blessings to remain."

Nonetheless, even as America in 2016 stood on the precipice of an election that threatened to establish "for ages the edicts of apostasy and the ways of godlessness," the course of history took a mysterious turn. The media, Democrats, Clinton, Obama, along with Republicans and even Trump himself, couldn't believe what happened. A "political earthquake" swept Trump into office—halting eight years of a Marxist, left-wing presidency that divided the nation, eroded national sovereignty, weakened the military, and undermined the constitutional foundation that helped make America a great and prosperous country. But, as Cahn told the crowd, "Donald Trump had not lived the life of a believer, and there was much concern among God's people. Can God use those who have not known or walked with God to accomplish the purposes of God? Can he choose them and anoint them to lead nations?"

In the Bible, God called the prophet Elisha to anoint the warrior Jehu to be king over Israel, even though Jehu didn't know God and was a "man of fiery passion." But God chose him and used him as a vessel to cause the shaking of a nation and the end of the dynasty of Ahab and Jezebel, the priests of Baal, and their evil influence. "And now we must pray for Donald Trump, that he will fully yield his life to be used as a vessel for the purposes of God," Cahn said. "God has now given a reprieve, a window of grace—to return. But what shall we do with that window?...The only way America will be great again...is for America to return to the God who made America great in the first place."[24]

Is the Trumpocalypse Coming?

Shortly after Cahn delivered this speech, President Trump faced the first major crisis of his presidency when North Korea conducted a series of successful nuclear and missile tests. North Korean leader Kim Jong-un threatened a "surprise attack" on America and "merciless ultra-precision strikes from ground, air, sea, and underwater." He threatened to reduce the United States to "ashes" if Trump fired a "single bullet" at North Korea. Afterward, the United States began deploying attack drones to South Korea, along with the controversial Terminal High Altitude Area Defense (THAAD) anti-missile system. Meanwhile, Trump urged China to do more to rein in North Korea. He tweeted that the United States would "solve the problem" with or without China's help. Shortly afterward, Trump ordered missile strikes against Syria in response to a chemical weapons attack on the Syrian people. Amid fears of war breaking out in Syria, North Korea, or elsewhere, Google searches for the term "World War III" hit the highest ever level.

In September 2017, James Stavridis, a retired Navy admiral and dean of the Fletcher School of Law and Diplomacy at Tufts University, estimated the chances of a conventional war with North Korea at fifty-fifty and the chances of nuclear war at 10 percent. "We are closer to a nuclear exchange than we have been at any time in the world's history with the single exception of the Cuban missile crisis," Stavridis said.

In a *Prophecy in the News* article, S. Douglas Woodward wrote that the realities of going to war with North Korea are complex. "Kim Jong Un has two big 'bodyguards' in Russia and China," Woodward wrote. "Going to war with Pyongyang makes war with the big boys a plausible outcome. One analyst, Joel Skousen (World Affairs brief) asserts that North Korea has always been the 'trigger mechanism' planned by the enemies of the United States to start World War III. That is, when Russia and China become fully capable and the U.S. power is sufficiently diminished, a war with North Korea will be the catalyst to launch a global war. From the vantage point of these Asian powers, WWIII promises to defeat democracy and Western-style capitalism once and for all. However, Skousen believes 'that they are not ready yet.' Essential new weapons are still two or more years away from production and deployment. Skousen's counsel: 'Trump must act now!'"[25]

As tensions on the Korean peninsula neared a breaking point, stories appeared in major publications pondering the prospect of a "global conflict—World War III." Former CIA military analyst Dr. Peter

Vincent Pry, chief of staff of the Congressional EMP Commission, wrote that the United States and its allies have long regarded the nuclear weapons programs of Iran, North Korea, and Pakistan as technologically backward. "If their assessment is wrong," he said, "and nuclear missile programs of rogue states are significantly more advanced technologically than Washington and media elites suppose—we could stumble into a nuclear Pearl Harbor." After returning from a trip to South Korea, U.S. representative Barbara Lee (D-CA) said, "We went to the DMZ, and I saw how close to nuclear war we really are."[26]

Meanwhile, some military analysts suspect that Russia, which has been accused of helping North Korea's nuclear weapons program, has long planned to use the rogue state as a trip wire to ignite a war with the West. Since the end of the Cold War, the public has assumed that the United States is the world's lone superpower and that its military could easily defeat any potential aggressors. Unfortunately, the balance of military power has shifted significantly in recent years unbeknownst to much of the public.[27]

As a result, Rabbi Jonathan Bernis believes America is facing an unprecedented array of threats from foreign nations and terrorist organizations. "Although [Trump] is focused on protecting the country, we are going to see terrorist activity," Bernis says. "Nuclear terrorist activity— a nuclear bomb in New York or Washington, DC—would be devastating. It would throw the world into turmoil, so that's a possibility. I think we have to watch Russia closely too. Any kind of crisis with Russia would spiral. I think Turkey continues to create danger for Israel, and when there is danger for Israel, there is danger for the world. So . . . something is going to give."[28]

Greg Laurie, pastor at the fifteen-thousand-member Harvest Christian Fellowship in Riverside, California, believes the fact that the United States and North Korea are absent from the book of Revelation may imply the two nations are decimated at some point in the prophetic timeline. Laurie explained: "We do not find the reigning superpower on the face of the earth anywhere in the last days' scenario. Other nations emerge. So where is America? I pray we are not out of the picture because we have been in some kind of nuclear conflict."[29]

John Hogue, a bestselling author and world-renowned Nostradamus scholar, is convinced that the prophecies of Nostradamus align with those of the Bavarian seer Matthias Stormberger and American mystic Edgar Cayce, who foresaw, detailed, and dated the advent of World Wars I and II. Hogue believes these seers and mystics predicted in equal detail a "Third World War that catches humanity off guard because at the time leaders and their news networks are promoting geopolitical myths based on denial of realities."

"[Nostradamus] gives two countdowns in two separate prophecies about this World War III scenario," Hogue says. "The short countdown is three years and seven months, and the long countdown is thirteen years." Hogue believes the countdown started with the new Cold War that began in April 2014 at the onset of the Ukrainian civil war. "Ukraine was the last straw, so the Russians said, 'We'll do something drastic,' and then they took Crimea back. The sanctions and countersanctions began the Ukrainian civil war, and that's when I thought, 'Oh my God. This is it. This is the beginning of the new Cold War that ends in a nuclear confrontation in three years and seven months, or in thirteen years, which would mean if it started around [April 2014] that means November of [2017] is the end of the short countdown, and then the year 2027 would be the end of the long countdown."[30]

Chapter Two

Nostradamus, Nuclear "Football," and Bible Codes

The great shameless, audacious bawler. He will be elected governor of the army: The boldness of his contention. The bridge broken, the city faint from fear.

—NOSTRADAMUS, *LES PROPHETIES*, CENTURY III, QUATRAIN 81[1]

How can I know that an order I receive to launch my missiles came from a sane president?

—U.S. AIR FORCE MAJOR HAROLD L. HERING, WHO WAS DISCHARGED
FROM THE AIR FORCE IN 1973 FOR RAISING THIS QUESTION WHILE
SERVING UNDER PRESIDENT RICHARD NIXON[2]

Peope across America and the world secretly wonder: Will President Trump keep us out of a major war, or will he in a fit of anger, like he fires off a tweet, push the nuclear button—firing multiple nuclear missiles at some enemy—and plunge us into World War III and start the Apocalypse predicted in Revelation?

Numerous psychiatrists, psychologists, and behavioral analysts have stepped forward to give us a psychological profile of Trump in the hope of answering this question.

As president of the United States and commander in chief of the armed forces, Trump has a military aide always with him. This highly trained officer is the carrier of the nuclear "football"—a metal briefcase dressed in black leather that contains numerous top secret codes and technologies that give Trump the sole authority and power to authorize a nuclear attack against the enemies of the United States.

"It is the closest modern-day equivalent of the medieval crown and scepter—a symbol of supreme authority," Michael Dobbs wrote in *Smithsonian* magazine. "Accompanying the commander in chief wherever he goes, the innocuous-looking briefcase is touted in movies and spy novels as the ultimate power accessory, a doomsday machine that could destroy the entire world."[3]

Paul McGuire Show: Nuclear Football

About a decade ago, I (Paul) did an hour-long interview on KBRT AM 740 for my nationally syndicated radio program, the *Paul McGuire Show*, with a top presidential military aide who talked to me in detail about the football. This aide told me that just one man, the president, has the power to launch an Armageddon-like nuclear strike.[4] He said although there is a "two-man rule" in ordering a nuclear attack, only the president has the authority to issue the order. The secretary of defense has the responsibility and power to verify it is an authentic order from the president, but he's not allowed to overrule the president's order. If the president is killed, a presidential succession plan determines the chain of command and who can order the launch of America's nuclear arsenal.

Critics of this system say there are no safeguards to determine if the president is sane when making this decision and not under extreme emotional duress or the influence of mind-altering substances. Major Hering raised this issue in 1973 at a time when President Nixon was acting erratically and drinking heavily during the Watergate scandal. It cost Hering his military career.[5]

Before the presidential election, Trump said that the use of nuclear weapons should be the "absolute last step." "I don't want to rule out anything," he said. "I will be the last to use nuclear weapons. It's a horror to use nuclear weapons. I will not be a happy trigger like some people might be. But I will never, ever rule it out."[6]

Nostradamus, Trump, and the Prophets

Since the beginning of mankind, the heads of all great empires have searched for answers about the future from supernatural sources—prophets, seers, clairvoyants, astrologers, sorcerers, and magicians.

The king of Babylon, Nebuchadnezzar, had a large inner advisory council consisting of powerful and proven prophets, seers, sorcerers, and astrologers. However, Nebuchadnezzar threatened to kill all of them because they could not describe to him, let alone interpret, a troubling dream he had regarding an "enormous, dazzling statue" featuring a head of gold, silver arms and chest, bronze thighs and belly, and feet of iron and clay (Dan. 2:31–33 NIV). Mysteriously, a young Hebrew prophet in their midst, Daniel, not only described the dream in incredible detail but also interpreted its meaning—helping shape the foreign and domestic policy of the Babylonian Empire. He told Nebuchadnezzar that the statue represented five powerful kingdoms—Babylon, Medo-Persia, Greece, Rome, and the revived Roman Empire—that would arise throughout history until God destroys the final one and replaces it with his heavenly kingdom (Dan. 2:29–47).

The Bible records the accounts of numerous prophets such as Elijah, Isaiah, Jeremiah, Ezekiel, Daniel, Joel, and Jonah who accurately predicted the future 100 percent of the time. Many of these prophecies have come true in history, and the rest will be fulfilled in the future.

"The Hebrew prophets were spokesmen for God," wrote Ed Hindson, dean of the Rawlings School of Divinity and Institute of Biblical Studies at Liberty University. "While the prophet preached to his own generation, he also predicted events in the future... Thus, the prophet was also called a 'seer' (Hebrew, *roeh*) because he could see future events before they happened. The Bible depicts the prophet as one who was admitted into the divine council chambers where God 'reveals His secret'" (Amos 3:7 NASB).[7]

The word *prophet* occurs only occasionally in the Old Testament before the time of Samuel—the founder of schools for prophets trained to serve as a moral check on kings and priests. These "oral prophets" performed their duties for three centuries before the "literary prophets" wrote the last seventeen prophetic books of the Old Testament.

In addition to prophets of the Old Testament, history records numerous other prophets, visionaries, astrologers, and seers who claimed to have seen into the future. These futurists have had an enormous impact on the world—regardless of whether their prophecies came true. One of the most widely read and famous prophets in human history is sixteenth-century physician, astrologer, and seer Nostradamus, who some say predicted not only Trump's election but that his presidency would initiate the countdown to the "end of the world."[8]

Did Nostradamus Foresee Trump Triggering the End of the World?

In 1556, King Henry II's queen, Catherine de' Medici summoned Nostradamus to the halls of power in Paris. Medici had discovered hints of threats to her family in his almanacs and asked him to draw up horoscopes for her children. A great admirer of his work, she later named him counselor and physician-in-ordinary to the king's court.[9]

While serving in this capacity, Nostradamus told her of a prophecy involving the king. It's detailed in *Les Propheties*—a ten-volume collection of 1,110 enigmatic, four-line poetic verses called quatrains that are organized into centuries. The prediction involved a "young lion" who would overcome the king in the field of battle. During the fight, the "young lion" would pierce the eye of his opponent through a "golden cage," resulting in his slow, cruel death. Nostradamus later warned the king to avoid jousting. But the king ignored the seer's warning, and three years later during a jousting tournament, an opponent pierced the king's golden visor, driving his lance deep into the king's brain. After ten agonizing days, King Henry II died from the resulting infection.[10]

The fulfillment of Nostradamus's prophecy catapulted him into a sixteenth-century literary sensation.[11] "That started Nostradamus on his notorious, some would say, career of fame that has carried him as a lively contradiction of controversy all the way to our times," says Nostradamus authority Hogue.[12]

Nostradamus went on to become the most widely read seer of the Renaissance. In the centuries since his death, his fame has only increased. Many Nostradamus experts have credited him with accurately predicting numerous pivotal events in history, from the French Revolution to the rise of the first two of three "Antichrists"—Napoleon Bonaparte and Adolf Hitler—to the September 11, 2001, terrorist attacks.[13]

"Interpreting Nostradamus is very much like working on a detective story," Mario Reading wrote in *Nostradamus: The Complete Prophecies for the Future.* "Following his filigrees of meaning through to a final, if tentative, conclusion, is an immensely satisfying work of deduction."[14]

In the months leading up to Trump's election, headlines in major media outlets heralded not only that Nostradamus predicted Trump's victory but that his election would be followed by the Third World War. Let's look at a couple of these headlines in the British tabloids:

- "'The Great Shameless, Audacious Bawler'—Donald Trump's Victory Was Predicted by Nostradamus Who Said It Would Bring

About the End of the World, Say Conspiracy Theorists" (Alison Maloney, *Sun*, November 11, 2016).

- "Donald Trump's Victory 'Predicted by Nostradamus Who Said It Would Bring About the End of the World'" (Chris Kitching, *Daily Mirror*, November 12, 2016).

Amid the hoopla, the History Channel broadcast the show *Nostradamus: Election 2016* a few days before the election. "There is a growing body of evidence that points to Nostradamus predicting the winner of this year's presidential election," the History Channel promo stated. "Now by breaking Nostradamus's code and searching for clues we can reveal that not only does he predict the outcome of this year's battle between Hillary Clinton and Donald [Trump], but he also foretells a time of great trouble in the wake of the historic election."[15]

Several stories highlighted Nostradamus's use of the term "false trumpet concealing madness"—speculating that this could be a reference to Trump. "Nostradamus predicted a third Antichrist would trigger Apocalypse," Maloney wrote. "Finally, Nostradamus writes, 'the Republic of the big city' will engage in costly military operations, ordered by the 'trumpet,' which has led to fears of nuclear war."

But Hogue—an empath who successfully predicted the winner of the popular vote in the last thirteen presidential elections—says Nostradamus's cryptic style and "nebulous verses" make it easy to subconsciously find what you're looking for. Although he appeared on this History Channel special, Hogue says he disagreed with the interpretations made by some guests. "I'd like to dispel a gathering myth about Trump being named in Nostradamus's 'trumpet' or 'bawler' verses," Hogue says. "Some people posing on TV as Nostradamus scholars can't avoid the lazy researcher's habit of picking a word here in one verse and there in another to patch together an interpretation that a simple reading of those verses, in their original sixteenth-century format, would upend."[16]

In one of several examples, Hogue cites Century III, Quatrain 81, which begins with, "The great shameless, audacious bawler..." It's translated in sixteenth-century French as: "The great crier, shameless (and) audacious, will be elected governor of the army; The boldness of his contention, the bridge broken (Pontefract), city and faint from fear." "You could apply this open-ended verse to Trump if you ignore line two, which says 'the great crier' (not 'bawler') is the 'governor of the army,'" Hogue explained. "The word *hardiesse* (boldness) could be an extension of the *Hadrie*—Henry IV anagram—applying this to the late 1500s, not today. *Pont rompu* (broken bridge) has been applied to someone who was commander of an army of Roundheads laying siege to the English city of Pontefract, Oliver Cromwell, in the 1640s."[17]

The Fourth Turning

While he hasn't uncovered any Nostradamus prophecies that he believes pertain to Trump, Hogue says Trump's presidency arrives at a momentous time in terms of the predictions of *The Man Who Saw Tomorrow*—the 1981 Nostradamus film narrated by the legendary actor Orson Welles.

"I'm still looking for that key in the case of Trump," says Hogue, who encouraged people in his 2015 book *Trump for President* to take him seriously because he's "in the race all the way to become president of the United States":

I would be very surprised that a man who is going to have such a significant—for better or worse—catalytic impact on change like this man will [is not mentioned in Nostradamus's quatrains]. Be that as it may, [Trump is] a very significant leader making tremendous change in the world that has not been seen since 1914 to 1919...I've been anticipating this in my books, telling people that

2014 to 2019 is going to be a very similar shake-up of structures, including the economic structure we now have. All that is going to be changed, upended and transformed, and by the time we pass out of 2019, we will not recognize the new world that we have created—somewhat for better and somewhat for worse.[18]

Hogue believes the prophecies of Nostradamus align with theories in the book *The Fourth Turning: An American Prophecy* by Neil Howe and William Strauss, which describes historical cycles that place America in the middle of an "unraveling period, on the brink of a crisis." Howe and Strauss identified an eighty-year cycle in American history marked by great crises—a "Fourth Turning." The crises include the American Revolution and the adoption of the U.S. Constitution (1774–1794), the Civil War (1860–1868), and the Depression and World War II (1929–1945). Following this pattern, they predicted another great crisis would occur between 2005 and 2025.

Around the year 2005, a sudden spark will catalyze a crisis mood... Real hardship will beset the land, with severe distress that could involve questions of class, race, nation, and empire... The very survival of the nation will feel at stake. Sometime before the year 2025, America will pass through a great gate in history, commensurate with the American Revolution, Civil War, and twin emergencies of the Great Depression and World War II. The risk of catastrophe will be very high. The nation could erupt into insurrection or civil violence, crack up geographically, or succumb to authoritarian rule. If there is war, it is likely to be one of maximum risk and effort—in other words, a *total war*. Every Fourth Turning has registered an upward ratchet in the technology of destruction, and in mankind's willingness to use it... This time, America will enter a Fourth Turning with the means to inflict unimaginable horrors and, perhaps, will confront adversaries who possess the same.[19]

Will the "Fourth Turning" Lead to Apocalypse?

As the Fourth Turning unfolds, Trump's presidency comes at a pivotal time in terms of the predictions of Nostradamus. This is especially true for those who believe the world is witnessing a convergence of prophetic signs. Over the centuries, much of Nostradamus's success as a "prophet" has been attributed to an ambiguous writing style infused with anagrams, obscure language, labyrinthine sentences, circular thinking, and poetry embedded with classical Greek and Latin grammatical devices, along with biblical words and phrases.[20]

The question, then, is this: Was Nostradamus just another Renaissance seer who periodically forecasted future events accurately, or was he something more—a complex man with a prophetic gift and deep fascination with the Bible whose predictions somehow corroborate those of the ancient prophets? As we watch what seems to be an alignment of the prophecies of Nostradamus and those within the Bible, it's an intriguing question to ask.

Considered a "Christianized Jew," Nostradamus was born in 1503 in Saint-Rémy, France, one of nine children of Jaume de Nostradame, a wealthy grain dealer and part-time notary of Jewish descent. His grandfather, Guy Gassonet, converted to Catholicism and changed his name to Nostradame to avoid persecution during the Inquisition. Nostradamus was tutored by his maternal grandfather, Jean de St. Remy, in the rudiments of Latin, Greek, Hebrew, and mathematics. It's believed that his grandfather introduced him to Kabbalah and astrology, along with teaching him the Old and New Testaments.

Experts believe much of Nostradamus's prophetic works are

paraphrases of ancient end-of-the-world prophecies, many Bible based, along with references to historical events and anthologies of omen reports—projected into the future with the "aid of comparative horoscopy." While Nostradamus was a student of the Bible, most theologians don't classify him as a prophet in the biblical mold because he used occult methods to forecast the future. This isn't to say that he couldn't predict the future, though. The Bible is full of examples of magicians, sorcerers, astrologers, mediums, and diviners, including those in the royal courts of Egypt and Babylon, who could imitate some miracles, though not all, and predict future events.[21]

Based on the culmination of decades of studying the works of Nostradamus, along with those of Stormberger and Cayce, Hogue believes the new Cold War that began in April 2014 marks the beginning of the countdown to World War III and "a full-scale thermonuclear exchange that kills two-thirds of the human race."[22]

"Stormberger and Nostradamus are the most prominent of a small group of seers one can define as 'World War Prophets,'" Hogue wrote in *A New Cold War: The Prophecies of Nostradamus, Stormberger, and Edgar Cayce.* "Looking back with hindsight at their documented predictions, they all share an undeniable accuracy presaging dates and details about the First and Second World Wars often centuries before these tragedies took place."[23]

The short countdown, Hogue believes, is three years and seven months, pointing toward November 2017—a date he now largely dismisses following Clinton's defeat in the 2016 presidential election. If Clinton had been elected, Hogue believes she would have brought the world to the "thermonuclear brink" by the end of 2017. The long countdown of thirteen years, however, culminates in 2027, and Hogue is quite concerned about the potential for nuclear conflict by then. This new cold war—what *Time* magazine called in its August 2014 cover story "Cold War II: The West Is Losing Putin's Dangerous Game"—began with sanctions and NATO encroachment on the Russian frontiers in April 2014 at the onset of the Ukrainian civil war.[24]

Ultimately, Hogue believes Nostradamus's prophecies predict that "Arab vassals fighting in Syria and Iraq" will drag the United States and Russia into a "direct shooting war that could go nuclear." Hogue explained, "He speaks of the *Barbare*, his metaphor for Barbary corsairs, the Islamic terrorists of his day, applied to Islamist terrorists in the future. They drag the Kings of the North (Russia and the U.S.) into a war."[25]

Two quatrains from Nostradamus's *Les Propheties* are key to understanding this prophecy:

Century II, Quatrain 89

One day the two greater leaders will become friends,
Their great power will be seen to increase;
The new land [America] will be at the height of its power,
To the bloody one the number is reported.[26]

Century V, Quatrain 78

The two will not remain allied for long,
Within thirteen years [they give in] to Barbare.
There will be such a loss on both sides,
That one will bless the Bark and cape [of the pope, of Peter][27]

Based on these and quatrains about the "great eagle kings," Hogue believes World War III will take the world by surprise following a "second cold war standoff between Russia and the U.S." Nostradamus often used animal totems to describe nations, and Hogue believes the countdown to World War III is linked to a time when both America and

Russia display eagles as their national totems. The United States adopted the bald eagle as its emblem in 1782. For decades, the Soviet Union used the red star with a hammer and sickle on a red banner as its totem. But following the dissolution of the Soviet Union, the Russian Federation in 1991 adopted an ensign of the czarist emblem of St. George slaying a dragon over a perched great golden and doubled-headed Russian eagle as the flag of Russia. Consequently, Hogue believes Nostradamus's countdown began after a failed attempt at friendship between the "eagle kings of the north"—the new cold war that began in 2014—and that within three years and seven months, or thirteen years, war ensues.[28]

"When the eagle kings go to war it's a big surprise," Hogue says. "They are undermined by *Barbare*, which is Nostradamus's way of describing in a metaphor what he would understand as the Islamic terrorists of his day, which were, of course, pirates that were constantly raiding and hijacking ships in the Mediterranean. Now they've moved on to hijacking jets and other things. Today, Russia and America both have a whole spiderweb of tangled vassals in the current fight over ISIS and Syria."

The Syrian civil war, which began in 2011, is one of several uprisings known as the Arab Spring that have spread violence across the Middle East, resulting in hundreds of thousands of deaths. "When you add the Syrians and the Iranians into the mix," Hogue says, "you've got a lot of ways in which two superpowers could get tangled up in a confrontation with each other over mistakes and miscalculations."

"Hidden Death" and "Dreadful Globes"

Another element of this prediction involves two quatrains that refer to "hidden death" and "dreadful globes," along with the "Aquilon-Eagle kings." Hogue believes these are references to a future nuclear war involving Russia and America.

54

Century V, Quatrain 8

There will be let loose living fire and hidden death,
Inside dreadful globes—horrible! frightful!
By night the city will be reduced to dust by the fleet,
The city on fire, helpful to the enemy.[29]

Century II, Quatrain 91

At sunrise one will see a great fire,
Noise and light extending towards the North [Aquilon in French—
the realms of America and Russia, signified here by their eagle
emblems]:
Within the earth, death and cries are heard,
Death awaiting them through weapons, fire and famine.[30]

The phrase "hidden death" is Nostradamus's way of describing radiation and is an example of the French seer "looking into the machinery of the future." "A fusion bomb, or a thermonuclear bomb, is an atomic-triggered bomb that sets off a hydrogen bomb, and it looks like a globe," Hogue says.

In other quatrains, Nostradamus spoke of a pattern of explosions that would start in the south and move north. "I find that rather chilling because the tactical plans of a thermonuclear exchange that Russia and America follow is that once [the ICBMs] come back into the atmosphere and start striking targets, they hit the southernmost targets of both countries first, and then slowly, slowly, walk up higher and higher toward the North Pole, and here is Nostradamus saying the same thing," Hogue says. "He talks about a world that is so diminished in population that there wouldn't be enough people to till the fields. He says two-thirds of the world will die in this war—the war and subsequent plagues and famines."

Even more unnerving, Nostradamus's prophecies note that the greatest killer isn't the nuclear exchange itself or even the nuclear fallout. "The greatest death-maker in thermonuclear war is the nuclear winter that with the smoke of thousands of cities will upset the climate to the point where food crop systems will fail," Hogue says. "I mean, it's a fact that if for some reason, America stopped exporting food, that immediately a hundred nations would go hungry. We have a very fragile system of agriculture. Famine is a very big theme with Nostradamus. It's all pretty scary stuff..."

Hogue is a proponent of the theory that Nostradamus believed the "future is not written in stone" and is "full of alternate futures." As a result, he believes World War III can be prevented if America and Russia follow the advice of Edgar Cayce, who foresaw Russia becoming the "hope of the world" if those nations could develop and maintain friendly relations.

Hogue believes that "...the same forces that are behind the scenes and really running the government—the corporate, multinational forces; those forces that profit immensely from creating cold wars and perpetual warfare—are trying very, very hard to co-opt President Trump." He explains that these forces are pushing Trump into a more aggressive stance with Russia to prevent a rapprochement between the two states. But he adds, "If we can make peace with Russia, we avoid this conflict."

Third Antichrist and Trumpet Judgments

Yet even as people pray that God will guide Trump in making wise decisions leading to peace, one of the most popular search terms on the Internet involves a loose interpretation of Nostradamus's prophecies claiming Trump is the "Third Antichrist."

Most Nostradamus scholars agree that he accurately predicted the rise of the first two "Antichrists"—Bonaparte and Hitler. Napoleon

Bonaparte rose through the ranks of the military during the French Revolution, crowned himself emperor after seizing political power in a coup d'état, and conquered much of Europe during the early nineteenth century. In the mid-twentieth century, Hitler's fascist policies led to World War II and the deaths of eleven million people, including the mass murder of six million Jews. Today, some people believe that Trump is the "third and final Antichrist, code named Mabus," that Nostradamus predicted would lead the world into the Apocalypse.[31]

"The First Antichrist was 'Napaulon Roy,'" Hogue says. "It's an anagram for 'Napoleon King,' or the angel who is the Destroyer from Revelation, which is Apollyon. Of course, the second anagram is 'Hister.' This is the ancient name of the river Danube. It was a common practice of Nostradamus to use geographical locations to mask a person."[32]

People have identified countless historical figures as the Antichrist. The list includes various Roman Catholic popes, Barack Obama, George W. Bush, Bill Clinton, Ronald Reagan, Saddam Hussein, Osama bin Laden, and innumerable others.

"A few weeks ago, I was reading a piece on President Trump's inner circle," wrote Eric Sapp of the Democratic consulting firm the Eleison Group. "The story talked about how Trump's son-in-law [Jared Kushner] saved the family fortune by selling their real estate holdings and investing them all in a single building: 666 Fifth Avenue . . . and how he then leveraged the profits from 666 Fifth Avenue to buy a new property adjoining the family's $666 million development in New Jersey. Want to guess how high the new building being built from the profits of 666 Fifth Avenue will be? Yup, 666 feet!"[33]

While Revelation 13:18 reveals the Antichrist's number is "666," more than 100 passages in the Bible provide specific details about the Antichrist's origin, nationality, character, and career. Most Bible scholars believe he will arise out of the "revived Roman Empire" shortly before or at the beginning of the Tribulation period. These scholars say the Antichrist could arise out of America, which was formed out of the nations of Europe, but it's far more likely that he'll emerge from "a future form of the Roman Empire that existed in [the apostle] John's day when he prophesied about the Antichrist's coming." In his book *The End: A Complete Overview of Bible Prophecy and the End of Days*, Mark Hitchcock, associate professor at Dallas Theological Seminary, wrote that the Antichrist won't be identified until after the Rapture and will "emerge from relative obscurity to take the international political scene by storm."

Jerry B. Jenkins, *New York Times* bestselling coauthor of the Left Behind series, says many people miss the fact that one of the Antichrist's major qualifications is that not only will he be beloved by nearly everyone but people will also think for a time that he is God reincarnate. He adds, "That should rule out the idea that any American politician could ever be the Antichrist. If roughly half the populace wants you out of office, that's hardly an endorsement of your divinity."[34]

Given what the Bible says about the Antichrist, we believe his identity will remain largely unknown until the Tribulation starts, or shortly before it begins.

While some question whether Trump is the Antichrist, many Christians believe he is instead paving the way for the second coming of Christ. "Trump's ideas meld perfectly with evangelical apocalyptic expectations as the battle of Armageddon nears," Gabriel Campanario wrote in the *Seattle Times*. "He promises to seize power and to use it for them. He claims he would restore religious liberty to evangelicals... He would defend Israel at all costs. He would fight abortion by adding conservative justices to the U.S. Supreme Court." After listing several other Trump policies dear to evangelicals, Campanario concludes, "If Armageddon is coming, and many evangelicals believe it is, there can be no one better to lead the United States than Donald Trump."[35]

Curiously, Nostradamus's prophecies make numerous references to a "trumpet," leading many to believe that the word may refer to Trump. Interestingly, the archaic English word for *trumpet* is *trump*. Revelation refers to the "trumpet judgments" and blowing of the "last trump," or trumpet. The Old Testament describes how a watchman would sit in a high tower to keep a lookout for approaching enemies. If he spotted the enemy, he would immediately blow a loud blast from a trumpet or shofar. A trumpet or "trump" is viewed biblically as a prophetic instrument of warning or announcement.

The "King of Terror"

In the 1550s, Nostradamus received warnings about a "third and final Antichrist" who would be revealed in the future. In Century X, Quatrain 72, he described the "King of Terror" who would appear on the world stage in "1999."

As was his practice, though, Nostradamus concealed information from the casual reader by making anagrams out of numbers. Hogue wrote, "If the month of 'September' is a lead, then '1999' could be a reverse code for the actual year, month, and day: 1999 = 9111. Thus, the prophecy means to say: In the year 9.11.1, September month, the great King of Terror comes from the sky."[36]

Considered Nostradamus's "most famous doomsday prediction," Hogue and many others believe it pertains to the September 11, 2001, terrorist attacks when Al Qaeda militants flew two hijacked airliners into the towers of the World Trade Center in New York City. Hogue also believes this prophecy is linked to the "Third Antichrist" and may mark the beginning of the "twenty-seven-year war of the Third Antichrist."[37]

"The Third Antichrist is also called Mabus by Nostradamus," Hogue wrote. "That's an anagram that fits a number of Middle Eastern dictators like Saddam Hussein of Iraq and terrorist leaders like Usama [Osama] bin Laden and the Caliph of the Islamic State. You can also get Mabus from decoding the names of the two previous U.S. presidents, G. W. Bush and Obama, who have waged war with all the above."[38]

However, Hogue says his study of Nostradamus's prophecies about the "Third Antichrist" revealed no link to Trump. "Mabus (the 'Third Antichrist') tends to have nothing to do with Trump because you can't translate him into that."

In *A New Cold War*, Hogue describes this prophetic puzzle as the "deadly doomsday riddle" and the "twenty-seven-year War of the Third Antichrist." He considers the four top candidates for the "Third Antichrist"—Hussein, bin Laden, Obama, and Bush—and how all four are "karmically entwined, drawn into the lands of the *barbare* in a struggle for Judeo-Christian or Islamic supremacy over the Middle East."

"The first is Saddam Hussein of Iraq," Hogue wrote. "Next is Osama [Usama] bin Laden, the dean of Jihad terrorism taught at his university of 'al-Qaeda' in Afghanistan. He's responsible for planning and inspiring the 9/11 attacks that inadvertently handed the neocons the Cold War on Terror guided by the last two top candidates, Presidents G. W. Bush and Barack Obama."[39]

This is one of the key Mabus quatrains:

Century II, Quatrain 62

Mabus will soon die, then will come,
A horrible undoing of people and animals,
At once one will see vengeance,
One hundred powers, third, famine, when the comet will pass.[40]

While he's still working on decoding this prophecy, Hogue believes the September 11, 2001, terrorist attacks—or Hussein's death in 2006 and possibly bin Laden's death in 2011—could also have marked the beginning of the "twenty-seven-year War of the Third Antichrist."

"Though his true name is occulted, the Third Antichrist's destiny is made clear," Hogue wrote. "Unlike the first two, he is the first to die in a war he initiates at the sign of a comet, or a rocket falling out of the skies. World War III begins when Mabus dies a sudden death. His act of terror unites a hundred nations in a war against what Nostradamus calls three Eastern kings secretly allied in opposition to the West. They would use piracy (hijacking?), ambush and subterfuge to wage war. Know the war has begun when hollow mountains of a great New City (yet to be built in Nostradamus' day) at latitude 45 in an unborn country he called Americh, or Amorica, will be attacked by a fire in the sky. The hollow mountains crafted by man will be seized and plunged into the boiling cauldron of their own debris clouds. After this happens, we will be living in the days of the last Antichrist."[41]

Bible Codes, Trump, and Messianic Era

As the world watches the beginning of the endgame of history and looks for God's promise to "pour out of my Spirit upon all flesh" (Acts 2:17–21 KJV), international Bible codes experts say biblical cryptograms not only predicted Trump's victory but also indicate that following a difficult period for the Jewish people, the "Moshiach," or Messianic era, will begin.[42]

Analyzing two sets of these ciphers before the election, Bible codes expert Rabbi Matityahu Glazerson claims to have found evidence that Trump would win the presidency, and that his victory would be connected to his support of Israel. In a table based off the book of Deuteronomy published in July 2016, Glazerson pointed to the word *Donald* in Hebrew letters next to the word *nasi*—Hebrew for president. In addition, Glazerson uncovered an abbreviation for *Artzot haBrit*, or the United States in Hebrew. He also found 8 Cheshvan 5777, the date on the Hebrew calendar for November 9, 2016—the first day Trump was president-elect. Glazerson views Trump in the mold of Cyrus the Great, who freed the Jews from Babylonian captivity, allowing them to rebuild the Temple in Jerusalem.

"In Hebrew, the word *Moshiach* [Messiah] means anointed," Dr. Rivkah Lambert Adler wrote in a Breaking Israel News story—"Bible Codes Predict Trump Win." "According to Rabbi Glazerson, 'Anybody who helps Israel, to build themselves, to settle property in their land,' is referred to as a kind of 'Moshiach.' Later in the video, Rabbi Glazerson shows where the word 'Moshiach' appears twice. He suggests that there is a connection between Trump's success and the eventual arrival of the Messiah."[43]

Bible codes experts Joe Gallis and Robert Wolf found that Trump's name, using biblical numerology, equals 424—Gematria for "Messiah for the House of David." Breaking Israel News feature writer Adam Eliyahu Berkowitz wrote, "This is not to say that Donald Trump is the Messiah, but that his presidency will usher in the Messianic era."[44]

These articles come as rabbis and others in recent years have claimed to have found hidden codes in the Bible. The three basic decoding systems include the Atbash Code, based on alphabetic inversion; Gematria, based on numerology; and a computer-driven code based on equidistant letter sequencing (ELS).[45]

Also, some believe the Zohar, a classic book of esoteric Jewish mysticism and the sacred text of Kabbalah, contains predictions regarding the Messianic era. Despite its growing popularity, Kabbalah and the Zohar have occult roots in Babylon, Egypt, and the antediluvian world. The belief systems of many of today's secret societies trace their origins to esoteric mysticism. In *Rule by Secrecy*, Jim Marrs, a former *Fort Worth Star-Telegram* investigative journalist and a *New York Times* bestselling author, explained that the mystical knowledge of Cabala, or Kabbalah, was passed down from Mesopotamia through Palestine into thirteenth-century Europe when the Zohar was first penned. "It has been stated how the Knights Templar brought Cabalistic knowledge back to Europe from the Holy Land at the time of the Crusades and that this knowledge was passed along through the alliance of the order and mason guilds," Marrs wrote. "It has also been documented that the hidden knowledge within the Cabala has been utilized through the centuries by nearly all secret societies, including Freemasonry, the Rosicrucians, and through the Illuminati on into modern groups."[46]

Curiously, the Bible codes phenomenon comes as three of the world's largest religions—Christianity, Islam, and Judaism—believe a Messiah, of some type, is about to appear.

Zohar Predicted Coming of the "Messiah"

In the Zohar, thirteenth-century rabbis speculated about the "Moshiach," predicting he would make himself known in the Hebrew year 5733, or 2012–2013, explained Thomas R. Horn, the bestselling author of *Petrus Romanus*, *Abaddon Ascending*, and *Zenith 2016*. "Oddly enough, Trump goes to Israel in 2012, decides not to run for U.S. president, meets with heads of state...and he starts talking to the Jewish people, telling them to vote for Benjamin Netanyahu and the Likud Party, which they did."[47]

Since then, about a dozen Jewish rabbis have said the Messianic era is imminent. But some key things need to happen for the Messiah figure— at least in the Jewish mind-set—to arrive. "You can't think of him like we [Christians] think of Messiah. We think of Messiah after the model of Jesus—he's the son of God, divine birth, and all that. That's not how the Jews look at the Messiah," Horn said. "They are looking for a political leader. In fact, Messiah to them means, 'The Anointed One,' and it goes back to the ancient days when they would anoint a king and recognize him as the man that God sent."

Traditionally, the Jews have looked for several things in the Moshiach.

"First, they are looking for somebody as a political figure who can lead decisive battles in defense of Israel," Horn said. "Second, they are looking that when the Messiah comes there will be an ingathering of the Jews from around the world back to the Holy Land. That's why the rabbis on the eve of this election went on television and said, 'We need to call Jews from around the world to come back to Jerusalem because the Messiah is here.' Third, they talked about when he arrives he's going to reinstitute Temple service."

Shortly after Trump won the election, the nascent Sanhedrin sent a letter to Trump and Putin asking them to use their influence to rebuild the Temple in Jerusalem. While the rabbis don't believe that Trump is the Messiah, Horn explained that they see him as a "forerunner" who is "going to start the message in the wilderness, and the Messiah is going to come in on his heels...So, they too believe that we are in the end times. They too believe that the Messiah is about to appear...but their Messiah is going to be a false Messiah. He's going to be the Antichrist. I also don't believe that Donald Trump is the Antichrist. So, I think the smart ones in Israel are looking at him right now and saying he is what we'd call John the Baptist. He is God's messenger."[48]

While Horn suggests the Messiah the rabbis are referring to is the Antichrist, we believe it's too early to say. While the Bible doesn't clearly state whether the Antichrist is a Jew or Gentile, most prophecy scholars believe he will be a Gentile who leads a European-based union of Gentile nations (Dan. 7:8–24) and makes a covenant with Israel that offers Gentile protection (Dan. 9:27), and that his rule is part of the "times of the Gentiles" and their domination over Israel (Luke 21:24). "These passages...do not specifically designate him as a Gentile," Ed Hindson wrote. "He could possibly be of Jewish origin or nationality and still be a European or American Jew who leads the final form taken by the one-world government of the last days."[49]

Mystical Gog and Magog Connection

Most Bible scholars believe the Temple won't be rebuilt until the Antichrist signs a seven-year peace treaty with Israel marking the beginning of the Tribulation. The Temple will be desecrated by the Antichrist at the midpoint of the Tribulation when he breaks his covenant with Israel by halting the sacrificial system (Dan. 9:27).

The apostle Paul wrote the Antichrist would enter the Temple and declare himself God. "He will oppose and will exalt himself over everything that is called God or is worshiped, so that he sets himself up in God's temple, proclaiming himself to be God" (2 Thess. 2:4 NIV).[50]

Before the start of the Tribulation or shortly thereafter, biblical scholars believe the "War of Gog and Magog" detailed in Ezekiel 38–39 will erupt. This war is believed to involve an invasion of Israel by a Russian-Iranian–led coalition of nations.[51]

In a strange twist on this prophecy, Adam Berkowitz wrote that a noted rabbi predicted more than two decades ago that North Korea would "become the nuclear key to the final war of Gog and Magog." Shortly before he died in 1994, Rabbi Levi Sa'adia Nachamanii, who accurately predicted the Six-Day War in 1967 and the Yom Kippur War in 1973, warned that North Korea posed the greatest danger to Israel. "Not Syria, not Persia (Iran), and not Babylon (Iraq), and not Gaddafi (Libya)," Nachamanii said. "Korea will arrive here."[52]

In making this prediction, the rabbi cited a reference in Deuteronomy 32:22 that "She'ol," or Hebrew for hell, would come to Israel. Strangely, "She'ol" is spelled in Hebrew the same way as Seoul, the capital of South Korea. The verse also mentions God's "fire," which the rabbi interpreted as a nuclear war in which North Korea will attack Seoul, unifying the nation, and later threaten Israel with nuclear attack. "At the time… no one even knew [North Korea] had a nuclear program," Berkowitz says. "They didn't start nuclear testing until 2006. People looked at

[Nachamanii] like—here's this big important rabbi who is saying you don't have to worry about all these enemies; the big one is North Korea—and people were like, 'He's nuts,' and now twenty-two years later, 'Oh, my goodness.'"

The rabbi's reference to North Korea has its source in the Zohar, which states Islam would rule the Middle East for thirteen hundred years, a century for every year until Ishmael was circumcised. Following that period, a country "from the edge of the earth" would be "aroused against Rome" and wage war against it for three months. While the earth doesn't have an edge, the international date line runs through North Korea. "An alliance between Iran and North Korea seems illogical, since the two nations have nothing in common, sharing neither a religion nor a border," Berkowitz wrote. "They seem to be united only in their hatred for the Western World, a commonality that has led them to cooperate on their intercontinental ballistic missile programs, and perhaps on their nuclear programs as well."[53]

For many years, military experts have suspected that North Korea and Iran have shared expertise when it comes to their missile programs. "The very first missiles we saw in Iran were simply copies of North Korean missiles," Jeffrey Lewis, a missile proliferation expert at the Middlebury Institute of International Studies, explained. "Over the years, we've seen photographs of North Korean and Iranian officials in each other's countries, and we've seen all kinds of common hardware."[54]

As the North Korean nuclear crisis intensified in the spring of 2017, Israeli defense minister Avigdor Liberman described North Korean leader Kim Jong-un as a madman who along with the leaders of Iran and Syria are part of an "insane and radical" gang bent on undermining international stability. In response, North Korea threatened Israel and any country that "dares hurt the dignity of its supreme leadership" with "merciless, thousand-fold punishment." At a special briefing, a senior

Israeli Defense Forces officer told journalists that the tensions between North Korea and the United States could impact Israel's security. He said Israel could bear the brunt of the North Korean nuclear crisis because the United States would likely divert security resources from the Middle East to Korea, leaving Israel vulnerable to attack.[55]

Chapter Three

Super-EMP Threat and "Daughter of Babylon"

In the end of days, there will be horrific violence all over the world, but the sign that the Messiah is truly imminent is when a war breaks out in the northern part of the world involving all the nations of the world.

—RABBI YOSEF BERGER[1]

For, lo, I will raise and cause to come up against Babylon an assembly of great nations from the north country, and they shall set themselves in array against her; from there she shall be taken; their arrows shall be as of a mighty expert man; none shall return in vain.

—JEREMIAH THE PROPHET (JEREMIAH 50:9 KJV)

In each generation, seventy-two Tzadikim, or "hidden righteous ones," receive the "Shekinah," or the "Divine Presence," according to the Talmud, the central text of Rabbinic Judaism.[2]

Not long ago, one of these Tzadikim, the renowned but reclusive century-old Torah scholar Rabbi Moshe Aharon HaKohen, contacted Rabbi Yosef Berger with an urgent message about the North Korean nuclear crisis. He had deciphered a fifteen-hundred-year-old book of esoteric teachings, uncovering a prophecy that the North Korean nuclear crisis would escalate into the "War of Gog and Magog" before arrival of the "Moshiach."[3]

The book containing HaKohen's discovery is called *Nevu'at ha-Yeled* ("The Prophecy of the Child"), which tells the story of a son born in northern Israel to childless parents who had been praying for a child. As he was born, he began revealing mystical secrets of the Torah that were supposed to remain hidden, including prophecies about the time before the Messianic era. The prophecies were recorded, and the child died at age twelve. The purpose of the *Nevu'at ha-Yeled* is to anticipate the coming of "Moshiach," along with the political and historical events and catastrophes that will bring about "his final revelation."[4]

"[HaKohen] contacted Rabbi Berger and said, 'You have to get the word out now. North Korea is the big one,'" says Adam Berkowitz of Breaking Israel News. "This 100-year-old hidden righteous man, a Tzadikim, sent an emissary to Rabbi Berger, saying…in the end of days there is going to be horrible violence, but the sign that the Messiah is truly imminent is when a war breaks out in the northern part of the world involving all the nations of the world, and he said it is very close to happening."[5]

Return of the Ten Lost Tribes

Based on his study of the *Nevu'at ha-Yeled*, a book written in cryptic Aramaic that is exceptionally difficult to understand, HaKohen told Berger that the nuclear crisis with North Korea is the first sign that the Messianic era is about to begin. The next sign is the return of the Ten Lost Tribes of Israel.

The Ten Lost Tribes of Israel were part of the original twelve Hebrew tribes who under the leadership of Joshua took possession of the Promised Land following Moses' death. In 930 BC, the ten tribes formed the independent Kingdom of Israel in the north while the other two tribes, Judah and Benjamin, created the Kingdom of Judah in the south. After the Assyrians conquered the northern kingdom in 721 BC, the ten tribes were gradually assimilated by other groups and disappeared from history. Nevertheless, a belief persisted that the tribes would be found one day.[6]

Through Jewish Voice Ministries International, Jonathan Bernis located some of the Ten Lost Tribes of Israel, including the black Jews of Ethiopia—the Beta Israel and Beta Avraham—the Bnei Menashe of India, and the Lemba of Zimbabwe. Many have followed Jewish traditions for centuries, and some have been genetically linked to the Israelites.

"One of the signs is that the Ten Lost Tribes are going to come back to help Israel with the war," Berkowitz says. "Who are the Ten Lost Tribes? I don't know, but I do know there are millions of Africans who are claiming to be a part of Israel, and their claims are being supported by genetic testing. Jews come in all colors." He added that genetic testing confirmed "an enormous number" of Jewish people in South America and India, and that millions "are coming to Israel claiming to be part of those lost tribes."

Dr. Rivkah Lambert Adler, a Jewish journalist who is doing research for a book on the subject, says her interviews with Christians and former Christians who are awakening to Torah and identify as Christian Zionists, Ephraimites, Noahides, and Gerim have led her to believe that Israel is witnessing the fulfillment of biblical prophecies regarding the return of the Ten Lost Tribes. She sees a developing pattern in which people gradually begin to realize they are part of the lost tribes and feel a strong desire "to come home and be reattached to the nation of Israel...Most of them believe that someday Yeshua will restore them to the nation of Israel, and then Yeshua will be proven to be the Messiah." Adler says the movement appears to have been around for twenty or thirty years and now seems to be picking up speed.[7]

Super-EMP Weapons Could Kill Nine in Ten Americans

The prophecies of Jewish mystics, along with those of seers such as Nostradamus, Edgar Cayce, and Matthias Stormberger, seem to align not only with the conclusions of many biblical prophecy scholars, but also with respected geopolitical, military, and intelligence experts.

Peter Vincent Pry, executive director of the EMP Task Force on National and Homeland Security, argues that the biggest threat facing America involves a combination "Super-EMP" and nuclear missile attack by North Korea—a scenario that could fulfill the end-time prophecies of Nostradamus and other seers and the biblical prophets.

Pry, author of *The Long Sunday: Nuclear EMP Attack Scenarios*, says evidence gathered by the commission indicates that North Korea has Super-EMP weapons embedded in satellites that orbit over North America. In 2009, South Korean military intelligence reportedly concluded, independently of the EMP Commission, that Russian scientists were in North Korea helping them to develop Super-EMP weapons. In 2012, a People's Republic of China military commentator stated that North Korea has Super-EMP weapons.

Nuclear electromagnetic pulse (EMP) weapons emit gamma rays that destroy electronics. If detonated at a high altitude, one or two of these weapons could render electronic devices nationwide useless—everything from smartphones and personal computers to automobiles and airplanes. Even more alarming, a Super-EMP attack could shut down the nation's electrical grid for an extended period because the grid is dependent upon thousands of high- and extra-high-voltage transformers. These transformers are the most critical component of the nation's electrical infrastructure. But nearly all of these transformers are imported, and America has only a few spares at any time. "Without this technological cornerstone of our modern electronic civilization, our society can't exist," Pry says. The transformers weigh hundreds of tons. To move one, bridges need to be reinforced and highways widened. "It's an enormous undertaking," Pry says. "Under good conditions, it takes months to replace one transformer, but under conditions where all critical infrastructure is destroyed, there is no food or water, the highways are blocked and there is rioting in the cities, who is going to come replace two thousand transformers?" Companies worldwide produce fewer than two hundred transformers annually, meaning it could take a decade to replace them. Pry added, "Basically, an EMP would re-create in the United States the conditions that exist in a Third World famine."

Experts say a Super-EMP attack could result in a national blackout lasting months to years—potentially resulting in the deaths of an estimated 90 percent of Americans within a year from starvation, societal collapse, diseases, "nuclear reactors going Fukushima," gas pipelines exploding, and the resulting firestorms in cities across the nation.[8]

Pry explained why the consequences of such an attack would be so devastating: "Three hundred and twenty million people cannot survive a year-long blackout that immediately stops the supply of water, that will exhaust the national food stockpile in thirty days, and paralyze the technologies necessary to our critical infrastructure that make it possible to sustain such a large population."[9]

"Super-Mighty Preemptive Strike"

In op-eds in the *Wall Street Journal*, the *Washington Times*, and the Hill, former CIA director R. James Woolsey and Pry wrote that senior national security officials in the Reagan and Clinton administrations warned that North Korea should be regarded as capable of delivering by satellite a small nuclear warhead, specifically designed to make a high-altitude EMP attack against the United States.[10]

These op-eds came amid a nuclear showdown between Trump and North Korean leader Kim Jong-un that garnered global headlines. North

Korea's vice minister Han Song-ryol said any sign of "reckless military aggression" by the United States would result in a preemptive strike against the United States with nuclear weapons. Kim threatened to reduce the United States to "ashes" and carry out a "super-mighty preemptive strike"—perhaps hinting at or signaling a Super-EMP attack on America.

Meanwhile, Trump threatened to "totally destroy" North Korea if necessary. He sent the USS *Carl Vinson*, USS *Ronald Reagan*, and USS *Nimitz* aircraft carriers to the waters off North Korea, along with battleships capable of shooting Tomahawk cruise missiles at the country's nuclear facilities. American B-1 bombers were positioned in Guam. Military officials dispatched the USS *Michigan*, a nuclear-powered submarine, to the waters off South Korea.[11]

Although North Korea is believed to possess only about twenty nuclear missiles and couldn't "trade blows with us in a normal nuclear exchange," Pry says North Korea's Super-EMP weapons could "eliminate us as a society." "It's a perfect asymmetric weapon because if you're a high-tech society like us, we're far more vulnerable to that kind of attack than North Korea is."

During Harvard University's Belfer Center for Science and International Affairs "Lurking Crises, Hidden Opportunities" conference in December 2016, William Tobey, director of the center's U.S.-Russia Initiative, said the "North Korea problem is about to get a lot worse. For the last twenty years, we've lived in a situation in which North Korea had a handful of nuclear weapons, but credible estimates now point toward Pyongyang having enough fissile material for as many as one hundred nuclear weapons over the next five or ten years."[12]

Obama Left America in a State of Maximum Vulnerability

Ironically, the North Korean nuclear standoff—arguably the world's worst nuclear crisis since the Cuban Missile Crisis in 1962—occurred as

President Obama was vacationing and kitesurfing on the British Virgin Islands while writing his memoirs for a reported $60 million. Pry said, "I prefer Trump and I supported Trump over Obama... That's because Obama left our country in a situation of maximum vulnerability. Our military forces are at their lowest point. He didn't do anything to protect our country against cyber or EMP attacks."[13]

Shortly after the election, the "Blob"—the nickname for "the Foreign Policy Establishment"—gathered at the "Lurking Crises, Hidden Opportunities" conference to discuss the challenges facing the Trump administration, including growing Russian aggression, nuclear proliferation, and terrorism. At the event, officials noted that America's nuclear arsenal of B-52s, B-2s, Trident submarines, and Minuteman III missiles is "dangerously outdated."[14]

During his campaign for president, Trump said the nation was on a "path of weakness" amid a "very scary nuclear world." "We have a military that's severely depleted," Trump said. "We have nuclear arsenals which are in very terrible shape. They don't even know if they work."[15]

Shortly after taking office, Trump mandated "a new Nuclear Posture Review to ensure that the United States nuclear deterrent is modern, robust, flexible, resilient, ready, and appropriately tailored to deter twenty-first-century threats and reassure our allies."

The Super-EMP threat was neglected in the Obama years. Following eight years of perseverance on Pry's part, Congress recently passed the Critical Infrastructure Protection Act to help protect Americans from an EMP attack. The act puts the EMP threat on the radar of the Department of Homeland Security, which is expected to launch a pilot project to show that the electric grid could be protected from an EMP attack in a cost-effective manner. The EMP Commission estimates it will cost about $2 billion to harden the nation's electric grid from an EMP attack. Pry is also working to educate the states about the threat. Several states, including Texas and Louisiana, have pending legislation.

Maine, Virginia, Arizona, and Florida have passed initiatives to protect their citizens from an EMP attack, and other states are showing interest.[16]

The Congressional EMP Commission estimates the nation's electrical grid could be protected in about three years, but many things could be done immediately to make improvements. Pry recommends that federal officials start a new "Manhattan Project"—the U.S. government research project that produced the first atomic bombs—to protect the grid on an emergency basis. "We ought not to tolerate North Korea orbiting any more satellites over us," Pry says. "We should shoot down the satellites they already have orbiting. We ought to have Super-EMP weapons the way the Russians and North Koreans do so that we can deter that with the threat of retaliation, or use them for preemptive purposes. This is the biggest threat our civilization faces. It's an imminent threat...We need to move quickly."

In *The Long Sunday*, Pry compares the poor state of the nation's military defenses to the weakness that invited aggression by Nazi Germany at the outbreak of World War II. He made these observations regarding the nation's vulnerabilities:[17]

- The U.S. Army has the lowest number of active-duty soldiers since World War II.
- The U.S. Navy has the smallest number of ships since 1915.
- The U.S. Air Force has the smallest air force in its history.
- America's strategic nuclear weapons are aging and obsolete compared to the new generation of nuclear weapons deployed by Russia and China.
- The United States ceded to China and Russia a virtual monopoly in tactical nuclear weapons, retaining only one hundred and eighty gravity bombs in Europe, while Russia has three thousand to eight thousand tactical nuclear weapons for battlefield use.

- North Korea now makes more nuclear weapons each year than the United States, which stopped making new nuclear weapons or replacing old ones with new models.
- NATO has become so militarily "hollow" that the U.S. Department of Defense and RAND Corporation say Russia could overtake NATO's frontline states in Poland and the Baltics in fewer than three days.
- Russia regularly makes nuclear threats and conducts military exercises against NATO and the United States.
- China and Russia, while paying lip service to the denuclearization of the Korean Peninsula, have helped North Korea develop nuclear missiles.
- Iran received $150 billion in sanctions relief from the United States and international community in exchange for a nuclear deal that "at best may delay Iran's development of nuclear weapons, while according to some experts Iran already has nuclear-armed missiles."

"All of the above looks like weakness, not only to many Western observers, but especially to the militant dictatorships that are Russia, China, North Korea, and Iran," Pry wrote.

In an article in the Hill, Pry wrote that although North Korea, Russia, and China have all made nuclear threats against the United States, most analysts dismiss these as mere "bluster" and "nuclear sabre rattling," not to be taken seriously. "One day, perhaps soon, this may well prove to be a fatal mistake for millions," Pry wrote. "In the West, generations of leaders and citizens have been educated that use of nuclear weapons is 'unthinkable' and the ultimate horror. Not so in Russia, China, and North Korea where their nuclear capabilities are publicly paraded, missile launches and exercises are televised as a show of strength, an important part of national pride."[18]

America's Number One Threat

Today, top military officials say Russia poses a far greater threat to the United States than many people assume. "Russia is the number one threat to the United States," Air Force secretary Deborah James said at the annual Reagan National Defense Forum in December 2016. Her concern was based primarily on Russia's nuclear power.[19]

A related concern about Russia, experts say, involves Russian president Putin's admiration of Tsargrad TV chief editor and commentator Aleksandr Dugin—described by *Foreign Affairs* magazine as "Putin's Brain" and by Breitbart News as "Putin's Rasputin." The owner of the new television station with twenty million viewers is Konstantin Malofeev, a multimillionaire described as Putin's "right-hand man." Before his move into the Russian political mainstream, Dugin was involved in "proto-Nazi mystical circles" and various secretive occult organizations. The former head of Moscow State University's sociology department, he is known for promoting Eurasianism, an ideology that has a "vision of unwinding the U.S.-led global order" and dreams of "revenge on the Western powers which brought about the collapse of the Soviet empire." Dugin once opined that "the American Empire should be destroyed. And at one point, it will be."

Robert Zubrin, in his *National Review* article "Dugin's Evil Theology," wrote that "Dugin is the mad philosopher who is redesigning the brains of much of the Russian government and public, filling their minds with a new hate-ridden totalitarian ideology whose consequences can only be catastrophic in the extreme, not only for Russia, but for the entire human race." In his book *The American Empire Should Be Destroyed—Aleksandr Dugin and the Perils of Immanentized Eschatology*, James D. Heiser, bishop of the Evangelical Lutheran Diocese of North America, wrote, "No matter how 'irrational,' Dugin's ideology now influences the foreign policy of one of the most significant regional powers in the modern world. When a man whose worldview is allegedly shaped by a 'fascination with the occult' proclaims that 'the American Empire [should] be destroyed' because it is at the center of the expansion of the 'kingdom of the Antichrist,' the real universe has been left behind in exchange for a 'counterverse' [in which] groups of men possessed by a gnostic ideology attempt to remake the world to conform to their fantasies."[20]

Dugin's geopolitical philosophies wouldn't mean much except that his ideology appears to have an impact on Putin's worldview. Russia has become increasingly aggressive in recent years. *Time* magazine described the renewed tensions between the geopolitical power blocs led by Russia and China and the United States and NATO as "Cold War II." For decades following the end of the Cold War in 1991, geopolitical and military experts thought the world was relatively safe from the threat of nuclear war, but that has changed. As Tobey said, "Russian President Putin [in 2005] described the collapse of the Soviet Union as the greatest geostrategic catastrophe of the twentieth century, a century that included two world wars involving both communism and Nazism."

Geopolitical experts agree that the global balance of military power has shifted toward an anti-American alliance of nations led by Russia. Some have expressed concerns about Russian defectors and other high-level officials in Russia and former Warsaw Pact countries who have claimed the former Soviet Union's ultimate strategy to subvert and destroy the United States continues even today. One of these individuals, former KGB officer Anatoliy Golitsyn, warned in his 1984 book *New Lies for Old* that the Soviet Union planned a massive campaign of deception that would include fake reforms and a fake collapse of communism designed to fool the West into thinking the Cold War had ended so it would reduce its nuclear forces, leaving it vulnerable to attack.[21]

These concerns come amid a massive military mobilization in Russia, along with threats of nuclear war. Russian media outlets have encouraged people to prepare for nuclear war by locating their nearest bomb shelters "before it's too late." In the fall of 2016, Russia conducted a nationwide civil defense drill involving forty million people—the largest since the Cold War—to prepare for catastrophes, including nuclear war. Further, Russia recently unveiled the "Satan 2" missile—or the Sarmat intercontinental ballistic missile—which "is capable of wiping out parts of the earth the size of Texas or France," according to the Russian state news outlet Sputnik. Paul Craig Roberts, a consultant to the U.S. Department of Defense, says, "One Russian SS-18 wipes out three-quarters of New York state for thousands of years. Five or six of these 'Satans' as they are known by the U.S. military, and the East Coast of the United States disappears."

Meanwhile, Russian defense ministry spokesman Viktor Baranetz said Moscow has been "seeding" nuclear bombs off the U.S. coastline that could trigger tsunamis. The missiles "dig themselves in and 'sleep' until they are given the command."[22]

In an open letter delivered to UN delegates gathered in the summer of 2017 to negotiate a nuclear weapons ban, thirty Nobel laureates, a former U.S. secretary of defense, and over three thousand scientists wrote that a nuclear war would likely kill most people on Earth. "The most horrible hazard is a nuclear-induced winter, in which the fires and smoke from as few as a thousand detonations might darken the atmosphere enough to trigger a global mini ice age with year-round winter-like conditions," they wrote. "This could cause a complete collapse of the global food system and apocalyptic unrest, potentially killing most people on Earth—even if the nuclear war involved only a small fraction of the roughly fourteen thousand nuclear weapons that today's nine nuclear powers control."[23]

Will America Perish Before the End Times?

As concerns grew about the possibility of nuclear war and a string of cat-astrophic hurricanes and other disasters pummeled America, dozens of faith leaders and Bible prophecy experts interviewed for *Trumpocalypse* concurred that the world is experiencing a convergence and acceleration in end-times signs. In an exclusive interview, Billy Graham explained that signs of the end of the age are converging for the "first time since Jesus made those predictions." Yet, Graham says the world believes that it will somehow work out its problems and that permanent peace will be achieved. "Permanent peace will come when the Prince of Peace comes back—not until then," says Graham. "We may have temporary peace— and the Christian is to work for peace—but ultimately the prophecy of Jesus will be fulfilled...At that time Jesus Christ, the Prince of Peace, will be crowned King of kings and Lord of lords. The church should be boldly proclaiming the deity and authority of Jesus as the powerful antidote to the present trend toward world chaos."[24]

In Matthew 24:32–35, Jesus told his disciples, "Now learn the parable from the fig tree: when its branch has already become tender and puts forth its leaves, you know that summer is near; so, you too, when you see all these things, recognize that He is near, right at the door. Truly I say to you, this generation will not pass away until all these things take place" (NASB). Many scholars believe the fig tree is a symbol of Israel and that the generation that witnessed the birth of Israel on May 14, 1948, is the "last generation" Christ spoke of in this passage.

The Bible speaks of a series of events preceding the Tribulation, including the rebirth of Israel (Ezek. 36–37), an increase in knowledge and travel (Dan. 12:4), the breakdown of morality along with the "fall-ing away" (2 Timothy 3:1–5; 2 Thess. 2:3), development of mark of the Beast technologies (Rev. 13:15–18), an increase in great earthquakes and other natural disasters (Luke 21:11, Mark 13:3–8), "wars and rumors of wars" (Matt. 24:6), the rise of globalism (Dan. 7:23–24), and the destruction of Russian-Islamic forces that invade Israel in the "War of Gog and Magog" (Ezek. 38–39).

Curiously, the Bible seems strangely quiet about the fate of America—the wealthiest, most powerful nation in history. If the world is indeed on the precipice of the end of days, it's perplexing that its sole superpower isn't mentioned in Scripture. For decades, Bible scholars have been puzzled by the apparent omission of the United States in the prophetic scenario. In explaining this situation, some say tens of millions of people will disappear in the Rapture—triggering a societal collapse. Others believe the nation will experience a catastrophic economic crash, a series of devastating natural disasters, or a surprise nuclear attack—eliminating or severely reducing America's role on the world stage as prophetic events unfold.

Over the last five decades, the "standard scenario" of Bible prophecy has reflected the views of popular prophecy writers Hal Lindsey (*The Late Great Planet Earth*), Tim LaHaye and Jerry B. Jenkins (Left Behind series), and Grant Jeffrey (*One Nation, Under Attack*; *The Next World War*). The basic premise is that America will decline as a world power, paving the way for the EU (revived Roman Empire) to dominate geopolitics. Then, the Antichrist will rise to power in Europe and lead an alliance of "ten kings."[25]

In *The Babylon Code*, we argued that the Antichrist and False Prophet will oversee a world government, instigate a cashless society, and impose a universal religion during the Tribulation. Revelation 16–19 describes this geopolitical, commercial, and religious system as "Mystery, Babylon" and "Babylon the Great." Currently, the globalist think tank Club of Rome and the UN divide the world into ten regions, including the EU, the "model for a projected Global Union." At some point, we believe something catastrophic may happen to America, paving the way for the rise of the Antichrist and False Prophet to oversee this global system, or that America will become part or even the head of this global system.[26]

As the world has watched Russia and North Korea threaten the United States with nuclear weapons, a growing number of prophecy experts believe the rise of the Antichrist and False Prophet could follow the destruction of America.

Is America the "Daughter of Babylon"?

Chuck Missler, former branch chief in the U.S. Air Force guided missiles department and founder of the Koinonia House ministry, says many who study Bible prophecy are disturbed that the role of the United States in the end times is unclear. "We're almost conspicuous in our absence of mention," Missler says. But he adds that after the description of Gog and Magog being crushed by God when they invade Israel in Ezekiel 38, there is a mention of an enigmatic third party that is destroyed along with them in Ezekiel 39:6—"Those that dwell securely in the coastlands or isles." Missler says, "There is some ambiguity of the Hebrew term used there, but the point is, it's a remote, pleasant place. And the question is, who is it talking about?" Missler goes on to speculate that "the United States is that third party" and that it is essentially destroyed by the weaponry of Magog.[27]

Along with Missler, S. Douglas Woodward, the late Times Square Church pastor David Wilkerson, and others believe prophecies regarding the "daughter of Babylon" and "Babylon the Great" in Isaiah 47, Jeremiah 50–51, and Revelation 17–18 suggest that America will sustain a nuclear attack, catapulting the world into chaos. Afterward, to preserve the "peace and security" of the planet, it's believed that the UN would likely assume full global power, create a world government, and usher in, either knowingly or unknowingly, the rule of the Antichrist and False Prophet.[28]

Many of these prophecy experts believe this attack will occur before or at the beginning of the Tribulation. Known as the "War of Gog and

Magog," the prophecy detailed in Ezekiel 38–39 involves a Russian-led confederation of nations that invade Israel in the end times. As it's interpreted, the prophecy involves a simultaneous attack by enemies from the "north parts" (Ezek. 38:15 KJV) on the United States and Israel.

In his book *Is Russia Destined to Nuke the U.S.?*, Woodward cites 220 biblical verses about an entity (a city, nation-state, or empire) known as the "daughter of Babylon" that will be destroyed like "Sodom and Gomorrah" (Isa. 13:19 NKJV). In Jeremiah 50:12, 50:23, 50:37, 51:7, and 51:13, the prophet describes the daughter of Babylon as "the hindermost" of nations (world's last superpower), "the hammer of the whole earth" (world's most powerful military), and the world's wealthiest country that is composed of a "mingled people" surrounded by "many waters"—terminology that parallels language in the book of Revelation regarding "that great city, Babylon, that mighty city! For in one hour is thy judgment come" (Rev. 18:10 KJV). The prophet Jeremiah describes how it was once a "golden cup" in the hands of God, but now is identified with sin and immorality.

In Ezekiel 38–39, the prophet wrote that when a coalition of nations, including many Middle Eastern countries, attacks Israel, an "evil thought" will enter the mind of its leader to also attack the "land of unwalled villages" and those who "dwell safely" in the "coastlands." Woodward wrote, "The notion that Israel and the U.S. would be attacked at the same time is not hard to fathom. Given that one is considered the Great Satan and the other, the Little Satan, a concurrent attack seems predictable, especially if the attacking parties were attempting to keep the U.S. from coming to the aid of Israel and were highly motivated by their hatred for the 'Zionists.'"

While America is destroyed, God intervenes in the attack on Israel, and the Russian-led coalition is "obliterated by the judgment of God." "The nations mentioned in Ezekiel 38 will team up [for this attack] and then there will be a time of perhaps three-and-a-half years before the Antichrist is able to coordinate the countries of Europe to form in effect the New World Order that will in fact come about as a result of America being destroyed and Russia being destroyed," Woodward says. "There will be a time period in which the world is in chaos, and out of that chaos will come order—the New World Order will finally be achieved."[29]

In One Hour Everything Is Going to Change

Wilkerson, the bestselling author of *The Cross and the Switchblade*, first detailed his vision of a nuclear attack on New York City and other American cities in his 1974 book *The Vision*. "The prophet Isaiah warns us that in the last days God is going to 'turn the world upside down,'" Wilkerson said in a 2007 sermon, "In One Hour Everything Is Going to Change." Revelation 18:19 says, "Woe! Woe to you, great city... In one hour she has been brought to ruin!" "Within that short span," Wilkerson says, "the whole world will witness fast-falling destruction upon a city and a nation, and the world will never be the same... Today, multitudes of secular prophets are saying a nuclear attack is inevitable. The target they mention most often is New York, but it could happen in any major city: London, Paris, Tel Aviv, Washington. Neither Isaiah nor John names the city upon which destructive judgment falls."[30]

Yet according to both biblical and secular prophets, judgment will fall. In one hour, God is going to change the entire world. Wilkerson explains:

A sudden cataclysmic event will strike, the first of the final judgments of God. This great event will cause the earth to reel... Once this happens, utter chaos will erupt. All civic activities will stop, and society will descend into massive disorder... Once this judgment strikes, it will devastate the economy... You may ask: "Why would the whole world change, if a nuclear attack occurs in just one city?" It will happen because of the fear of retaliation. If a rogue nation sends such an attack, you can be sure that within hours that nation will be wiped out. Consider the plan Israel has in place, known as the Samson Option. The moment a nuclear warhead is launched against them, within moments Israel will unleash nuclear missiles to devastate the capital cities of all enemy states. The world has become a ticking bomb, and time is quickly running out.

Chapter Four

Deep State Coup and Occult Explosion

Well, I found some examples that I've seen firsthand in Washington—evidence, the influence of occultism, certainly witchcraft...You have a lot of witchcraft. You have a lot of hedonism. You have all the issues. When I think of Sodom and Gomorrah I often think of Washington, DC, in the same thought.

—LIEUTENANT COLONEL BOB MAGINNIS (RETIRED), SENIOR FELLOW
FOR NATIONAL SECURITY AT THE FAMILY RESEARCH COUNCIL[1]

Have nothing to do with the fruitless deeds of darkness, but rather expose them.

—APOSTLE PAUL (EPHESIANS 5:11 NIV)

In what was perhaps the strangest presidential election in American history, the headlines shortly before Election Day 2016 hinted at the dark underbelly of a "diabolical scandal"—one that involves not just Bill and Hillary Clinton, but the "Deep State" and occult elite globally:[2]

- "Is Hillary Clinton the Antichrist or an Illuminati Witch?" (Jennifer LeClaire, Charisma News, August 11, 2016).
- "Witchcraft on the Campaign Trail" (Stacy Schiff, *New York Times*, October 30, 2016).

- "No, John Podesta Didn't Drink Bodily Fluids at a Secret Satanist Dinner" (Abby Ohlheiser, *Washington Post*, November 4, 2016).
- "The Devil Is a Woman: Ben Carson Ties Hillary Clinton to Lucifer as GOP Swaps Campaign for Witch Trial" (Gideon Resnick, the Daily Beast, July 20, 2016).

These stunning headlines had to do with a WikiLeaks-released e-mail in which the brother of Clinton's campaign chairman, John Podesta, invited him to attend the "Spirit Cooking" dinner of performance artist Marina Abramović. The articles also involved speculation by former presidential candidate Dr. Ben Carson at the Republican National Convention about a "Democratic-Satanic alliance." During the convention, Carson—now Trump's secretary of housing and urban development—spoke about Saul Alinsky, the Democratic socialist who dedicated his book *Rules for Radicals* to Lucifer. Clinton wrote her undergraduate thesis about Alinsky and interviewed him before he died. "Are we willing to elect as president someone who has as their role model somebody who acknowledges Lucifer?" Carson asked. "If we continue to allow [secular progressives] to take God out of our lives, God will remove himself from us."[3]

These allegations of widespread occult influence in Washington, DC, came amid growing concerns about a "Deep State coup" and an explosion in occult phenomenon in America and worldwide.[4]

"The Deep State, although there's no precise or scientific definition, generally refers to the agencies in Washington that are permanent power factions," Glenn Greenwald, a Pulitzer Prize–winning journalist, told Amy Goodman on *Democracy Now!* "They typically exercise their power in secret, in the dark, and so they're barely subject to democratic accountability, if they're subject to it at all. It's agencies like the CIA, the NSA, and the other intelligence agencies that are essentially designed to disseminate disinformation and deceit and propaganda, and have a long history of doing not only that, but also have a long history of the world's worst war crimes, atrocities, and death squads."[5]

The concept of the "Deep State" can be traced to President Dwight D. Eisenhower's warning in his farewell address in 1961 about the growing power of the "military-industrial complex." Eisenhower's remarks followed the publication of the 1956 book *The Power Elite*, which argued that America's power is concentrated in the "military-industrial complex," Wall Street, and the Pentagon. Today, the Deep State refers to the "entrenched networks hostile to Trump," including a "silent coup" under way at the behest of Obama—operating from a "bunker" less than two miles from the White House—and his army of thirty thousand "agitators…who will fight his Republican successor at every turn of his historic presidency." The concept exploded into the national consciousness shortly before the election as Trump alleged that Obama had wiretapped telephones at Trump Tower.[6]

The controversy intensified in the initial months of Trump's presidency amid calls by some House Democrats for his impeachment in the wake of his firing of FBI director James Comey. Critics called the firing obstruction of justice because Trump had allegedly asked Comey to drop an investigation into his former national security adviser Michael Flynn amid a congressional probe of Russian interference in the election. In tweets, Trump described the investigation as the "single greatest witch hunt of a politician in American history!"[7]

By the summer of 2017, an investigation by the Senate Committee on Homeland Security and Governmental Affairs found the Trump administration was facing an unprecedented wave of national security leaks appearing in the press at least once a day—far more than either the Obama or Bush administrations had experienced at the same point.[8]

Syndicated columnist Pat Buchanan, the White House communications director under Reagan, told Fox Business that the Establishment "octopus," which includes the media and the Deep State, is attempting to destroy Trump. "What they want to do is cancel the returns from last November, and basically overturn the election of a man who they could not defeat at the polls."[9]

The Occult Revival

On top of concerns over a Deep State coup, America is simultaneously experiencing a resurgence in the occult, Satanism, and witchcraft—one of the world's fastest-growing religions today. This pervasive occult influence has infused Washington, DC, the media, and Hollywood and is flaunted before tens of millions of people globally during events such as the Super Bowl and Grammy Awards. From the recent opening of the Satanic Temple in Salem, Massachusetts, and the reproduction of the arch of the Temple of Baal in New York City, London, and Dubai at the World Government Summit, to CERN's attempts to contact entities in other dimensions and a spike in exorcisms, it seems the world has gone mad and is ready to meet the "deceiver of the whole world" incarnate.[10]

"We are having an incredible outpouring of occult things, of various alternative religions that are occult-based like Wicca, and even the Satanic Temple group that is getting so much press," says Rev. William "Bill" Schnoebelen, a biblical authority on alternative religions and the occult and former Druidic high priest. "When I was into this stuff in the 1960s, it was all kind of in the closet. It's now out in the open and it's been mainstreamed...We have turned the reins of the culture over to Hollywood, and it's been a disaster because the media, for the most part, are entirely owned by the Illuminati. All these different entertainers— Miley Cyrus, Madonna, and whatnot—are totally sold out to the devil's agenda, and because of that, they have this enormous influence on the culture, especially with younger people, and we are losing this battle."[11]

This sharp rise in satanic influence comes several decades after *Time* magazine chronicled the modern reawakening of this devilish movement in its 1972 cover story "The Occult Revival: Satan Returns." The article coincided with the release of Hal Lindsey's bestseller *Satan Is Alive and Well on Planet Earth*. While working on West Coast college campuses in the 1960s, Lindsey witnessed a "paradigm shift in thinking" in which students moved from rejecting the supernatural to believing in occult phenomena. Professors and students became involved in psychic research, parapsychology, extrasensory perception, mystic philosophies, Eastern religions, astrology, illicit drugs, witchcraft, black magic, and fortunetelling. "By 1965 this became the 'in vogue' thing among professors and students, particularly at the University of California at Berkeley," Lindsey wrote in 2002. "They still rejected things supernatural in Christianity, but they blindly accepted supernatural experiences associated with the practice of the occult. National news magazines, TV shows, movies, all began to reflect the acceptance of the supernatural in the occult."

In her 2015 *Time* magazine article—"The Evolution of Modern Satanism in the United States"—Lily Rothman wrote that the existence of Satanists as an organized, public group in the United States "can be largely traced to one man: Anton Szandor La Vey, author of 1969's *The Satanic Bible*. La Vey founded the Church of Satan in 1966 in San Francisco...In 1978, the U.S. Army even included the group in the manual of 'Religious Requirements and Practices' delivered to its hundreds of chaplains."[12]

Today, the demoniacal movement La Vey helped resurrect grows increasingly stronger as the fallen archangel Lucifer, his demonic host, and secret society minions revel in what is arguably a new heyday of satanic evil as the phantasmagorical prophecies of Revelation come into clear focus.

"People look at movies like *The Sorcerer's Apprentice* and *Doctor Strange*, and they think, 'Oh, well, this is just fantasy,'" Schnoebelen says. "No, this is not fantasy. This stuff is real, except the source behind it is demonic. People at the Temple of Set and other groups are working to bring in a dark age in which old dark gods are going to come back and take over the planet." Schnoebelen explains that these groups use several orders of magic to open portals into other dimensions. And that now they have an "enormous, multibillion dollar technological facility at the border of Switzerland and France called CERN that is trying to do this."

CERN: Shiva—the Destroyer

CERN, the European Organization for Nuclear Research, operates the largest particle physics laboratory in the world. It's home to the Large Hadron Collider, an enormous device used to smash subatomic particles into each other to re-create conditions at the beginning of time. CERN's scientists are also working to decipher the mysteries of antimatter. In 2013, they discovered Higgs boson—the "God Particle." In a study published in *Physical Review Letters*, physicists claimed that "portals" may link our physical reality to an unseen one containing dark matter and energy. Physicists are concerned that CERN's work could create a microscopic black hole that could implode the Earth. In *Starmus*, world-renowned physicist Stephen Hawking explained the "God Particle" could become unstable and potentially destroy the entire universe. Several years ago, Sergio Bertolucci, CERN's director of research and scientific computing, remarked that CERN might open portals into other dimensions. "Out of this door might come something, or we might send something through it," Bertolucci speculated.

Perhaps in a case of fiction predicting reality, the buzz in some circles now is about CERN's paranormal associations, including the statue of Shiva—the Hindu god of destruction known as "the Destroyer"—displayed near CERN's headquarters. The bronze statue depicts Shiva performing the tandava dance involving the "preservation of all life and existence, and the termination of all life and existence." Even more ominously, a portion of CERN is built atop a town that in Roman times was called Apolliacum. Its temple was dedicated to Apollyon—the "Destroyer." Apollyon is the "angel of the bottomless pit" mentioned in Revelation 9:11. Further, CERN has a "circular logo with three clockwise tails as the layering of three '6' numerals"—or 666, the number of the Beast.[13]

"It's just bizarre that science has come to be a servant of evil," Schnoebelen says. "In the book of Revelation, it talks about how the key to the bottomless pit is given to an angel...and the destroyer—Abaddon/Apollyon—is going to emerge and come forth with these locust-like armies. That's very much what these people [at CERN] are trying to do...They think if they can get enough demonic entities and fallen celestial beings on their side that they can beat the armies of heaven when the Battle of Armageddon finally occurs."

Temple of Baal, Satan Clubs, and Exorcisms

Following its erection at New York City Hall, in London's Trafalgar Square, and in Florence, Italy, at the G7 Summit, a reconstructed version of Palmyra's Triumphal Arch—the arch of the Temple of Baal—was displayed at the World Government Summit in Dubai in early 2017. The summit featured more than one hundred internationally known speakers, including UN secretary-general Antonio Guterres, International Monetary Fund managing director Christine Lagarde, and SpaceX and Tesla chief executive officer Elon Musk. The original arch stood for two thousand years in Palmyra, Syria, in front of the pagan Temple of Baal, or Temple of Bel, until ISIS destroyed it in 2015. The Institute for Digital Archaeology, working with Harvard and Oxford Universities, created the twenty-eight-meter-tall replica of the arch using original photographs, 3-D printing technology, and robots. "And, of course, 'Bel' and 'Baal' are synonymous, and both titles can be traced all the way back to ancient Babylon and a very evil ruler named Nimrod," Michael Snyder explained. "Nimrod was the great king of the very first 'world government' in the post-Flood world...So, it seems more than a little strange that an arch with links to Nimrod has been erected to honor a summit devoted to the promotion of 'world government' in our day...Nimrod's world government in ancient times attempted to push God out of the picture, and the same thing is true with the globalists of today...Donald Trump stands opposed to this twisted dream, and that is why the globalists hate him so much."[14]

Meanwhile, several decades after La Vey founded the Church of Satan in 1966, a new group called the Satanic Temple has grown significantly since its founding in 2013 with one hundred thousand members worldwide. In 2016, it opened its headquarters in an 1881 Victorian house in Salem, Massachusetts—the historic home of the Salem witch trials. The religious freedom campaign group generated headlines in 2016 after launching "After School Satan Clubs." The Satanic Club said the clubs would focus on teaching children "critical reasoning, independent-thinking, fun, and freethought." Travis Weber wrote in a Family Research Council article, "The Satanic Temple has already agitated in the name of its 'religion' by creating a gigantic bronze statue of Baphomet for the lawn of the Oklahoma State House, opening city council meetings with satanic incantations, [and] distributing coloring books featuring the dark lord to schools across the country." In 2017, the Satanic Temple convinced officials in Belle Plaine, Minnesota, to let them place a monument at a veterans' park.[15]

The occult's growing impact on society has been accompanied by a "huge increase" in exorcisms. Two of America's most active exorcists—Father Gary Thomas and Father Vincent Lampert—are now having trouble keeping up with demand for their services. "In lengthy interviews with the *Telegraph*, the two exorcists discuss how the increase in drug and pornography addiction, failure of the mental healthcare system, and a rise in popularity of 'pagan activities,' such as using a Ouija board to summon the dead, are among the factors contributing to the huge increase in demand for the Rite."[16]

Meanwhile, witches gathered worldwide at midnight in early 2017 to cast binding spells on Trump in the hope of banishing him from office. They pledged to cast spells on each crescent moon until Trump is no longer president. In response, Breitbart called on Christians to say prayers to protect the president from the "Bind Trump" spell.[17]

"A lot of what we're seeing play out is a visible reflection of what is taking place in the invisible world," says Billy Graham's evangelist daughter Anne Graham Lotz. She explains that a great battle is raging in the invisible world between the forces of Satan and God. "And if we're at the end of the age…the enemy knows his time is short, and so I feel like the invisible world is in turmoil." Lotz urges Christians to pray for the president. "I would pray that God would give him wisdom, and patience and self-control, that he would give him good counselors…that he would turn to God and that he would find God at his hard moments when he needs help and strength and wisdom."[18]

The apostle Paul warned that the primary battle we face is against "principalities, against powers, against the rulers of the darkness of this age" (Eph. 6:12 NKJV).

While many Christians assume witchcraft is just theater with incantations, the supernatural power released into the world by these ceremonies is real. The Bible teaches that one of the secrets of "Mystery Babylon" is the ability to use witchcraft to reconfigure reality. We should take to heart Paul's final exhortation and instructions on how to engage in spiritual warfare: "Put on the whole armor of God, that you may be able to stand against the wiles of the devil" (Eph. 6:10–11 NKJV).

As America moves from a post-Christian nation to a New Age, Marxist, and Eastern mystical one, we can expect to see an even greater increase in this intense spiritual battle.

"There is no question that we're engaged in spiritual battle and warfare," says Jack Graham, pastor of the forty-thousand-member Prestonwood Baptist Church in Plano, Texas. "Satan is real and his powers of darkness are seen so vividly across the earth, whether we're talking about ISIS and terrorism, the redefinition of marriage, or sixty million babies aborted...and we're facing increasing dangers in our generation. This very well could be the terminal generation."[19]

"Mystery, Babylon" and Globalism

For many years, an odd mix of investigative journalists, whistleblowers, prophecy experts, and others warned of the dangers of globalism—sounding the alarm that the wealthy elite and secret societies were planning a global coup to launch a world state, cashless society, and New Age–Illuminati-based religious system.

But their warnings were largely met with indifference and disbelief. The government, mainstream media, and academia labeled these claims "conspiracy theories." However, Lance deHaven-Smith, a professor of public administration and policy at Florida State University, wrote in *Conspiracy Theory in America* that the term "conspiracy theory" was created by the CIA in 1967 as propaganda to encourage the media to lambast "conspiracy theories," infuse the term with "powerfully negative associations," and discourage investigation into government corruption scandals. DeHaven-Smith wrote, "From the nation's beginning, Americans were fearful of secret plots by political insiders to subvert constitutional governance."[20]

The CIA campaign to dupe the media and public began to unravel shortly after Trump announced his run for president in June 2015. Beginning that summer, Trump tapped into the zeitgeist of the nation by explaining to the public that the system was rigged against them "for the benefit of shadowy forces in the news media, the banks, and the government," Liam Stack wrote in the *New York Times*. "Hillary says things can't change," Trump tweeted in June 2016. "I say they have to change. It's a choice between Americanism and her corrupt globalism."[21]

Joseph E. Uscinski, an associate professor of political science at the University of Miami and coauthor of *American Conspiracy Theories*, says, "There were two candidates that referenced conspiracy theories frequently in their campaigns. One was Donald Trump, who if you put all of his conspiracy theories together, what you sort of get is a conspiracy theory that our political elites are aligned with foreign interests rather than with the American people's interests…Bernie Sanders, on the other hand, believed that a small group of people—the 1 percent—control our entire economy and political systems, and to quote him, he believes that they have a 'greed that knows no end by making it hard for us to survive.'"[22]

Trump's focus on the evils of globalism helps explain why he won the election—a feat that stunned the world and, in many ways, defies logical and natural explanations. It's also one of the reasons why so many evangelical Christians believe God raised up this imperfect man in an act of mercy following their intercessory prayers. God chose Trump because he has the will, knowledge, and warrior spirit to confront the great evil that has penetrated the highest levels of power in America.

Trump champions the things that please God's heart on many levels, including his opposition to globalism. As we revealed in *The Babylon Code*, globalism has its roots in ancient Babylon—an archetype of the Antichrist's end-time empire, which was ruled by the first world dictator Nimrod in a Luciferian rebellion against God. That's why God judged it and left the account in Genesis 11 as a warning for our world today.

Babylon plays a key role as both an instrument and a target of God's judgment in Isaiah, Jeremiah, Ezekiel, and Daniel—and then reappears in Revelation 17–18 as "Mystery, Babylon" and "Babylon the Great." In

Revelation 17:5 (NKJV) an angel shows the apostle John an abominable woman sitting on a scarlet beast, "And on her forehead a name was written:

MYSTERY, BABYLON THE GREAT, THE MOTHER OF HARLOTS AND OF THE ABOMINATIONS OF THE EARTH."

The prophetic riddle of "Mystery, Babylon" and "Babylon the Great" is considered one of the Bible's greatest mysteries. It reveals how an interlocking network of transnational corporations, international banks, government agencies, think tanks, foundations, and secret societies is working to create a global government, cashless society, and universal religion as predicted by the prophets. During the Tribulation, the Antichrist and False Prophet will rise to power, controlling "Mystery, Babylon"—the worldwide religious system—and "Babylon the Great," the global geopolitical and economic system.

Babylon is second only to Jerusalem as the most-mentioned city in the Bible. The Bible mentions Babylon nearly three hundred times, and one out of ten verses in Revelation is about Babylon. Revelation 17–18 is devoted entirely to Babylon and its destruction in the end times. As Mark Hitchcock wrote, "Babylon holds a key place in the mind of God and in his final plan for the ages."[23]

Globalism Is Spiritual and Demonic at Its Core

The evils of globalism, like abortion, deeply grieve the heart of God. In an article that went viral prior to the 2016 presidential election, Skyline Church pastor Jim Garlow wrote that few people understand the true significance of globalism. "Trump opposes globalism," Garlow wrote.

"Hillary thrives on it. Globalism is far more than 'geographical' or 'eliminating national borders and boundaries.' It is spiritual and demonic at its core. Few—very few—understand this. This is quite likely one of the main reasons why Trump is hated."[24]

Trump is one of the few politicians who is at war with globalism. Most of the Republicans and Democrats, along with Obama and the Clintons, for all intents and purposes, are on the payroll of the wealthy corporate elite. They sold America down the river long ago—as did their EU counterparts—with numerous trade treaties that promote globalism. Today, Babylon is rising again as the Luciferian order ascends to power with plans to require everyone to take the mark of the Beast. The goal of this one-world system is the reawakening of "Mystery, Babylon" with just two classes of people—the occult rulers and essentially a large slave class perpetually in debt to them.

The entire occult system of world politics, government, intelligence, finance, media, entertainment, and academia is at war with Trump because he is the chief threat to their power and plans. Meanwhile, the Deep State is involved in a coup to overthrow Trump by orchestrating his impeachment over allegations of Russian interference in the 2016 election. In a *Foreign Affairs* article titled "3 Ways to Get Rid of President Trump Before 2020," Rosa Brooks, a law professor at Georgetown University and a former senior adviser at the U.S. State Department, raised the possibility of having Trump declared mentally unfit, or a military coup, to topple his presidency. "In these dark days, some around the globe are finding solace in the 25th Amendment to the Constitution," Brooks wrote. "This previously obscure amendment states that 'the Vice President and a majority of...the principal officers of the executive departments' can declare the president 'unable to discharge the powers and duties of his office,' in which case 'the Vice President shall immediately assume the powers and duties of the office as Acting President... [Another] possibility is one that until recently I would have

98

said was unthinkable in the United States of America: a military coup, or at least a refusal by military leaders to obey certain orders."[25]

Despite such virulent opposition, if God's people will turn to the Lord in humble repentance and prayer, we believe God will give Trump a long series of unprecedented, miraculous victories that will radically transform America. A political and spiritual battle of gargantuan proportions is raging behind the scenes. As we've pointed out, the Deep State is thoroughly intertwined with the occult elite, just as similar forces have been operative in all the great empires of history. This battle explains why the world is experiencing an upsurge in demonic activity in the political, entertainment, and media realms. Satanists, witches, and Illuminists in high places are waging a supernatural war against Trump, America, and the world, as "Mystery, Babylon" arises again in our time.

Archetypal Forces of Good and Evil

Man's original blueprint for how a society and the world should be managed was drawn in ancient Babylon when the occult elite organized the first worldwide political, economic, and religious system. An essential secret of "Mystery, Babylon"—long kept hidden from the masses—is that it is a control system designed to corral about 99 percent of humanity into a global class of debt slaves who live exclusively to serve the interests of the elite 1 percent. However, for "Mystery, Babylon" to function properly, the 99 percent must not realize that they are in effect slaves to the occult ruling class.

Beginning in ancient Babylon—the birthplace of the world's mystery religions—the elite established a template by which they could control people, government, and economics through occult power, a debt-based economic system, and the worship of Lucifer. The occult elite view themselves as "god-kings." The term "Illuminati bloodlines" refers to the belief that certain families born thousands of years ago are genetically descended from entities who visited Earth from outer space or another dimension, but whom the Bible describes as fallen angels.

The best-known of the purported thirteen Illuminati families, according to the special publication *Secret Societies: The Truth Revealed*, are the Rothschilds and Rockefellers. In his book *Our Occulted History: Do the Global Elite Conceal Ancient Aliens?*, Jim Marrs wrote that the Rothschilds believe they are descended from Nimrod, the great-grandson of Noah. In this belief system, the "Anunnaki/Nefilim," according to interpretations of ancient stone tablets from Sumer, are extraterrestrials who visited Earth in "fantastic flying machines" long ago and manipulated the "DNA of primitives on Earth"—creating "kings and dynasties" among "the new hybrids." The term "Nefilim" is the biblical "Nephilim." A growing number of Bible scholars say Nephilim were the offspring of women and fallen angels as described in Genesis 6:1–4, Numbers 13:30–33, and Jude 4–8. "The practice of dynastic kingship based on a royal lineage traceable to the gods has affected nations and governments up to the present day, as evidenced by the fact that the Rothschilds of today claim kinship with Nimrod," Marrs wrote.

In his seminal book on the Nephilim, *The Omega Conspiracy: Satan's Last Assault on God's Kingdom*, the late Dr. I. D. E. Thomas, pastor of the United Community Church in Glendale, California, wrote that "strong biblical evidence" indicates Genesis 6:1–4 "refers to the bizarre union between extraterrestrials and the women of Earth." "The Nephilim were the superhuman offspring of the union, and they appeared on this planet just before the great Flood," Thomas wrote. "In fact, their existence and vile corruption of the world was the main reason for the catastrophe. Their kind was destroyed along with the rest of mankind in the Flood. Only Noah and his family escaped their contamination and hence were saved. Yet, centuries later, the Nephilim emerged again, this time on a more limited scale in the land of Canaan (Numbers 13:2, 25–33). As before, God ordered their destruction... Evidence indicates that some of these Nephilim survived the second extermination. If so, where are they today?"[26]

The elite's belief system helps explain why occult groups are so obsessed with ancient astrological sciences. Some Bible scholars believe the Tower of Babel was an astrological temple designed to worship the "sky gods," or fallen angels. The Babylonian word *Bab-ilu* means the "Gate of God." Today, many biblical experts believe the Tower of Babel was an interdimensional portal that allowed extradimensional entities to enter our world.[27]

Pause for a moment and read the Tower of Babel account in Genesis 11:1–8 to glean the implications of what God was saying.

Tower of Babel: The Portal to the Gods?

In his article "Revisiting the Tower of Babel," *Prophecy Watchers* magazine editor in chief Gary Stearman wrote that God didn't view the construction of the tower as "merely a monument to pride... They were apparently about to realize some success in penetrating the dimensional veil that separates some aspect of heaven from the earth! This 'tower' would enable men to realize their darkest imaginings. And what had they imagined to do? Simply to renew their contact with the 'sons of God' [fallen angels] as their predecessors had done before the Flood... Today, the laboratories of intelligentsia are deeply preoccupied with scaling the dimensional wall, once again. They are on the verge of penetrating the veil that lies between earth and the invisible heavens."[28]

Today, the worlds of science and science fiction are merging. It wasn't long ago that a theory about ancient astronauts genetically seeding our planet—popularized by Erich von Däniken in his 1968 cult classic *Chariots of the Gods*—was considered a kind of fairy tale. Today, it's known as *panspermia* and is one of the theories of the origin of life on Earth. This idea, now accepted by some modern scientists, goes back to "Mystery,

Babylon" and involves secret occult teachings on accessing supernatural power. This secret knowledge was passed down from empire to empire for thousands of years through a network of secret societies and occult religious movements.

The "New Aeon" of Secret Societies

Since ancient Babylon, secret societies have pushed for what British occultist Aleister Crowley called the "New Aeon"—the Age of Aquarius, the mythological Golden Age, the fulfillment of what is known in occult circles as the "Plan."[29]

Throughout history, members of secret societies have wielded enormous influence over the world's most powerful empires. The *Newsweek* publication "Secret Societies: Infiltrating the Inner Circle" lists the names of the better-known secret societies: Druids, the Order of the Assassins, Knights Templar, Rosicrucians, and the Bavarian Illuminati. Semisecret societies like the Freemasons, Yale University's Skull and Bones, Bohemian Grove, Bilderberg Group, Council on Foreign Relations, Trilateral Commission, and Club of Rome are often the topic of books, films, and media articles. Among these groups, the Bavarian Illuminati—a historical secret society founded May 1, 1776, by Adam Weishaupt, a professor at the University of Ingolstadt—has captured the world's imagination and has been the focus of blockbuster books like Dan Brown's *Angels and Demons* and *The Da Vinci Code* and films like *Lara Croft: Tomb Raider*. Celebrities often flash the Illuminati "pyramid signal" in music videos and during concerts.

"Other celebrities, such as Rihanna, Madonna, Lady Gaga, Katy Perry, and Beyoncé, have added to the clamor over Illuminati infiltration of the entertainment industry by being pictured with Illuminati symbols and words," Jim Marrs wrote in *The Illuminati: The Secret Society That Hijacked the World*. "Whenever a celebrity dies unexpectedly, such as

Heath Ledger and Michael Jackson, the elusive Illuminati is blamed. Others drop hints of their lives being controlled by the Order. Beyoncé has admitted in interviews to being guided by a separate personality named Sasha Fierce... Many believed Jay Z was connected to the Illuminati when he was pictured wearing a black sweatshirt with the words 'Do what thou wilt,' the Assassin maxim that passed through the Illuminati to Crowley's OTO... Madonna, who released a record entitled 'Illuminati,' said, 'People often accuse me of being a member of the Illuminati, but the thing is, I know who the real Illuminati are.'" While Bavarian ruler Duke Karl Theodor banned the Illuminati and other secret societies in 1784, researchers believe the "Illuminati went underground at the end of the eighteenth century" and still exists today.[30]

Following Theodor's ban, the Illuminati merged with Freemasonry—an organization with six million members worldwide that traces its origins to the Tower of Babel and the Mystery Schools of Greece and Egypt. Marrs wrote that the Illuminati serves as the "connective tissue between ancient and modern secret societies" and attracts the attention of "corporate leaders, high-level society members, European royalty, and even intelligence agencies." He wrote that most Freemasons "look at their brotherhood as little different from that of the Lion's Club, the Optimists, or the Chamber of Commerce," and are unaware of the inner core of the "Illuminated Freemasons."[31]

"The Illuminati began as a secret society under the direction of Jesuit priests," wrote American businessman Robert Kiyosaki, who coauthored with Trump *Why We Want You to Be Rich*.

Later, a council of five men, one for each of the points on the pentagram, formed what was called The Ancient and Illuminated Seers of Bavaria. They were high-order Luciferian-Freemasons, thoroughly immersed in mysticism and eastern mental disciplines, seeking to develop the super powers of the mind. Their alleged plan and purpose is world domination for their lord—which is the fallen Lucifer...Organizations such as the United Nations, the International Monetary Fund, the World Bank, and the International Criminal Court are seen as tentacles of the Illuminati. The Illuminati are the driving force behind the brainwashing of the mindless masses, blatant mind control, manipulation of beliefs, scientific dumbing-down of society, chemical poisoning of food, water, and air; also, the Illuminati are revealed to have total and complete control over all the mainstream media of the modern world, all the information, all the food, all the money, most of the world's military forces...The Illuminati have a private board of elite, interlocking delegates who control the world's major banks. They create inflations, recessions, depressions, and manipulate the world markets, supporting certain leaders and coups and undermining others to achieve their overall goals. The goal behind the Illuminati conspiracy is to create and then manage crises that will eventually convince the masses that globalism, with its centralized economic control and one-world religious ethic, are the necessary solution to the world's woes. This structure, usually known as The New World Order, will of course be ruled by the Illuminati.[32]

Based on decades of collective research resulting in this book and our bestselling globalism expose *The Babylon Code*, we believe the evidence is overwhelming that an occult network has infiltrated the highest levels of government, business, religion, and academia to create a global government, cashless society, and universal religion.

Before this new global system goes live, though, these powerful groups must eliminate the Christian church, or infiltrate it so that its theology is largely humanist, Marxist, and New Age—transforming Christianity into an agent of occult Marxist globalism. In what could be confirmation that these occult groups are close to achieving this goal, a Barna Group survey found only 17 percent of Christians who attend church regularly have a biblical worldview today. The study found that 61 percent of practicing Christians agree with ideas rooted in New Spirituality, 54 percent resonate with postmodernist views, 36 percent accept ideas associated with Marxism, and 29 percent believe in ideas based on secularism. The authors wrote that "almost three in 10 (28 percent) practicing Christians strongly agree that 'all people pray to the same god or spirit, no matter what name they use for that spiritual being.'"[33]

The sea change in worldviews of Christians can be traced to ideas introduced a century ago by Fabian socialists such as H. G. Wells, author of *The New World Order*; philosopher Bertrand Russell; economist John Maynard Keynes, the father of modern economic theory; novelist Aldous Huxley, author of *Brave New World*; and biologist Julian Huxley, the first director general of the UN's UNESCO. Many of these figures secretly belonged to elite occult societies. Socialist activist Beatrice Webb played a prominent role in creating the Fabian Society and later helped found the prestigious London School of Economics.[34]

The Fabian socialists and other globalists were financed by the world's wealthiest banking families, who were members of secret societies. Their goal was to use UNESCO to control mass communications such as newspapers, magazines, television, and radio—and the Internet and social media today—to brainwash the masses into accepting global governance. They sought to use communications, along with indoctrination, social engineering, and scientific mind control, to create an Orwellian form of groupthink in which people believe the same thing.[35]

In his 1958 nonfiction book *Brave New World Revisited*, Aldous Huxley concluded that the planet was already becoming like the dystopian fictional world he wrote of in *Brave New World*—a world literature classic about an "unequal, technologically advanced future where humans are genetically bred, socially indoctrinated, and pharmaceutically anesthetized to passively uphold an authoritarian ruling order." Huxley wrote, "Under a scientific dictator education will really work—with the result that most men and women will grow up to love their servitude and will never dream of revolution. There seems to be no good reason why a thoroughly scientific dictatorship should ever be overthrown."[36]

What Huxley meant was that with truly effective, scientific mind control, the elite could program the masses to be, in effect, their political, economic, and spiritual slaves, and they wouldn't consciously know this. A correct understanding of the biblical account of "Mystery, Babylon" shows it to be an occult dictatorship, or scientific dictatorship, that rules the masses. The two terms are interchangeable because the ancient super civilizations like Babylon viewed science, magic, technology, and mathematics as all one thing. That's why Sir Arthur C. Clarke, a futurist and author of the classic *2001: A Space Odyssey*, said, "Magic's just science that we don't understand yet." Clarke wasn't trying to be clever; he knew that at the highest level of human understanding we are only dealing with one system—the unseen one beyond what we call reality.[37]

Elite Rule via Vast Fortunes

The wealthy corporate elite rule the world through their vast fortunes, such as those of international banking families like the Rothschilds. While Bankrate.com estimates the Rothschild family's net worth at $400 billion, some researchers believe the extended family's actual net worth could total tens of trillions of dollars—secretly spread out among legions of descendants and hidden in various investment groups, estates, and multinational corporations.[38]

In his book *The Conspirators' Hierarchy: The Committee of 300*, former MI6 intelligence agent John Coleman calls the world's "ultimate controlling body" the "Committee of 300"—explaining that the Rothschild and Rockefeller families, along with British royalty and "Britain's hierarchy," are among its leading members. Other members include the old families of Venetian and European Black Nobility, the American Eastern Liberal Establishment, Freemasonry, Skull and Bones, the Illuminati, the "Nine Unknown Men," Lucis Trust (originally the Lucifer Publishing Company), International Monetary Fund, Bank of International Settlements, World Bank, and United Nations.

"The Committee of 300, although in existence for 150 years, did not take on its present form until around 1897," Coleman wrote. "It was always given to issuing orders through other fronts, such as its Royal Institute of International Affairs (RIIA). When it was decided that a super-body would control European affairs, the RIIA founded the Tavistock Institute, which in turn created the Club of Rome and then NATO…The power exercised by these important personages and the corporations, television stations, newspapers, insurance companies, and banks they represent, match in size and strength, the power and prestige of at least five European countries…These nice, very proper English gentlemen are in reality, utterly ruthless. They will invade every nation and seize its wealth to protect their privileged way of life. It is this class of British aristocracy, and their American cousins, whose fortunes are inextricably woven and intertwined with the drug trade, the gold, diamond, and arms trades, banking, commerce, industry and oil, the news media and entertainment industries, who will be in the elite class of the New World Order—one world government."[39]

The elite rule Europe and its endless colonies by controlling the monetary systems of nations through central banks. Until recently, most people thought central banks like the Federal Reserve were official governmental banking institutions. They didn't know that the central banks in the United States, United Kingdom, France, Italy, and most nations are owned by a handful of extremely wealthy families who put people who will follow their orders without hesitation into the highest positions of power.

"Deep State"—the Invisible Government

The terms "invisible government," "shadow government," and more recently "Deep State" have been used to describe the secretive, occult, and international banking and business families that control financial institutions, both political parties, and cabals within various intelligence agencies in Britain and America. Edward L. Bernays, a pioneer in the field of propaganda, spoke of the "invisible government" as the "true ruling power of our country." He said, "We are governed, our minds are molded, our tastes formed, our ideas suggested, largely by men we have never heard of."[40]

"The political process of the United States of America [is] under attack by intelligence agencies and individuals in those agencies," U.S. representative Dennis Kucinich (D-OH) said. "You have politicization of agencies that is resulting in leaks from anonymous, unknown people, and the intention is to take down a president. Now, this is very dangerous to America. It's a threat to our republic; it constitutes a clear and present danger to our way of life."[41]

Emotional Contagion

One of the reasons why the Deep State has been able to hide in plain sight is because it controls the mainstream media in the United States. Despite the growing evidence of its existence, the media largely denies this reality. David Remnick, editor of the *New Yorker*, wrote an article titled, "There Is No Deep State: The Problem in Washington Is Not a Conspiracy Against the President; It's the President Himself." Like the "thought police" in George Orwell's *1984*—a classic book about a dystopian future where critical thought is suppressed by a totalitarian regime—the Deep State uses the media to program the population according to the dictates of Big Brother and tell people in effect that "WAR IS PEACE," "FREEDOM IS SLAVERY," and "IGNORANCE IS STRENGTH."[42]

Many of the largest social media platforms are used by the Deep State for surveillance and to influence the masses. Many people think social media is just for personal fun and networking with friends, family, and business associates. However, this innocent activity enables powerful computer networks to create detailed profiles of people's political and moral beliefs and buying habits, as well as a deep analysis of their psychological conflicts, emotional problems, and pretty much anything Big Brother wants to know.

Most people don't understand the true extent of surveillance now occurring. For at least a decade, digital flat-screen televisions, cell phones and smartphones, laptop computers, and most devices with a camera and microphone could be used to spy on you without your knowledge. Even if the power on one of these devices was off, you could still be recorded by supercomputers collecting "mega-data" for potential use later.

These technologies are also used to transform people's belief systems and create powerful external changes in the political and cultural environment of a nation. By using complex psychological strategies, revolutions and regime changes are now instigated via social media. A computer-generated emotional contagion spreads intense emotions such as fear and anger, triggering betrayal and revolution through social media.

Growing numbers of thinking Americans are realizing that their nation is no longer ruled by "We the People." Instead, we are ruled by the Deep State—the government within the government.

Who Really Runs the World?

The existence of the Deep State and how it works is tied into the question, "Who actually runs and controls this world?" The answer is not one that modern intellectuals, geopolitical analysts, and university professors want to hear. The reality is that a powerful fallen angel named Lucifer is the temporary god of this world.

This transfer of power to Lucifer happened when Adam and Eve disobeyed God in the Garden of Eden and activated the "law of sin and death" (Rom. 8:2). At that moment, Lucifer, who was plotting to overthrow the throne of God, temporarily became the god of this world. Although this assertion is considered a myth by many sophisticated elites, it is what is known as the "final reality"—meaning it is a truth not contingent on anyone's beliefs, fashions, or opinions.

Ironically, many of the world's secretive, occult elite who publicly claim to be secular humanists privately believe in the existence of a supernatural world and the power of Lucifer and worship him through various rituals. The highest-level Luciferians are members of groups such as the Illuminati, or what some call *Illuminati Mystery Babylon*. Today, they still maintain the control grid their ancestors created in ancient Babylon to rule over humanity. It is no coincidence that "Mystery, Babylon" is a central topic in the last few chapters of the Bible. The book of Revelation describes the final great events that will bring history to consummation and the role that "Mystery, Babylon" will play.[43]

Winston Churchill wrote in a 1920 article in the *Illustrated Sunday Herald* that modern attempts to overthrow and reconstitute society had been growing for over a century. He added, "[The Illuminati] has been the mainspring of every subversive movement during the nineteenth century; and now at last this band of extraordinary personalities from the underworld of the great cities of Europe and America have gripped the Russian people by the hair of their heads and have become practically the undisputed masters of that enormous empire."[44]

In summary, when you delve into the Deep State and intelligence agencies of various nations, you see a clear connection between the elite, international banking and business families, and a spectrum of occult societies such as the Illuminati. Like it or not, these are the people and groups who rule our world.

Chapter Five

The Great Mass Deception

For this reason God sends them a powerful delusion so that they will believe the lie and so that all will be condemned who have not believed the truth but have delighted in wickedness.

—APOSTLE PAUL (2 THESS. 2:11–12 NIV)

The New Age lie is simply: We all need to welcome and accept a one-world leader to rule over all of us, submit to a one-world government, merge with a one-world economy and universal payment system, combine all religions into one under a one-world religious system, and thereby create and establish a "New Golden Age" for humanity; a time of universal peace like never before.

—PASTOR BILLY CRONE

We live in the time predicted by the ancient Hebrew prophets and prophesied by Jesus Christ and his apostles—an era of mass deception unparalleled in human history.

Today, the level of deceit, subterfuge and disinformation in politics, media, Hollywood, business, academia, and religion is truly mind-boggling. The "Mystery, Babylon" thought-control matrix is fully operational. In today's occult-entangled and technology-addicted culture, it's not hard to envision how the world and church could be duped by what is known in prophecy circles as "the Great Deception."[1]

In recent years, Bible scholars have offered different theories about what "powerful delusion" could persuade humanity to embrace the occult religion of the Antichrist in partnership with a world government.[2]

"Scripture does warn about a coming world ruler who will appear and will be like an angel of light, as Paul warns us, and yet he will end up bringing great destruction," Bill Schnoebelen says. "If you look at the New Age movement and the Illuminati, what they are trying to do is exactly what is prophesied in the book of Revelation—the idea that the Beast, this man, will deceive the nations and set up an idolatrous system."[3]

Prophecy experts speculate that this sophisticated deception might involve the work CERN is doing to open an interdimensional portal along with occult predictions of a transhumanist messiah, or a "false Jewish messiah," who enthrones himself as God in the rebuilt Temple in Jerusalem. He could be a New Age messiah with appeal to all world religions, or even a religious leader boasting of contact with extraterrestrials who have come to save the world from nuclear annihilation or climate change—promising to help humanity make the next evolutionary, spiritual, and technological leap forward.[4]

The Deception of the Elect

Jesus issued this warning: "For false christs and false prophets will arise and perform great signs and wonders, so as to lead astray, if possible, even the elect" (Matt. 24:24 ESV). The apostle Paul also warned of "false apostles," "deceitful workmen," and servants of Satan who "disguise themselves as servants of righteousness" (2 Cor. 11:15 ESV). The Bible further warns of the *apostasia*, or "the apostasy"—"a falling away" (2 Thess. 2:3 KJV).

Most theologians believe Paul is talking about a great falling away from the fundamental doctrines of the faith such as the virgin birth of Christ, salvation through faith in Christ, and the second coming of Christ. "The great apostasy" refers to a rejection and turning away from the Word of God in the last days by those who call themselves Christians and the church. Paul warns that "evildoers and impostors will go from bad to worse, deceiving and being deceived" (2 Tim. 3:13 NIV).

In *The Coming Apostasy: Exposing the Sabotage of Christianity from Within*, Mark Hitchcock and Jeff Kinley wrote that the world is now living in "days of rampant, surging, encroaching apostasy." Today, believers are witnessing Satan's subtle sabotage of Christianity and the church, using false teachers to undermine the work of God. These apostates are entrenched in nearly all major church denominations and have "overrun most theological seminaries in what is nothing short of a landslide." "Every aspect of Christianity is under sustained attack," they wrote. "Doctrinal underpinnings are being challenged and jettisoned at an accelerated pace. We are witnessing a startling departure from the truth on the part of individuals, churches, and even entire denominations." The reality is that many ministers are not preaching the "true gospel" and some are denying the central doctrines of the Christian faith, including a denial of Jesus' second coming and claiming that Scripture is not the inerrant, infallible Word of God. They decide for themselves that some portions of the Bible are optional or outdated.[5]

Derek P. Gilbert, host of *SkyWatchTV*, says research shows only 9 percent of Americans—and 19 percent of born-again Christians—have a biblical worldview, and even less understand Bible prophecy at a time when most churches no longer teach about the end times.[6]

"Maybe that's why Jesus said there would be a deception in the end times that would be so effective it would lead astray even the elect, if it were possible," Gilbert says. He speaks of Satan's "psyops," which is a psychological operation or military tactic "to change what a person or group of people believe with the end goal being to change how they behave, to change what they do. The enemy has been doing that since the garden when the serpent lied to Eve and Adam...Today, there are multiple facets to this deception. The enemy is playing eleven-dimensional chess while we're playing checkers in two dimensions so we are totally out of our depth if we try to fight them on our own terms." Gilbert adds that many Christians do not believe Christ will literally return to Earth or they are so ignorant of biblical prophecy or uncomfortable with apocalyptic images that they simply ignore the whole subject. "They just have some sort of vague belief that things are going to work out just fine and the world will just get better and better until somehow then God comes back and sets up his kingdom—ignoring all the stuff in between that has been prophesied to take place before Christ returns and establishes his reign on Earth. I think the biblical ignorance of Christians is part of this deception."

The Aquarian Conspiracy: "The Great Apostasy"

This quantum rise in mass deception—"the great apostasy"—involves several significant factors, including:

- Ministers not teaching the whole counsel of God's Word. Prophecy experts estimate that seven out of ten—and perhaps as many as nine out of ten—pulpits in America are largely silent about Bible prophecy. Today, 100 million American church members have little or no understanding of Bible prophecy.[7]
- A drop in personal and family Bible studies.
- Minimal exposure to biblical truths in the media, especially Christian television and radio. In recent decades, we've seen less teaching of the whole counsel of God on Christian media in favor of entertainment-style programming.

- Indoctrination by Hollywood, media, and the secular educational system designed to erode trust in the Bible as the inspired Word of God.
- A UN campaign to infuse youth with a "universal spirituality (i.e., the occult)."[8]

Billy Crone, pastor and founder of Get a Life Ministries, says the great apostasy can largely be traced to several decades of UN-sponsored New Age propaganda spread by the media, Hollywood, the public educational system, and the government. While many may think the New Age phenomenon peaked in the 1970s and 1980s, the movement has since "blanketed our whole planet, smothering one and all into accepting their core tenets." Crone explained that celebrity Oprah Winfrey—a possible Democratic presidential candidate in 2020 who is considered the most influential woman in the world—is one of the biggest "New Age Priestesses on the planet" spreading these spiritual beliefs worldwide.[9]

The New Age movement, or the "New Age" of love and light, derives its name from Helena Petrovna Blavatsky, cofounder of the Theosophical Society, who announced a coming New Age in the late nineteenth century. Blavatsky believed that theosophists should assist in the evolution of humanity by working with the Ascended Masters of the Great White Brotherhood—the "world's hidden leaders." In the 1940s, one of her successors, Alice A. Bailey, predicted the coming of a "world savior"—Master Maitreya. In the 1970s, theosophist David Spangler developed the basic concept of the modern movement when he claimed the Age of Aquarius had initiated the New Age. As an architect of the movement, Spangler wrote a series of books—starting with *Revelation: The Birth of a New Age*—attracting many leaders from occult and metaphysical organizations.[10]

In 1922, Alice and Foster Bailey created the Lucifer Publishing Company—now called Lucis Trust—to publish the book *Initiation*

Human and Solar about the "ancient myth of Lucifer." Today, Lucis Trust—located for many years on the UN grounds in New York City— works to spread information about and foster support for UN programs. "[Lucis Trust is] currently working with governments around the world," Crone says. "The UN is one of the biggest governmental authorities on the planet disseminating New Age teachings. In fact, you can go to the UN's website and find out who is helping to disseminate their literature. It's Lucis Trust. It's New Agers. Their indoctrination has never stopped. They just have different tools at their fingertips now with people like Oprah, and if you throw in Hollywood, then the whole planet is being prepared to receive this New Age lie."[11]

These are some of the core tenets of New Age beliefs:[12]

- Everything—the earth, people, plants, and animals—is god.
- Everyone can attain "Christ-consciousness."
- Mankind is destroying the earth, and unless it changes, "Mother Earth" will be forced to destroy humanity. The biggest culprit of this destruction is Christianity because the Bible says people have dominion over the earth.
- Sin is nonexistent, as is hell, so there is no need to repent of sin.
- Jesus is just one of many great teachers, including Muhammad, Buddha, and Confucius.
- People should seek guidance from "the spirit world" through chan- nelers, psychics, palm readers, meditation, extraterrestrials, and departed relatives.
- Global peace will only be obtained through the New World Order, a universal monetary system, and a one-world leader.
- Lucifer is a "good guy" who wants to save us.

A recent *Christianity Today* article noted the New Age movement moved "into the mainstream" in the 1990s and infiltrated the "daily world of business," and today New Age bookstores, along with the business sections of mainstream bookstores, routinely feature "New Age–tinted titles" such as pop guru Deepak Chopra's *The Seven Spiritual Laws of Success.*

A recent Barna Group survey found 61 percent of regular church attendees agree with ideas rooted in New Spirituality—the contemporary term for the New Age movement. The survey also found 28 percent of practicing Christians strongly agree that "all people pray to the same god or spirit, no matter what name they use for that spiritual being." Further, research by the University of Notre Dame and Harvard University found that nearly two-thirds of evangelicals under age thirty-five now believe non-Christians can go to heaven.

"Most people don't realize how far reaching [the New Age movement] really is," Crone says. "Part of that is because the apostasy of the church is in high gear and most churches today aren't even preaching the Bible, let alone all the Bible…How in the world did [these New Age beliefs] get into the church? I think part of their methodology was to infect the church."[13]

Hollywood Media Mind Control

On some levels, there is collusion, or conspiracy, between the mainstream media, Hollywood, government, and the Deep State regarding the mass deception of the public through New Age and other highly sophisticated methods of brainwashing and mind control. When we use the word *conspiracy* we aren't talking about powerful people in darkened rooms with giant pentagrams carefully plotting how to control the hive. But there is an organized political, social, and spiritual campaign under way to radically transform our world into something completely unrecognizable—a dark and terrifying planet few of us can truly imagine.

It's naive not to believe that powerful individuals within the major power centers of society—Hollywood, media, government, academia, religion, and science—are committed to brainwashing the masses into believing lies about reality, human nature, and behavior. They are already planning to persuade humanity to go along—willingly or unwillingly—with the elite's socialist-utopian vision of the future.

Why would they do that? The secretive ruling elite want to turn our world into a global socialist or communist state, which will enable them to acquire dictatorial power and amass even greater wealth. Their globalist game plan has nothing to do with what is fair or best for everyone. It is strictly about what is better for them, because they literally view themselves as the rulers of the planet and see us as "useless eaters" who exist to serve them. Many will find this difficult to accept, because they have been brainwashed to believe the globalist elite want to share their wealth and a create a better world for all mankind. Unfortunately, that is a total lie and not even on the menu.[14]

Do you really think when a major politician such as Hillary Clinton described a large segment of American voters as "deplorables" that her remark was just a slip of the tongue? This is what Clinton said at a LGBT fund-raiser before introducing actress Barbra Streisand: "To just be grossly generalistic, you can put half of Trump supporters into what I call the basket of deplorables. Right? Racist, sexist, homophobic, xenophobic, Islamophobic, you name it."[15] That's how the globalist elite view much of the world. They speak of the need to "cull the herd"—a truly chilling turn of phrase.

Do the Elite Want to Reduce Global Population to 500 Million?

Many high-profile elite leaders have spoken openly about the need to toss out traditional ideas of right and wrong and simply embrace the concept that they must do whatever is necessary to survive and prosper, even if it means killing off the masses in a wholesale fashion. In *Population Control: How Corporate Owners Are Killing Us*, Jim Marrs claims a small group of extremely wealthy people in control of key industries— food, weapons, oil, pharmaceuticals, and media—plan to cut the world's population to 500 million "by whatever means necessary and make a profit from it." This shocking claim is openly exhibited on the Georgia Guidestones, four sixteen-foot-tall stone monuments in Georgia commissioned in 1979 by a man using the pseudonym R. C. Christian. The astrological alignment of the stones is reminiscent of the alignments of similar monuments worldwide associated with secret societies like the Freemasons, Druids, and Mystery Schools of ancient Greece and Egypt. Ponder some of the messages below the title, *Let These Be Guidestones to the Age of Reason*:[16]

MAINTAIN HUMANITY UNDER 500,000,000 IN PERPETUAL BALANCE WITH NATURE.

UNITE HUMANITY WITH A LIVING NEW LANGUAGE.

BE NOT A CANCER ON THE EARTH—LEAVE ROOM FOR NATURE—LEAVE ROOM FOR NATURE.

Throughout the world, Marrs wrote, "entire populations" are being "culled for profit and control." "Elites have used the so-called GOD syndicate—Guns, Oil, and Drugs—as well as toxic air, water, food, and medicines, and of course, the toxic financial system on which the whole master plan depends—to reduce the world's population," Marrs explains.

This is due to the belief of the global elite that the basis of all the world's problems is overpopulation—just too many people using the earth's limited resources. We now live in a culture of death and decay that has been imposed upon us by a small group of wealthy elites that publicly espouses involuntary population reduction. We're being killed by chemicals, genetically modified organisms (GMOs), dyes, additives, plastics, tainted water, and polluted air...Precious few recognize that we are being psychologically programmed by a mass media controlled by a mere handful of corporate owners. This handful of multinational media corporations, many with interlocking directors and owners, control everything we see and hear, from movies, TV, and newspapers to satellite networks, magazines, even book clubs and billboards. Indeed, the complicity of the mass media ensures that we cannot protest the population reduction that threatens our very lives...Collectively, they call themselves "globalists," men and women who have a right to dominate based on wealth, heritage, and bloodline...And they have a plan to control the globe, one formulated many years ago within secretive societies in both Britain and the U.S. It depends on killing most of us.[17]

The globalist belief that overpopulation is humanity's most pressing problem can be largely traced to the publication of Stanford University biologist Paul Ehrlich's 1968 book *The Population Bomb* in which he supported the notion of "triage"—meaning nations would be ranked by their ability to feed themselves, and food aid would be cut off to countries deemed overpopulated. Recently, actor Tom Hanks—the star of Dan Brown's *Inferno*—seemed to endorse the Malthusian theory of overpopulation. The central plot of the movie involves an evil scientist who tries to release a virus to kill off the world's excess population. In an interview on NBC's *Today* show, Hanks said he was taught by his college history professor that "eventually, the world will have too many people in it in order to subsist on its own." Hanks added, "And actually the math does add up."

Stunningly, many members of the elite have said that they would like to see the globe's population cut significantly. Paul Watson, founder of the Sea Shepherd Conservation Society, said the world needs to "radically and intelligently reduce human population to fewer than one billion" and "eliminate nationalism...and become Earthlings" that recognize other species on Earth as fellow Earthlings. Ted Turner, American media mogul and founder of CNN, said the world's population should be reduced to 250 million to 350 million. In 1981, England's Prince Philip, husband of Queen Elizabeth II and a prominent globalist, told *People* magazine that overpopulation is humanity's biggest long-term threat to survival. "If it isn't controlled voluntarily, it will be controlled involuntarily by an increase in disease, starvation, and war." In 1988, he opined, "In the event that I'm reincarnated, I would like to return as a deadly virus, in order to contribute something to solve overpopulation."[18]

It's difficult to believe that many of the elite think this way, but they do. Ominously, Microsoft founder Bill Gates, one of the richest men in the world, warned recently in an interview with the *Telegraph* that "intentionally caused epidemics could kill hundreds of millions of people thanks to genetic engineering advances proceeding at a "mind-blowing rate."[19]

Occult Invasion of the Church and Society

In the first century, the apostle John warned believers that in the centuries ahead the "spirit of antichrist" would work to undermine and deny the truth about Christ.

In 1979, Willis W. Harman, a "metaphysical futurist," Stanford University professor, and president of the Institute of Noetic Sciences, addressed the nation's leading evangelical scholars at a major Christian college. Harman had previously directed research at the Stanford

Research Institute on "how Western man could be deliberately turned into an Eastern mystic/psychic." He addressed the group on the topic "A Utopian Perspective on the Future," in which he advocated a broadening of the concept of science to include the New Age, psychic abilities, and the occult—all of which are forbidden in the Bible. "Once-taboo areas of science—notably sleep and dreams, creativity, hypnosis, unconscious processes, psychosomatic theories of illness—have become legitimatized," Harman said. He also promoted the exploration of psychic phenomena, altered states of consciousness, meditation, and contemplation "via biofeedback training and other routes."[20]

Over the last five decades, new forms of spiritual deception have come into existence through scientific mind control of the masses. A key organization that specializes in indoctrination and social engineering is the Tavistock Institute of Human Relations in the United Kingdom. Officially established in 1947 with funding from the Rockefeller Foundation, Tavistock is a kind of psychological warfare institute that has used mind-control techniques to radically transform the belief systems of entire nations. In what he described as the "Aquarian Conspiracy," former MI6 intelligence agent John Coleman claimed the Illuminati—the Committee of 300 and the Tavistock Institute—helped turn the Beatles into a musical sensation and engineered the 1960s countercul-ture revolution that transformed the global culture. Coleman wrote:

The phenomenon of the Beatles was not a spontaneous rebellion by youth against the old social system. Instead it was a carefully crafted plot to introduce by a conspiratorial body which could not be identified, a highly destructive and divisive element into a large population group targeted for change against its will. New words and new phrases—prepared by Tavistock—were introduced to America along with the Beatles. Words such as "rock" in relation to music sounds, "teenager," "cool," "discovered," and "pop music" were a lexicon of disguised code words signifying the acceptance of drugs had arrived with and accompanied the Beatles wherever they went, to be "discovered" by "teenagers."[21]

In *Tavistock Institute: Social Engineering the Masses*, investigative journalist and bestselling author Daniel Estulin wrote that the Tavistock Institute is part of an "interlocked juggernaut" consisting of think tanks and research centers such as the RAND Corporation, the Wharton School, Harvard Business School, London School of Economics, Esalen Institute, and the Geneva-based International Foundation for Development Alternatives—"the first full-time Age of Aquarius graduate school, charged with teaching behavior modification for high-level executives from *Fortune*'s top 500 companies." "Make no mistake, everything from the New Left to Watergate to Vietnam to Pentagon Papers to the insane hippies, the anti-war movement and the drug-rock counterculture were pre-planned social engineering projects," Estulin wrote. "Over the period of half a century, tens of billions of dollars have been allocated by the government of the United States with surreptitious help from think tanks and foundations aligned with Tavistock to fund the work of these groups."[22]

The first Marxist-oriented research center, the Institute for Social Research—also known as the Frankfurt School—was founded in Germany in 1923. Curiously, Frankfurt was the headquarters of Illuminized Freemasonry and the birthplace of Mayer Amschel Rothschild, founder of the famed banking dynasty that researchers claim financed the Bavarian Illuminati and later funded "robber barons like Rockefeller and Morgan," and British businessman Cecil Rhodes, "who founded the Round Table groups, a precursor of the Council on Foreign Relations and its offshoot, The Trilateral Commission." Members of the Frankfurt School sought to develop a theory of society based on Marxism. They, along with the Tavistock Institute, were instrumental in aligning

America and the EU with their Marxist vision of state control and management of the economy. These organizations have worked to create new forms of state-run capitalism—a euphemism for socialism, which became wildly popular among youth during the presidential campaign of Vermont senator Bernie Sanders, a self-proclaimed socialist.

Marxism, socialism, communism, and progressivism are designed to destroy the individuality of men and women created in God's image. The goal is to create a hive mind where everyone thinks the same. In Marxism and its variants, the infinite, personal, living God of the universe is replaced by the state or the "collective." This permits totalitarianism under a godless state.

The Frankfurt School, whose representatives later occupied key positions in important American universities like Harvard University and the University of California, Berkeley, understood the importance of controlling the media in producing "massification." Ultimately, ideas like massification, collectivism, conformity, and the New Age movement were designed by a secretive occult elite to control the masses. All these concepts contradict God's plan for humanity. They are the pillars of what is really a new kind of religion—a religion that believes the state collective replaces God, man is nothing more than a biological machine, and there is no absolute right or wrong.

The great irony is that many communist leaders were secretly involved in the occult. For instance, German philosopher Karl Marx, who published *The Communist Manifesto* and wrote *Das Kapital*, was a purported Satanist.[23]

Progressivism: Path to a World Government

The work of the Tavistock Institute and Frankfurt School to secretly steer the course of world events is a continuation of the mass manipulation tactics of Fabian socialists such as H. G. Wells, Bertrand Russell,

Aldous Huxley, Julian Huxley, and others who planned the New World Order—a global socialist system of governance and finance.

The problem with progressives and their goal, according to *New York Times* bestselling author David Horowitz, is that "they live in an imaginary future. They have no idea what human beings are like, the controls that human beings need to have placed on them, their natural tendencies which are selfish, self-centered, egocentric, and deceitful. All these human traits have been with us for five thousand years of history... The beginning of governmental philosophy is how do you channel these basic instincts that human beings have, that are part of their nature, into productive, creative, peaceful, and cooperative forces. The market is one way and private property is another, and I think the American political system is the third. But progressives never think of that stuff. They think people are good, and all they have to do is take down the whole system around them and everything will be hunky-dory. Progressives are very dangerous... Progressivism is just another name for communism. What is their essential platform? Redistribution of wealth. Take it from the people who have earned it—the creative people, the people who have worked hard—and give it to the lazy and the shiftless and the antisocial. That's the progressive agenda."[24] Of course, not all poor people are "lazy, shiftless, or antisocial." Many hardworking people encounter illness, disaster, or other financial losses that are not their fault. And it is right for a just society to provide a safety net for the truly needy. But the progressive agenda makes no such distinction. It aims to level the wealth of American families in a way that will wipe out the middle class.

In 1952, Bertrand Russell wrote about the vital importance of mass psychology tactics to achieve progressive goals in his book *Impact of Science on Society*. Mass psychology is far more than political brainwashing; it's a modern technique rooted in occultism designed to create mass spiritual deception. In the last days, it will play a key role in getting people to worship the Antichrist as god and join the world superstate that the book of Revelation warns us about.

Russell, who worked closely with the Frankfurt School, advocated brainwashing youth at young ages to maximize the effectiveness of this campaign of mass deception. This indoctrination has been going on in America and countries throughout the world for decades now. This explains why countless millions of children and adults no longer believe in God, the Bible, or right or wrong. The primary goal of the Frankfurt School was and is to use the sexual impulse as a method of weakening Christian nations like America, destroying biblical and family values. This is a partial list of those goals:[25]

1. Continually create racial conflicts.
2. Teach sex and homosexuality to young children.
3. Create massive immigration to destroy national identity.
4. Promote heavy drinking.
5. Make people dependent on the state for benefits.
6. Control and dumb down people through the media.
7. Promote breakdown of the family.
8. Destroy Christianity by infiltrating its institutions and emptying its churches.
9. Destroy patriotism and the concept of nationalism and the independent nation-state.
10. Attack the authority of the father. Endless television shows and movies portray the father as weak and incompetent. Rebrand the feminine mother as the true authority figure in a marriage and promote the mother, single or married, as a superwoman—beautiful, sexually attractive, career driven, having multiple affairs.

All you need to do is turn on your television and watch these goals being played out right before our eyes.

In *Impact of Science on Society*, Russell wrote that the secular educational system held the most promise for indoctrinating youth: "The social psychologists of the future will have a number of classes of school children on whom they will try different methods of producing an unshakable conviction that snow is black. Various results will soon be arrived at. First, that the influence of home is obstructive. Second, that not much can be done unless indoctrination begins before the age of ten. Third, that verses set to music and repeatedly intoned are very effective."[26]

Notice how the Tavistock Institute created the "sex, drugs, and rock 'n' roll" counterculture through groups like the Beatles, Rolling Stones, the Who, Led Zeppelin, and others by playing their albums endlessly to countless millions of people with "verses set to music and repeatedly intoned." The British rock 'n' roll invasion was a Tavistock-engineered mind-control program, and the lyrics of groups like the Beatles—who many thought sang, "Smoke pot, smoke pot, everybody smoke pot" in "I Am the Walrus"—incited millions to light up marijuana joints.[27]

Today we are engulfed in a mostly godless society characterized by its "hookup culture," widespread adultery, homosexual lifestyles, an epidemic of addiction, high crime, unemployment and incarceration rates, and rising levels of poverty and homelessness. It's not hard to see just how successful the globalist elites have been in their effort to undermine the Judeo-Christian foundations of the West and pave the way for the Great Deception.

"In the 1930s America had the Great Depression," Franklin Graham noted. "Now we have the Great Deception. Hollywood and media moguls want you to think sin is okay, even something to celebrate. It's not. Sin has a price, and the price is death—spiritual death. God is the righteous judge and the Bible says He is 'standing at the door.' One day, 'says the Lord, every knee shall bow to Me, and every tongue shall confess'" (Rom. 14:11 ESV).[28]

Our world is being prepared to accept a one-world leader who will oversee a global government, economy, and religious system. Even more disturbing, we are being conditioned in numerous ways to accept what the Bible calls "666"—the mark of the Beast. This infamous mark could be a microchip, biochip, or nanochip implant, a chip integrated into our genetic coding system, an electronic tattoo, or any number of similar technologies that governments, corporations, and universities are rolling out worldwide today.

The Bible speaks of the False Prophet who will control the global economic system and religion—the predominant methods of controlling humankind since the beginning of civilization. During the second half of the Tribulation, to buy or sell or conduct any business transactions, people will be required to receive the mark of the Beast. Those who refuse will face tremendous difficulty and persecution, and most will be executed. To take the mark, people will be required to reject Jesus Christ as Lord and pledge to worship the Antichrist as god. The Bible warns that those who do so will ultimately be cast into the "lake of fire" (Rev. 19:20 KJV).

As the occult elite work to set the stage for the launch of the "Mystery, Babylon" system, we can expect sophisticated deceptions to play even greater roles in preparing the world for the "powerful delusion" that will fool "even the elect."

Jan Markell, founder of Olive Tree Ministries, says, "What the Bible talks about is an end-time giving heed to the doctrines of demons, an end-time giving heed to unsound doctrine. This has happened since the beginning of time, but the Bible indicates it's going to pick up great steam in the last days, and there will be a great apostasy and even the elect will be deceived."[29]

Part II

GLOBALISM VS. NATIONALISM

Chapter Six

The Trump Revolution

Then, in 2016, the earth shifted beneath our feet. The rebellion started as a quiet protest, spoken by families of all colors and creeds—families who just wanted a fair shot for their children, and a fair hearing for their concerns. But then the quiet voices became a loud chorus—as thousands of citizens now spoke out together, from cities small and large, all across our country.

—PRESIDENT DONALD J. TRUMP,
JOINT SESSION OF CONGRESS ADDRESS[1]

Former Vice President Joe Biden blamed his own party for losing the 2016 election, telling a crowd at the University of Pennsylvania that Democrats ignored one of its core ideals during the campaign: maintaining "a burgeoning middle class."

—JESSICA CHASMAR, *WASHINGTON TIMES*[2]

When Donald Trump walked onstage to run for the office of president of the United States, he stepped into a vacuum and filled the political void with an electrifying presence and skills honed as a reality TV superstar on NBC's *The Apprentice*.

Trump's shoot-from-the-hip style, his belief that America can be great again, his success as a billionaire real estate and resort developer, with his properties prominently displaying the word "TRUMP" in gold, his giant stature, eccentric hairstyle, and red power tie contrasting with the subdued ties of the other candidates, was like no candidate Americans had yet seen. His supermodel wife and daughters and handsome, articulate sons lit stages and TV screens across the country. Trump's son-in-law, Jared Kushner, spoke of closing the ultimate deal, a peace treaty that protects Jerusalem. He conducted record-breaking campaign tours, flying to countless American cities in his own private jet, which appeared larger and more powerful than Air Force One. His strong support of Christian values and evangelical Christians, and his funny, in-your-face, powerful speeches where he calls out the media by name for disseminating "fake news" and shames them for not showing the size of his enormous crowds gave cathartic expression to the feelings of America's middle class. It was a new kind of campaign that rocked America, the mainstream media, the Republican and Democratic parties, and the world.

During the election, a large demographic of Americans—moderate Democrats, independents, and Republicans—were generally ignored by the Washington political strategists and pollsters, creating a massive void. But Trump's magnetic personality and message filled that space as he moved like rolling thunder across America with a completely new message not created by tired political strategists and advertising agencies. Trump's key players kept saying, "Let Trump be Trump," which meant trampling political correctness and breaking every rule in the book.[3]

While other candidates struggled to find their unique brand, Trump long ago created his brand—simply "TRUMP." Never in the history of American politics had any presidential candidate so infuriated the mainstream media, whose ratings and advertising revenues went through the roof when he appeared on their networks. Hollywood, the Democratic National Committee, and the elite classes looked down their noses at

Trump and his nationalistic beliefs. To top it all off, Trump took on Pope Francis, saying it was "disgraceful" for a religious leader to suggest he was "not a Christian" for his plan to build a wall along the Mexican border. "I am proud to be a Christian, and as president I will not allow Christianity to be consistently attacked and weakened, unlike what is happening now, with our current president," Trump said during the campaign.[4]

Trump's style, personality, aggressiveness, and genuine belief that with the help of the American people he could "Make America Great Again" caught fire and quickly launched what is now called "the Trump Revolution." And among evangelical Christians it helped ignite what Franklin Graham calls the "Christian revolution."[5]

In 2016 Graham conducted a fifty-state Decision America Tour that attracted hundreds of thousands of people to the steps and front lawns of state capitols across the nation to pray for America.[6] At the rallies, Graham called on believers to pray, live righteous lives, share the good news, get involved in the political process, and run for office at all levels of government. "No one should think that electing Donald Trump will fix our country. America is still a sin-saturated and divided nation, and Trump himself is a leader with human flaws," Graham said, shortly after completing the tour. He went on to compare America's political chaos today with that of 1860, when, like Trump:

The man who emerged to become the next president had very limited Washington experience, was considered uncouth by a significant part of the electorate, and won the election without a majority of the popular vote. Abraham Lincoln became one of our most effective presidents, and several years into his presidency a well-known pastor in New York pinpointed the reason: "The prayers of God's people made President Lincoln what he was to the nation." Donald Trump is, of course, a far different man than Lincoln, and the conflicts and issues in our country today are entirely different than in 1860. But we know that God can use any leader. We as God's people can have a huge impact if we take our responsibility seriously and are diligent "always to pray and not lose heart" (Luke 18:1 ESV).[7]

Boston Tea Party Redux?

The movement that brought Trump to power involves significant historical, cultural, and spiritual dynamics. First, millions of Americans came to realize that they could no longer afford the American dream. They were terrified of losing their homes, health care, jobs, and way of life. Second, they foresaw little hope of positive change for them, their children, and grandchildren. All they saw coming out of Washington were globalist policies, job-killing environmental regulations, social engineering programs, failing educational programs like Common Core that were not preparing their children for better-paying future jobs, and endless inane regulations that made it practically impossible to start their own businesses. What they saw in Washington was a bunch of tap-dancing Democratic and Republican politicians from Ivy League schools playing golf, jumping on jets for fancy vacations, and going out for expensive lunches.

Former Vice President Joe Biden said the Democrats lost the election because they ignored struggling middle-class workers. "This is the first campaign that I can recall where my party did not talk about what it always stood for, and that is how to maintain a burgeoning middle class," Biden said. "You didn't hear a single solitary sentence in the last campaign about that guy working on the assembly line making 60,000 bucks a year and a wife making $32,000 as a hostess in a restaurant and…they've got two kids and they can't make it and they're scared. They're frightened, because they're not stupid." While globalization has been a "phenomenal success" on a macroeconomic level, Biden said it's also "left a lot of people behind."[8]

As it was during the American Revolution's Boston Tea Party when high taxes and regulations from Great Britain had become oppressive, in 2016 millions of Americans were ready to revolt, not with guns and bombs, but peacefully with their votes. They were looking for a leader, and Trump filled the role with a philosophy that promised to deliver on making dramatic changes in our government.

The political pundits and strategists completely missed how Trump connected to the heart of the evangelical Christian movement in America. They thought this alliance would be impossible because of Trump's billionaire playboy image and past. When a recording of Trump making highly vulgar comments about women was released, his enemies thought they had severed his ties with evangelicals. While certainly offended, many evangelicals exhibited a biblical maturity that the media didn't expect. Although they didn't approve of what he said, they focused on the bigger picture. Trump championed evangelical concerns and promised to change laws and policies that previous administrations had crafted to muzzle and marginalize evangelicals. Trump's willingness to partner with evangelicals helped ignite the "Christian revolution."[9]

This revolution came on the heels of the populist Tea Party movement that began in 2009 in the wake of Obama's election and took its name from the historic Boston Tea Party. In the ensuing years, working- and middle-class people became "disgusted with the status quo" as they lost their jobs and homes. "So there really was a revolt against the Establishment," S. Douglas Woodward says. "This is something Donald Trump picked up on and it's something the Democratic Party, or the Republican Establishment, didn't pick up on." Woodward explained that in the 2016 election, people revolted not only against repressive economic policies, but also against globalism, "endless wars in Iraq and Afghanistan," and fake news to advance the mainstream media's agenda.

"I think Donald Trump represented a kind of anti-Establishment candidate, and to me Trump represented a victory of really a third party. He really wasn't a Republican and he wasn't a Democrat...This is what is called populism. It's a revolt of the people against the Establishment." Woodward added that the voters felt that the government was no longer "of the people, by the people, or for the people," which meant "it's time that we change our government."[10]

Reality TV Star or God-Called President?

Never in the history of the United States and perhaps in the history of the world has any nation experienced anything quite like "the Trump Revolution."

"Revolution will be in the air in 2017," wrote Daniel Franklin, editor of the *Economist*'s "The World in 2017" issue. "Americans have already voted for game-changing disruption. The dramatic election of Donald Trump as president means that the insurrection will be led from the White House, with both chambers of Congress also in Republican hands...Britain, meanwhile, will formally launch its proceedings for divorce from the European Union, which will be bitterly fought over at home and abroad."[11]

This global uprising gained real traction about the time Trump started his campaign for the presidency. He's a natural and highly gifted communicator who developed a powerful emotional bond with his followers. Trump pulled this off because he was being himself and being real in a way only a guy from Queens who made it big in Manhattan could do. When Trump spoke, the physical and electronic distance between the television viewer and himself disappeared. He was there in your living room talking to you personally.

Trump honed his communication skills as one of the world's biggest reality TV stars on *The Apprentice* when his unique style of on-camera presentation began to come alive. After the show started airing in 2004, it quickly became the number one program on television, making ratings history. *The Apprentice* aired for fourteen seasons. In 2012, *Forbes* ranked Trump number fourteen in the world on their top one hundred celebrity list. Trump is one of only two people twice named to ABC's Barbara Walter's *Most Fascinating People* special. He has been in the "spotlight nearly all of his adult life," wrote the authors of *Trump Revealed: An American Journey of Ambition, Ego, Money and Power*. "He was still in his thirties when he became a single-name celebrity, like Madonna or Beyoncé, like a rock star or a president, his name, in ALL CAPS, gold plated, on buildings and airplanes and shirts and wine bottles (even though he says he's never had a drink in his life)," the authors wrote. "More than three decades before he decided he wanted to be president, he showed up on Gallup's list of the ten men Americans most admired, running behind only the pope and some presidents."[12]

Shortly after his election, *Time* magazine featured Trump on its cover as "Person of the Year." "The revolution he stirred feels fully American, with its echoes of populists past, of Andrew Jackson and Huey Long and, at its most sinister, Joe McCarthy and Charles Coughlin," *Time* editor Nancy Gibbs wrote. "His appeal—part hope, part snarl—dissolved party lines and dispatched the two reigning dynasties of U.S. politics. Yet his victory mirrors the ascent of nationalists across the world, from Britain to the Philippines, and taps forces far more powerful than one man's message."[13]

On *The Apprentice*, Trump perfected his skills to revolutionize political speeches in which, without the use of a teleprompter, his "straight from the heart" style would pack out large stadiums, giant auditoriums, and massive airplane hangars with huge crowds inspired by his radical message.

Trump didn't come with the typical sterilized political speech that is the product of surveys, demographic research, political strategists, and public relations teams. Instead, he said what he said because it was passionately felt and he believed in it. As a result, it deeply resonated with working- and middle-class people who were desperately hurting, having watched their incomes stagnate, good-paying jobs outsourced, and hundreds of thousands of manufacturing and other high-paying jobs leave the United States. This was the direct result of globalism and numerous trade treaties enacted by the Republican and Democratic elite.

Until Trump came on the scene, all these topics were largely ignored by the mainstream media and politicians. The corporate media and both political parties were so removed from the bitter realities experienced by voters that when Trump began to speak about these hardships, it was as if millions of Americans who had been suffocating finally caught their breath.

Most of the mainstream media and political elite chose to remain clueless as to the plight of a huge segment of the American public whose children may never get the opportunities and jobs available in better days. The moment Trump stepped onto the global stage, a rush of oxygen began to fill their lungs, and at that very second there was bond, a kind of blood oath between Trump and the American people. It was this bond and the deep sense that Trump was not just another politician that created a loyalty to a leader that many people knew they could trust—and it exploded into life as "the Trump Revolution."

The movement had begun, and the crowds were unprecedented and enormous. During the campaign, much of the mainstream media deliberately used camera angles to conceal the size and passion of the crowds by only giving Trump close-up shots. However, many Americans stopped trusting much of the mainstream media years ago, so when Trump called out the specific names of the networks who refused to show the size of his crowds, it energized his supporters like rocket fuel.

The American people had never seen a conservative candidate stand fearless in front of the media attacks and then go on the offensive.

Trump broke every rule in the book by completely reinventing political rallies, speeches, and debates. Day after day he appeared at giant rallies in multiple cities, flying in his own private jet emblazoned with the giant letters "TRUMP." On arrival, the herculean Trump bolted down the stairs of the jet wearing his red baseball hat, which bore the words "Make America Great Again." Although most of the mainstream media networks detested what he stood for, they covered him anyway because he spiked their ratings.

In response to massive negative attack ads by his Republican primary opponents, Trump did the unthinkable, using his wit, communication skills, and natural comedic talents to unmask them by giving them pet names like "Low Energy Jeb" for former Florida governor Jeb Bush, whose powerful family has a vast network of the highest-level contacts in politics, finance, and industry with nearly unlimited financial resources. Trump, who self-financed much of his campaign, could never compete with that level of power and money, so he improvised.

The unexpected impact of this humor was how it exposed the true personalities, actions, and beliefs of America's so-called conservative political elite and their globalist connections. Trump's theatrics brought in a massive American and global audience of viewers throughout the campaign. Not only did he draw in politically interested viewers; he brought in a worldwide audience that found him more interesting and entertaining than network programming.

Underneath all the fireworks and showmanship, Trump was deftly communicating his unique core beliefs—to secure our borders, assert "Americanism, not globalism," create new high-paying jobs, and bring American companies and manufacturing plants back into the United States. Those beliefs also included protecting and strengthening our unique form of government with its Constitution and Bill of Rights, the Protestant work ethic, and Christianity.[14]

"We will always support our evangelical community, and defend your right, and the right of all Americans, to follow and to live by the teachings of their faith," Trump told those gathered at the Faith and Freedom Coalition's "Road to Majority" Conference. He went on to say:

As you know, we're under siege. You understand that. But we will come out bigger and better and stronger than ever...I signed, as I promised I would, a new executive action to protect religious liberty in America...This executive order directs the IRS not to unfairly target churches and religious organizations for political speech...As long as I'm president, no one is going to stop you from practicing your faith or from preaching what is in your heart...We want [our pastors'] voices in our public discourse. And we want our children to know the blessings of God. Schools should not be a place that drives out faith and religion, but that should welcome faith and religion with wide, open, beautiful arms. Faith inspires us to be better, to be stronger, to be more caring and giving, and more determined to act in selfless and courageous defense of what is good and what is right...We will end the discrimination against people of faith. Our government will once again celebrate and protect religious freedom."[15]

It is Trump's commitment to strengthen America's Judeo-Christian foundations that led many faith leaders to support his presidency. "The real reason was I felt God told me to support him," says Sid Roth, a Messianic Jew and host of *It's Supernatural!* "It was confirmed when I had a meeting with him with about six other pastors. It was a small meeting in his office. I observed what I believe he's going to be—a father of our nation. When I got there, I saw a different man than I saw on television...I saw his heart. I saw love coming from him. I saw his concern for people...I want to see Donald Trump fulfill his destiny, and that is to cause America to be unified and to have freedom of religion."[16]

"You Can't Outtop Abraham Lincoln"

The son of wealthy real estate developer Fred Trump and Scottish immigrant Mary Anne (Macleod) Trump, Donald John Trump was born June 14, 1946, in Queens, New York. Trump's father was the son of a German immigrant, Friedrich Drumpf, who was raised in a wine-producing village in southwest Germany and immigrated to the United States in 1885. When he arrived in New York, an immigration officer spelled his name "Trumpf" on entry documents. When he became a citizen a year later, the naturalization papers were made out to Friedrich Trump.

Friedrich operated a restaurant in Seattle, worked as a Wall Street barber, went into the real estate business, and left his family a considerable estate when he died at age forty-nine during a flu epidemic. His widow, Elizabeth, made herself head of the family business, E. Trump & Son. Her son Fred took over the business at her death.

Growing up in Queens, Donald Trump learned "the art of the deal through osmosis" from his father, Fred Trump, who built and operated middle-income apartments. "I learned about toughness in a very tough business," Trump wrote in his 1987 bestseller *The Art of the Deal*.[17]

In 1955, after graduating from Sunday school at his family's Presbyterian church, the future president's mother presented him with what became his family Bible. Six decades later, Trump took the oath of office by placing his hand on that Bible, along with the one President Abraham Lincoln used at his inauguration.

Trump grew up in a time in Queens when, in the eyes of most Americans, the United States was still the greatest nation on earth. Most Queens residents were proud of their country, and many were veterans who served in World Wars I and II. At that time, most people believed in God, went to a church or synagogue, and attempted, however imperfectly, to live moral lives.

When he was thirteen, Trump's parents enrolled him in the New York Military Academy, where he was nicknamed "the Trumpet." "I was a very assertive, aggressive kid," Trump wrote. "I liked to stir things up, and I liked to test people." By the time he graduated in 1964, Trump had become a star athlete and a student leader. He then enrolled at Fordham University and later transferred to the Wharton School of Finance at the University of Pennsylvania, graduating with a degree in economics in 1968.[18]

He soon went to work at the Trump Organization—helping to increase its holdings of rental housing and honing his "deal-making chops." By the mid-1970s, the young mogul could be found regularly in the *New York Times*. "He is tall, lean and blond, with dazzling white teeth, and he looks ever so much like Robert Redford," Judy Klemesrud wrote in an article. "He rides around town in a chauffeured silver Cadillac with his initials, DJT, on the plates. He dates slinky fashion models, belongs to the most elegant clubs and, at only thirty years of age, estimates that he is worth 'more than $200 million.'"[19]

During these years, Trump bought and renovated and built several hotel complexes and apartment towers in Manhattan. In 1977, he married model Ivana Zelnickova Winklmayr. Norman Vincent Peale—a mentor to Trump—married the couple at New York's Marble Collegiate Church. Peale predicted Trump would become "the greatest builder of our time." Two years later, Trump leased a site on Fifth Avenue for a $200 million apartment-retail complex dubbed Trump Tower. The fifty-eight-story building—featuring a six-story atrium lined with pink marble and an eighty-foot waterfall—attracted celebrity renters and brought him national attention. In 1985, he bought Mar-a-Lago, a historic 128-room oceanfront mansion in Palm Beach, Florida, known as "the Jewel of Palm Beach." From 1983 to 1990, he built and purchased properties in New York City and opened casinos in Atlantic City, including Trump Plaza and Trump Taj Mahal, which publicists called the "Eighth Wonder of the Modern World."[20]

Two years later, following a highly publicized divorce from Ivana Trump, he married model Marla Maples. The following year, he became co-owner of the Empire State Building. Then, in 1996, Trump partnered with NBC to buy the Miss Universe Organization, which handles the Miss America, Miss USA, and Miss Teen USA beauty pageants. Trump and Maples divorced in 1997.[21]

In 1999, Trump changed his party affiliation from Republican to Reform Party to run for president in 2000. He withdrew from the race and later rejoined the Republican Party. In the early part of this century, he developed several major hotel and residential complexes, including Trump World Tower in New York City, Trump International Hotel & Tower in Chicago, and Trump International Hotel Las Vegas. His portfolio further includes eighteen signature golf courses in America and abroad.

In 2004, Trump joined forces with Mark Burnett Productions and NBC to produce and star in the reality TV show *The Apprentice*. In 2007, NBC's president Ben Silverman said it had become "the most successful reality series ever on NBC." Trump's celebrity "peaked with the premiere of *The Apprentice*, a reality show that put Trump in charge of a board room full of hopeful employees willing to do anything for a job with the mogul," wrote the authors of a *Newsweek* special that described Trump as "the most famous man ever to be elected president."[22]

The following year, in a highly publicized and lavish wedding, Trump married his current wife, Slovenian model Melania Knauss. In 2009, Trump resigned from the board of Trump Entertainment Resorts, which operated several Atlantic City casinos, shortly before the company filed for bankruptcy under Chapter 11. In 2015, with the blessings of his family, he announced that he would run for president on a platform emphasizing the creation of jobs, replacement of Obamacare, greater border security, and enhanced foreign relations. "I can be more presidential than any president that this country has ever had, except for Abraham Lincoln, because...you can't outtop Abraham Lincoln," Trump told his family.[23]

Trump outlined his vision in his book *Crippled America: How to Make America Great Again*. "America needs to start winning again," Trump wrote. "Nobody likes a loser and nobody likes to be bullied. Yet, here we stand today, the greatest superpower on Earth, and everyone is eating our lunch. That's not winning...A lot of people were encouraging me to speak out, and I realized that with my well-known success story and record of building residential and office buildings and developing public spaces—all the while accumulating personal wealth—I could inspire people to help create the most massive turnaround in American history."[24]

God and Donald Trump

The topic of President Trump's faith has been a mysterious one, both during his campaign for president and after his election.

Trump has long identified as a Presbyterian, and since his election, he's increasingly made references to God in his speeches and taken steps to cultivate a good relationship with Christian leaders and Christian media. In one of his first interviews as president, Trump told Christian Broadcasting Network's David Brody that he's "always felt the need to pray." He realized that as president, his decisions no longer involve whether to erect a new building; they involve "questions of massive life and death...So, God comes into it even more so."[25]

Though Trump may be a fledgling Christian, signs that he is now taking his faith seriously are highly encouraging. He has surrounded himself with strong Christian leaders and advisers. Prior to the election, Dr. James Dobson, founder of Focus on the Family, wrote an article noting that Paula White, senior pastor of New Destiny Christian Center in Apopka, Florida, had reportedly led Trump to Christ. "Only the Lord knows the condition of a person's heart," Dobson wrote. "But there are many Christian leaders who are serving on a faith advisory committee for Trump in the future. I am among them. There are about twenty-five of us that include Jerry Falwell, Jr., Robert Jeffress, Jack Graham, Ben Carson, James Robison, Michele Bachmann, and many others…How will that play out if Trump becomes president? I don't know. It is a good start, I would think."[26]

Apparently, Trump's faith advisory council did indeed make a good start. Jim Garlow, pastor of Skyline Church in San Diego and a member of the White House faith advisory council, said of Trump, "I do sense there is clearly a growing in the faith. [In May 2017] the White House faith advisory council met in the White House for a dinner with the president. I wasn't sure if he'd just be there for five minutes and leave. None of us knew, but he stayed with us for two hours…and my biggest takeaway from the evening was how remarkably comfortable he was with us." Garlow added that there were "some very encouraging evidences of spiritual growth taking place in his life. I listened very carefully to [Trump] and he spoke as a man who is understanding the nature of God, who grasps the significance of spiritual truth in our nation. I came away quite encouraged with the progress I've seen to this point."[27]

While only God knows for certain the state of Trump's faith, he has committed and taken steps to enact policies, laws, and programs that permit and promote major principles of the Bible. Perhaps his most important action has been to approve policies that make it legal once again for any person to practice his or her faith without fear of incrimination or harassment by the government. According to Deuteronomy 28, the net effect of this upon individuals, communities, and nations is the blessings of God economically, sociologically, and in countless other ways.

While Trump never claimed to be an evangelical Christian during his campaign, as many Republican candidates often do with little or no evidence of their conversion, Trump began to speak out in politically incorrect ways about the spiritual decline of America, and affirmed the historical reality that America was formed by our Bible-believing Christian forefathers who built this country on biblical values, the Protestant work ethic, and a great deal of prayer.

Although the mainstream media were working around the clock to destroy Trump as a candidate, tens of millions of evangelical Christians resonated with his message of sincerity and fearlessness and knew that he was a man who would keep his campaign promises and fight for Christian and American values. They clung to the hope that God has a special plan for America. Most evangelical Christians believe in Bible prophecy, and they understand that we are now in the last days. By the millions, they had a deep intuitive sense that America needed a strong president who would not be afraid to stand up for America and do the right thing as the last days unfold.

What the mainstream media, political elite from both parties, and globalists will never understand is that when evangelical Christians saw Trump on television, their hearts told them that Trump is the man God has chosen for this hour. They were not just responding to the encouragement of respected Christian leaders like Franklin Graham who believe God called Trump to be president. The biggest factor in motivating tens of millions of evangelical Christians to vote for Trump came from this deep intuitive sense that Trump was the man God had raised up for this particular hour. This is the reason why Trump is now president of the United States.

Is Trump an Authoritarian President?

While many are hopeful that God is using Trump to help America fulfill its prophetic destiny, the all-out assault on him by the mainstream media, the Deep State, progressives, and Democrats is intensifying with claims that Trump has authoritarian tendencies.

In his article in the *New Yorker*, "The Frankfurt School Knew Trump Was Coming," Alex Ross wrote that the school developed the concept of "the Authoritarian Personality"—a psychological and sociological profile of the "potentially fascistic individual"—and posed the possibility that a situation would arise in the future in which "large numbers of people would be susceptible to his psychological manipulation."[28]

Ross wrote that Frankfurt School member and German philosopher Theodor W. Adorno, coauthor of the 1950 book *The Authoritarian Personality*, "believed that the greatest danger to American democracy lay in the mass-culture apparatus of film, radio, and television. Indeed, in his view, this apparatus operates in dictatorial fashion even when no dictatorship is in place: it enforces conformity, quiets dissent, mutes thought...With the election of Donald Trump, the latent threat of American authoritarianism is on the verge of being realized...Now a businessman turned reality-show star has been elected president. Like it or not, Trump is as much a pop-culture phenomenon as he is a political one."

In a psychological profile of Trump in the *Atlantic*—"The Mind of Donald Trump"—Dan P. McAdams, a professor of psychology at Northwestern University, wrote that during and after World War II psychologists conceived of the "authoritarian personality as a pattern of attitudes and values revolving around adherence to society's traditional norms, submission to authorities who personify or reinforce those norms, and antipathy—to the point of hatred and aggression—toward those who either challenge in-group norms or lie outside their orbit." Among white Americans, McAdams wrote, high scores on measures of authoritarianism are associated with prejudice against various "out-groups," including homosexuals, immigrants, African Americans, and Muslims. "Authoritarianism is also associated with suspiciousness of the humanities and the arts, and with cognitive rigidity, militaristic sentiments, and Christian fundamentalism. When individuals with authoritarian proclivities

149

fear that their way of life is being threatened, they may turn to strong leaders who promise to keep them safe—leaders like Donald Trump."[29]

These articles come amid growing concerns, predominantly among progressives, Democrats, and the mainstream media, that Trump is an authoritarian—a leader who "values order and control over personal freedom and seeks to concentrate power."[30]

However, like many claims progressives have made about Trump, this one is weak too in terms of supporting evidence.

So where can we look to find evidence of this authoritarian tendency toward control and concentrated power? I (Paul) speak at large multiracial churches across the nation consisting of a mix of Hispanics, African Americans, Asians, whites, and other groups. And what I see are thousands of people bonded together as one in the body of Christ and loving one another in the agape love of Jesus. I've never seen the mainstream media cover these meetings. Also, as I speak at churches and Bible prophecy conferences around America and the world, I meet large numbers of evangelicals who are artists, actors, directors, novelists, sculptors, dancers, painters, and singers, and I don't see any animosity by Christians toward those in the arts. However, I do see large numbers of Christians attempting to enter the entertainment industry here in Hollywood, and once the industry discovers they are conservatives and Christians, they are shunned in a manner worse than during the era of the Hollywood blacklist when entertainment professionals were denied employment because of suspected communist ties. It's well-known among Christians in Hollywood that if you want to work in the entertainment industry you'd better hide your faith unless you're already a superstar.

In movies, television shows, and other forms of entertainment, Christians are often ridiculed, demonized, attacked, and mocked. Most of the time, they are depicted as outwardly pious, but secretly psychotic—a sociopath, serial killer, or rapist. This happens so often it's become a cliché.

Hollywood and the media have indoctrinated people to believe that sincere evangelical Christians are authoritarians or potential terrorists. Why else would evangelical Christians who are peaceful and law abiding show up on so many government watch lists?

Clearly, the progressives' accusation of authoritarianism against conservative Christians and Trump is a classic case of the pot calling the kettle black. Christians exhibit strong affinity with minorities, the humanities, and people in the arts, while the mainstream media, Hollywood, and Democrats exhibit an extremely repressive authoritarian attitude toward Christians. These progressives have no tolerance for conservative thought or practice, and they use every venue available to excoriate Christians and the president they helped to elect.

Will Trump Defeat the Neo-Marxist Revolution?

Countless mainstream media, television networks, newspapers, magazines, and online news sites are collectively chanting the mantra that Trump has dangerous Nazi- and Adolf Hitler–like psychological tendencies.

In her CNN article "Trump Is Following the Authoritarian Playbook," Ruth Ben-Ghiat wrote, "I have spent decades studying authoritarian and fascist regimes and saw in Trump a deeply familiar figure: the strongman who cultivates a bond with followers based on loyalty to him as a person rather than to a party or set of principles. Such individuals inevitably seek to adapt the political office they inhabit to serve their needs. They are clear from the start about this intention, refusing to submit to shared customs and norms—such as releasing tax returns— that would mean they were submitting to the will of the political class. Anyone who believes that Trump will morph into anything resembling a traditional politician will be sorely disappointed. Authoritarians never pivot."[31]

However, what Ben-Ghiat is not telling you is that the theory about "the Authoritarian Personality" originates with the Frankfurt School, and she omits the most important historical fact about this theory—the agenda behind it. As we noted in the previous chapter, the psychological theories and research that came out of the Frankfurt School were designed to ignite a Marxist cultural revolution to take down America by destroying Christianity, traditional marriage and the nuclear family, biblical moral values, and patriotism.

The Frankfurt School launched their Marxist cultural revolution through venues like political correctness, education, media, arts, literature, sex, religion, and psychology. These Marxist professors partnered with Austrian neurologist Sigmund Freud, who developed the theory of psychoanalysis. Together, they created the still-popular theory that the repression of sexual urges of any kind, especially through Christian or biblical teachings and a strong father-centered family structure, creates severe psychological problems that give rise to phenomena such as "the Authoritarian Personality."

One of the primary tenets of Marxism and communism is to destroy the concept of the individual and replace it with groupthink where people find their identities by being part of the team, group, or collective. Individuality is considered a product of capitalism and Christianity. In the ideal Marxist society, the individual disappears, the collective emerges, and the state replaces God.

A strong individual leader who has enough self-confidence to be fearless and doesn't need the approval of the collective is a direct threat to Marxism. This is because the Authoritarian Leader possesses the power, along with the people who follow him, to stop or overthrow a Marxist revolution. The primary motive for the creation of the Authoritarian Leader theory is to use it as a powerful weapon in the world of public opinion to frighten the masses into thinking that a strong leader like Trump will ultimately become a Nazi-like fascist dictator. This argument has been used constantly by the American left and is an attempt to demonize strong leaders in the political arena or any center of power.

However imperfect Trump is, the reason for the intensity of the attacks we've seen against him—the rioting, recounts, death threats, and accusations of collusion with the Russians—is that he's now standing in the way of the globalist, New Age, and Marxist revolution.

The Plot to Assassinate the President

During the summer of 2017, I (Paul) saw a picture on the front page of the Drudge Report featuring evangelical Christian leaders praying for President Trump in the Oval Office.

The photo showed two hands on Trump's shoulder—one a man's hand and the other a woman's—and the two hands wore matching wedding rings. I recognized the wedding rings as those of Rodney and Adonica Howard-Browne, whom I had met a year prior when I was a guest on his television show and spoke at his church—the River at Tampa Bay.

Immediately after reading the article, I called Howard-Browne to ask for his spiritual perspective on whether he felt Trump was receptive to the Christian leaders and the prayer. He said that when they arrived in Washington for the meeting, they were first told that Trump wouldn't be able to meet with them, due to his busy schedule. But when Trump was alerted that the Christian leaders were at the White House he invited them into the Oval Office.

Howard-Browne reported that Trump greeted the pastors with outstretched hands and a big smile on his face and said, "Here is where the real power is!" I asked Howard-Browne what he sensed spiritually in the room when he prayed for the president, and whether Trump received the prayer. This is a phrase used by evangelical ministers. A spiritually sensitive minister can sense if the person being prayed for is being resistant or rebellious. He responded to my question saying, "I literally shook under the power of God when I was praying for Trump." I understood that to mean that not only was the president receptive to their prayers, but there were matters of extreme gravity and urgency occurring in the spiritual world.

I recognize that in certain Christian circles, Howard-Browne is somewhat controversial. Over the decades, I've had the opportunity to develop close relationships with many of the nation's most well-known Christian leaders such as Dr. D. James Kennedy, Dr. Jack Hayford, Pastor Chuck Smith, Pat Robertson, Dr. Tim and Beverly LaHaye, Dr. Bill Bright, Dr. James Dobson, and Chuck Missler. In that time, I've rarely encountered a man or woman whom God is using who some people don't think is controversial. I know Howard-Browne to be a man of integrity. He's also extremely knowledgeable and educated on matters of geopolitics, economics, central banks and the Federal Reserve, and other subjects that require a rare level of sophistication to comprehend. In addition, I observed that he has strong character in that he has been married to his wife, Adonica, for thirty-seven years, and his ministry buses in large numbers of African Americans from the inner cities each week to attend his church and be fed and ministered to. Many of these people, due to extreme poverty, are involved in gangs, drugs, prostitution, and other things, but Howard-Browne and his wife reach out to them.

I tell you all this to validate the veracity of what I'm about to reveal. As Howard-Browne and I continued our phone conversation, he began to share with me something very private and asked me not to reveal it until he made the story public. He told me that while at the White House, he encountered a very high-ranking Republican leader who told him secretly that there is "a plot on Capitol Hill to remove Trump suddenly from office" and that this leader specifically meant via assassination and not impeachment or indictment.

At the time, Howard-Browne had recently issued a generic message asking people on Twitter to pray for the president. He told me that the U.S. Secret Service was waiting in his outer office to conduct an investigative interview about the assassination plot on the president's life. Howard-Browne was careful about what he said to me, and he said he was going to release certain information to the media and via social media. I told him we would be praying for him and President Trump. About an hour after our call, he released information about a Capitol Hill assassination plot on the president's life and the need to pray for the president.

Greatest Crisis in the History of Mankind

This plot to assassinate the leader of the free world comes as the world is in the greatest crisis in the history of mankind. Humanity is facing the prospect of World War III, Super-EMP attacks by rogue states, food shortages and famine, supervolcanoes, giant earthquakes, terrorism, child sex trafficking, the European immigration crisis, along with globalism and trade treaties that are negatively impacting the working and middle class in the United States, the EU, and other parts of the world.

The economic standard of living for ordinary people in America is plateaued or declining, while the Orwellian–Big Brother surveillance state continues to grow—monitoring nearly everything we do and say. In the United States, the number of Americans experiencing serious depression and anxiety because of their declining economic fortunes is approaching record levels. The "Youth Misery Index" rose to its highest point in history during Obama's time in office as millennials found themselves saddled with more debt and fewer job opportunities than before. Americans are concerned about the future for their children and themselves, the loss of spirituality and moral values, degradation of the environment, contamination of food and water, and the continual erosion of their constitutional rights.[32]

The answer to why America is in chaos is not a complex one. It is because it gradually began to reject the ideas, beliefs, and philosophies that made it great. Ideas have consequences. And bad ideas have bad consequences.

Beginning in the early 1900s, America slowly began to turn its back on the original Judeo-Christian principles of our Founding Fathers that had made America the greatest nation on earth. While not all our Founding Fathers were Bible-believing Christians, our Constitution, Bill of Rights, and Declaration of Independence flowed directly out of a biblical worldview that our "Creator" has given us "certain unalienable Rights, that among these are Life, Liberty and the pursuit of Happiness."[33]

The foundational truth from this statement is that it is God who has given us our rights—not man or any man-made form of human government. This makes the American system of government different from that of every other nation on earth, where freedoms and liberties are granted by men and man-made institutions and can be taken away at the whims of man.

What then is the key to America's greatness? It is the fact that the Pilgrims and Puritans who came to America in the 1600s in search of religious freedom entered a covenant with God based on the one he made with ancient Israel recorded in Deuteronomy 28:1–2: "Now it shall come to pass, if you diligently obey the voice of the Lord your God, to observe carefully all His commandments which I command you today, that the Lord your God will set you high above all nations of the earth. And all these blessings shall come upon you and overtake you, because you obey the voice of the Lord your God" (NKJV).

From a theological standpoint, America isn't Israel, and this covenant was made specifically with Israel. However, the Pilgrims and Puritans were deep scholars of the Old Testament and by faith based their covenant with God on Deuteronomy 28. It appears from history that God did honor this covenant with America. However, just like Israel, America didn't keep the covenant perfectly. The second half of Deuteronomy 28 outlines a list of specific curses for violating the covenant.

America is guilty of numerous sins, including our violation of numerous treaties with Native Americans, the theft of their land and slaughter of their people, the enslavement of African Americans, and the murder of sixty million babies through the sin of abortion. Nevertheless, there have been various degrees of repentance, and it appears God may be giving America one final opportunity to be used as a light to the world and as a global platform for the preaching of the gospel. It is within this spiritual context that many evangelical Christians view Trump, however imperfect, as being raised up by God to drive back powerful forces that are seeking to destroy Christianity, the preaching of the good news, and the teachings of Jesus Christ.

The Powers Behind World Revolutions

The American Revolution in 1776 with its biblically influenced Declaration of Independence originated with the strong biblical worldview of the Pilgrims and Puritans. Without the influence of the Bible and the first Great Awakening in the early 1700s, there would have been no American Revolution or United States of America. The American Revolution was a direct expression of the Christian revolution that preceded it.

Shortly after the American Revolution, a humanistic revolution swept the streets of France in 1789 when revolutionaries overthrew the government, leading to the Reign of Terror when King Louis XVI, Marie Antoinette, and thousands of people, mostly aristocrats, were murdered or executed via the guillotine.

Unlike the American Revolution, the French Revolution was based on a philosophy centered on human logic, reason, and knowledge. That philosophy was known as the Enlightenment, which promoted the idea that the enlightened, or "illuminated" man, could be like a god and solve all of mankind's problems. The hidden force behind the Enlightenment and the French Revolution was the Illuminati, which embodied the belief that man is a god and that the energies of Lucifer, not Christ, would lead the world into the New World Order.

"Contrary to some conventional accounts, the French Revolution was not a spontaneous uprising of the downtrodden public," Marrs wrote in *The Illuminati*. "Once popularly believed to have begun due to a public uprising over lack of food and government representation, the record is quite clear that the revolution was instigated by cells of French Masonry and the German Illuminati, often intermingled. It was plainly a major world event inspired by secret society machinations. *The New Encyclopaedia Britannica* reported that in France there arose a political system and a philosophical outlook that no longer took Christianity for granted, that in fact explicitly opposed it... The brotherhood taught by such groups as the Freemasons, members of secret fraternal societies, and the Illuminati, a rationalist secret society, provided a rival to the Catholic sense of community." The French Revolution lasted for a decade until Napoleon Bonaparte seized control in 1799. "Hundreds of thousands had died of starvation, war, violence, and the guillotine," Marrs wrote. "The dream of the Illuminati was realized—the power of both the monarchy and the monolithic church had been largely destroyed."[34]

It was also the teachings of the Illuminati that ignited a series of revolutions that resulted in an estimated ninety-four million deaths in the twentieth century—the Bolshevik Revolution in Russia in 1917 followed by the communist revolutions in China, North Korea, and other countries. This isn't counting the twenty-eight million deaths resulting from the fascist regime of Adolf Hitler's National Socialism (Nazi) movement.[35]

The philosophical fruits of man-centered and humanistic revolutions have never led to a "workers' paradise," "social justice," or the fair redistribution of wealth by a benevolent collectivist state. The results were always, without exception, widespread misery and mass deaths by starvation and slaughter, and total loss of freedom through communist, socialist, and totalitarian regimes.

The American Revolution, unlike all the humanist-inspired revolutions, produced freedom, economic prosperity, a prosperous middle class, and the American dream. The contrast between the two philosophical ideas could not be more obvious. The only potential reason that so many millions of people around the world are blinded to this reality is that there exists a sinister force at work, a secretive ruling oligarchy, which according to Fabian socialists like Aldous Huxley, has covertly established a "scientific dictatorship" using scientific mind-control techniques on the masses.

We know this to be true from statements made by British philosopher Bertrand Russell, former national security adviser Zbigniew Brzezinski, American social philosopher B. F. Skinner, and numerous Frankfurt School–influenced intellectuals. These individuals, in conjunction with clandestine organizations such as the Bilderberg Group, Bohemian Grove, Illuminati, Yale's Skull and Bones, and Freemasonry, compose a global and secretive occult elite who are building a global government, cashless society, and New Age–based religious system. The globalist revolution under way around the world and its dream of a utopian one-world government is the direct continuation of the humanist and socialist philosophies that sparked the nightmares of the French Revolution and subsequent revolutions of the twentieth century. And in the end, it will produce the exact same results. The book of Revelation describes precisely what those results will be.

"Are the globalists now pushing for a world state? Of course, they are!" said the late Tim LaHaye. "And they have been ever since World War I ended when President Woodrow Wilson in 1919 tried to get the U.S. Congress to join the other nations of the world in starting the

League of Nations with the dream of a world organization that would assure 'world peace.' Our Congress had enough sense to defeat that pipe dream." LaHaye went on to say that the one-world dream did not die, and the massive horrors of World War II gave the globalists an opportunity to revive it with the creation of the United Nations in 1945 to "assure a world of peace." But "wars and rumors of wars" continued with conflicts in Korea, Vietnam, and the Middle East while cruel dictators arose throughout the world. And now we have unthinkably powerful weapons of mass destruction delivered by systems that "travel faster than the speed of sound." LaHaye observed, "All this produces a world more dangerous than before with no solution in sight. It is easy to see how a smooth-talking 'man of sin' will arise with more promises of 'world peace in our time' and deceive the nations for a worse period during the last three and a half years of the Tribulation described in the book of Revelation."[36]

The Christian Revolution

It appears, based off a study of his speeches, interviews, and the books he's written, that at some point Trump gained a basic understanding of the New World Order and its conflict with the Constitution, Bill of Rights, and the American dream.

Whether Trump fully realized what he was walking into when he began to openly challenge and confront globalism and the New World Order, the result was that all hell broke loose against him, his family, and his policies. An endless assault was launched by the mainstream media, Hollywood celebrities, cultural leaders, university professors, and activist groups. This was not the result of a spontaneous uprising. It was and is a highly strategic attack that has endless financing behind it.

In light of this concerted effort to quash a duly elected leader, the question must be asked: Is it the globalist elite—"the shadow government"—that really controls the world, or is it "We the People"? Today, just five globalist corporations—down from fifty in 1983—own most of the media, and most Republican and Democratic politicians bow to their bidding. The all-out and unprecedented full-scale war against Trump has no other explanation.[37]

This brings us back to the Trump Revolution and what Franklin Graham called the "Christian Revolution." Since the time of presidential candidate Arizona senator Barry Goldwater and President Ronald Reagan, there has been endless talk about a conservative revolution, but it has never come. A secular conservative revolution has never happened and will never happen because mere conservatism does not have the intellectual, philosophical, and spiritual power to grab hold of men's hearts and minds. However, Marxism does have this power because Marxism, though destructive and deceptive, is a forceful political, philosophical, and spiritual movement.

While a simply conservative revolution can never succeed, a revolution inspired by Christianity certainly can, because it draws its energies from the existence of the biblical God, the reality of the resurrection of Jesus Christ and his second coming, the truth of the Word of God, and the power of the Holy Spirit.

It's these factors, and these alone, that ignited the American Revolution. A true "Christian Revolution" can never happen unless the church, individual Christians, and Christian leaders really believe what they are teaching and then act upon it. Only a holy fire can ignite the hearts of men and women. Mere intellectual acknowledgment of the truth of the gospel will never release the explosive energies of heaven. The human heart, mind, and will must be absolutely gripped with the truthfulness of God's existence and his purpose for their lives and the destiny of mankind. When and only when this happens will the Christian Revolution occur and radically change our world.

Chapter Seven

Battle Against the Globalist Elite

We got here because we switched from a policy of Americanism—
focusing on what's good for America's middle class—to a policy of
globalism, focusing on how to make money for large corporations
who can move their wealth and workers to foreign countries all to
the detriment of the American worker and the American economy.

—DONALD J. TRUMP, CAMPAIGN SPEECH, JUNE 2016[1]

That is the whole election, right there!

—MATT DRUDGE, FOUNDER OF THE DRUDGE REPORT,

IN REACTION TO TRUMP'S SPEECH[2]

It's among the strangest and most famous stories in the Bible—an
ancient tower reaching into the heavens constructed by the multitudes
at the behest of the infamous tyrant Nimrod, the king of Babylon.

Long considered a "mythological tower" by *Encyclopaedia Britannica*,
the Tower of Babel is back in the spotlight following a recent Smithsonian Channel special claiming the biblical account is accurate, based
on ruins of the ancient megastructure uncovered in modern-day Iraq.
The special also features the discovery of an ancient tablet depicting the
Tower of Babel, giving significant credence to the biblical tale.[3]

"Inside the legendary city of Babylon in modern-day Iraq lie the remains of a vast structure, which ancient records suggest was the Tower of Babel," according to the Smithsonian Channel. "Is it possible that this biblical stairway to heaven actually existed? Experts think it did, and thanks to satellite technology and new discoveries, they have pinpointed exactly where the legendary tower once stood, and what it looked like."[4]

The sixth-century BC tablet depicts the massive structure as a ziggurat. The inscription reads: "Tower of Temple of Babylon." It also shows a large figure near the tower wearing a conical helmet and holding a staff. An inscription states that he mobilized people from "far-flung lands" to "construct this building."

"As an Assyriologist, I don't deal in the Bible, and I am not a religious person, but in this case, I can say there is an actual building which does seem to be the inspiration for the biblical narrative," University of London professor of Babylonian Andrew R. George explained.[5]

Origins of Globalism

The history of globalism—and the anti-globalization movement that led to Brexit and ultimately catapulted Trump into the White House—began at the Tower of Babel in Genesis 11 where we read about the first world government. Under the charismatic and almost superhuman leader, Nimrod, the world became "one" in ancient Babylon—a super-civilization built and ruled by the occult elite.

At the time, humanity spoke one language and came together to create a utopia a few generations after Noah's flood. Armed with the power of their "oneness," they sought to build the first New World Order. However, the living God of the universe knew their motives and final goal. As they built the tower, he disrupted their work by confusing the languages of the workers. The project ground to a halt and humanity eventually dispersed over the face of the earth.

God judged the world's first world government because he understood that it was motivated by humanity's desire to join Lucifer's rebellion and become as gods—the original sin the devil used to tempt Adam and Eve in the Garden of Eden. In Revelation 17–18, the Apostle John warned that this Luciferian system—"Mystery, Babylon"—would return in the end times as Satan and his followers staged one final rebellion to overthrow God's kingdom—a revolt that began long ago when Lucifer declared, "I will be like the Most High" (Isa. 14:14 NKJV).

Since ancient Babylon, the secretive occult system known as "Mystery, Babylon" has enabled the Luciferian elite to rule the great kingdoms and empires of history and dream of world domination. In ancient Egypt, the pharaoh aimed to rule "all that the sun encircles." The ancient Chinese and Japanese emperors wanted to rule "all under Heaven." Greek historian Polybius believed that a government ruling over the Mediterranean world would be a "marvelous" achievement. The same dream existed in the Roman Empire, which arose out of the ideas and pagan rites of ancient Babylon. The Roman Caesars, like their predecessors in Babylon and Egypt, wanted to dominate the world by creating a political, monetary, and religious system.[6]

In all the great kingdoms of history—described by the prophet Daniel as the four "beasts" (the Babylonian, Medo-Persian, Greek, and Roman Empires)—pagan religious beliefs played major roles. In each empire, priests, sorcerers, and astrologers served as close advisers to the rulers. Many of them were the true power behind the throne, manipulating the leaders through sorcery and crafty counsel.[7]

In the Roman Empire, the emperor was worshipped as God and served as the leader of the state-sponsored pagan priesthood. Christianity grew rapidly despite severe persecution in the first few centuries following Christ's death and resurrection. Emperor Constantine professed a conversion to Christianity and played an influential role in the

AD 313 Edict of Milan, decreeing tolerance for Christianity throughout his empire. Though the de facto head of Christianity, Constantine continued to oversee the pagan religion of Rome.[8]

Rome still worshipped Apollo the sun god, which experts believe is Nimrod with a new name in a different culture. In Egypt, Nimrod became known as the sun god Ra, who is linked to the All-Seeing Eye of Horus, inspiration for the eye above the pyramid on the back of the dollar bill. The story of Nimrod evolved to become the story of Ra, Osiris, Apollo, and other deities in various cultures. While his account is embroiled in controversy today, Scottish minister Alexander Hislop wrote in his 1858 book *The Two Babylons* that Nimrod married a beautiful prostitute named Semiramis. Shortly after becoming pregnant with his child, Semiramis killed him. Afterward, she claimed the child was a reincarnation of Nimrod and named him Tammuz. The Babylonian religion of Ishtar worshipped both Semiramis and Tammuz. Semiramis, according to Jewish, Christian, and Islamic traditions and legends, became a goddess, starting the mother-goddess religions that spread throughout the world. As these religions spread, the names were changed from one country to another. In Egypt, the mother and her child Tammuz became known as Isis and Horus; in Greece, Ceres/Irene and Plutus; and in Rome, Fortuna and Jupiter. Thus, the satanic Babylonian religion spread throughout the earth.

Semiramis is described as "the Mother of Harlots" in Revelation 17:5, Hislop argued. While Semiramis isn't mentioned in the Bible directly, Ezekiel speaks of her son Tammuz (Ezek. 8:14), Jeremiah objects to the heathen practice of offering cakes to the "Queen of Heaven" (Jer. 7:18, 44:17–19), and respected Bible scholar John F. Walvoord described her as the wife of Nimrod, who "headed up the mystery religion that characterized Babylon."[9]

Globalism: The "Cause Célèbre"

Today, "Mystery, Babylon" is rising again as contemporary globalism with the existence of a globalist elite and their dream of a world socialist government. The several secretive organizations, corporations, banks, law schools, think tanks, and foundations we have previously identified are investing massive resources in this goal.

Chuck Missler says of globalism, "There is no question about the fact that it's become the cause célèbre of the day, and it's also a very dangerous one because that's the one that the leadership is going to usurp, and its ultimate path will be a form of global tyranny."[10]

Not coincidentally, the growing popularity of globalism is linked to an anti-biblical worldview that involves the push for same-sex marriage, dismantling the institution of marriage, abortion, New Age and occult beliefs, and a decline in morals. "The biblical perspective that God has laid out is very antithetical to the kinds of things that globalists aspire to," Missler says. "But it's no surprise because the Bible talks about how this globalism appeal is going to be the very instrument that will be used to enslave people."

The widespread acceptance of globalism and its anti-biblical positions didn't appear out of nowhere. Some of the world's most prominent figures have promoted globalism and the creation of a world government, including iconic broadcast journalist Walter Cronkite, theoretical physicist Albert Einstein, author and biochemistry professor Isaac Asimov, Soviet statesman Mikhail Gorbachev, UN assistant secretary-general Robert Muller, historian Bertrand Russell, U.S. president Harry S. Truman, Fabian socialist and author H. G. Wells, evolutionary biologist Richard Dawkins, cosmologist Carl Sagan, and British prime minister Winston Churchill.[11]

"Unless we establish some form of world government, it will not be possible for us to avert a World War III in the future," Churchill said in

1945. The following year, Einstein wrote: "A world government must be created which is able to solve conflicts between nations by judicial decision. This government must be based on a clear-cut constitution which is approved by the governments and the nations and which gives it the sole disposition of offensive weapons."[12]

More recently, Microsoft founder Bill Gates said that a global government is "urgently needed" to address such problems as extreme poverty, climate change, famine, and the potential of a global epidemic.[13]

Today, we see the prototypes for the return of Babylon in the UN and the EU—believed by many biblical researchers to be the revived Roman Empire foreseen by the prophet Daniel. Viewed by globalists as a model for the "Global Union," the EU and the dream of a utopian world government originated in modern times with one of the greatest open secrets in history. The long-term goals in *The Communist Manifesto*—the 1848 pamphlet by Karl Marx and Friedrich Engels—are largely the same as those in Adam Weishaupt's *The Illuminati Manifesto*.

The Illuminati's goals included the creation of a New World Order, abolition of national governments, inheritance, private property, national sovereignty, patriotism, individual homes and family life, along with all established religions. In comparison, in their ten steps to create an "ideal state," Marx and Engels included abolition of private property and inheritance, a graduated income tax, confiscation of property of dissidents and immigrants, creation of a central bank, centralization of communications and transportation, control over factories and farm production, central ownership of capital, and a free education to indoctrinate children. "The goals of Russian communists and Karl Marx were largely the same goals of the Illuminati and continental Freemasonry," Marrs wrote. "They were almost identical to the major platform goals of Hitler's National Socialists (Nazis), indicating they all stemmed from a common source."[14]

In *The Illuminati Manifesto*, the world's most secret occult group mapped out their plan for a Luciferian world government—a New World Order for the exclusive benefit of the super-rich. The rest of mankind would be enslaved or disposed of.

The true purpose of Marxism and communism was never social justice or the fair redistribution of wealth and property. Its founders knew they couldn't publicly announce their plan to create an all-powerful totalitarian world government, so they found softer words to convince the masses that this would be in their best interest. Given the deaths of tens of millions of people in the twentieth century's communist revolutions and Hitler's National Socialism movement resulting in World War II and the Holocaust, this would seem a formidable task. But the ruling elite, the oligarchy, the "scientific dictatorship," the Illuminati, or whatever you choose to call them, really believe that the masses are genetically inferior and can be deceived by a well-funded campaign of carefully crafted messaging and subliminal and overt scientific mind control.

Remember, the elite are completely convinced of the validity of Darwin's theory of evolution in which certain races and genetic lines are vastly superior to others. That's why the occult ruling families are obsessed with having their children breed within certain genetic lines to preserve their superiority.

In the early twentieth century, the Rockefeller family funded eugenics programs—the science of selective breeding. The term was coined in the late 1800s by British natural scientist Francis Galton, who, influenced by Darwin's theory, proposed a system allowing "the more suitable races or strains of blood a better chance of prevailing speedily over the less suitable." Many political leaders and scientists supported eugenics, but it failed as a science after the Nazis used it to justify exterminating millions of people in the Holocaust in their quest for a "master race."[15]

While the Rockefellers were experimenting with eugenics, Margaret Sanger, founder of Planned Parenthood, expressed the belief that certain races are genetically superior and inferior. In her book *Pivot of Civilization*, Sanger referred to immigrants, African Americans, and poor people as "human weeds," "reckless breeders," and "spawning...human beings who never should have been born." Today, Planned Parenthood operates the nation's largest chain of abortion clinics, and nearly 80 percent are in minority neighborhoods. Since 1973, abortion has reduced the black population by over 25 percent.[16]

In their contempt for the masses, the elite believe they can proceed with their programs of eugenics, economic control, and globalization because they are convinced we are intellectually inferior and are quite content with endless sports and television shows, movies and videos, social media, partying, taking drugs (the reason behind the legalization of marijuana), and easily available pornography.

The Occult Roots of the New World Order

The elite's belief in their genetic superiority played a role in the rise of Hitler and Nazi Germany. The Thule Gesellschaft, or Thule Society—an order of purported Satanists who practiced black magic with a heritage stretching back to the medieval Teutonic Knights that employed the swastika as their symbol—was formed in 1918 in Munich, Germany. Prominent members and associates, including Hitler, later became Nazi leaders. With the help of secret occult societies, Hitler—whom some researchers claim was an Illuminati operative with a "Jewish background linked to the Rothschilds"—gained power, created the world's first "DNA dictatorship," and began the mass extermination of six million Jews and others he considered inferior genetically.[17]

Before and during the war, Hitler gained access to highly advanced technologies that placed the Nazis years ahead of the United States in terms of rockets and other military programs. Nazi scientists conducted advanced experimentation in genetic breeding, performing the most horrific and monstrous biological and scientific mind-control experiments on people.[18]

Even as he watched the collapse of the Third Reich at the end of World War II, Hitler believed that the Fourth Reich would rise again in the form of the New World Order, and that an EU-like organization would be a key step in that process. He wrote an unpublished and untitled book in 1928 known today as *New World Order*. In 1940, Fabian socialist H. G. Wells wrote his own *The New World Order*, popularizing the phrase. The book advocated unification of the nations of the world to end war and bring global peace. Since the late eighteenth century, when the Illuminati first called for the New World Order, many globalists have openly advocated its creation, including President Woodrow Wilson, Vice President Nelson Rockefeller, Secretary of State Henry Kissinger, President George H. W. Bush, British prime minister Tony Blair, Soviet leader Mikhail Gorbachev, banker David Rockefeller, and Vice President Joe Biden.

"The world's elite deal in only one commodity—power," Marrs wrote in *The Rise of the Fourth Reich: The Secret Societies That Threaten to Take Over America*. "They seek to gain and maintain the controlling power that comes from great wealth, usually gained through the monopoly of ownership over basic resources. Politics and social issues matter little to the globalist ruling elite, who move smoothly between corporate business and government service...It is this unswerving attention to commerce and banking that lies behind nearly all modern events. It is the basis for a 'New World Order' mentioned by both Hitler and former President George H. W. Bush."[19]

Over the last century, the elite have engaged in a massive, covert campaign to prepare humanity for the New World Order. The first major step was the creation of the EU with the Treaty of Rome in 1957. The treaty established the European Economic Community, or Common Market. The EU, now comprising twenty-eight member states with a population of over 510 million people, was officially created by the Maastricht Treaty in 1993. "Interestingly enough, the Nazis' attempt at central control through the economic sector produced the early stages of a united Europe so sought by Hitler," Marrs wrote. "George McGhee, a member of the secretive Bilderberg Group and former U.S. ambassador to West Germany, acknowledged that 'the Treaty of Rome, which brought the Common Market into being, was nurtured at Bilderberg meetings.'...The 1942 Nazi vision of a unified Europe had become a reality."[20]

Behind the creation of the EU were powerful Masonic and Illuminati forces, the financing of international banking families, the CIA and MI6, and a vast globalist elite network led by "David Rockefeller's and Zbigniew Brzezinski's Trilateral Commission," experts contend. As the EU began to form, the elite spent massive sums of money to convince people of its necessity as part of a sweeping clandestine plan to create a world state.[21]

Two decades before the Treaty of Rome, in both the United States and Europe, the very thought of a global state reminded people of the communist goal to establish an all-powerful communist world government. After World War II, the idea became more palatable—though still resisted by many—in a world shocked by the horrors of the bloodiest conflict in history.

Today, the threats of World War III, cataclysmic climate change, economic Armageddon, and terrorism are key tools in manufacturing public consensus to bring about a global government. The elite behind the EU, such as French politician Jean Monnet—one of the founding fathers of the EU along with "United States of Europe" advocate Winston Churchill—used a series of carefully worded trade treaties to establish the EU as a kind of soft totalitarian government that rules over its member states.[22]

Now, elite globalists are continuing to use international trade treaties, climate change agreements, and transnational laws that weaken national sovereignty and NATO as strategies to create regional global governments. Among these is the proposed North American Union, consisting of Canada, Mexico, and the United States, which will ultimately be merged into a world government.

In 2016, President Obama met with Canadian prime minister Justin Trudeau and Mexican president Enrique Peña Nieto to form a new "Partnership Action Plan" modeled after Obama's Clean Power Plan. In a statement, the proposed North American Union had been renamed the North American Climate, Clean Energy, and Environmental Partnership, which sets "us firmly on the path to a more sustainable future." The elite often change the names of organizations and programs once they become controversial and attract public concern.[23]

"The steps that led to the creation of the European Union are unsurprisingly similar to the steps being taken to create the North American Union today," Patrick Wood, an expert in elite globalization policies wrote in *Technocracy Rising: The Trojan Horse of Global Transformation.* "As with the EU, lies, deceit and confusion are the principal tools used to keep an unsuspecting citizenry in the dark while they forge ahead without mandate, accountability or oversight."[24]

Meanwhile, the Lisbon Treaty—an international agreement that amended the Maastricht Treaty and Treaties of Rome to streamline the institutions that govern the EU—is being used by globalists as an effective method of keeping EU nations in line. Critics are warning of the "Sovietization" of the EU, which operates like a bureaucratic dictatorship. Trump and many Americans have leveled similar criticism at "the swamp" in Washington, DC. Soon, his supporters were calling on him to follow through on his promise to "drain the swamp"—to root out the unelected special interests influencing the government and weakening America's sovereignty because they are controlled by a consortium of groups funded by the globalist elite.[25]

Babylon Rising in Plain Sight

The occult elite who secretly rule the UN, the EU, and most of the world are no longer hiding their goals and beliefs. While many Christians and others don't believe globalism, trade treaties, and supranational government bodies are a real threat to their freedom, the EU openly proclaims who and what they are via the symbolism and imagery of ancient Babylon on display at EU buildings and in murals, paintings, statues, stamps, and posters.

The symbols of Babylon are widespread throughout Europe. For instance, right in front of the EU headquarters building in Brussels, Belgium is a giant metallic statue of the goddess Europa riding a bull—an image reminiscent of the whore of Babylon riding the beast of Revelation 17:3–5. Further, the engraving on the EU's euro and many of its official documents, including stamps, depicts Europa riding on the back of the mythological beast Minos. The harlot image is also depicted on a large painting on the dome of the building and on a mural at the European Parliament building in Strasbourg, France.[26]

Meanwhile, the parliament building in Strasbourg is a modern architectural replica of the Tower of Babel known as "the Tower of Eurobabel." An EU poster features artist Pieter Bruegel's painting of the Tower of Babel with the slogan "Europe: Many Tongues, One Voice."

The heads of the EU know exactly what all these biblical symbols mean, and they are using them intentionally because they are communicating a message.

Ironically, while many evangelical leaders don't study or teach biblical prophecies, the most powerful people in the world are sending the message that the EU is the resurrection of the spirit of Babylon. They are communicating via paintings, architecture, and statuary that "Mystery, Babylon" is rising again.

"As a backdrop, keep in mind that when Christ came at his first coming the Jewish leaders missed the signs of the times. We must not make the same mistake," Ron Rhodes says. "We've been given signs of the times in biblical prophecies, and it's important that we understand them so we can deduce the fact that we are in fact living in the end times. What are some of those signs? First, we are witnessing a tremendous escalation in apostasy... Secondly, we are witnessing major steps toward globalism. We already see globalist policies emerging in commerce and banking, trade, business, manufacturing, environmentalism, education, agriculture, the entertainment industry, publishing, and so much more. The other thing we're seeing with globalism is directly related to the multiple, cascading problems facing humanity." Rhodes cites Middle East conflicts, terrorism, ISIS, overpopulation, starvation, and cyber warfare as evidence the world is spinning out of control, causing people to yearn for a strong leader to "take control and make sense of the world." He warns that "he's not going to have a badge that says 'Antichrist.' He's going to be a very charismatic leader who will be a political genius and an economic genius and a religious genius, and he will seem to be just the ticket—just what we need to solve the world's problems."[27]

Seven in Ten People Support World Government

Today, it seems the world is primed to meet this charming enchanter—the world's long-awaited false messiah. Astonishingly, at a time when dozens of prophecy experts interviewed for *Trumpocalypse* agree the world stage is set for the arrival of the Antichrist, a new poll found overwhelming support for the creation of a world government authority.

The survey, commissioned by the Global Challenges Foundation, included 8,101 people in Australia, Brazil, China, Germany, India, South Africa, the United Kingdom, and the United States. It found that 71 percent think a "new supranational organization should be created to make enforceable global decisions to address global risks." The poll also found that 62 percent of people now view themselves as "global citizens." "As world leaders gather for the G7 Summit [in the summer of 2017], they should be aware that citizens across the planet are yearning for them to collaborate and work harder to find solutions for these critical threats to humanity," Mats Andersson, the foundation's vice-chairman, explained.[28]

The movement to create a global government has gained widespread and surprising public support, but the concept is often sold to people in sugarcoated terms such as "globalization," "globalism," "global governance," being a good "global citizen," and "one world"—part of the name of the new One World Trade Center, the Manhattan skyscraper that replaced the World Trade Center destroyed in the September 11, 2001, terrorist attacks.

Globalists and federalist groups around the world, including the World Constitution and Parliament Association, which drafted the Earth Constitution, are part of a growing movement to create a global government through bodies like the United Nations, trade treaties, transnational laws, the "global citizens" campaign, and the biggest enticement in the candy jar—a government-provided "universal basic income" for global citizens. This renewed interest in a global state comes amid vast technological progress, economic globalization, and heightening fears of a climate change "tipping point" and nuclear war. For the first time in history, the Internet, globalization, air travel, mark of the Beast technologies, and the surveillance state have made a world government a realistic possibility.[29]

Strangely, the Global Challenges Foundation in its "Global Catastrophic Risks" report named a "global totalitarian state" among the top threats facing humanity. Others include nuclear warfare, catastrophic climate change, ecological collapse, a doomsday asteroid, supervolcano eruption, and artificial intelligence gone amok.[30]

In a section of the "Existential Risk" report by Oxford University's

Global Priorities Project about "global totalitarianism," the authors noted that during the twentieth century, citizens of several nations lived for a time under "extremely brutal and oppressive regimes." "Between them, these states killed more than one hundred million people, and sought total control over their citizens," the authors wrote. "Previous totalitarian states have not been particularly durable chiefly due to the problem of ensuring orderly transition between leaders, and to external competition from other more liberal and successful states. However, there is a non-negligible chance that the world will come to be dominated by one or a handful of totalitarian states." The authors explain that if this were to happen, without competition the state would become deeply entrenched, surveillance would be easy, and the quality of government would decrease. "In addition," the authors conclude, "a long future under a particularly brutal global totalitarian state could arguably be worse than complete extinction."[31]

John Fonte, a Hudson Institute fellow and the author of *Sovereignty or Submission: Will Americans Rule Themselves or Be Ruled by Others*, says globalists are working methodically to create international laws, rules, and institutions that are "supranational," or "above the Constitution of the United States," as part of a plan to create the legal framework for a worldwide federal system or global state. "This is being funded—you know, follow the money—by leading American foundations like the Ford Foundation and the Rockefeller Foundation," Fonte says. "They are promoting global governance. So is the European Union. So are many global corporations. Look on the websites and read the mission statements of the Fortune 500. They claim that they are global companies. They are not multinational companies that are based in the United States."[32]

"In explaining global governance," Fonte wrote, "[former Obama official Anne-Marie] Slaughter argues that nation-states should cede sovereign authority to supranational institutions, such as the International

Criminal Court. Slaughter maintains that such transnational networks 'can perform many of the functions of a world government—legislation, administration, and adjudication—without the form,' thereby creating an effective global rule of law."[33]

The concept of world government is gaining popularity because people believe world peace and justice can be achieved only through a global political authority, which sets up acceptance of the lavish promises of a charismatic leader who will turn out to be the prophesied instrument of Satan who brings on the end times.

Global Citizens: "Blueprint for a United World"

As part of a campaign to persuade people worldwide to think of themselves as global citizens, the organization named Global Citizen hosts regular "Global Citizen Festivals" and Earth Days in major cities worldwide. Beginning in 2012, these massive events have attracted tens of thousands of people and dozens of world leaders, celebrities, and activists. Global Citizen defines itself as a "social action platform for a global generation that wants to solve the world's biggest challenges," including ending "extreme poverty by 2030." The celebrities, bands, and world leaders have included Beyoncé, Jay Z, Ed Sheeran, Rihanna, Usher, Demi Lovato, Hugh Jackman, Coldplay, Metallica, comedian Stephen Colbert, Nobel laureate Malala Yousafzai, UN messenger of peace and actor Leonardo DiCaprio, U2 lead singer and ONE cofounder Bono, Sir Richard Branson, former UN secretary-general Ban Ki-moon, Bill and Melinda Gates, World Bank Group president Jim Yong Kim, Swedish prime minister Stefan Löfven, U.S. senator Chris Coons (D-DE), and U.S. representative Charlie Dent (R-PA).[34]

In many ways, these celebrities and world leaders are following in the footsteps of the late Beatle John Lennon and former president Obama. In his signature song "Imagine," Lennon urged his fans to imagine a world without nations and borders and called for the "world to be as one." Lennon believed that patriotism and nationalism were the causes of war. He viewed himself as a citizen of the world and influenced millions of people to think like him.[35]

In 2008, while speaking before a massive crowd in Berlin, Obama referred to himself as "a proud citizen of the United States, and a fellow citizen of the world...But the burdens of global citizenship continue to bind us together." Previous presidents never would have used those words, but through a subtle indoctrination process involving celebrities and powerful memes introduced into the global lexicon, times have changed.[36]

This campaign of change culminated in September 2015 when the "Global Citizen Festival" was held shortly before world leaders met in New York City to vote on the UN plan "Transforming Our World: The 2030 Agenda for Sustainable Development." The plan is the follow-up to the UN plan known as the "Millennium Development Goals" and shares much of the rhetoric and agenda with the highly controversial Agenda 21 plan. The conference was followed a few months later by the Paris climate-change summit when 196 nations agreed to address climate change. At the UN meeting on sustainable development, Obama, Pope Francis, and the UN General Assembly approved the sweeping document that experts say puts the world on the fast track to a global government. The preamble calls for a "new universal agenda" for all humanity, and the authors wrote that the next fifteen years will be "some of the most transformative in human history." Critics describe the plan as an "undisguised roadmap to global socialism and corporatism/fascism."[37]

In his article "This Happened in September," Idaho congressional candidate Michael Snyder noted the UN has seventeen goals it plans to achieve over the next fifteen years. "Virtually every nation on the planet has willingly signed on to this new agenda, and you are expected to participate whether you like it or not," wrote Snyder. "The elite want a one-world government, a one-world economic system and a one-world religion. But they are not going to achieve these things by conquest. Rather, they want everyone to sign up for these new systems willingly. The 'global goals' are a template for a united world. To many, the 'utopia' that the elite are promising sounds quite promising. But for those that know what time it is, this call for a 'united world' is very, very chilling."[38]

Masquerade for a One-World Order

In effect, the UN plan is masquerading as a global movement to end poverty through "sustainable development" and "social justice." They expect to accomplish this through socialist wealth redistribution by transferring the wealth of hardworking middle- and working-class people in America and other nations to poor countries worldwide.

Goal number ten of the UN's "2030 Agenda" calls on the UN and national governments to "reduce inequality within and among countries." The agreement states this will "only be possible if wealth is shared and income inequality is addressed." The UN is calling for international socialism to reduce inequality among the nations. This means that even if nations like America work harder and smarter, they are not allowed to keep their higher incomes. Using classic Marxist principles, all wealth must be redistributed "equally." Who will ensure wealth is distributed equally? The answer will likely be the giant UN bureaucracy with a long track record of failure. What is usually left out of these one-world socialist plans is the fact that the "1 percent"—the superwealthy—will not be forced to give up their wealth.[39]

"In simpler terms, Western taxpayers should prepare to be fleeced so that their wealth can be redistributed internationally as their own economies are cut down to size by Big Government," Alex Newman wrote in his "UN Agenda 2030: A Recipe for Global Socialism" article. "Of course, as has been the case for generations, most of the wealth extracted from the productive sector will be redistributed to the UN and Third World regimes—not the victims of those regimes, impoverished largely through domestic socialist/totalitarian policies imposed by the same corrupt regimes to be propped up with more Western aid under Agenda 2030."[40]

Consider the mathematical insanity of this proposal. Today, middle- and working-class people often need to work more than one job just to maintain the same level of economic well-being that one job produced several decades ago. Since 1967, the percentage of Americans in the middle class (households earning $35,000 to $100,000 a year) has dropped from 53 percent to 43 percent. At the same time, the percentage of Americans in the upper class (households earning over $100,000 annually) increased from 7 percent to 22 percent. Meanwhile, an Oxfam report, "An Economy for the 1%," found how the wealth of the poorest half of the world's population (3.6 billion people) fell by a trillion dollars (38 percent) since 2010 while the wealth of the richest sixty-two people increased by over half a trillion dollars. "Power and privilege are being used to rig the system to increase the gap between the richest and the rest of us to levels we have not seen before," Raymond C. Offenheiser, president of Oxfam America, said.[41]

Another Oxfam report found that the richest 1 percent now own 99 percent of global wealth. This being the case, then why are they asking the remaining 99 percent of the population who only control 1 percent of the wealth to pay for their plan? How is that fair or equal?

Of course, it's not even remotely fair or equal, but through public education programs developed by UNESCO and constant propaganda from the globalist-controlled media, the masses have been blinded to the obvious. Do you really think the "1 percent" globalist elite are going to pay for this UN plan? Of course not.

These "sustainable development" rules, laws, and taxes—and the whole ruse of ending poverty—are simply designed to further reduce the standard of living among middle- and working-class people so that soon there will just be one large, compliant, and obedient lower class and a tiny, super-rich upper class. Patrick Wood wrote, "Sustainable development is a Trojan horse that looks good on the outside but is filled with highly toxic and militant policies on the inside. It promises a utopian dream that it cannot possibly deliver."[42]

Today, globalists are using a variety of strategies in their quest to create some form of world government through "global governance," Fonte says. For instance, Pope Francis recently called for the creation of a "Global Public Authority" to address climate change and help in "the development of poor countries and regions." This appeal echoes one Pope Benedict XVI made in a 2009 encyclical proposing a "kind of super-UN to deal with the world's economic problems and injustices," according to the *Guardian*. "There are forces within the European Union and within the American elite at leading law schools trying to establish global governance," Fonte says. "They have said it openly. They are not going to do this by force. They are going to do it by judicial fiat—a judge says you've got to do X, Y, and Z. We're a law-abiding people, so we usually go along with judges. The law changes. You can see the whole definition of marriage changing within a four-year period. All of a sudden what was normal for thousands of years is now considered racist or bigoted... I think there will be an attempt [to create a 'single global authority']. The UN is attempting to do something. Whether it will be successful, I really don't know, but nothing good can come from it.[43]

"Americanism, Not Globalism, Will Be Our Credo"

This campaign by the globalist elite to gain approval for "Global Public Authority" is a battle over the future of mankind.

The early realization among the public of what was really happening began with the anti-globalization movement that has its roots in the 1960s counterculture with the early environmental movement, the punk rock 'n' roll movement, and social anarchism. The anti-globalization movement reemerged in the 1990s in response to neoliberal globalization—policies that helped corporations maximize their profits with little regard for their employees. In the profit-focused world created by these policies, the government safety net was weakened. A "new social Darwinism" communicated the message that "only the strong and remarkable survive." A "permanent insecurity" in income and living conditions was created, unemployment, welfare, and pension benefits were cut, the retirement age was increased, and private retirement plans such as 401(k)s were encouraged. This rapid transformation in the global economy became known as "turbo-capitalism."[44]

The anti-globalization movement received significant media coverage during protests at the World Trade Organization meeting in Seattle, Washington, in 1999, at the International Monetary Fund and World Bank gatherings in 2000, and at the G8 (Group of Eight) meeting in Genoa, Italy, in 2001. But it wasn't until after the global recession in the late 2000s when millions of people had lost their jobs and homes that the movement began to capture the public's imagination with the Occupy Wall Street protests that began in 2011.

The protests received global media coverage and inspired a wider movement against economic inequality, greed, and corruption. The protesters slogan "We are the 99 percent" had to do with the inequitable wealth distribution between the richest 1 percent and the other 99 percent of the population. The protests soon spread nationwide to banks, corporate headquarters, and college campuses. Similar ones erupted worldwide as word spread virally on social media, including the Arab Spring, and protests in the United Kingdom, Greece, Spain, Chile, and India.

However, the term "anti-globalization movement" can be misleading because many of its adherents believe in social justice through a global government in synch with Gaia, or Mother Earth—viewed as the personification of the Earth with a living consciousness. As such, they are on board with sustainable development and the Paris climate change agreement. This side of the anti-globalization movement believes in a mystical approach to utopia, but doesn't seem to comprehend the darker realities and hidden agenda of the secret societies and "shadow governments" across the world. They are right and even astute in their understanding of the dangers posed by the ruling elite and their desire to control resources and wealth and effectively enslave humanity through financial institutions and free trade agreements. But like the hippies and the counterculture, they are largely unaware that they are pawns of the financial elite and are secretly controlled and financed by them.

The anti-globalization movement took the world by surprise in the summer of 2016 when more than thirty million people in the United Kingdom voted 52 percent to 48 percent in a referendum to leave the EU in what became known as "Brexit." A few days later, Trump endorsed the UK decision to leave the EU, predicting similar populist movements throughout the West. Trump connected the vote to the political climate in the United States. "I think people really see a big parallel," Trump said. "And not only the United States, but other countries. People want to take their country back."[45]

A month later at the Republican National Convention when he accepted his party's nomination for president, Trump expressed the central strategy of his campaign. "The most important difference between our plan and that of our opponents, is that our plan will put America first," Trump said. "Americanism, not globalism, will be our credo."[46]

The spirit of Brexit, like the spirit of freedom that birthed it, swept the European nations in the ensuing months. However, during the presidential election in the fall of 2016, something happened that never should have happened. It appeared as a fluke to the political analysts, media pundits, and political strategists on the left and right. But, as things turned out, it was far more than a fluke. It was the beginning of the revolution of Americanism versus globalism.

Rebirth of the American Dream

Trump not only defied reality; he helped create a new reality for America. Unlike many of the political elite who come from wealthy dynasties and live in the nation's most secluded and private wealthy enclaves, Trump is largely a self-made billionaire from Queens, New York, who wasn't raised among the elite, unless you consider Jamaica Estates, Queens, as a kind of Beverly Hills, which it's not.

Jamaica Estates is an upper-middle-class neighborhood, and the Trump family interacted with the middle class and working class of Queens. With the help of some serious seed money from his father, Trump became successful the old-fashioned way—by working hard and smart. When he entered the election process as a candidate, the overwhelming conclusion among the media, Democrats, and Republicans was that he might provide some amusement, but he was not a serious contender.

The big money early on was on people like Jeb Bush, Marco Rubio, and maybe Ted Cruz. Trump wasn't a "politician" like these candidates. But he was a powerful communicator who knew how to bond with people in minutes, and a business entrepreneur who survived and thrived by understanding marketing, customer service, profits, cutting costs without cutting quality, good management, leveraging, competition, deal making, sophisticated financial strategies, and what he called *The Art of the Deal*—the title of his bestselling book.

Although he had an advantage because his father trained him and gave him money to help launch out on his own, it wasn't a silver spoon in his mouth. His father expected Trump to make it happen. Unlike most politicians, Trump didn't come from a superwealthy political dynasty like Jeb Bush or receive major backing from powerful globalist special interest groups. Trump, although educated in prestigious schools, was also educated on the streets of Queens. In Queens, Trump learned what other politicians from both parties never learned and never had, and that was "street smarts." Queens instills you with a cutting edge and an instinct for survival. It was also in Queens that Trump learned patriotism and acquired a love for America, the value of hard work, discipline, the importance of the American Constitution and the Bill of Rights, and a respect for God and Christianity, even though he wasn't particularly religious for much of his life.

In a sense, Trump became the "killer" that his father taught him to be. To the working- and middle-class people of Queens, "killer" doesn't mean harming someone; it's a street term that means you need to be tough or you're going to get walked on.

When Trump entered the election process he saw that America had become weak because of corruption and that our nation was being walked on. He set out with a simple vision—"Make America Great Again"—because he understood what America's greatness is all about. He understood that the real purpose of globalism and trade treaties was to allow the globalist elite to economically pillage our nation and merge us into a one-world government. Trump clearly believed in Americanism over globalism. Unlike a lot of his competitors, it wasn't an act; it was straight from the heart, and millions of Americans could feel it.

"A Hard-Nosed Prophetic Cyrus"

One of those Americans was business consultant Lance Wallnau. Before the election, Wallnau was one of several evangelical Christian leaders who believed against the odds that Trump would become America's forty-fifth president. Wallnau contends that Trump is "God's answer" to rescue the United States from the emerging tyrannical "one-world order."[47] "Trump is literally an individual raised up like a Cyrus candidate for the sake of God's people, Israel, and the church," Wallnau explained.[48]

However, dark forces are resisting Trump's mission to vanquish the emerging global order paving the way for the Antichrist. "What Trump did in his inaugural address was he punched the globalist one-world movement in the nose," Wallnau said. He noted that Trump said he would not do deals with special interest groups "to fund their globalist agendas. From now on, every deal that is done benefits the United States when the United States is in it. He was sending a signal to the one-world order. Everybody focuses on Islamic extremism. Islamic extremism is dangerous because they want a caliphate, a unified Islamic state. More dangerous than that is what's happened in Europe and what happened in the United States as progressives began to remove religion as a foundation and replace [it with] the elite intelligence of man and science... gradually assimilating us all into a one-world economy. That's where the Antichrist comes from."

At a time when the "door was closing," judgment was coming upon America, and the nation's economy was spiraling "out of existence," God gave America "a hard-nosed prophetic Cyrus who stands there at the door and says, 'No, there is going to be an extension of peace and grace on America,'" Wallnau said. "This battle is global. Every Christian in the world knows it. They were praying in Africa for this election. Every Christian nation knows. If America goes down, tyranny comes up... This is a world order battle. Expect it to be played out at a world order level."

Chapter Eight

The Illuminati's Secret Plan

The league of the ten kings is the cooperative commonwealth of mankind, the natural and proper form of human government. The Atlantis, therefore, is the archetype or pattern of right government... Plato['s]... ideal king was... descended of a divine race; that is, he belonged to the Order of the Illumined... Here then, is a pattern of world government to insure the prosperity of all peoples and activate the preservation of the peace.

—MANLY P. HALL, A LEADING ESOTERIC SCHOLAR,
IN *THE SECRET DESTINY OF AMERICA*[1]

From the highest spiritual Being upon our planet, through the graded spiritual groups of enlightened and perfected men... the tide of the new life sweeps. The Plan is ready for immediate application and intelligent implementing; the workers are there...

—ALICE BAILEY, FOUNDER OF LUCIS TRUST,
IN *THE EXTERNALIZATION OF THE HIERARCHY*[2]

"Who can hide in secret places so that I cannot see them?" declares the Lord. "Do not I fill heaven and earth?" declares the Lord.

—JEREMIAH THE PROPHET, JEREMIAH 23:24 (NIV)[3]

At 120 Wall Street in New York City, the Arcane School at Lucis Trust—formerly Lucifer Publishing Company—is working on behalf of the "spiritual Hierarchy of the planet" to carry out the "Plan" to create the "New World Order."[4]

Lucis Trust defines the "Hierarchy" as the "inner spiritual governance of the world led by enlightened beings." It's also known as the "society of Illumined Minds." Lucifer is known as the "Light Bringer, the Illumined One."[5]

As astounding as this may seem given its obvious occult connotations, it's all detailed on the website of Lucis Trust, a nongovernmental organization that has "consultative status" with the United Nations Economic and Social Council and whose political lobby, World Goodwill, is accredited by the UN Department of Public Information.

Since its founding in 1922, Lucis Trust and World Goodwill "have given their support through meditation, educational materials, and seminars, by highlighting the importance of the UN's goals and activities as they represent the voices of the peoples and nations of the world." Even more astonishing, World Goodwill notes there is "widespread expectation" that as the world approaches the "Age of Maitreya," the "World Teacher and present head of the spiritual Hierarchy, the Christ, will reappear among humanity to sound the keynote of a new age." In *The Reappearance of the Christ*, Alice Bailey—an esoteric author and founder of Lucis Trust—wrote that the "second coming of the Christ, as the world Teacher for the age of Aquarius" is "the same great Identity in all the world religions."[6]

"The one thing which humanity needs today is the realization that there is a Plan which is definitely working out through all world happenings, and that all that has occurred in man's historical past, and all that has happened lately, is assuredly in line with that Plan," Bailey wrote in *The Externalization of the Hierarchy*.[7]

Illuminati, Trump, and the "Plan"

As many of you discovered in *The Babylon Code* with its extensive documentation, the Illuminati is as real today as it was in 1776 when its founder, University of Ingolstadt professor Adam Weishaupt, first called for a "New World Order through Revolution." Today, the Illuminati network—operating through countless front groups and an interconnected web of multinational corporations, international banks, government agencies, think tanks, foundations, and secret societies—is believed to be in the final stages of implementing its Plan to launch the New World Order. Illuminati whistle-blowers and others claim this could start soon with an engineered financial collapse, outbreak of war, or a sophisticated global deception involving a "fake Antichrist" before the "fake Second Coming of Christ." We'll delve more into these claims later.[8]

At this urgent time, we must ask: Is Trump on the inside or outside of the Illuminati? Or is Trump being unknowingly used by the Illuminati? A man as perceptive as Trump would know if he is being played, or perhaps he's attempting to play them. But the bigger question is: Has Trump been raised up by a power greater than the power behind the Illuminati?

In nations like the United States, the Illuminati controls the highest seats of power. However, there exists a greater power than the Illuminati, and that is the power of the living God of the universe. What if to fulfill his prophetic plan, God raised up Trump for such a time as this?

Many people in America bristle at such talk. But God is a sovereign king who chooses whom he will, and in God's sovereign election, he doesn't ask for man's opinion, nor does he need to conform to man's expectations. We'll explore these matters in this chapter.

First, let's take a closer look at the connection between the "Plan," the New Age movement, and the world's most infamous secret society.

In his 1989 book *Guardians of the Grail*, J. R. Church, founder of the *Prophecy in the News* ministry, magazine, and syndicated television show, put together the pieces of the puzzle, arguing the Illuminati is "bigger than ever" and closely connected to the New Age movement. "Most important of all, [the Illuminati] is being promoted in this decade as a New Age movement," Church wrote. "This powerful organization is dedicated to the establishment of world government and vows to soon introduce a single dictator to sit upon the throne of this world. To this agree the words of the prophets—they call him Antichrist."[9]

World Leaders Trained to Carry Out the Plan

The Plan was developed by Luciferian and New Age leaders, many of whom were influenced by famous Russian occult teacher and Theosophical Society cofounder Helena Blavatsky. Her teachings have impacted New Age, occult, political, and economic leaders throughout the world, including the Rothschilds, Rockefellers, Henry Kissinger, and Adolf Hitler. It was Blavatsky's disciple Bailey who later set up Lucis Trust to train and disciple world leaders in the Plan.[10]

In her 1983 book *The Hidden Dangers of the Rainbow: The New Age Movement and Our Coming Age of Barbarism*, Michigan attorney and Christian activist Constance Cumbey wrote that those working to carry out the Plan are "in every city and institution in the world." They are at the United Nations, in prominent scientific, legal, and medical circles, and even at the "congressional and cabinet levels of the United States government." "According to New Age sources, the New Age movement is a worldwide network," Cumbey wrote. "It consists of tens of thousands of cooperating organizations. Their primary goal or the secret behind their 'unity-in-diversity' is the formation of a 'New World Order.'...Carefully structured along the lines set forth in the Alice Bailey writings, it includes organizations teaching mind control, holistic health, esoteric philosophy, scientific workers, political workers, and organizations dedicated to peace and world goodwill."[11]

Cumbey believes the New Age movement meets the "scriptural requirements" for the Antichrist and the movement that will facilitate his rise to power.[12]

In an exclusive interview for *Trumpocalypse*, Cumbey said she believes the New Age-Illuminati elite are planning to use Trump "as an excuse for globalization." "They are using populism, Brexit, and Donald Trump as an excuse for why they need to bring things together quickly. Are they going to succeed this time? I don't know. The timetable is in God's hands. If God's ready we'd better be too."[13]

The Plan to establish a Luciferian world order involves some of the most powerful and influential institutions on earth. The UN and its leaders are fully behind the Plan, and most of their policies, programs, and treaties are designed to implement it. In 1933, Bailey predicted that the "'World Federation of Nations' will be...taking rapid shape by 2025."[14]

"They plan on the world being organized into a system of continents through global governance," Cumbey says. "The European Union is one of the prototypes. They also want a 'New World Religion.'...Those who don't are cancer cells in the global brain that need to be eradicated. And the New Age Messiah they cheerfully admit is not Jesus."

The UN plan "Transforming Our World: The 2030 Agenda for Sustainable Development" is a critical component of the Plan, Cumbey says. "Sustainable development has been one of their very big pushes, and it's the New Age heart and core of their plan. The way things have been shaping up also involves the outcome-based education and Common Core curriculum that we've heard so much about."

New Age Network Follows the Plan Like a Recipe

The United Nations was established in October 1945 following the end of World War II. The UN replaced its predecessor, the League of Nations, which was created by the Treaty of Versailles in 1919 and disbanded in 1946.[15]

The UN's worldview was largely inspired by the occult teachings of New Age visionary and "UN apparatchik" Bailey. She created several organizations under Lucis Trust (Lucis Publishing Company, World Goodwill, Arcane School, and Triangles) to teach world leaders what was communicated to her telepathically by Tibetan "Master" Djwhal Khul—a representative of the "Hierarchy." Before it moved to its address on Wall Street, Lucis Trust was located at 866 United Nations Plaza, New York.[16]

"This whole thing started with the Theosophical Society back in the late 1800s with Madame Blavatsky," Bill Schnoebelen says. "She wrote two massive books—*Isis Unveiled* and *The Secret Doctrine*—that detailed how there is to be this 'Plan' put forward for a one-world religion led behind the scenes by these ascended celestial beings." As a former Illuminist, Schnoebelen says he used to pray for the success of the Plan, but Cumbey's book helped him get out of the occult. "Frankly," he says, "the UN is a spiritual citadel of evil."[17]

Since its inception, the Arcane School at Lucis Trust has trained tens of thousands of people for "active New Age discipleship and leadership," Cumbey wrote. "It may safely be said that Lucis Trust is truly the brains—at least from an occult planning basis—of the New Age movement...Her instructions to New Age 'disciples' have been followed like recipes."[18]

As part of its work to prepare humanity for the "reappearance of the Christ," Lucis Trust today serves in a "referral capacity" for the

"Worldwide Network of Servers," consisting of countless organizations listed on its website.[19]

"On the international political scene, the United Nations has supplied a platform for New Age promoters through supporting or otherwise abetting New Age organizations such as Planetary Citizens," Philip H. Lochhaas wrote in *New Age Movement*. "Founded by Donald Keys, a longtime UN consultant, its headquarters were once housed in the UN building. Robert Muller, a retired assistant secretary-general of the UN, is a New Age activist who believes the UN will play an important role in global transformation."[20]

Bailey wrote more than two dozen books to lay the foundations for the New Age movement and included specific instructions from her "Master" on how to carry out the Plan. "Step by step they plotted the coming 'New Age,' with instructions for the institution of the necessary New World Order," Cumbey wrote. "Plans for religious wars, forced redistribution of the world's resources, Luciferic initiations, mass planetary initiations, theology for the New World Religion, [nuclear] disarmament campaign, and elimination or sealing away of obstinate religious orthodoxies—all were covered extensively in the Alice Bailey writings. Even the 'sacredness' of the number of the beast—666—was covered in at least two places."[21]

It becomes clear in reading Bailey's books that the Plan is designed to rid the world of true Christianity, create a watered-down "New Age Christianity-Lite," and replace the biblical worldview predominant in Western culture with a New Age–Illuminati worldview.

Carolyn Hamlett, a former Illuminati member who was raised in the Luciferian organization and was responsible for implementing the Plan, says its real author is Satan. Luciferians have been working from generation to generation to "tear down Judeo-Christian values, bring strife, war, famine, and chaos so they can offer their solution for global peace." Their hidden agenda is to unveil "Lucifer's 'Christ' as global ruler." Ultimately, this Plan calls for killing Christians to free the world of the restraining influence they "impose on the collective spirituality of the human race," Hamlett says. "At this point, I think the world is pretty much taken over…These are [Illuminati] people at the top levels. In fact, they are much more evil today than [several decades ago]. The point is what is the power behind them…It's Satan's spiritual Hierarchy."[22]

The Illuminati is carrying out the Plan in three stages, and "one of the last sections has to do with 9/11," Hamlett says. "It's to get the entire world prepared to want to have what they call the 'Christ' in global power. They work little by little, very patiently. Like a frog in the pot, you bring it slowly to a boil. They don't want people to recognize that anything is up…But they are getting impatient, and so they are probably going to try to push things."

Hamlett says the Plan involves a "fake Antichrist" followed by a "fake Second Coming of Christ" to deceive people into accepting the "most Illuminated one of all"—the Antichrist. But Hamlett believes God "has a plan that is going to empower the church." She says, "God is keeping certain things secret until it actually happens…God has a phenomenal plan that is going to defeat Satan's plans."

Common Core: Targeting Our Youth

In her books, Bailey stressed the importance of targeting youth, knowing if children were indoctrinated with a New Age worldview, the Plan would become a normal part of life for future generations. Muller, along with Julian Huxley, first head of the United Nations Educational, Scientific, and Cultural Organization (UNESCO), created the "World Core Curriculum"—a "sort of pro-UN Common Core for the world"—to create a globalist education program for children worldwide.

Today, most Christian parents have no idea that the Common Core curriculum their children are taught in schools is simply an updated version of occult teachings created by Bailey, who received the information from her enigmatic Hierarchy guide.

Pastor Billy Crone says, "The UN has been working with the National Education Association to basically carry out the UN agenda. They've been disseminating it to America, not just through the media...and not just through politics, but also in American schools through the NEA, and they did it by continually changing the terminology. First, you had the UN plan called Goals 2000, then it turned into No Child Left Behind, and now it's called Common Core...They have been in control of indoctrinating American students for decades into this UN plan for global governance, global religion, etc. The UN is full-blown New Age." Crone adds that people don't take New Age practices seriously and will not until they "see the big picture of where the Bible tells us this is all headed."[23]

The UN "2030 Agenda" outlines seventeen "Sustainable Development Goals" detailing its vision for using children as "agents of change" in what the Council on Foreign Relations describes as its "global development agenda." The plan promotes the use of schools to indoctrinate youth with a new set of values in preparation for the new "sustainable" world order. Former UN secretary-general Ban Ki-moon and UNESCO director-general Irina Bokova said at the World Education Forum in South Korea in 2015 that globalized schools worldwide need to reshape children's values to create "global citizens."

This global indoctrination campaign originated with Bailey's instructions to her New Age disciples in the 1940s to target children below the age of ten, especially from the elite classes of society, and liberate them from Judeo-Christian values. Since then, we've witnessed the impact of Bailey's program because children from elite families now occupy the highest positions in politics, government, business, law, media, and education, and largely run the UN, International Monetary Fund, World

Bank, and countless other influential organizations, government agencies, and corporations. They are making policy decisions based on secular humanism, New Age ideas, occult concepts, and concealed Luciferianism. This explains why business and media moguls such as Ted Turner and Oprah Winfrey, along with many American presidents and global leaders, think the way they do. The covert rise of the New Age movement to such a dominant position in the world is especially ominous given that Winfrey recently told Bloomberg's David Rubenstein that she may consider a presidential run in 2020.[24]

Election 2020: Trump vs. Oprah?

Remarkably, a poll by Public Policy Polling found Winfrey could beat Trump. "Reports have conflicted on whether she's really interested, but for what it's worth, Oprah Winfrey has a 49/33 favorability rating nationally and would lead Donald Trump 47–40 in a hypothetical 2020 presidential contest," the survey found.[25]

Given how closely world events are now tracking with the Plan, Crone says it's intriguing that one of the most famous New Age promoters on the planet may make a bid for the White House. "If you look at the New Age, and the ways they are indoctrinating people, whether it be environmentalism, the fitness movement, and even the vegetarian movement, certainly, Oprah and other female figures are promoting this," Crone says. "The one thing they have in common is they want us to go back to a matriarchal instead of patriarchal worship of Father God. If you look at environmentalism, which basically has the same tenets as New Age, it's that we all need to worship Mother Earth or we're going to be destroyed...If you look at feminism it's 'We need to get rid of this male, patriarchal figure—this God, this Father God, and Jesus. We need to get back to Gaia worship, goddess worship,' and that's part and parcel of this."

Crone notes that Revelation 17 tells us that it's a woman who rides the Beast. He adds, "Who is the Beast? He's the Antichrist. He's the political figure that draws the world's governments under his control. So... you have this one-world female entity, a global religious figure, riding the one-world governmental system, working hand in hand."

Trade Treaty Hornswoggle

The true goal of the globalist elite is to destroy national sovereignty and nationalism. One of the most effective ways to accomplish that is through the passage of secret trade treaties.

For decades, the EU passed a series of seemingly harmless trade treaties involving steel and coal. An architect of the EU, Jean Monnet—president of the High Authority of the European Coal and Steel Community—said the goal was to incrementally insert seemingly harmless legal agreements into each trade pact that would quietly assemble the legal framework to end the national sovereignty of European nations like Great Britain, France, and Germany.[26]

One day, Europeans woke up and realized that all their former rights as citizens of independent European nations had been stolen, and they were under the control of a European super state. Their politicians and media had sold them down the river.

In America, major politicians from both political parties boasted in recent years that globalist trade treaties would usher our nation into a new golden age of opportunity for everyone, but the opposite happened as the economy began to hemorrhage jobs and manufacturing.

One of the most controversial of these proposed treaties was the Transatlantic Trade and Investment Partnership (TTIP), which WikiLeaks described as the "hyper-secret Euro-American trade pact." U.S. attorney general Jeff Sessions said TTIP would create a "secret Pacific Union" that would compromise America's sovereignty and transfer power to "an elite set who dream of writing rules in foreign capitals." Sessions explained, "To read the trade agreement is to know that, if Congress adopts the fast track, it will have preapproved a vast delegation of sovereign authority to an international union, with growing powers over the lives of ordinary Americans."[27]

A WikiLeaks release stated that the TTIP and two similar treaties "aim to create a new international legal regime that will allow transnational corporations to bypass domestic courts, evade environmental protections, police the internet on behalf of the content industry, limit the availability of affordable generic medicines, and drastically curtail each country's legislative sovereignty."[28]

It appears the plan is to weaken America's sovereignty to generate larger profits. The phrase "police the internet on behalf of the content industry" is a reference to the decision by the Obama administration in October 2015, with the support of major U.S. technology companies, to relinquish control over key Internet architecture and move it outside the protections of the Constitution—promoting Orwellian censorship. Afterward, Chinese President Xi Jinping called for "global governance" of the World Wide Web. Communist China, which oversees the world's strictest online censorship regime, has been pushing for global control of the Internet and a crackdown on online freedom for many years.[29]

Top Secret: The Bilderberg Group

The mainstream media has largely censored serious reports about these trade treaties and America's relinquishment of key facets of the Internet, along with burying coverage of the secretive Bilderberg meetings.

Each year since 1954, the three-day conference is attended by over one hundred of the world's most influential bankers, politicians, government officials, and economists. This has included people such as Bill Clinton, Hillary Clinton, George H. W. Bush, Henry Kissinger, David

Rockefeller, Zbigniew Brzezinski, Tony Blair, Christine Lagarde, and others. The conference is held at luxurious hotels in Europe and North America amid high security where the most powerful individuals in the world engage in "informal discussions about major issues facing the world."[30]

Jim Marrs says Bilderberg is the "inner core" of secretive organizations such as the Council on Foreign Relations, Royal Institute of International Affairs, and Trilateral Commission where the world's most powerful people meet to decide global policies. "They are so secretive they don't really have a name," Marrs says. "The name Bilderberger comes from the fact that they were publicly identified meeting at the Bilderberg Hotel [in Oosterbeek, the Netherlands]. They were founded by Prince Bernhard who had been a former [Nazi] SS officer, and that has led to a lot of people suspecting that this is a gathering of world corporate and banking leaders—and, of course, they are trying to argue that it's just a social gathering; they just get together, drink expensive champagne, and swap stories—but . . . policies discussed at the Bilderberg meetings all too often become public policies of national entities like the United States, England, etc."[31]

Daniel Estulin, bestselling author of *The True Story of the Bilderberg Group*, says the "biggest scandal" involving Bilderberg is it was "heavily populated by people who came out of the old, World War II Nazi apparatus who were basically cleaned up and dusted off and then employed or deployed to [oversee] hard-core, Cold War, anti-Soviet structures in the West. Bilderberg is a medium, a means of bringing together, the financial institutions which are the world's most powerful and predatory financial interests," Estulin says. "Members of this organization come and go, but the system itself has not changed in the decades since it was first created. You can even go further back in time to its roots in all the secret organizations. It's a self-perpetuating system, a virtual spiderweb of interlocking financial, political, economic and industry interests."[32]

The Bilderberg meeting was held in Chantilly, Virginia, in 2017, just a few miles west of the White House. Its top issue for discussion: "The Trump Administration: A Progress Report." This is interesting because Bilderberg is very concerned that Trump might attempt to block their globalist agenda. The following topics of discussion come directly from Bilderberg:[33]

1. The Trump administration: A progress report
2. Trans-Atlantic relations: options and scenarios
3. The Trans-Atlantic defense alliance: bullets, bytes, and bucks
4. The direction of the EU
5. Can globalization be slowed down?
6. Jobs, income and unrealized expectations
7. The war on information
8. Why is populism growing?
9. Russia in the international order
10. The Near East
11. Nuclear proliferation
12. China
13. Current events

A quick glance at the topics reveals their top priority is making sure their globalist agenda proceeds without any unexpected interruptions. Trump is the center of attention because he campaigned on anti-globalist and anti–trade treaty issues. Besides Trump, Bilderberg is focused on a couple of key issues:

Can globalization be slowed down?

The implication is that their globalist agenda could be slowed down. This reveals two things: First, they very much want to proceed with their agenda as fast as possible. They have a sense of urgency. Second, they are very much aware of the geopolitical, economic, populist, and nationalist forces that represent a potential threat to their real agenda.

Jobs, income, and unrealized expectations.

Bilderberg is composed of highly intelligent and well-informed members. They're completely aware that the economic decline of the middle and working classes in America and other countries is driving an awareness of their globalist agenda and played a major part in Trump winning the presidency, Brexit, and the growth of populism in Europe. They understand that social media and the Internet have been key to spreading public awareness. In fact, recent reports by Gallup and the Government & Public Sector Practice found trust in central governments had reached an all-time low as citizens with "almost unlimited access to information" via social media and the Internet had become "increasingly angry" over globalization. The report noted "pent-up anger at elites they believe to be out of touch" and that "populism and extremism have become more mainstream." Consequently, in partnership with giant technology companies, the elite are now vastly increasing censorship and control of information on the Internet.[34]

The Bilderberg elite also understand that the middle and working classes are now aware, largely because of Trump, how globalism and trade treaties have severely impacted "jobs, income, and unrealized expectations" in America and Europe. Hidden beneath those words exists an oligarchical belief system that the middle and working classes have been spoiled in the past and now have unrealistic expectations about their futures.

The Obama administration tipped its hand in revealing the attitude of the elite when a U.S. attorney said that "Americans have no reasonable expectation of privacy" on their cell phones. The administration simply revealed the attitude that the "deplorables" have no right to privacy based on the consensus of the elite, not the Constitution.[35]

It's likely that the globalist elite will make no real effort to increase the number of better-paying jobs or take real steps to make it possible for people to realize their dreams. This is contrary to their basic goal of creating a world socialist government. We can expect cosmetic solutions that appear to solve these problems. But the major emphasis will be on social engineering and propaganda through movies, television, radio, arts, education, celebrity statements, and novels designed to program Americans to be happy with less.

In short, it is inconceivable that the promoters of the New World Order will make any real changes to increase incomes, provide better jobs, and empower people to improve their lives. Instead, they will promote a one-world socialist government as the answer to social injustice, income inequality, and unrealized expectations. This is a game they have been playing for a long time, and they are very good at it. Reread George Orwell's *1984*: "Freedom Is Slavery."

Skull and Bones: "Illuminati in Disguise"?

Another highly secretive group of globalists who have wielded enormous influence over American politics is Yale University's Skull and Bones.

Known also as Chapter 322, the "Brotherhood of Death," "The Order," and "Bones," this secret fraternal order was brought from Germany to Yale in 1832 by students William Huntington Russell and Alphonso Taft, secretary of war under President Ulysses S. Grant. Taft is the father of President William Howard Taft. Given the similarity of its symbols and rites to those of the Bavarian Illuminati, researchers believe Skull and Bones is a "modern reincarnation of the Order."[36]

A pamphlet by a rival secret society about an 1876 investigation into

Skull and Bones noted that Russell formed a "warm friendship with a leading member of a German society"—leading to speculation that the German occult society was the Bavarian Illuminati or some reiteration of it. "Returning to campus, he used that organization, in which secrecy was paramount, as a blueprint for his own," Buster Brown wrote in the *Atlantic*. Antony Sutton, a senior fellow at the Hoover Institution at Stanford University, also argued that Skull and Bones has its roots in the Bavarian Illuminati,[37] as did M. J. Stephey in his *Time* article "A Brief History of the Skull & Bones Society."[38]

The ranks of Skull and Bones members have included some of the most influential people in the United States and an "unprecedented number of government officials who have furthered the globalist aims of their brethren." This includes former CIA director and president George H. W. Bush; former president George W. Bush; former secretary of state John Kerry; *Time, Life,* and *Fortune* publisher Henry Luce; *National Review* founder William F. Buckley Jr.; J. Richardson Dilworth, a long-time manager of the Rockefeller fortune; various CIA officials, Fortune 500 chief executive officers, and many politicians.[39]

"Bonesmen have gone on to manage the Carnegie, Rockefeller, and Ford Foundations, all of which are involved in international relations, international business, and politics," wrote the authors of *Secret Societies: The Truth Revealed*. "Bonesmen have played key roles in the Central Intelligence Agency and the Council on Foreign Relations—an organization that meets to discuss and develop ideas about how the United States should implement its foreign policy...Bonesmen also developed the CIA—and became some of the first leaders of that organization as well."[40]

Curiously, the occult symbols for Skull and Bones are the same as those used by the Nazi Death Head Division and are found on Nazi uniforms, belt buckles, hats, and rings. These symbols have their roots in ancient occult and secret societies. The official skull-and-crossbones emblem of Skull and Bones is also the official crest of the Illuminati, journalist Ron Rosenbaum, a former Yale student, wrote in an *Esquire* article. "Other researchers agree that the Order is merely the Illuminati in disguise, since Masonic emblems, symbols, German slogans, even the layout of their initiation room, are all identical to those found in Masonic lodges in Germany associated with the Illuminati," Marrs wrote in *The Rise of the Fourth Reich*.[41]

As an author, I (Paul) was previously very skeptical about Skull and Bones until I read an article over a decade ago that actress Jane Fonda's ex-husband, the late Tom Hayden—a longtime California senator, counterculture activist, and member of the University of Michigan secret society the Druids—wrote about two "Bonesmen," George W. Bush and John Kerry, running for president in 2004. "I don't consider myself a conspiracy nut, but is it really all right that four decades after the egalitarian Sixties, and some 225 years since the Declaration of Independence, the American voters' choices in 2004 are two Bonesmen?" Hayden wrote in Yale's *Politic*.[42]

The fact that a highly respected leader of the left believed that there existed an occult secret society involving the Bushes, Kerry, and many of the most powerful people in U.S. politics challenged me to stop rejecting it as a "conspiracy theory" and do research into Skull and Bones.

In fact, as authors of this book and *The Babylon Code*, we remain highly skeptical of most "conspiracy theories," although, as we noted earlier, the term was likely invented by the CIA to discourage journalists from investigating government scandals and discovering the "true rulers of the world." "While secrecy is a vital part of Illuminati theology, it is not the ultimate goal, which is keeping the whole plan 'unbelievable' to the public," Marrs wrote. "Control over the mass media plays a huge role in this."[43]

Despite our extreme care in vetting the credibility of our sources and skepticism about secret societies, we must admit we were surprised to discover that some of the most powerful people in American politics belong to a secret society with links to Nazi Germany.

Following World War II, a U.S. intelligence program known as Operation Paperclip brought over 1,600 Nazi scientists into America. These scientists were given new identities and positions of great power in the military-industrial complex. They brought with them their occult and Satanic beliefs. Today, the descendants of these Nazi scientists occupy positions of great prominence in the government, corporate, and scientific sectors in America.[44]

"Both Nazi science and ideology were brought to America in the aftermath of World War II with the aid and assistance of the very same self-styled globalists who created National Socialism in the first place," Marrs wrote. "Their agenda matches that of the old Bavarian Illuminati... Working with the same financiers and capitalists that had helped create German Nazism, these globalists began laying the foundation for a Fourth Reich. Conspiracy researchers have long suspected that one element of this German influence has been centered in the secretive Skull and Bones fraternity on the campus of Yale University... Utilizing the stolen wealth of Europe... men with both Nazi backgrounds and Nazi mentality wormed their way into corporate America, slowly buying up and consolidating companies into giant multinational conglomerates."[45]

NATO: Rise of the Fourth Reich?

Is Hitler's vision of the "Fourth Reich" coming to pass today? Many biblical theologians believe that the prophet Daniel's predictions about the "fourth beast"—the "revived Roman Empire"—pertain to the EU, a "unique and essential partner" of NATO.[46]

Daniel supernaturally interpreted King Nebuchadnezzar's dream, revealing that in the last days the world would be ruled by a global government. The Bible contains about twenty-five hundred precise prophecies, many of which have been fulfilled with 100 percent accuracy—making the Bible unique among all other spiritual books. In interpreting the King of Babylon's dream, Daniel predicted the coming of four subsequent world empires followed by a fifth world kingdom known as the "fourth beast" or "revived Roman Empire." These are the five:

1. Babylonia
2. Medo-Persia
3. Greece
4. Rome
5. Revived Roman Empire

Today, the EU is situated in the same geographic area controlled by the ancient Roman Empire. This region was also controlled by Hitler and his Third Reich, which borrowed many ideas and architecture from the Roman Empire, as did America and Great Britain. Like ancient Babylon, the Roman Empire was in many respects the New World Order of its time.

Daniel explained that in the last days a "fourth beast"—the "revived Roman Empire"—would rule the world. It will totally control all facets of life on earth through the establishment of a one-world government, economy, and religion.

However, Daniel 2 indicates that the revived Roman Empire will be like "iron mixed with clay," meaning it is built upon a fragile geopolitical foundation of alliances that are not normally cohesive.

"Heading the revived Roman Empire will be a man of such magnetism, such power, and such influence, that he will for a time be the greatest dictator the world has ever known," Hal Lindsey wrote in *The Late Great Planet Earth*. "He will be the completely godless, diabolically evil 'future fuehrer.' "[47]

Many Bible scholars believe this figure will arise out of the EU and will take control of NATO to solidify his military control over Europe and ultimately the world. Promising peace initially, the Antichrist will ultimately plunge the world into total war.

On his visit to NATO, Trump publicly chastised various EU member nations for not paying what they should for their defense. But Trump expressed his support for a "NATO of the future" that "would be even stronger than it is today." What Trump understood and the mainstream media ignored is that the United States pays the lion's share of NATO's budget as it does with the UN and many globalist agreements. Trump's support of NATO indicated a political softening of his original message. When running for president, Trump described NATO as "obsolete."[48]

Students of Bible prophecy understand that NATO could one day be a threat to American sovereignty. Under the NATO treaty, the United States is bound to treat an attack on any country in the NATO alliance as if it were an attack on the United States. This essentially takes the power to declare war away from Congress, which has been given that authority under the Constitution. One day this could draw America into a devastating war outside of its control.

Manchurian Candidate: Is Trump Part of the "Plan"?

This brings us back to questions we posed at the beginning of this chapter. What is Trump's connection to the Illuminati? Is he being unwittingly used by them? Is he a "Manchurian Candidate" the globalists have placed in power to preside over an economic catastrophe—staged or otherwise—or some other disaster or deception to pave the way for the New World Order? Or has Trump been raised up by God to confront the Illuminati's "Plan"?

Recently, different commentators have speculated that Trump's election provides globalists with the perfect opportunity to create the New

World Order.[49] They believe the world is confronted by an intensifying economic crisis of such magnitude that it can't be fixed with the current system of central banking and fiat currencies. Consequently, this crisis is expected to erupt—perhaps soon—into either a global depression or massive hyperinflation. While this could be inevitable given the world's record levels of debt, some commentators believe the globalist elite could stage an "engineered collapse." In either event, the Trump administration would be blamed, and the "surge of national populism which elected Mr. Trump would be discredited," wrote Edwin Vieira Jr., an attorney in Virginia who has argued cases before the U.S. Supreme Court.

"And the mass of Americans who supported him will be left disconsolate, depressed, and politically disarmed in the face of the globalists' taunt that 'we told you so'—leading to the ascendancy of the Globalist International's candidates in the next congressional and presidential elections; and then to the enactment of legislation, ratification of treaties, and signing of 'executive orders' and other decrees necessary and sufficient to secure the final victory of globalism over Americanism," Vieira wrote. "Some analysts and commentators even go so far as to impugn Mr. Trump as actually nothing less than a 'Manchurian Candidate' deviously put up by the Globalist International in order to preside over the catastrophe as its own front-man. Others argue that, although the Globalist International was truly surprised by Mr. Trump's election, it immediately realized that it could turn his presidency to its own advantage by accelerating the arrival of the inevitable catastrophe during the next few years."

In the event Trump is a "Manchurian Candidate," Vieira believes America is in dire straits unless the "deplorables" take decisive action to invoke their right set forth in the Declaration of Independence to throw off a despotic government to "provide New Guards for their future security." He wrote, "Without far more evidence than anyone has adduced to date, I am unwilling to entertain the 'Manchurian Candidate' thesis, or to conclude that a 'Declaration of Independence situation' now confronts this country with the desperate choice to do or to die."

Billy Crone has pondered similar scenarios, noting American presidents often "play the Christian card" at first, but later it turns out that's not quite the reality.[50]

Meanwhile, Crone says he wouldn't be surprised if a "false flag" event is blamed on Christians and that becomes the "nail in the coffin as to why they need to round us up and get rid of us. They are going to create a crisis and that will be the switch." Crone speculates that the crisis could be a stock market crash blamed on Trump, America getting nuked, an assassination, or some other catastrophe. "They control the economy. They can shut that thing down in a second."

These concerns mirror those of Illuminati whistle-blowers, including "Svali," a registered nurse who claims she was born into an Illuminati bloodline and escaped the Illuminati cult where she worked as a high-level programmer. She alleges the highest levels of politics, military, and the financial world are "heavily Illuminati occupied and controlled" and that the Illuminati works closely with the CIA and Freemasonry, and about 1 percent of the population in the United States is "Illuminati or Illuminati assets." She claims that the United States has been divided into seven major regions with hidden military compounds used to train Illuminati personnel in military techniques "in preparation for the ultimate collapse of government."

"Why? Because the Illuminists believe that our government, as we know it, as well as the governments of most nations around the world, are destined to collapse," she explained. "The Illuminati has planned first for a financial collapse that will make the Great Depression look like a picnic... Next there will be a military takeover, region by region, as the government declares a state of emergency and martial law."[51]

While the body of evidence compiled in *Trumpocalypse* suggests the globalist elite are planning some type of engineered financial meltdown, war, or other event to fulfill the Plan, we don't think Trump is a Manchurian Candidate or a dupe in their scheme. Rather, we believe God has raised him up "for such a time as this" (Esther 4:14 MEV) to fulfill God's prophetic plans no matter what type of multi-faceted stratagem the elite plan to foist on the world.

War of the Secret Societies

Before Trump's election, a theory was disseminated across the Internet claiming there is an ongoing war for America and the world between two powerful factions of Freemasonry. These commentators believe that Trump's support comes from a large patriotic group within Freemasonry that believes in making America great again.[52]

This group is a kind of "America First" faction that believes America has a unique role to play in the New World Order as the *New Atlantis*. This is the title of a scientific-utopian book by Sir Francis Bacon, the lord chancellor of England and head of the Rosicrucian Order who played an instrumental role in America's creation in the early 1600s. This segment of Freemasonry is believed to include Christians and others sympathetic to Judeo-Christian beliefs. Some are reportedly direct descendants of George Washington, Thomas Jefferson, Andrew Jackson, and others who believed in Divine Providence.

The second faction is a globalist "Illuminized Freemasonry" that has been the primary driver behind a one-world government, religion, and economic system. This faction is believed to be controlled by international banking families whom researchers claim instigated the French and communist revolutions and many wars, and are now attempting to radically transform America into a socialist state to be merged into the coming one-world order.

If it's true that a secret societies war is under way for the control of

America, then it would be essential to know if Trump is associated with Freemasonry. These commentators suggest that Trump is connected to high-level Scottish Rite Freemasonry who believe America has a special destiny as the leading force in the world.

Trump's link to Freemasonry is through his "mentor"—Rev. Norman Vincent Peale, author of the 1952 motivational bestseller *The Power of Positive Thinking* and pastor at New York's Marble Collegiate Church. Trump attended the church with his parents periodically. It was the place of his first wedding and the funerals of his parents. Peale, who is listed as a thirty-third-degree Mason on the Scottish Rite of Freemasonry website, is the only person other than his father whom Trump described as a mentor. "I still remember [Peale's] sermons," Trump told the Iowa Family Leadership Summit in July 2015. "You could listen to him all day long. And when you left the church, you were disappointed it was over. He was the greatest guy."[53]

Throughout history, both the Illuminati and Freemasons have used the motto "Order Out of Chaos" as a mechanism to generate radical political change. The motto is often combined with a red painting of a mythological Phoenix, which is burned alive, dies, and then resurrects supernaturally from the dead. The Phoenix symbolizes the New World Order. On the back of the U.S. dollar bill exists a picture of a bird that most people believe is an eagle. However, many researchers believe it's the Phoenix. This symbolism goes back to Bacon, who believed America was destined to be the New Atlantis. An important part of Masonic teaching is that the country would resurrect from the dead after being destroyed. According to Bacon, this rebirth would be the birth of the New World Order with America as its head. Obviously, Bacon did not foresee America being destroyed permanently, but rather as having a unique destiny among the nations.[54]

So, is Trump leading a second American Revolution against the globalist and Illuminati bloodline families? Or is he being used by the

Illuminati as part of their classic Hegelian dialectic strategy of conflict between thesis and antithesis to create the chaos necessary to bring about radical change and move America and the world into synthesis?

The difficulty we have in believing that Trump is just a pawn in an Illuminati strategy is that the globalist elite, mainstream media, and politicians didn't expect Trump to have any real chance at winning the presidency. The level of animosity that continues to be leveled at him by the globalist elite, Hollywood, and the media is way too intense to suggest that he's just a pawn in their game.

Further, the claim that there is some kind of war over America between the "good Freemasons" and the Illuminati-aligned branches is problematic because the Scottish Rite continues to play a major part in the New World Order. On top of this, some have questioned whether Trump is secretly part of the Deep State because he has hired members of the Council on Foreign Relations to work in his administration and met with former secretary of state Henry Kissinger, a member of banker David Rockefeller's Trilateral Commission and one of the most powerful globalists in the world.

However, Trump understands that if he wants to accomplish anything, he must work with the most powerful people in the world even though he opposes their goals.

"He's Not Part of the Club"

Former members of secret societies say Trump doesn't exhibit any of the telltale signs of the Illuminati like other high-level politicians do.

"I was in the Illuminati," Schnoebelen says. "[Trump] is totally opposed to everything the Illuminati wants and he is also very much an outsider. Newt Gingrich said, 'He's not part of the club, he hasn't been through the initiation.' It means he's not been illuminated, and he's kind of got where he's gotten to on his own without the help of the

Brotherhood. So, I'm hopeful. I know the guy is flawed. He certainly has a lot of sin in his background. Supposedly, he's been led to Christ, and obviously he's a young believer, but he understands the stakes of what it means to turn this country around."[55]

Before the election, Gingrich, who has attended events at the secretive Bohemian Club, said that the Establishment is afraid of Trump because he's not associated with any secret societies: "He's an outsider, he's not them, he's not part of the club, he's uncontrollable, he hasn't been through the initiation rites, he didn't belong to the secret society."[56]

Chapter Nine

The Economic Reset

Essentially, what we believe is needed is a reset of the way in which the economy grows around the world... The final reset is the structural reforms that we have been calling for not just in advanced economies, but also in the emerging market economies... That's the set of measures that could reset going forward.

—CHRISTINE LAGARDE, MANAGING DIRECTOR,

INTERNATIONAL MONETARY FUND[1]

Who controls the issuance of money controls the government!

—NATHAN MEYER ROTHSCHILD, SON OF THE FOUNDER OF THE

ROTHSCHILD BANKING DYNASTY[2]

In early 2014, International Monetary Fund managing director Christine Lagarde delivered a speech at the National Press Club in Washington, DC, making enigmatic statements, even using the term "magic," and talking about numerology.

Pundits labeled concerns about her speech as "conspiracy theories," but occult experts believe she was subtly communicating a message on behalf of the elite regarding the future of the global financial system. A couple of weeks later during a Bloomberg interview at the World

Economic Forum, she spoke on why it's important to "reset" the global economy.[3]

To understand what she meant, think of what happens when you reset a computer; you reboot the system from scratch. Resetting the global economy means shutting down the old economic system of fiat currencies and rebooting up to a cashless society with microchip implants.

Here we are reproducing intact part of Lagarde's Bloomberg interview. While you may find the language and references somewhat confusing, the import is stunningly clear:

Now, I'm going to test your numerology skills by asking you to think about the magic seven, okay? Most of you will know that seven is quite a number in all sorts of themes, religions. And I'm sure that you can compress numbers as well. So, if we think about 2014, all right, I'm just giving you 2014, you drop the zero, 14, two times 7. Okay, that's just by way of example, and we're going to carry on. So, 2014 will be a milestone and hopefully a magic year in many respects. It will mark the 100th anniversary of the First World War back in 1914. It will note the 70th anniversary, drop the zero, seven—of the Breton Woods conference that actually gave birth to the IMF. And it will be the 25th anniversary of the fall of the Berlin Wall, 25th, okay? It will also mark the 7th anniversary of the financial market jitters that quickly turned into the greatest global economic calamity since the Great Depression.[4]

In this talk, Lagarde communicated her belief—and by implication, the financial elite's beliefs—in the occult, magic, and numerology. Many members of the highest-level international banking families who control the global economic system are members of secretive organizations that make decisions and plans based on numerology.

In shorthand, this is what Lagarde was communicating:

- The financial elite met at Bretton Woods to rebuild the international monetary system after World War II, and that occurred seventy years before she made this speech.
- It was also the twenty-fifth anniversary of the fall of the Berlin Wall. If you add two plus five, it equals seven. Also, 2014 marked the seventh anniversary of the real estate market crash and global economy calamity.

These three figures line up horizontally, if you "drop the zero," to 777, an important occult number used by British occultist Aleister Crowley—author of *777 and Other Qabalistic Writings of Aleister Crowley*—along with many occult groups. In her talk, Lagarde deliberately didn't use the number 666—the number of the Beast—because it would have been too obvious. But experts believe 777 is a cloaked reference to the elite's plans for the coming cashless society.[5]

Why? In occult circles, seven is the number of perfection—a solution to a problem. Three years after Lagarde's occult numerological speech, Trump was inaugurated president of the United States. On his first day as president, Trump was seventy years, seven months, and seven days old. This adds up to 777, the number of perfection in numerology. And it happened during year 5777 on the Hebrew calendar.

So, was Lagarde's speech a coded message to the Illuminati and other secret societies to get ready for the Trump presidency and the "Plan" for a staged economic collapse that would push the global financial reset button?[6]

Without question, many of the international financial moguls who control the global economic system are members of secret societies and communicate much of what they do through numerology and esoteric symbolism. Look at the cover of the January 2017 issue of *The Economist*, which is partially owned by the Rothschild family. It's layered with tarot cards, including the Trump Judgment card, the Death card featuring a nuclear mushroom cloud, and the Hermit card depicting the mass of humanity carrying red and blue flags, protesting trade treaties and the EU, and walking blissfully off the financial cliff.[7]

Some experts in occult symbolism believe the cover reinforces the concept of paranormal activity and reveals that despite humanity's protests of globalism through Brexit and Trump's election, the world is going over the cliff anyway. The elite plan to unleash a financial collapse on Trump's watch, blame it on principles of nationalism, and then carry out their Plan with the blessings of a world traumatized by a cataclysmic financial meltdown.

One cannot conclude from the statements or symbols of the Illuminati that Trump is playing their game, though. Nevertheless, one should assume that the Illuminati and other secret societies have already penetrated the Trump administration and other high-level positions in the federal government. The Illuminati has largely controlled American politics and our financial system since the Federal Reserve Act of 1913 and exerted a powerful influence over America long before then. As counterintuitive as it may seem in our technological age, this tenebrous secret society, as Marrs argued in *The Illuminati*, has "hijacked the world."

Evidence of Illuminati influence turns up in the most unexpected places. Consider the Illuminati symbolism on the back of the US dollar. Look at the pattern of thirteens with the stars, leaves, arrows, and layers of bricks in the pyramid. The thirteen-step unfinished pyramid with the all-seeing eye is a prominent Illuminati symbol. The motto above the pyramid, *Annuit coeptis*—interpreted as "God has favored our undertakings"—has thirteen letters, traces to Virgil's *Aeneid* and *Georgics*, and involves a "prayer requesting or invoking aid from the pagan god Jupiter." The Latin numerals at the base of the pyramid denote the year of the signing of the Declaration of Independence, 1776, the same year as the founding of Illuminati. The motto on the Great Seal is *Novus ordo seclorum*. It translates as "A new order of the ages," although many interpret it as "New World Order." Finally, the thirteen-letter traditional motto of America on the banner above the eagle, or the Phoenix, is *E pluribus unum*, Latin for "Out of many, one." "Overtly, the number thirteen was used to reflect the number of the original colonies," Robert Hieronimus, co-Mason and expert on the Great Seal, wrote in *Founding Fathers, Secret Societies: Freemasons, Illuminati, Rosicrucians, and the Decoding of the Great Seal.* "Covertly, however, the number thirteen is part of the magical numerology of the dollar bill... The secret geometry and the magical history of the symbols on the dollar bill firmly connect it, and therefore the Great Seal, with the Freemasonic and Rosicrucian influences of the Founding Fathers."[8]

A World Currency in 2018?

The 2017 cover of the *Economist* comes nearly three decades after its 1988 cover featured a red Phoenix standing amid a burning pile of money with the headline "Get Ready for a World Currency." Around the Phoenix's neck was a chain holding a coin with the year "2018" minted on it.[9]

As the back of the dollar bill and the *Economist* covers reveal, the occult elite often use numerology, symbols, and secret writing to communicate powerful messages. Was this cover such a message? Given the fast pace at which the world is now rushing toward a cashless society, it's easy to envision the elite rolling out a new world currency and microchip implants in the not-too-distant future.

Since ancient Babylon when bankers first loaned money created out of thin air and charged interest, the occult elite have understood the "magic of money manipulation." Today's modern credit-debit system originated in ancient Babylon. "Many of these early 'protobanks' dealt primarily in coin and bullion, much of their business being money changing and the supplying of foreign and domestic coin of the correct weight and fineness," according to *Encyclopaedia Britannica*.[10]

The economic system in ancient Babylon was based on sorcery. Money was and is nothing more than occult magic because it's a mechanism of creating wealth out of nothing. The economic system in ancient Babylon was an integral part of the secrets of "Mystery, Babylon," whose elite created a satanic monetary system in which money or coinage wasn't backed by anything of tangible value such as land, livestock, or gold. This money was loaned to individuals and nations for usury or interest.

The purpose of the Babylonian money system, or "mammon," was to control nations and individuals through a debt-slavery system because, as the Bible says, the "borrower is slave to the lender" (Prov. 22:7 NIV). The monetary system of "Mystery, Babylon" was passed by elite secret societies from empire to empire and kingdom to kingdom for thousands of years. It's no accident that the wealthiest banking families in the world are members of the Illuminati and other secret societies. Throughout human history, the occult elite have clearly understood that those who control the money control the world.

"A Short Trip to Tyranny"

A recent cover story in *Newsmax* magazine—"The Plan to Abolish Cash"—highlighted concerns of prominent economists about the campaign for a cashless society. In the article, *Newsmax* senior editor David A. Patten wrote that governments around the world are beginning to ban cash, and the United States is moving in this direction too. This will mean "total surveillance" of financial transactions by governments. "The anti-cash crusaders want to render paper money as obsolete as the 8-track cassette tape," Patten wrote. "Based on what's been happening around the globe, they might just be able to do it. The United Nations, multinational banks, charitable foundations, and credit-card companies are all stepping up their campaign to dethrone King Cash." The Bill & Melinda Gates Foundation supports a cashless society and is a leading member of the "Better Than Cash Alliance"—a group of multinational credit card companies, charitable foundations, and sovereign governments based out of the UN.[11]

A Gallup poll found that 62 percent of Americans expect the United States to go cashless during their lifetimes. "They express these views as more Americans make payments from an expanding menu of electronic options, and fewer make cash transactions, and as younger populations are becoming more comfortable without cash in their pockets," according to Gallup.[12]

This trend has set off alarms among conservatives, especially free market and libertarian economists. "They warn that declaring a war on cash could send society on a short trip to tyranny," Patten wrote.

Larry White, a senior fellow at the libertarian Cato Institute, says the push for a cashless society is largely being driven by major credit card companies that stand to make substantial profits, along with governments looking to increase tax revenues. Of course, it's all being done in the name of fighting black markets, tax evasion, and a variety of crimes enabled by cash.[13]

"There have been governments who have used their access to people's financial records to suppress their political enemies," White says. "It has a chilling effect on people if everything they do is subject to surveillance by the government. The presumption ought to be that people are entitled to privacy unless there is evidence that they have committed a crime. But we've made crimes of just ordinary depositing and withdrawing of cash, transporting of cash, or using cash to buy big-ticket items in some countries, so that's worrisome. It enables a kind of Big Brother state to pry into the details of people's lives."

It's Just a Matter of Time

The elite's campaign to create a cashless society comes amid staggering levels of global debt. An IMF report by two Harvard University professors found that debt levels in the Western world are approaching a "two-century high-water mark," and the "endgame of the global financial crisis" will require a "restructuring" of the world's economic system.[14]

A report by the Institute for International Finance found global debt is $217 trillion and climbing. That's 327 percent of the world's annual economic output.[15]

The amount of debt is "larger than the estimates of the total wealth on planet Earth," Chuck Missler says. "It doesn't take great scholarship to realize that's unstable, it can't endure, and those debts will never be repaid by any legitimate currency. So, there is an implosion or collapse of some kind that is inevitable."[16]

Why is it that the global debt and our national debt continue to expand to such dangerous levels? The reason is, debt is the primary way that a group of international banking families and financial moguls rule the world. The Federal Reserve and the central banks are giant banks owned by these families, according to researchers.[17]

When America was founded, there was no private banking consortium known as the Federal Reserve. The U.S. government acted as its own Federal Reserve, as the Constitution requires. If Congress had followed the Constitution, we would not have $20 trillion in national debt to pay interest on. Today, more than 99 percent of the world's population lives in countries under the control of central banks.[18]

The United States didn't rack up $20 trillion in debt by accident. The Federal Reserve System was created to put America into debt. Its creation began with secret meetings in the early twentieth century at American banker J. P. Morgan's Jekyll Island Hunt Club off the coast of Georgia. These meetings involved banker Paul Warburg and others who owned as much as one-fourth of the world's wealth. They agreed not to say the words "central" or "bank," and that the central bank they created would appear to be an official agency of the U.S. government. Later, these men helped elect Princeton University president Woodrow Wilson as president of the United States. On December 23, 1913, the day before Christmas Eve, when most members of Congress were home and people were enjoying the holidays, Wilson signed the Federal Reserve Act into law, placing our entire monetary system into the hands of a private banking cartel. At the time, Congressman Charles A. Lindbergh Sr. said, "This [Federal Reserve Act] establishes the most gigantic trust on earth. When the President signs this bill, the invisible government of the monetary power will be legalized...The worst legislative crime of the ages is perpetrated by this banking and currency bill." By law we are not allowed to know the actual names of the Federal Reserve's international banking families, their assets, or their policies. Essentially, we're not allowed to ask any questions. That's always a bad sign.[19]

Since the Federal Reserve was established, America's national debt has grown five-thousand-fold and the value of the dollar has declined by 98 percent. Some experts believe the elite's goal is to destroy the dollar as the world's reserve currency, and then amid the ensuing chaos, replace it with a globalist-run monetary authority. Perhaps that's the economic "reset" the IMF has in mind.

The Big One: The Coming Crash

James G. Rickards, author of *The Road to Ruin: The Global Elites' Secret Plan for the Next Financial Crisis*, believes the financial "system is very vulnerable to collapse and it will collapse sooner than later." Rickards adds that the elite have laid the groundwork for a successor system. He claims they are stockpiling hard assets and plan to lock down the global financial system in a "sudden American collapse" that leaves stock exchanges closed, ATMs shut down, and money market funds frozen. He calls this "the Big One"—what a *Forbes* columnist described as "the coming crash of 2018," although it's unclear how the writer arrived at that year. "You can see a global financial collapse coming," Rickards said. "From there...how do you put things back together again? There aren't that many choices. One is the gold standard, one is the special drawing rights." Special drawing rights (SDRs) is a world currency issued by the IMF during past crises. In the event of a severe economic crisis, the IMF could issue SDRs—the "New World Money"—to keep the international monetary system afloat.[20]

Peter Schiff, an economist and chief executive officer of Euro Pacific Capital, agrees the financial system is in a "big bubble" that is "going to burst." "It will have a terrible impact," Schiff says. "Americans are able to live beyond their means because of the overvalued dollar. When the dollar collapses, Americans will no longer have that luxury. Our standard of living will be greatly reduced."[21]

Investor Jim Rogers, chairman of Rogers Holdings and Beeland Interests, Inc., told *Forbes* that bubbles are happening in multiple parts of the economy. "Right now, all types of debts are making historic highs, and everyone is convinced that they cannot lose money in bonds...The world has had economic problems every five to ten years. We had a problem in 2008 because of debt, and the debt is much higher now. Thus, it is going to be an even worse problem than before." In an interview with Business Insider, Rogers said the crash is "going to be the biggest in my lifetime."[22]

The disturbing fact is that none of this had to happen. According to Article I, Section 8, of the U.S. Constitution, Congress was expressly given the authority to "coin Money, regulate the Value thereof, and of foreign Coin, and fix the Standard of Weights and Measures." Our elected representatives violated the Constitution when they passed the Federal Reserve Act. The big secret about the way our monetary system really operates is that the Federal Reserve prints money from nothing. There is nothing of actual value like gold or silver backing up printed dollars, coins, and digital money. After the Federal Reserve prints money from nothing, the federal government borrows it from the Federal Reserve and spends it into circulation. The federal government then owes the Federal Reserve the money it borrowed—plus interest.[23]

Before the passage of the Federal Reserve Act, the United States government created its own money, wasn't in debt, and didn't have to pay gargantuan sums of interest. The Federal Reserve Act made America the greatest debtor nation on earth to a private group of international bankers who have total control over our economy. This single decision to illegally pass the Federal Reserve Act has made the American people in effect debt slaves to a small group of international bankers.

Danielle DiMartino Booth, founder of the economic consulting firm Money Strong, LLC and former adviser to the president of the Federal Reserve Bank of Dallas, wrote in *Fed Up: An Insider's Take on Why the Federal Reserve Is Bad for America* that the era of financial deregulation championed by former Federal Reserve Chairman Alan Greenspan and the policies of his successors Ben Bernanke and Janet Yellen to lower interest rates to zero and use quantitative easing to "flood America with easy money" enriched the wealthy at the expense of everyone else, inflated economic bubbles that decimated the retirement savings of working- and middle-class Americans, ballooned America's "shadow unemployment" rate to 23 percent, and created a situation in which nearly half of males and 36 percent of females ages eighteen to thirty-four are living with their parents, unable to afford the high cost of living on their own. "The Fed's experiment has widened the inequality gap, angering millions of people who bought into the American dream and know it's being stripped away from them," Booth wrote. "The ostentatiousness with which the so-called one percent has flaunted its wealth has fueled the rise of anger and extremism, leading to the presidential campaigns of Bernie Sanders on the left and Donald Trump on the right."[24]

Bible Prophecy and the Future of America

The elite's insatiable desire for more wealth, power, and pleasure is part of an enormous spiritual battle that involves Trump and the prophetic destiny of America. Many biblical scholars debate whether America is mentioned in Bible prophecy. Scripture does contain references that could be interpreted as pertaining to America, and we're convinced that America has an important part to play in the last days. When America was founded by Bible-believing Pilgrims and Puritans in the early 1600s, they entered a covenant with God based on his covenant with Israel through Abraham (see Deut. 28).

God promised to pour out tremendous blessings on Israel economically, militarily, and in all areas of their lives. The condition for receiving these blessings was obeying God and following his commandments. Although this covenant was specifically made to the nation of Israel, we believe God also chose to honor the covenant the Pilgrims and Puritans made with God, which, like his covenant with Israel, was based on Deuteronomy 28. America, like Israel, is a flawed and imperfect nation. We have committed serious abominations before the Lord, such as our sinful treatment of Native Americans, slavery of African Americans, and the abortion of sixty million babies.

Despite our imperfections, most Americans adhered to Christian values and chose to worship Jesus and obey his commandments. As a result, God raised up America above the nations of the world, and it has only been during the last several decades as millions of Americans turned their backs on God and worshipped the idols of pleasure and prosperity that God's hand has been removed to a significant degree from our nation.

But God originally raised up America for a special purpose in the last days, and he is waiting for his people to turn to him and repent of their sins so that he can move powerfully through America.

Will America Fulfill Its Destiny?

Despite Trump's many imperfections, millions of Christians believe God has raised him up to "Make America Great Again" by helping it to fulfill its prophetic destiny. But for God to use America, he must restore to whatever degree America's economic power, which was intentionally brought down by an anti-American and anti-Christian globalist elite.

Trump is under constant attack because he represents a serious threat to the globalist elite and their plans to create a New World Order and merge our nation into the North American Union, rendering our Constitution and Bill of Rights null and void. In America, we have freedom of religion, speech, and the press; the right to bear arms; and freedom from unreasonable search and seizure. We must diligently protect these rights, along with our economy, global influence, state-of-the-art technologies, creativity, and unique American can-do mind-set. These assets are vital to fulfill the prophetic role God intended America to play in the last days, and that is to serve as a global platform for preaching the gospel, making disciples of all nations, and doing what Jesus said in Luke 19:13: "Occupy till I come" (KJV). In God's prophetic plan, America is to become the base for spreading biblical revival around the world.

America must have a president who truly desires to use his power to allow these things to happen, and the only president in our lives who is poised to do that is Trump. In recent decades, no other Republican or Democratic president has been willing to confront the globalist elites' plans to create a global superstate.

It is our sincere prayer that Trump recognizes not only the great blessings that flow from obedience to God, but also the potential chastisement or curse that follows disobedience. It is the responsibility of every true believer in Christ to continually lift Trump up in prayer, along with his family and administration, and ask the Lord to supernaturally strengthen, protect, and guide him.

A Voice "Speaking to Me Like a Trumpet"

Christine Lagarde's occult remarks represent the secretive beliefs of the wealthiest and most powerful people in the world. Many are not the secular humanists or atheists they pretend to be publicly. The elite at the top of the Illuminati pyramid are worshippers of Lucifer and "Mystery, Babylon."

Lagarde's announcement of a global economic reset was a kind of coded message to the world's financial elite that they are planning a monumental change in the global economic system. The timing of her remarks reveals much about the nature of the reset. It means the world is moving rapidly toward a global superstate and cashless society.

Jesus warned us in Revelation that the Luciferian control system of "Mystery, Babylon" would arise again in the end times. In Revelation 4 (NIV), the apostle John saw a "door standing open in heaven," and a voice "speaking to me like a trumpet said, 'Come up here, and I will show you what must take place after this.'" John was supernaturally taken into a dimension outside of space and time known as the spiritual world or invisible realm, where God revealed to him in chapters 17–18 the future rise of geopolitical and economic Babylon, also known as "the great harlot."

"And there came one of the seven angels who had the seven bowls, and talked with me, saying unto me, Come here; I will show unto you the judgment of the great harlot that sits upon many waters: With whom the kings of the earth have committed fornication, and the inhabitants of the earth have been made drunk with the wine of her fornication" (Rev. 17:1–2 KJV 2000).

We read here about the global economic system empowered by Lucifer that allowed the wealthiest and most powerful people on earth to gain their wealth and power by fornicating with the "the great harlot." God then carried John to a different location in this dimension where he saw the name of the woman revealed.

"On her forehead a name was written, a mystery, 'BABYLON THE GREAT, THE MOTHER OF HARLOTS AND OF THE ABOMINATIONS OF THE EARTH.' And I saw the woman drunk with the blood of the saints, and with the blood of the witnesses of Jesus" (Rev. 17:5–6 NASB).

The Mark and "Blood of the Saints"

Over the last two millennia, more than seventy million Christians have been killed for their faith in Christ, and that trend is increasing today as certain religions believe it is their duty to behead and murder Christians. Of those seventy million martyrs, the Center for the Study of Global Christianity estimates half were killed in the twentieth century under fascist and communist regimes. Today, about one hundred thousand Christians are killed each year.[25]

As the prophetic time clock advances, we're going to see the killing and beheading of countless millions of Christians. During the Tribulation, Revelation 13 tells us that the Antichrist will require everyone to accept the mark of the Beast. Without it, people won't be able to earn a living or buy the necessities of life. To receive the microchip implant, electronic tattoo, or whatever technology ends up as the mark of the Beast, a person must publicly renounce Jesus Christ as Lord and worship the Antichrist. Those who refuse will be beheaded.

Revelation 17 tells us that this global government known as "Mystery, Babylon" will be "drunk with the blood of the saints." The apostle John wrote that God would severely judge "Mystery, Babylon" and all those who join her system to a kind of cosmic prison—what the Bible describes as the "lake of fire" (Rev. 20:15 KJV), a place of everlasting torment.

We are now quickly approaching the time when the Luciferian elite are planning to bring online a global government, cashless society, and universal religion. To do this, they have said repeatedly that they need to create a borderless world and get rid of independent, sovereign nation-states. "The sovereignty of states must be subordinated to international law and international institutions," wrote George Soros, a Hungarian American business magnate who is one of the richest people in the world and a supporter of progressive social causes. "We need some global system of political decision-making. In short, we need a global society to support our global economy."[26]

This global system, whether it's headed up by the UN, NATO, or some other entity, will use all its military resources and futuristic technologies to try to stop Jesus Christ's prophesied return to Earth. But Jesus will defeat the Antichrist, False Prophet, Satan, and all their forces during the Battle of Armageddon. Christ will then reign from Jerusalem, the new capital of planet Earth (Rev. 19:11–16, 21:1–4).

The Bible is clear that there will be no permanent peace in the world until the "Prince of Peace" returns to "set up His Glorious Kingdom of Peace and it will last for one thousand years." The late Tim LaHaye explained that Christ will "enforce peace, justice, and true freedom while Satan is sealed and bound 'in the bottomless pit' (Rev. 20:2–3) where he can 'deceive the nations no more until the thousand years are ended.'"[27]

Will the Reset Result in a Cyborg Future?

It remains to be seen if America and the world will experience a global economic meltdown and financial reset with a cashless society and microchip implant in 2018, as Lagarde and others predicted. It could occur a decade or more in the future. But we know that the goal of the globalist elite is to bring in their cashless society and microchip implants as soon as possible, because they have stated this in writing and in speeches many times.

Throughout the world, companies are already implanting their employees with microchips. The implants replace keys and various cards people carry. A recent *Daily Mail* article noted that 150 employees at a Swedish start-up were microchipped: "The syringe slides in between the thumb and index finger. Then, with a click, a microchip is injected in the employee's hand. Another 'cyborg' is created."[28]

Australia is the first country to begin microchipping its population. At first, the microchipping plan was limited to its health care system. "It may sound like sci-fi, but hundreds of Australians are turning themselves into super-humans who can unlock doors, turn on lights, and log into computers with a wave of the hand," Emma Reynolds wrote in an article for *News Corp Australia.* "The microchips, which are the size of a grain of rice, can act like a business card and transfer contact details to smartphones, and hold complex medical data." Meanwhile, A Wisconsin company announced it had become the first business in the United States to offer optional microchip implants for employees beginning August 1, 2017. Officials at Three Square Market (32M), a River Falls–based software design company, said the chips are implanted underneath the skin between the thumb and forefinger, allowing employees to pay for food and drinks in the company's break room, open security doors, and log into their computers without passwords or special cards. "Eventually, this technology will become standardized, allowing you to use this as your passport, public transit, all purchasing opportunities, etc.," Todd Westby, CEO of 32M, said. "We see chip technology as the next evolution in payment systems, much like micro markets have steadily replaced vending machines."[29]

Meanwhile, Tesla and SpaceX tech mogul Elon Musk is planning to unveil new computers that connect directly to the human brain via a "neural lace"—a wireless mesh that serves as an interface between a computing device and the brain that would be injected into the jugular and carried via the blood to the cortical neurons. "Creating a neural lace is the thing that really matters for humanity to achieve symbiosis with machines," Musk tweeted. Critics have expressed concerns that such technologies could be exploited. "The technology would allow governments and corporations to exert a level of control which most people would consider terrifying," Jasper Hamill wrote in the *Sun*.[30]

Most likely, the microchip implant, "neural lace," or whatever technology ultimately becomes the mark of the Beast will emerge incrementally over time because several other things need to happen before one of these technologies becomes the infamous mark.

A Transhuman Antichrist?

In Revelation, we learn some key details about the Antichrist. First, we discover that he is called the "beast" (Rev. 13:1). Later, we learn that he is given power and authority by the "dragon." The dragon is Satan, who bodily possesses the Antichrist. Also, we learn the Antichrist has powerful enemies, because he's killed and then supernaturally healed in what appears to be a counterfeit resurrection (Rev. 13:3–4).

Revelation 13:5 tells us the Antichrist is given a supernatural ability to speak "great things and blasphemies." This implies that, like Adolf Hitler, who was demonically possessed, the Antichrist will have supernatural charisma and capture mankind's imagination with his talk about the New Age of "love and light" on earth. Unlike the powerful and forceful style in which Hitler spoke, when Satan speaks through the Antichrist, it may be in an entertaining Hollywood style suitable for our time. Ultimately, the Antichrist will directly challenge God and wage war with all true believers in Christ, overcoming them with his supernatural ability to turn the world against them.

The Antichrist will speak with such mind-expanding power that he will completely win over the hearts and minds of humanity through a spiritual seduction that puts them into a trancelike state. Every person who lives on Earth whose names are not written in the Book of Life will worship him as if he was God.

This is because only those people who have placed their faith in Jesus are truly "born again" and will be able to withstand his preternatural power and lies. Only those people who have the Spirit of Truth living inside them will have the ability to resist and see through the deceptions of the Antichrist.

The Antichrist will be the head of the world government during the Tribulation, but the Bible also tells us about the second "beast" known as the False Prophet. He will come off like a harmless lamb, but speaks like the "dragon" (Rev. 13:11).

The False Prophet, who will be head of the religious and economic systems, will use his power to cause the world to worship the Antichrist as God. He will have the ability to create powerful counterfeit miracles, signs, and wonders, including giving life to the "image of the beast."

Although the Bible is not definitive here, one must ask whether occult sciences and modern technologies are used by the False Prophet. During the counterfeit resurrection of the Antichrist, it appears that an image of the beast is resurrected. Could that image come from highly advanced virtual reality technologies, a lifelike robot, clone, cyborg, android, or a combination of the Antichrist's biological being integrated with a cyborg or robotic body—a transhuman Antichrist?

Transhumanism is a popular and growing movement to overcome the body's limitations through technology and achieve a form of immortality through artificial intelligence. It is heavily funded by billionaire philanthropists. WikiLeaks head Julian Assange predicted that people will be able to upload their consciousness to an artificial intelligence and "live forever" as part of a simulation. "It's like a religion for atheists," Assange explained. Ray Kurzweil, director of engineering at Google and author of *The Singularity Is Near*, predicts humans will become hybrids by the 2030s—a time when he expects human brains will be able to connect directly to the cloud, where thousands of computers will augment people's intelligence. "Our thinking then will be a hybrid of biological and non-biological thinking," Kurzweil predicted.[31]

Currently, DARPA (Defense Advanced Research Projects Agency), a U.S. Department of Defense agency, is developing a "brain chip" for soldiers that will permit "precision communication between the brain and the digital world." The proposed technology is similar to Musk's "neural lace." Musk's company, Neuralink, estimates the "Matrix-style technology" will be available to everyone in eight to ten years.[32]

These developing technologies open up all kinds of possibilities that could easily mesh with the prophecies in Revelation concerning the Antichrist, his False Prophet, and their Plan to reset the world's governmental, economic, and religious systems.

Toward a Psychocivilized Society

The elite have been planning the global economic reset, cashless society, and mark of the Beast for decades. They started developing technologies for a cashless society after World War II. In the 1950s and 1960s, Jose Delgado began experiments using permanent brain implants in bulls, primates, and human beings. Delgado wrote his infamous 1971 book, *Physical Control of the Mind—Toward a Psychocivilized Society*, with the goal of controlling people in a global society with electronic implants controlled by radio signals.

In a 1965 interview with the *New York Times*, Delgado, director of neuropsychiatry at the Yale University School of Medicine, revealed the future of his human experimentation: "The individual may think that the most important reality is his own existence, but this is only his personal point of view. This lacks historical perspective. Man does not have the right to develop his own mind. This kind of liberal orientation has great appeal. We must electronically control the brain. Someday armies and generals will be controlled by electric stimulation of the brain."[33]

Delgado's words should terrify you because they represent the thinking of the elite ruling our world. The same concepts have been expressed publicly by Zbigniew Brzezinski, executive director of the Trilateral Commission, and many other members of the elite. They have long been developing these technologies designed to implant every person on planet Earth with a microchip, biochip, nanochip, "neural lace," or devices embedded into people's genetic coding system.[34]

The purpose of the implants is twofold: First, electronic mind control. Second, creating a cashless society by requiring an implant to participate in the global economy.

With tiny microchip implants that store vast amounts of information, the possibility now exists for the first time in history to create the mark of the Beast system that would provide the Antichrist and False Prophet not only economic control over humanity, but also control of what people think, believe, and do. That's a truly chilling thought that should shock our conscience and awaken us to just how late the hour is.

Just as the prophet Daniel foresaw an explosion of knowledge at the "time of the end" (Dan. 12:4 NIV), today's microchip implant technologies are light-years ahead of what Delgado developed several decades ago.

Former DARPA director and now Google executive Regina Dugan attended the secretive Bilderberg conference in Austria in 2015 to discuss artificial intelligence. Dugan reported that the company was working on a microchip inside a pill that people could swallow to obtain the "superpower" of their body acting as authentication for cell phones, cars, doors, and other devices. Critics accused Google of having an unusually close relationship with "military leadership" after hiring Dugan.[35]

Following the September 11, 2001, terrorist attacks, John Poindexter, former national security adviser to President Reagan, became head of the newly created Information Awareness Office at DARPA. At the time, civil libertarians expressed concerns that the program was a super-spy agency that would use advanced technologies to spy on Americans. To make matters worse, the agency chose the ominous logo of a pyramid with an all-seeing eye sending out rays of light, spying on everyone on earth. The pyramid image came from the back of the dollar bill—a symbol of the Illuminati. "They might just as well have used the motto 'We Spy on Absolutely Everybody,'" Tim Dowling wrote in the *Guardian*.[36]

The All-Seeing Eye of the Illuminati

As the authors of *Trumpocalypse*, we believe it's important to know the truth about the all-seeing eye because it opens the door to a plethora of truths that are essential in understanding occult influences in the worlds of government, finance, media, entertainment, academia, and religion.

Since its founding, the Illuminati has used symbols to convey information secretly to its members. Some of these symbols can be traced back to the Knights Templar; the Assassins; and the Mystery Schools of Greece, Egypt, and Babylon. One of its key symbols is the All-Seeing Eye of Horus, also known as the eye of the sun god Ra, an ancient Egyptian symbol. As an occult icon, the all-seeing eye ultimately symbolizes Lucifer, the prince of this world system, who is described in Isaiah 14:12 (NIV) as the "morning star." In Hebrew, the word is *Heylel*, meaning "shining one" or "light bearer."[37]

Lucifer in effect created the all-seeing eye in Genesis 3:5 when in the Garden of Eden, he deceived Adam and Eve, promising them if they disobeyed God they would become "as gods." "For God doth know that in the day ye eat thereof, then your eyes shall be opened, and ye shall be as gods, knowing good and evil." When they ate the forbidden fruit, the Bible says their eyes were opened. The word for eye in Hebrew is *ayin*, meaning the singular eye of their understanding was opened regarding the knowledge of good and evil. They became gods in the sense that they could make their own choices in terms of good and evil.

This brings us to the occult and mystical meaning of the supernatural third eye of enlightenment and understanding, a prominent belief in ancient Babylon, Egypt, and other super civilizations. In Buddhism and Hinduism, followers often paint a third eye between their left and right eyes to represent spiritual enlightenment. The ancient mystery religions taught that the third eye, when activated through meditation, rituals, and hallucinogenic herbs, enabled them to see into the spiritual world. According to this belief system, men and women whose third eye is opened can see the coming of the New Age of "love and light"—the New World Order.

Students of Bible prophecy, though, understand that the concept of the third eye is occultic and designed to prepare the world for the coming of the Antichrist. An invisible, ruling Luciferian elite on earth are members of secret societies and believe they are gods. They believe they have the right to exercise total control over everyone's lives. This is what Plato meant when he referenced the ten god-kings, or philosopher-kings, who ruled the legendary supercivilization of Atlantis. It's also what writer Aldous Huxley referred to as the "scientific dictatorship" and what some now refer to as the technocratic elite.

Illuminati's Endgame

The endgame of the Illuminati is to enslave the world through a satanic one-world government, economic system, and religion, and force the world to worship the Antichrist—the incarnation of Satan.

To accomplish this, they will create a global financial system that consists of a cashless society and microchip implant that everyone on planet Earth must receive to buy or sell. However, before a person can receive the mark of the Beast, he or she must publicly renounce Christ as Lord and openly pledge to worship the Antichrist as God.

If they do that, they will participate in the global economic system during the Tribulation period. If they refuse, they will be beheaded. However, the Bible says those martyrs, or Tribulation saints, will be honored for their sacrifice during the Millennium.

"I saw the souls of those who had been beheaded because of their testimony about Jesus and because of the word of God. They had not worshiped the beast or its image and had not received its mark on their foreheads or their hands. They came to life and reigned with Christ a thousand years" (Rev. 20:4 NIV).

Part III

NINEVEH MOMENT

Chapter Ten

King Cyrus and the Third Temple

We are poised to rebuild the Temple. The political conditions today, in which the two most important national leaders in the world support the Jewish right to Jerusalem as their spiritual inheritance, is historically unprecedented.

—SANHEDRIN RABBI HILLEL WEISS IN A LETTER ASKING PRESIDENT
TRUMP AND RUSSIAN PRESIDENT PUTIN TO HELP ISRAEL
BUILD THE THIRD TEMPLE

Yesterday, I visited the Western Wall, and marveled at the monument to God's presence and man's perseverance. I was humbled to place my hand upon the wall and to pray in that holy space for wisdom from God.

—PRESIDENT TRUMP DURING A VISIT TO THE WESTERN WALL[1]

That's exactly the reason I came here—to pray for the Temple to be built again.

—RUSSIAN PRESIDENT PUTIN IN REMARKS TO A BYSTANDER
AT THE WESTERN WALL[2]

Possessing the only key, famed Israeli archaeologist Eli Shukron unlocked the gate leading to an underground sanctuary dating to the First Temple period—guiding Bob Cornuke, the "Christian Indiana

Jones," into a highly secured complex below the Jerusalem Walls—City of David National Park.[3] Few individuals have been allowed to view this mysterious archaeological dig underneath Mount Zion.

"We do not know exactly what it is, but it is from the First Temple period and possibly even before. This is the only worship area in the City of David," Shukron told Cornuke, an FBI-trained investigator and president of the Bible Archaeology, Research and Exploration Institute who has spent decades traveling the globe in search of evidence to solve biblical mysteries.

Shukron, director of excavations at the City of David, has been digging in the twelve-acre area beyond the southern wall of the old city of Jerusalem since 1995. He showed Cornuke a carved-out hole in the stone floor for an olive press to make olive oil. As he looked at it, Cornuke's heart and mind raced, and he thought of Leviticus 21:12: "Nor shall he go out of the sanctuary, nor profane the sanctuary of his God: for the consecration of the anointing oil of his God is upon him." He recalled that the Hebrew high priest was forbidden to leave the sanctuary of the Temple once oil was sprinkled on him.

Shukron pointed out a hand-cut channel running the full length of the room. "This is a channel for blood and, as you can see, this room is raised," he explained. "It is here there was an altar for sacrificing small animals, such as sheep. The blood went onto the floor over there and the animals were tied up here." He walked over to a corner and poked his fingers through a hole. "This is where a ring was set to tie up the animal being slaughtered. Everything is perfect...I knew that something happened here, [but] I did not know what. When I started to clean it, I began to understand. This is the place of something huge and we are in the heart of it. This is an area of worship and praying and a place where people connected with God. And from that we understand what happened here in the time of the First Temple period and even before."

Shukron pointed out that the room is about ten meters from the

Gihon Spring, which would have been used to wash away the blood of sacrificed animals. "You have everything together here close to the spring, close to the water, living water—and we know that a place of worship of God is near to water," Shukron said. "This is the foundation of the earth that connects with God."

As he stood in stunned silence, Cornuke realized that he might be somewhere deep inside Solomon's Temple near the flowing Gihon Spring where Solomon was crowned king of Israel. It's the only natural water source in the area big enough to wash away massive flows of blood from animal sacrifices.

In his book *Temple: Amazing New Discoveries That Change Everything About the Location of Solomon's Temple*—which is shaking up long-held traditions regarding the location of the first two temples—Cornuke cites many biblical references and quotes from ancient historians to augment his argument that the original temples were constructed in the City of David, not the nearby thirty-six-acre Temple Mount—the location of the Dome of the Rock and al-Aqsa Mosque, Islam's third-holiest site.

Cornuke pointed out that this is where the Jewish historian Josephus, the Greek historian Eusebius, and the Bible all placed the temple. "[The Gihon Spring] comes up underground and travels through Hezekiah's Tunnel and dumps out into the Pool of Siloam. It's very interesting because you need to have water for the priests to clean themselves to be able to go in and do temple functions and services. On the Temple Mount where the big gold dome is, where I think the Roman Fort Antonia was, there is no water coming up from the ground."[4]

Contrary to widely held beliefs that the original temples were located on the Temple Mount, Cornuke claims the preponderance of the evidence reveals the original temples were in the City of David. If Cornuke's theory is true, it would be one of the greatest archaeological discoveries in history, with world-changing ramifications.[5]

What Did Jesus Say About the Temple?

While Cornuke's theory contradicts a thousand years of Jewish tradition and the opinions of leading biblical scholars and archaeologists, if proven true, it could pave the way for the construction of the Third Temple and the fulfillment of major end-time prophecies.

A growing number of prophecy experts and archaeologists say the evidence is mounting that Solomon's Temple wasn't built on the Temple Mount but rather in the City of David on land now controlled by Israel. If the theory proves correct, it means the Third Temple could be built in the ancient City of David, which is about six hundred meters south of the Temple Mount.

The Temple Mount is considered the third most holy site in all of Islam after Mecca and Medina. "This is the area where they feel that Muhammad went to heaven aboard his horse named Barack, interestingly enough," Cornuke says. "They claim if any Jew ever comes up there and puts so much as a shovel to ground that 1.2 billion Muslims will be rallied in an assault to annihilate all Israel . . . This is the most dangerous piece of real estate on planet Earth."

The Dome of the Rock has occupied the Temple Mount since about AD 692 following the Muslim conquest of Jerusalem fifty-five years earlier. The Arab caliph Abd al-Malik built the Dome of the Rock on that site mostly because it overshadowed the Church of the Holy Sepulcher, where Jesus is believed to have risen from the dead. The Temple Mount is in Jerusalem's Old City and is considered a holy place by Muslims, Jews, and Christians. Many believe the Temple was built on top of Mount Moriah and is the place where Abraham brought his son Isaac to be sacrificed. Some believe it's the site of the Foundation Stone, the Holy of Holies, where God gathered dust to create Adam. The dome sits atop a massive foundation built about two thousand years ago.

Traditions dating to the Crusades a millennium ago hold that the Temple Mount was the site of Solomon's Temple, which the Babylonians destroyed in 586 BC. A more modest temple was built by Judah governor Zerubbabel in 516 BC. From 37 BC to AD 4, Herod the Great built Herod's Temple, although it wasn't finished until AD 64. Following a violent insurrection against Rome by the radical Jewish sect the Zealots, Roman general Titus crushed the revolt, and both Jerusalem and Herod's Temple were destroyed in AD 70. Herod's Temple was a massive rebuilding of the Zerubbabel temple, so both are referred to as the Second Temple in Judaism.[6]

The apostle Matthew described the destruction of Herod's Temple in Matthew 24:1–2 (NIV): "Jesus left the temple and was walking away when his disciples came up to him to call his attention to its buildings. 'Do you see all these things?' he asked. 'Truly I tell you, not one stone here will be left on another; every one will be thrown down.'"

Retired U.S. Army brigadier general Norman H. Andersson, a West Point graduate with a doctorate in Christian leadership and author of *Jerusalem's Temple Now!: Political, Military, Economic, and Religious Implications*, raises the question, if "not one stone will be left on another," how can the Western Wall be what's left of Herod's Temple? The implication being, the temple must have been somewhere else.

Over the years, about a dozen locations have been proposed for the original temples. "But...," Andersson says, "you'll find that the archaeologists from the Israel Antiquities Authority talk about structures in the City of David definitely dated to the First and Second Temple periods." He notes that while they are reluctant to come out and state that these religious platforms and edifices were part of the First or Second Temples, they insist that they date to that period of time. "So that leads you then to the notion that the true location, as Cornuke said, is probably the City of David, which is owned and controlled by the mayor of Jerusalem. And if the modern-day Israeli people want to rebuild the Temple, then they could put it in what may have been the true location of Solomon's Temple or the Zerubbabel Temple."[7]

Evidence of the Temple in the City of David

Cornuke says Jesus' statement in Matthew 24:1–2 that "not one stone here will be left on another; every one will be thrown down" is key to his argument. While Jesus' words suggest "total annihilation of the Temple," Cornuke notes that today there are massive stone blocks by the thousands set in the wall supporting the Temple Mount platform. "Now people will say, 'Well, that's the foundational walls around the Temple, so that wouldn't be thrown down.' No, [Jesus] is walking away...and when you're walking away from the Temple you're looking out into the distance, probably from a lower elevation, and Jesus says, 'Do you see all these things?...Truly I tell you, not one stone here will be left on another; every one will be thrown down.' He's looking at all these things pertaining to the Temple—the buildings, the retaining wall, everything," Cornuke says. "In fact, in AD 70, the Temple was indeed destroyed by Roman General Titus. And Josephus wrote...'No one would even know a Temple was there.' In other words, it's just a barren field that was completely and totally annihilated."

Cornuke believes the huge wall now rising on the Temple Mount is not a remnant of the temple but what's left of a Roman fortress—Fort Antonia—that once housed the mighty Tenth Legion consisting of six thousand Roman soldiers and four thousand support personnel. "In Jerusalem today, no one has found one block from the Roman fort...," Cornuke says. "Now you've got to understand that the Roman fort was there from just before the time of Christ and afterward for around three hundred years."

Eleazar ben Jair was a commander of the Jewish rebels at Masada. In about AD 73, Josephus quoted him regarding the destruction of Jerusalem and Herod's Temple, saying, "It is now demolished to the very foundations, and hath nothing left but that monument of it preserved, I mean the camp of those [the Romans] that hath destroyed it, which still dwells upon its ruins." Cornuke explains, "This guy is saying...that the Roman fortress survived, and I surmise, Ernest Martin surmised, and several other top scholars now surmise, that the Roman fortress is in fact where you have the gold dome today."

In other words, the foundation of the Temple Mount and the Western Wall are what's left of the Roman fortress, not Herod's Temple, Cornuke claims. The massive structure on the Temple Mount has all the hallmarks of a Roman fortress, not a Jewish temple. He adds that it makes no sense that the Romans would build a small fortress beneath the Jewish temple on the Temple Mount when they could seize the strategic high ground for their military fortress.[8]

Cornuke's claim seems to align with the prophecy of Micah 3:12 (NIV): "Zion [the city of David] will be plowed like a field, Jerusalem will become a heap of rubble, the temple hill a mound overgrown with thickets."

Stronghold of Zion

To bolster his argument, Cornuke cites many Bible verses, including 2 Samuel 5:6–10 (NKJV), which notes that King David "took the stronghold of Zion (that is, the City of David)" shortly after he was anointed king of Israel. Cornuke says this passage is key to "solving the riddle as to where the true temple is located." At the time, the City of David was about twelve acres in size, had a population of about two thousand people, and was home to a Jebusite fortress. After capturing the city from the Jebusites, David took up residence in the old Jebusite fortress called Zion. Toward the end of his reign, an angel of the Lord killed seventy thousand Hebrews as judgment for David's sins, but halted the slaughter at God's command at the "threshing floor of Araunah the Jebusite" (2 Sam. 24:16 NKJV). The angel then told David to buy from Araunah land for a threshing floor to build "an altar to the Lord" (2 Sam. 24:18–25). Cornuke says this is a "huge clue for the Temple location" because 2 Chronicles 3:1 (NKJV) states, "Now Solomon began to build the house of the Lord at Jerusalem on Mount Moriah, where the Lord had appeared to his father David, at the place that David had prepared on the threshing floor of Ornan (Araunah) the Jebusite."[9]

"This verse conclusively says that the Temple will be built in the strict boundary of the City of David at the place of the threshing floor bought from the Jebusite," Cornuke explained. "That can only be in the City of David, and this makes it impossible for the temples to be have been on the Temple Mount."[10]

The Jewish temples were built and subsequently destroyed, and no traces of them remain. As Jews faced persecution throughout the Roman Empire, the Diaspora, or scattering of the Jews, began and knowledge of the location of the destroyed temples vanished in the mists of time. Since the "stronghold of Zion" was in the City of David, Zion vanished as well. For nearly two millennia, Zion and the City of David "laid silently together, buried in a forgotten tomb of earth," Cornuke explained.[11]

In piecing this puzzle together, Cornuke found numerous biblical clues throughout Scripture in the form of verses equating "Zion" with "my holy mountain," and the location of the original temples. He cites more than a dozen verses, including Joel 2:1 and 3:17, Psalm 2:6, 65: 1–4, and Isaiah 2:3. In addition, numerous ancient historians spoke of the "inexhaustible reservoir of water" within the Temple, including Roman historian Tacitus, along with supporting references in the Dead Sea Scrolls.

"You have to realize that everybody, that every Jew who goes to the Western Wailing Wall, he was brought there by his father, and his father was brought there by his father, and his father was brought there by his father, and so this is a place that is considered holy to them," Cornuke says. "They've believed it so long that it would be very hard for them to ever consider the City of David as the place for the Temple, even though the Bible specifically, and the Tanakh specifically, says that's the place where it is."

"The Kryptonite of Bible Archaeology"

If Cornuke is correct, the implications are staggering. He describes this as "the kryptonite of Bible archaeology."[12]

When he's spoken to Jews about his theory on the Temple Mount, Cornuke says those over age forty wouldn't even discuss it. "It's heresy to them to even consider that." Yet most younger Jews and tour guides have been open to the possibility.

"Archaeologists who are of great fame and note have given us great encouragement to continue our work," Cornuke says. These include California State University at Fullerton Professor of History Emeritus George Giacumakis, who is one of the leading scholars in the world; Chuck Missler; Dr. William P. Welty (associate editor of the ISV Bible); and calls, e-mails, and letters from other scholars over the world "saying, 'Hey, I think you're right.' Pastors, one after another, saying, 'I'm reading your book, and I think you're right.'"

Andersson says a growing number of people are concluding Cornuke could be right. He says there's a groundswell in the number of Christians and Jews who "think the City of David theory makes the most sense of everything." He adds, "Now, when are we going to reach the tipping point—when everybody says, 'Aw, forget the Temple Mount. Let's just go ahead and build it on the land we own and control, and we'll build it there in the City of David'—that's the question."

High-ranking political and military figures in Israel have told Andersson that the movement to build the Third Temple is gaining significant momentum. Officials estimate it will cost about $2 billion. They have said that "when our religious leaders tell us that we should build the

Temple, then we here at the Knesset will look at it to find out what we as politicians need to do."

"There are members of Knesset that actually talk about rebuilding the Holy Temple," Rabbi Chaim Richman, international director of the Temple Institute, told CBN News. "Twenty years ago these people wouldn't have been given a moment on prime-time television to say these things. They would have been laughed out."[13]

The Temple Institute, based in the Old City of Jerusalem, has spent years painstakingly preparing the necessary sacred vessels in accordance with biblical instructions—the golden crown of the High Priest, the seven-branched Menorah, the golden Incense Altar, the golden Table of Showbread, musical instruments, among other items—for Temple service. Additionally, a pure line of red heifers is ready to consecrate the Temple. "I also have an unconfirmed rumor that they have been cutting the stones for the Temple, and that they are using the right kind of marble and the right kind of granite, and the stones are actually being stored in warehouses in Israel," Andersson says.

Lost Ark of the Covenant: "Nobody Asked a Jew"

Surprisingly, Richman claims the Ark of the Covenant isn't lost, as many presume. "The real one is hidden about a kilometer from here, in underground chambers created during the time of Solomon," Richman told the *Telegraph*. "It's true. Jews have an unbroken chain of recorded information, passed down from generation to generation, which indicates its exact location. There is a big fascination with finding the lost ark, but nobody asked a Jew. We have known where it is for thousands of years. It could be reached if we excavated the Temple Mount, but that area is controlled by Muslims."[14]

Of course, that's a big sticking point with explosive potential. The Temple Institute would like to build the Third Temple on the Temple

Mount, one of the most contested spots on the planet. Jews revere the Temple Mount as the location of their two destroyed temples and pray daily for its reconstruction. The competing claims between Jews and Muslims have resulted in riots on the Temple Mount in which many people have been killed. The Third Temple has been one of the key sticking points that has kept the two sides from reaching the long-elusive peace agreement.

The effort by the Temple Institute to build the Third Temple is beginning to capture the imagination of the public. As of the deadline for *Trumpocalypse*, the Temple Institute had 20,000 subscribers on You-Tube, more than 192,000 fans on its Facebook page, and over 24,000 subscribers to its e-mail newsletter.

Trump: A Modern King Cyrus?

Today, significant numbers of evangelical Christians believe God has called Trump to be like a modern King Cyrus—described in Isaiah 45:1 as God's "anointed"—to help rescue and save America and protect Israel.

One reason Christians are comparing Trump to the Persian king is because the Sanhedrin recently asked Trump to help Israel rebuild the Jewish Temple, and Trump asked his Jewish son-in-law, Jared Kushner, to help negotiate a peace agreement between Israel and the Palestinians. Many American presidents have tried to negotiate this peace agreement over the decades, but the dream of the Third Temple has been one of the sticking points with Muslims.

Assuming the Persian throne in about 559 BC, Cyrus carved out a vast empire stretching from the Aegean Sea to India. After conquering the Babylonian Empire, the people in the capital welcomed him, viewing him as a liberator instead of a conqueror. In 539 BC, Cyrus issued his famed decree (2 Chron. 36:22–23, Ezra 1:1–4) that released the Jews from seventy years of captivity in Babylon.[15]

This allowed the Jews to return to their land and rebuild the Temple. In *The Antiquities of the Jews, Book XI,* Josephus wrote: "And these things God did afford them; for he stirred up the mind of Cyrus, and made him write this throughout all Asia: 'Thus saith Cyrus the king: Since God Almighty hath appointed me to be king of the habitable earth, I believe that he is that God which the nation of the Israelites worship; for indeed he foretold my name by the prophets, and that I should build him a house at Jerusalem, in the country of Judea.' "[16]

Josephus further wrote, "This was known to Cyrus by his reading the book which Isaiah left behind him of his prophecies; for this prophet said that God had spoken thus to him in a secret vision: 'My will is, that Cyrus, whom I have appointed to be king over many and great nations, send back my people to their own land, and build my Temple.' This was foretold by Isaiah one hundred and forty years before the Temple was demolished."[17]

When Cyrus read this prophecy, he recognized the supernatural power of God's prophets to predict not only the future but even his name. Cyrus then had a passionate desire to fulfill what was written in the biblical prophecies about him.[18]

Like Cyrus, Trump is not a Jew. Yet just as God used Cyrus to help his people rebuild their temple, many believe God may use Trump in some similar way.

Trump's Mission to Release America's Prophetic Destiny

Today, many Christians believe God has anointed Trump for a specific mission to fulfill as president in releasing America's prophetic destiny in the last days. Among those missions is continuing the role that America has played in being Israel's strongest and only true ally.

Millions of American Christians believe God gave the Jews the physical land of Israel as part of an "everlasting covenant" that God made with Abraham and his descendants (1 Chron. 16:17 ESV). They also believe that God will bless those nations and people who bless Israel.

Many evangelicals believe one of the reasons why God has blessed America is because America has chosen to bless Israel. In his article "Is Trump a False Cyrus?" in the *Jerusalem Post*, Benjamin Glatt wrote: "One can only believe that the leader that now stands at the front of the Cyrus movement is none other than U.S. President Donald Trump. Never has there been a leader since the times of Cyrus that has declared so emphatically his desire to help Israel. As if he was being directly spoken to through God, already on the campaign trail Trump said he would recognize Jerusalem as the 'eternal capital of the Jewish people,' and on one occasion he declared himself to be 'totally pro-Israel.' "[19]

Trump, like other U.S. presidents, was raised up by God to this position. This overarching principle is laid out in Daniel 2:21 (NKJV): "He removes kings and raises up kings." However, not every president is willing to put aside his own agenda and obey what God requires of him.

Our presidents have been raised up by God for a variety of reasons and have different callings. Biblical scholars, Jewish rabbis, and Bible-believing pastors from a variety of Christian denominations—along with respected Christian leaders such as Dr. James Dobson, founder of Focus on the Family; Stephen E. Strang, founder of *Charisma* magazine and author of *God and Donald Trump*; and many others—firmly believe that God has raised up Trump to lead America and the world on behalf of God, and that Trump has a special calling that sets him apart from other presidents and world leaders.

Lieutenant General William G. "Jerry" Boykin, executive vice president of the Family Research Council and former deputy undersecretary of defense for intelligence under President George W. Bush, is a trained expert in Marxist insurgencies and believes America is currently in the latter stages of a dangerous Marxist insurgency or revolution. Not long ago, I (Paul) attended a major Bible prophecy conference where both

General Boykin and I were to speak. I asked Boykin privately if there was any truth to the "conspiracy theories" about FEMA or other government or military branches having secretly built reeducation camps, which are essentially concentration camps where millions of Bible-believing Christians who have secretly been put on watch lists would be rounded up and sent if martial law was declared.[20]

Boykin, taking great care in what he revealed, replied, "Paul...if you had asked me this question twenty years ago I would have said absolutely not. But today large numbers of military leaders who hold high-level positions in the different branches of the military have very serious concerns about the real purpose of these camps."

It's for this and other reasons that Christian leaders believe Trump was raised up by God for a very important purpose, and that in the divine plan of God, the United States will play a special role in the prophetic time we are now in—the last days.

Christians who have educated themselves to the lessons of history and read their Bibles understand that America is under siege, and powerful people and institutions are attempting a coup d'état in the United States. Currently, there are plans to remove Trump from office either through impeachment, drummed-up charges, assassination, or creating the false narrative that he is psychologically unbalanced and could fire off thermonuclear missiles at an enemy state just as easily as he fires off fiery tweets about his enemies.

MK Ultra, "Big Nurse," and the Cuckoo's Nest

Many of Trump's enemies operate in secrecy but are very powerful and could use existing laws to remove him from office by declaring him mentally unfit. In the former Soviet Union and other communist nations, those who didn't agree with the official communist ideology were diagnosed as insane and could be sent to a mental hospital indefinitely, where they received high-voltage electroshock therapy that would wipe out their memories. Then with the use of powerful mind-altering drugs, these dissidents would be reprogrammed using the same techniques employed in MK Ultra and the Monarch mind-control programs.

This politicization of psychiatry allows a totalitarian state to destroy and control its enemies through this form of psychological assassination. This is one of the major premises of George Orwell's novel *1984* and Aldous Huxley's *Brave New World*. It's also a theme in Ken Kesey's *One Flew Over the Cuckoo's Nest,* in which a character named Nurse Ratched ran a mental hospital controlling everyone through drugs. Kesey was saying that America had become one giant mental hospital controlled by the "Big Nurse," who represented a soft totalitarian government that used drugs to control the people.

During the election, it was clear that people trained in psychological warfare were using a psyops campaign to try to destroy Trump. The usual psyops process involves seeding the American people's consciousness with subconscious messages. Shortly after Trump's election, I (Paul) began reading articles in which psychologists questioned Trump's sanity. Then after the Russian election collusion story began to implode, the new psyops of Trump being mentally unstable emerged.

The essential thesis is that Trump sometimes says erratic things in his tweets, which proves that he's psychologically unstable and that he could press the nuke button at any moment and plunge the world into a nuclear apocalypse of biblical proportions.

Why Trump Is a Threat to Globalists

Many Christians believe God raised up Trump because they believe in biblical prophecies and see them unfolding right in front of their eyes.

Trump, along with former congressman Ron Paul, his son U.S. senator Rand Paul (R-KY), U.S. senator Ted Cruz (R-TX), and a few others, exposed to ordinary Americans the hidden agenda of globalism—which involves a secret plan to use stealth trade treaties to essentially steal the wealth of working- and middle-class people and send it to Third World countries.

But all-too-few people seem to get the message. Today, many Americans are so dumbed down by the indoctrination of television shows, movies, celebrities, media, public schools, and universities that they are largely incapable of deep critical thinking. For instance, many Americans admire the late Beatle John Lennon, whose song "Imagine," which *Rolling Stone* ranked number three on its list of "The 500 Greatest Songs of All Time," has done much to brainwash several generations into believing that an atheistic global government would be a utopian paradise. This song has played an instrumental role in the world's embrace of globalism.[21]

Lennon briefly became a born-again Christian in 1977 but later rejected Christ and described himself as a "born again pagan." Ironically, he was tragically gunned down in front of his exclusive Manhattan apartment building in 1980 by a man some believe was programmed through the MK Ultra program as a CIA "sleeper" assassin, as fictionalized in the 1962 and 2004 films *The Manchurian Candidate*. Lennon's assassination at age forty not only immortalized him as a peace-loving visionary and "figure of colossal symbolic importance," but also helped solidify "Imagine" as the defining statement of our age. In "Imagine," Lennon wrote an anthem of praise to the New World Order, singing about no more nationalism, borders, Christian religion, heaven or hell, and everyone sharing equally in the wealth. Yet when Lennon died he had a net worth of $800 million. Once while Lennon was complaining about soaring business expenses, an aide reminded him, "Imagine no possessions," to which Lennon quipped, "It's only a bloody song."[22]

Former MI6 intelligence agent John Coleman, author of *The Conspirators' Hierarchy*, claims Lennon was catapulted to international stardom, along with the rest of the Beatles, via a secret Tavistock Institute mind-control program designed to weaken and eventually destroy Christianity, Judeo-Christian moral values, the traditional family, and patriotism. This psyops promoted drugs, New Age and Eastern mystical religions, socialism, and free sex—"if it feels good, do it"—and helped create the 1960s counterculture and sexual revolution. Many of these people now occupy some of the world's most powerful positions in politics, media, Hollywood, religion, and academia.[23]

Today, the Trump administration, with the support of many political and faith leaders and tens of millions of Christians in America and worldwide, is working to reverse the damage inflicted by these types of covert indoctrination campaigns. Faith leaders say there is only so much Trump can do, and they are encouraging believers in America and worldwide to get involved in politics and in other ways to fight the agenda of the globalist elite.

"I think the danger is that we view Donald Trump as the answer rather than as an opportunity because Donald Trump doesn't have the solutions the United States or the world needs," Rabbi Jonathan Bernis says. "The church does. Believers do. And I think God... may be giving us an opportunity for our voices to be heard in a greater way because of the left elitist agenda to silence the voice of Christians and those who really adhere to or proclaim a Judeo-Christian ethic or values... This is a Nineveh Moment certainly for America, and I think we need to take advantage of it."[24]

We'll explore the "Nineveh Moment" in more detail in the Conclusion, but it's important to recognize the significance of the joint prophetic destinies of Israel and America in the last days. Today, many people resent the term "American exceptionalism." But America is exceptional. American exceptionalism is not due to any inherent virtue in the American people. In fact, the case could be made that the sins of America are far worse than those of any other nation.

American exceptionalism comes from many foundational facts

regarding its history. America and Israel are the only two nations in history that made deep covenants with God. In the case of Israel, God reached out to them through Abraham and unilaterally entered an "everlasting covenant" (1 Chron. 16:17 KJV). In the case of America, the strong biblical believers who settled America in the 1600s likewise made a covenant with God based on the one he made with ancient Israel.

Leader of the "Cyrus Movement"

Today, the leader who is seeking to uphold the covenant the Pilgrims made with God and is standing at the forefront of the "Cyrus movement" is none other than President Trump. No leader since King Cyrus has declared so emphatically his desire to help Israel. On the campaign trail, Trump said he would recognize Jerusalem as the "eternal capital of the Jewish people."[25]

In a recent speech to Christians United for Israel, Vice President Mike Pence promised that Trump will keep his promise to move the American embassy from Tel Aviv to Jerusalem. "It is not a question of if, it is only when," Pence said. "President Trump and I stand with Israel for the same reason every freedom-loving American stand with Israel: because her cause is our cause, her values are our values, and her fight is our fight."[26]

Trump's role as the Cyrus of this generation may not be to bring peace to the Middle East or even to help Israel build the Third Temple. Perhaps his role is move the embassy to Jerusalem and convince the nations of the world that this is Israel's undisputed capital—something that hasn't been agreed upon since the time of King Solomon.

"It's important because God gave Jerusalem to be the capital of Israel for the Jewish people," Sid Roth says. "The world is maneuvering to make Jerusalem a combined ownership of three different religions, but the prophet Joel says end-time judgments come on nations as a result of dividing up God's land...Psalms 105:8–11 says God gives the land of Israel to the Jewish people—and he uses three different adjectives—'forever,' 'everlasting,' and for 'a thousand generations.'"[27]

Israel Is the Epicenter of Bible Prophecy

The fact is, Israel is the center of Bible prophecy, and it will ultimately be the focus of the entire world, as predicted by the prophets.

When Israel was officially re-formed as a nation in 1948, that was God's prophetic "super sign" that the last of the last days had begun. Since the Israelis returned to their land, major conflicts, wars, and terrorism have surrounded Israel, which has been the center of just about every geopolitical conflict in the Middle East.

According to Scripture, Israel has been placed in the center of the cyclone in the last days, and it will be under almost constant pressure and attack until Jesus returns for his millennial reign.

Today, the primary force driving the hatred and contention over Israel is extremist Islamic nations like Iran and Syria, along with terrorist groups like ISIS and Al Qaeda, not to mention the continual conflict with Palestinians over West Bank occupation.

A month after his election, Trump strongly criticized the UN following the landmark Security Council vote that condemned ongoing construction of Israeli Jewish settlements in the West Bank. Trump said, "When do you see the United Nations solving problems? They don't. They cause problems."[28]

The Globalist Synthesis of Europe

Many EU nations are allowing entrance of hundreds of thousands of militant Islamic extremist men from Syria and other countries with inadequate vetting. This has resulted in an increase in terrorist attacks, anti-Jewish attacks, and rapes of women in the EU.

It appears the elite have a hidden agenda to radically transform Europe and overturn its Judeo-Christian values by allowing this mass immigration. The elite's game plan is to destroy patriotism, the independent nation-state, and what is left of Judeo-Christian values in the EU. By allowing the mass immigration of Islamic extremists into Europe, the elite are employing the Hegelian dialectic of "manufactured crisis"—the raising up of two conflicting opposites known as thesis and antithesis—to create the new order based on synthesis. The various EU nations with their Judeo-Christian values and culture are the "thesis," and the Islamic extremists with their militant culture and Sharia law are the "antithesis." As these two groups continue to clash, it serves the purpose of creating a one-world, globalist Europe based on "synthesis"—the blending of the two cultures.

The same process was at work in the United States until Trump was elected. One of his first actions was to begin intensive vetting to identity and remove suspected militant Islamic extremists. Obviously, securing our borders is a top priority for a responsible political leader.

"We've got two hundred million jihadis in the world," Pastor Michael Youssef says. "We have twelve thousand members of ISIS in Europe alone…I'm absolutely convinced there is no stopping Islamization and Sharia Law. [The experts] think it's just a matter of ten or fifteen years and they will be the vast majority of Europe." Youssef spoke of the incredible blindness of the left-wing progressive feminists uniting with their militant Muslim "sisters" to protest Trump's inauguration in Washington: "I guess it's sort of a blindness of biblical proportions when you get the left uniting together with [militant] Islamists."[29]

"All Israel Will Be Saved"

Prior to Jesus ruling from Jerusalem during the Millennium, the nations of the world will form an alliance under the control of the Antichrist and False Prophet. They will vainly attempt to stop the return of Christ and the armies of heaven in a military attack employing humanity's most futuristic, high-tech weapons.

During the horrific Battle of Armageddon on the plains of Megiddo, Jesus will triumph against Satan, his armies of fallen angels, and all those who chose to follow him by receiving the mark of the Beast. At that time, the final deliverance of the Jews as God's chosen people will occur. Every nation on Earth that joined the New World Order—or "Mystery, Babylon"—will be destroyed at Armageddon.

The veils will fall off the eyes of the Jews, and they will have a supernatural revelation that Jesus is Israel's Messiah. At that moment, "all Israel will be saved" (Rom. 11:26 NIV). The prophet Zechariah predicted this time thousands of years ago.

"It shall be in that day that I will seek to destroy all the nations that come against Jerusalem. And I will pour on the house of David and on the inhabitants of Jerusalem the Spirit of grace and supplication; then they will look on Me whom they pierced. Yes, they will mourn for Him as one mourns for his only son, and grieve for Him as one grieves for a firstborn" (Zech. 12:9–10 NKJV).

During this time of national restoration in Israel, God will supernaturally cleanse the land. He will cause the false prophets to leave the land, including the False Prophet and the "unclean spirit" of disbelief that has controlled Israel for thousands of years.

In fulfillment of Bible prophecy regarding "the day of the Lord," the feet of Jesus will touch down on the Mount of Olives—the place where he ascended to heaven following his resurrection—and the topography of the land will be radically altered by a supernatural earthquake.

"And in that day His feet will stand on the Mount of Olives, which faces Jerusalem on the east. And the Mount of Olives shall be split in two, from east to west, making a very large valley; Half of the mountain shall move toward the north and half of it toward the south... And the Lord shall be King over all the earth" (Zech. 14:4–9 NKJV).

The Everlasting Covenant

The Arab-Israeli conflict began over four thousand years ago. At that time, the nations of the world were largely pagan and engaged in all kinds of practices in rebellion against God. They worshipped pagan gods with names like Baal and Moloch and sacrificed their children by placing them on the red-hot metallic hands of these idols. These pagans also worshipped the female goddess Asherah through orgies and the use of mind-altering drugs and music. All these practices and the worship of false gods were forbidden by the biblical God.[30]

God wanted to reach the lost people of these pagan nations. To accomplish this, he raised up a man named Abraham from Ur of the Chaldees, a prominent Sumerian city. God entered an "everlasting covenant" with Abraham to give the land of Israel to Abraham's descendants forever. The covenant was based entirely on the faithfulness of God and his willingness to uphold the covenant. It was not dependent on Israel's spiritual performance. They could not lose the promise of the covenant even if they failed to keep the law or disobeyed God's commandments.

This means the fact that the displaced Jews returned to the land of Israel in a state of spiritual unbelief, idolatry, and immorality is proof that it is the faithfulness of God, and not the performance of men and women, that guarantees the Jews' divine right to possess the land. In fact, numerous Old Testament prophets predicted that the Jews would return to the land in unbelief and not necessarily in obedience to the law.

This should silence critics who maintain that the Jews no longer have the right to the land based on their disobedience. The false doctrine of replacement theology teaches that the Christian church has replaced Israel; the Abrahamic covenant has been given to the church, and the church has the right to possess Israel. This goes against a central biblical teaching that salvation is by faith and not through works or performance.

This principle also applies to how and why God appoints and raises up both Christian and secular leaders. Trump was not raised up by God based on his perfection in obeying all the laws of God. Trump, like King David, is an imperfect man. Yet God called David "a man after my own heart, who will do all my will" (Acts 13:22 NKJV). This was said after David had committed adultery and murder and lied. It was not that God was indifferent to those sins. In fact, although God completely forgave him, David paid a serious price for those sins that included rebellion and murder among his sons. But God's evaluation of David was based on far deeper factors.

Trump Is Taking on the Armies of Hell

In the same way, many Christian leaders believe Trump has been chosen by God, not because of his outstanding morality or Christian virtues, but specifically to be a champion for God's people in the last days as a totally evil and Luciferian New World Order seeks to control and dominate mankind.

God has given Trump very unusual gifts in terms of leadership, strategy, fearlessness, boldness, wisdom, and a vision for what America is supposed to be that is lacking from the majority of secular and Christian leaders.

Like King David, Trump is a warrior who has literally taken on the armies of hell that have illegally seized the highest places in government, intelligence, and the mainstream media, and he has the boldness to "drain the swamp" in Washington, where many influential political leaders are largely controlled by demonic powers.

As a billionaire, Trump knows many of the elite who are members of secret societies and control much of the world's wealth. Yet he's willing to stand for a sovereign America, the Bill of Rights, and the Constitution. Therefore, he's under constant and unprecedented assault from elite globalists who attack him through their control of America's most influential leaders and institutions.

Most born-again Christians who renew their minds regularly with the Word of God and seek God through prayer can see this quite clearly. They also know that Trump faces great danger because he's dared to expose and confront the elite's illegal control of the monetary system through globalism, trade treaties, and governmental agencies that are violating the Constitution and Bill of Rights.

As such, Trump is under a very real threat of assassination. President John F. Kennedy was assassinated not long after he issued a debt-free currency and began publicly speaking out about the secret societies that control our nation and monetary system. Kennedy defied the unconstitutional powers of the Federal Reserve, took back the constitutional power of "We the People," and ordered the government to print its own money. Kennedy was brutally killed in a very public manner not long afterward.[31]

The only other president called by God to stand up against the international banking families and secret societies was President Abraham Lincoln. Lincoln was assassinated in a secret plot because he dared to take constitutional control of our monetary system and began printing money issued by the United States government. John Wilkes Booth—an actor, Confederate secret agent, and member of the Knights of the Golden Circle secret society who had connections to international bankers—killed Lincoln under highly mysterious circumstances.[32]

Israel, Trump, and the Third Temple

A president who truly supports Israel opens America up to receive the enormous blessings of God. Genesis 12:3 says, "I will bless them who bless you and curse him who curses you, and in you all families of the earth will be blessed" (MEV).

We believe God is using Trump on behalf of God's people, both Jews and Christians, in ways similar to his use of King Cyrus, who delivered the Jews from Babylon. Trump is being used by God to deliver Christians from the New World Order and to help defend the Jews.

So far, Trump hasn't spoken about the Sanhedrin's request that he and Putin help build the Third Temple, although Putin reportedly expressed his support during a visit to the Western Wall.

If Trump truly has a calling like Cyrus, is it possible that God could use this real estate mogul turned president to help facilitate the greatest building project in modern history?

When Trump visited Israel in May 2017, the nascent Sanhedrin sent another letter calling on him to pray for world peace at the Wall: "We hope that you will decide to go up to the Temple Mount, Mount Moriah, to the proper areas, and by doing so, you will merit the blessings of King Solomon, who founded the Temple with the intention that foreign leaders will come from afar to bring peace to their lands. If that is indeed your intention, there is but one way to do this: to declare the raising up of the Temple as a universal human goal within the sanctified biblically defined boundaries."[33] Trump did visit the Western Wall, and he was the first sitting American president to do so.

Despite the evidence he's unearthed that he believes points to the location of the original temples in the City of David, Bob Cornuke says it's unlikely that Israeli officials will build the Third Temple there. Instead, he believes the Third Temple will be a large tent, or a "tabernacle," as described in Exodus 26, erected somewhere on the Temple Mount.

"The Third Temple is called the Tribulation Temple," Cornuke says. "And then there is another Temple following that that I call the Millennial Temple where Christ will reign and rule from for a thousand years. I believe the Third Temple, the Tribulation Temple where the Antichrist goes in and declares himself God, could possibly be on the Temple Mount because [the Bible] says the Antichrist is so slick, so smart, so unbelievably creative and charismatic, that he'll be able to broker a peace deal."

Cornuke says he understands a tent tabernacle has been prepared for this purpose that could be erected in a few days on a small corner of the massive, thirty-six-acre Temple Mount. A temporary tabernacle, like the "tent of meeting" in 1 Samuel 2:22 (MEV), would be more amenable in the Muslim world.

"I think they will accept a tent," Cornuke says. "If you put up a tent in the Muslim world, it means it's migratory, so they won't be that freaked out. The Antichrist will somehow persuade the Arabs that this is something that is good for the peace of everybody...That will last for three and a half years until the Antichrist goes into the portable tent...and he will say, 'I am God, and stop Temple worshipping.' That will trigger the next three and a half years of the Tribulation, which is going to be a very, very, very horrendous time frame."

"Bright, Shiny White and (Coming) Down from Heaven"

Andersson agrees that the Bible indicates there will be the Third Temple followed by the Millennial Temple. But instead of a tabernacle tent erected on the Temple Mount, he believes the Third Temple will be built in the City of David. He believes this temple "that could be built in our lifetimes, may become the Tribulation Temple." He adds, "Now the final Temple, the last Temple, the Millennial Temple, is supposed to be, from what I understand, bright, shiny white and is a kilometer by a kilometer by a kilometer, and it comes down from heaven and it's already built."

Conclusion

Last Trump or Nineveh Moment?

So, why don't we just pray for America? For all the people in America, and the future of this great country. And when you pray, pray with confidence, because I truly do believe, in those ancient words, spoken millennia ago, and enshrined in the heart of every American...And if His people, who are called by His name, will humble themselves and pray, He'll do like He's always done in the long and storied history of this land. He'll hear from heaven, and He'll heal this land.

—VICE PRESIDENT MIKE PENCE, FAITH AND FREEDOM COALITION'S
ROAD TO MAJORITY CONFERENCE[1]

Our world is desperately seeking answers to the deepest questions of life—answers that can only be found in the gospel. That is the reason for my hope, that there can be changed hearts and a changed society as we yield ourselves to Christ.

—BILLY GRAHAM, "AMERICA'S PASTOR," IN AN EXCLUSIVE INTERVIEW[2]

Several years ago, Billy Graham—the beloved, world-renowned evangelist—penned a prophetic letter to America.[3] In it, Graham lamented the downward spiral of the country's moral standards, the "idolatry of worshipping false gods such as technology and sex," and the nation's unconcern for tens of millions of aborted babies.[4]

"Self-centered indulgence, pride, and a lack of shame over sin are now emblems of the American lifestyle...," Graham wrote. "Yet, the farther we get from God, the more the world spirals out of control. My heart aches for America and its deceived people. The wonderful news is that our Lord is a God of mercy, and He responds to repentance. In Jonah's day, Nineveh was the lone superpower of its time—wealthy, unconcerned, and self-centered. When the prophet Jonah finally traveled to Nineveh and proclaimed God's warning, people heard and repented. I believe the same thing can happen once again, this time in our nation."

Inspired by the letter and Graham's subsequent *My Hope America* broadcast during the week of November 7, 2013—his ninety-fifth birthday—tens of thousands of Christians spent the next several years encouraging America to turn back to God. As the 2016 presidential election approached, this effort accelerated significantly, and dozens of major faith leaders raised the alarm that the nation's future was at stake and the most momentous election in modern history would set a path for generations to come.

We believe Billy Graham's prophetic words are coming true, and Jesus is now reaching out to America and the world, inviting us to return to him. Some faith leaders are calling this our "Nineveh Moment." We believe if we repent and turn back to God, that America will go on to fulfill its destiny to take the good news to the ends of the earth for one final, great end-times revival.

The story of Jonah is an apt description of much of the church today. While polls show eight in ten evangelical Christians believe we're living in the biblical end times, pastors are largely silent about what's happening and reluctant to speak up—just like Jonah. In the biblical story, the prophet Jonah was wary of delivering God's warning to the wicked people of Nineveh, one of Israel's greatest enemies. Yet, when he obeyed, following God's prodding and after spending three days in the belly of a whale, the people of Nineveh repented and God relented from judging them for another century.

"The United States is going to have to turn from its evil ways...," Billy Graham said in an exclusive interview. "First, we need to repent of our sin and turn back to God; that's the biblical admonition through the Old and New Testaments. Second, we need faith to believe. And then obedience. God gave us the Ten Commandments, which we need to take seriously. But we have no power within ourselves to live up to them. That's where the gospel of Christ comes, in giving us a supernatural power to live that kind of life. It's much easier for me to talk about the love of God, and it's very difficult to tell a person, if you don't repent you're going to hell. But that's exactly the way it is...We need spiritual renewal now. And it can begin today in each one of our lives, as we repent before God and yield ourselves to him and his Word."[5]

Anne Graham Lotz, Billy Graham's daughter and chair of the National Day of Prayer, says this could be our "Nineveh Moment." She cites Joel 2:12–13 (NIV), where God says, "'return to me with all your heart, with fasting and weeping and mourning. Rend your heart and not your garments.'" "In other words," Lotz says, "stop giving lip service and just being sort of glib with things, but you truly grieve over your sin, you repent, you return to God. He says, 'Who knows? He may turn and relent and leave behind a blessing'" (Joel 2:14 NIV).[6]

When Billy Graham Goes to Heaven

The Grahams' remarks come as Billy Graham is approaching the age of 100—an extraordinary phenomenon that Graham Lotz believes may be connected to the Second Coming of Christ.

Billy Graham told his son Franklin Graham several years ago that he believed God may allow him to live to be 100 years old. In 2016, Graham Lotz told a group of pastors that the fact that her father is still alive might have something to do with the "return of Jesus."

Graham Lotz says her father's life and ministry have been very unique in history. "There hasn't been anything like it, and just as his life was global in scope and very significant, I believe his death will be also. It just stands to reason that God used his life and God will use his death if he takes him before Jesus comes back." Graham Lotz says her mother went to heaven ten years ago, and many people in her family thought their father would follow quickly because "they were so entwined, so in love—that he'd be here ten years later, I never would have thought that. So, then I know my father's life is in God's hands, and I believe the Bible says that our days are numbered, so for whatever reason God's purpose for Daddy isn't finished. I'll tell you [Troy] what I based it on. I told him [Billy Graham] this years ago. In studying Genesis 5, there is a genealogy, and when Methuselah was born—he lived the longest of anybody on earth—and his name means, 'When he died it shall come.' "

Extrabiblical tradition maintains that Methuselah died seven days before his grandson Noah and his family escaped the Great Flood in a giant wooden ark. Like Noah, Billy Graham spent his life calling people to repentance, and his sermons on the Second Coming of Christ were seen and heard by tens of millions of people worldwide over many decades. It took Noah 120 years to build the ark. "He had been preaching righteousness and warning people, and telling them that judgment was coming and that they needed to come into the ark and be saved," Graham Lotz says. "So, then you wonder if Methuselah died, and then Noah is there in the door of the ark, preaching salvation in the Old Testament sense, inviting people to come into the ark and be saved from the Flood that was coming. The Bible tells us Noah went into the ark and it was seven days later before God closed the door. So, for seven days he's getting everything settled and then the New Testament tells us he was a preacher of righteousness. We also know that when Jacob died they mourned for him for seven days. And so, was that a mourning period for Methuselah in which God was also speaking to the world that he loved, inviting them to be saved from the judgment that he knew was coming? I don't know if that is right or not, but we know that judgment came. We know that all the people who refused to come into the ark were destroyed. They came under God's judgment because they hadn't accepted his offer of salvation. So, I told Daddy years ago I wonder if his life would sort of be like that when he goes to heaven."

When her father dies, Graham Lotz says there will be worldwide mourning. "I would expect that there will be programs and things that would be on the news about his life," Graham Lotz says. "I would expect also that because they are giving biographical sketches, or going through his life story, that they would have to give the gospel, too. I don't know how you could talk about Billy Graham and describe him without talking about the gospel and the cross of Jesus. And so that makes me wonder will there be a time when the world, in a time of mourning and they are focused on Billy Graham, but more than that they are focused on the gospel, and it will be one more time God has in reaching out to the whole world. Matthew 24:14 says when the gospel is preached to the whole world then the end will come, and there are many ways today that the gospel is being preached to the whole world. I've just wondered if God is holding Daddy for whatever time heaven thinks will be the most effective time to take him to heaven, and then at that moment one more time the gospel will be preached to the whole world."

National Day of Repentance

Throughout American history, presidents have often called for a Day of Humiliation, Fasting, and Prayer and a Day of Prayer. During the colonial era from 1607 to 1776, the Pilgrims and colonists often declared these special days during droughts, attacks by Native Americans, and threats from other nations.[7] In 1668, the Virginia House of Burgesses in Jamestown declared the first Day of Humiliation, Fasting, and Prayer to "implore God's mercy." In the ensuing decades, the colonists often fasted, prayed, and asked God for forgiveness. During the Revolutionary War period, the practice increased markedly.

On April 15, 1775, just four days before the Battle of Lexington, the Massachusetts Provincial Congress, led by John Hancock, declared a Day of Fasting, Prayer, and Humiliation to "ward off the impending judgments." As the war intensified, General George Washington ordered a similar day to implore God to "pardon our manifold sins and wickedness, and that it would please Him to bless the Continental army with His divine favor and protection." After winning the Revolutionary War, Massachusetts governor John Hancock mandated a Day of Thanksgiving and Prayer.

At the height of the Civil War on March 30, 1863, President Abraham Lincoln proclaimed a National Day of Humiliation, Fasting, and Prayer: "The awful calamity of civil war...may be but a punishment inflicted upon us for our presumptuous sins to the needful end of our national reformation as a whole people... We have forgotten God... We have vainly imagined, in the deceitfulness of our hearts, that all these blessings were produced by some superior wisdom and virtue of our own. Intoxicated with unbroken success, we have become... too proud to pray to the God that made us! It behooves us then to humble ourselves before the offended Power, to confess our national sins."

President Lincoln was the last president to call for a National Day of Humiliation, Fasting, and Prayer. Since then, several presidents have called for a Day of Prayer, but none have called for America to humble itself before God and repent of its sins.

Now, as we approach the 155th anniversary of Lincoln's National Day of Humiliation, Fasting, and Prayer in 2018, faith leaders are urging President Trump to address the nation and world in a globally televised event from the Oval Office as part of a Sacred Solemn Assembly National Day of Repentance. Kevin Jessip, founder and president of the Global Strategic Alliance, a ministry seeking to restore Judeo-Christian values that is helping coordinate the event, has asked Anne Graham Lotz and Rabbi

Jonathan Cahn to lead the nation in a period of prayer and fasting prior to the president's proclamation. "On this national day of reconciliation and restoration, political and faith leaders will repent of America's sins and call the nation and world back to God," Jessip says. "Many nations will watch America's repentant heart, and as the Holy Spirit moves, many nations are also expected to turn back to God in repentance as well." As envisioned, during the daylong event, political and faith leaders would also talk about the historical foundations of America and how the Word of God is the "blueprint for American freedom," Jessip says.

"On that day, we'll have Judeo-Christian leaders and state legislators and members of Congress coming across a platform and repenting for the sins of the nation—abortion, murder, rape, idolatry, witchcraft, all of these things," says Jessip, the great-grandson of Charlie Robinson, a circuit-riding preacher in Arkansas in the early 1900s who was instrumental in forming the worldwide Assemblies of God denomination.[8]

All the great spiritual revivals in history began with one idea: Repent and turn back to God. God makes it clear that failure to obey this command will result in judgment. The nation of Israel is an example of the tendency of people to revert to their sinful ways and forget God. At least seven times in the Old Testament, the same cycle repeated: blessing, disobedience, warning, judgment, and repentance. After giving the Israelites numerous chances to repent, God finally left them to their own devices, allowing them to be conquered and deported by their enemies.

Twelve revival movements are detailed in the Old Testament. While each is different, four common factors preceded each revival:

1. A tragic declension. Each Old Testament revival was preceded by a period of moral and spiritual decline. For example, the revival in Exodus 32–33 was preceded by the worship of the golden calf.
2. A righteous judgment from God. Without exception, Old Testament revivals were preceded by some form of judgment.

3. The raising up of an immensely burdened leader. In each case, God raised up a leader who was deeply concerned about the moral and spiritual needs of his people.

4. An extraordinary action the people were required to undertake. While this action varies from revival to revival, it usually involved a solemn assembly filled with prayer, fasting, and heartfelt repentance.

"I believe it's almost like a process," says Jessip, a descendant of "Pilgrim Fathers" pastor John Robinson, who provided spiritual guidance to the Pilgrims before their journey to America aboard the *Mayflower*. "It starts with number one, repentance; number two, reconciliation; number three, restoration; number four, revival; and number five, reformation. We see this in the story of the Prodigal Son. We see it throughout the Scriptures, so in other words you can't have national restoration without national repentance…And so, this is the key, and when the national leader of the free world calls for it while leading the nation in repentance, that's the day the world will watch as God restores a nation, reconciles a nation, and then revival will begin as the church is awakened."

Pastor Jim Garlow is very optimistic about this exceptional event. "We are calling the Church to repent for its failure to be the Church so much of the time…We're in an era where we need to see people stand boldly on the truths of God's Word and proclaim it, because what we do is condemn [unbelievers] to complete destruction if we don't point the way of renewal of their hearts with the power of the gospel…So, I pray we have a whole generation raised up out of a Day of Repentance [to ignite awakening]."⁹

Rabbi Jonathan Bernis, host of *Jewish Voice with Jonathan Bernis*, agrees a day of repentance is urgently needed. "That would be one of the greatest steps we could take as a nation to restore the favor of God."¹⁰

The Great End-Times Revival

A National Day of Repentance comes as many Christians say they are witnessing signs of what they believe could be the beginning of a spiritual awakening in America and many parts of the world, especially China and Africa.

They cite Acts 2:17–21 (NIV), where Peter quotes the prophet Joel saying, "In the last days, God says, I will pour out my Spirit on all people. Your sons and daughters will prophesy, your young men will see visions, your old men will dream dreams...I will show wonders in the heavens above and signs on the earth below...And everyone who calls on the name of the Lord will be saved." Many Christian leaders believe those days are upon us.

As Youth with a Mission Founder Loren Cunningham notes, there is a five-hundred-year pattern in history of major moves of God, including the Protestant Reformation initiated by Martin Luther in 1517. He says, "We are poised for the greatest spiritual awakening the world has ever known."[11]

Other faith leaders are reporting pockets of revival throughout the United States. Anne Graham Lotz says, "I'm on these prayer networks and prayer calls—and there are thousands of people praying earnestly for revival in this nation. So, God may hear our prayers. There are already pockets of revival, whether it's a church here or a community there."[12]

Sid Roth, of the highly rated television show *It's Supernatural!*, is convinced that an increased openness of the Jewish people to the gospel is a sign the world is entering a time known as the "fullness of the Gentiles" (Luke 21:24, Rom. 11:25) when "the spiritual blinders will fall off the Jewish people and they will accept their Messiah and fulfill their destiny to evangelize the world."[13]

"I believe Israel is absolutely pregnant for the greatest revival in Israel's history and in the world's history," Roth says. "What does God say? 'I've made you a light to the Gentiles.' I believe the Jews out of Israel with the technologies Israel has are going to lead the world shortly in technology, and use those technologies to evangelize the world. I also believe there will be a beginning of a release of the greatest glory of the presence of God in history."[14]

Soul Harvest

The late Tim LaHaye said he was unaware of any biblical prophecies that forecast a spiritual awakening prior to the Tribulation period. "However, prophecy does indicate there will be an enormous 'soul harvest' after God commissions the 144,000 [Jews from all the tribes of Israel] at the beginning of the Tribulation that according to Revelation 7 will see 'a multitude which no man can number from all over the world come to faith in Jesus.' "[15] However, LaHaye believed there could well be a great spiritual awakening prior to the Tribulation because of the "longsuffering and merciful" nature of God as he identified himself to Moses in Exodus 34:6.

In the Olivet Discourse, Jesus predicted that one of the signs of the approaching end would be that "this gospel of the kingdom will be preached in the whole world as a testimony to all nations, and then the end will come" (Matt. 24:14 NIV).

LaHaye believed there were signs indicating that we are approaching the time when the gospel will reach all the people in the world. He cited "the amazing moving of the Spirit of God among indigenous groups who had never heard the gospel before but now are turning to Christ in great numbers...Like the number of Jews in both Israel and America accepting him as their Messiah and the report of the former bureau chief of *Time* magazine in China, claiming that the Chinese were professing to receive Christ an average of 30,000 a week in that communist-dominated country. When we study the many signs of the times of Christ's soon return, we realize it is later than we think to fulfill our Lord's Great Commission to spread the gospel to every creature." LaHaye urged all Christians to engage in personal evangelism, saying, "We may well be the last generation to reach the lost and share in the great harvest of souls that we have good reason to expect may come to faith in our lifetime."

"The Greatest Supernatural Awakening in the History of Mankind"

Based on current trends and population growth projections, the Pew Research Center predicts that the percentage of Christians worldwide will remain at 31.4 percent between 2010 and 2050, rising from 2.17 billion people to 2.92 billion people. During that period in the United States, Christians are expected to decline from more than three-quarters of the population to two-thirds amid the rise of the "nones"—a shorthand term denoting people who are atheists, agnostics, or "nothing in particular." Europe's Christian population is expected to shrink from 553 million to 454 million in the coming decades. And the geographic concentration of Christians will shift dramatically; by 2050, four out of every ten Christians in the world will live in sub-Saharan Africa.[16]

However, Pew researchers say many factors could alter these trajectories. One would be an end-times revival. Also, if a large share of China's population were to switch to Christianity, that shift alone "could bolster Christianity's current position as the world's most populous religion," the Pew researchers wrote. "At present, about 5 percent of China's population is estimated to be Christian, and more than 50 percent is religiously unaffiliated. But if Christianity expands in China in the decades to come—as some experts predict—then by 2050, the global numbers of Christians may be higher than projected."

China is currently on course to become the "world's most Christian nation." Since the reopening of churches following Chinese Communist Party chairman Mao Tse-tung's death in 1976, the number of Christians in China has skyrocketed. Fenggang Yang, a professor of sociology at Purdue University and author of *Religion in China: Survival and Revival Under Communist Rule*, estimates the number of Christians in China will swell to 247 million by 2030, surpassing the United States and other nations as the largest Christian congregation in the world.[17]

In his book *Final Fire: Is the Next Great Awakening Right Around the Corner?*, Thomas R. Horn, chief executive officer of SkyWatchTV, wrote that he believes the "greatest supernatural awakening in the history of mankind" is coming, and it may follow a weapon of mass destruction attack on America or a military conflict, although he prays that's not the case.[18]

"You read the book of Judges, and over and over it says, 'And Israel forgot the Lord their God and went whoring after idols.' And then what happens? God allows some harsh circumstances; they go into captivity, or there is a famine, or a war. Something happens and it triggers an act of repentance." He cites 2 Chronicles 7:14 (NIV), which says, "If my people, who are called by my name, will humble themselves and pray and seek my face and turn from their wicked ways, then I will hear from heaven, and I will forgive their sin and will heal their land."[19]

The Coming Tempest

Faith leaders agree that something historic and supernatural is happening in America. The election of President Trump isn't just another election of the leader of the free world. Trump's presidency comes at a critical point on God's prophetic timetable—a time when many believe God is preparing the world for the coming tempest.

Many are hearing the rumblings of a gathering storm and are getting their houses in order. Something strange and unprecedented is going on in the world. People can sense it. Social media is filled with their voices, dreams, and visions. Many believe judgment is coming unless we return to God. Many believe the greatest awakening in history is coming too.

Some believe this is the prelude to "the last trump" (1 Cor. 15:52 KJV). On the other hand, many also believe this is the world's "Nineveh Moment."

As people watch events placing the planet on the fast track to the end of the age, we've sought in *Trumpocalypse* not only to open people's eyes to the dangers ahead but also to offer a road map and guide for how to prepare personally, spiritually, and financially.

In the last part of this final chapter, Paul McGuire—based on decades of prayer, Bible study, research, and ministry experience—offers concise wisdom and prophetic insights to help you prepare for what many believe lies ahead: the economic "reset," a cashless society, and a mighty spiritual awakening that will radically change all our lives.

A Christian Manifesto II
A Prophetic Message of Hope from Paul McGuire

We believe that America has a unique destiny in the last days, and that your personal destiny is directly connected to America's destiny.

We also believe in "American exceptionalism," meaning that America is uniquely different than other nations, not because Americans are in any way superior or more virtuous but because of the covenant God made with the Pilgrims and Puritans who settled America in the 1600s.

It's on this basis of a supernatural covenant that God planned a unique destiny for America at the end of the age. However, in many covenants, the two parties have conditions to fulfill. The covenant the Pilgrims and Puritans entered was based on the covenant God made with Israel through Moses in Deuteronomy 28, known as "the blessings and curses." To receive the enormous blessings of the covenant made via the Pilgrims and Puritans, America—like Israel in the original covenant—needs to worship and obey the true God of the Bible. If those conditions are met, then God will use America to spread a last-days global revival.

At this present moment, America, its political leaders, our president, and all true Christians who are walking in the supernatural with God are engaged in the most intense spiritual battle in human history. We are literally in a fight for the heart and soul of America. Today, millions of people believe that despite his human limitations, President Trump represents the answers to the prayers of millions of Christians over the last few decades. Trump represents an act of divine grace upon America, and God has raised him up due to his willingness to confront a very evil and corrupt system, both in America and around the world. This evil within the system has, to a significant degree, taken control of the elites in both political parties and throughout the upper levels of government in America.

God wants to use America, but he will not put up with its pervasive evil and corruption. The reason all hell is breaking loose upon Trump with a viciousness never experienced by any other politician is because he has chosen to confront the beast—the Hydra—within that system.

However, neither Trump nor any other politician is our messiah. History has shown that monsters have arisen whenever a nation or people look to their leader as a god or messiah. Since Trump is a human like the rest of us, it's the divine responsibility of all believers to obey the call of God at this hour and engage in intense prayer and fasting.

Our present corrupt and evil system arose primarily as the result of the passiveness of the church and those who call themselves Christians. As we read in 1 Peter 4:17 (KJV), "Judgment must begin at the house of God," which means among Christians and the church. It's not the responsibility of unbelievers to pray, fast, and evangelize. That's solely the responsibility of the church.

As such, if we wish to see a biblical revival or a Third Great Awakening, genuine repentance must begin in the house of the Lord. It's a grievous sin for Christians to point their fingers at unbelievers and condemn them for their sins. Jesus did not call us to condemn people, but to evangelize them in love. When Jesus enters their hearts, he will give them a new nature.

We are to stand for the love of God, along with his righteousness and holiness, and the primary way that we do that is living a righteous, loving, and holy life before a culture that long ago rejected Christ. Those who have spiritual ears can hear and those who have spiritual eyes can see that the Lord is now calling his church to repent of their sins. And it will be upon the basis of that repentance that the Lord will honor the prayers, fasting, and intercession of America.

You Are Alive at the Most Momentous Time in History

The spiritual principles that will unlock the destiny of America are the same spiritual tools that will unlock your destiny. You are living in the most important period in human history, a time predicted in detail by the Old Testament prophets and in New Testament passages such as the book of Revelation.[20]

The book of Revelation discloses heavenly mysteries involving Bible prophecy and end-time events. The infinite personal living God of the universe exists in a dimension outside of space and time, and that's why he can constantly see and know what is in the future. Being the creator of time, he has had access to knowledge of all events that occur in all of time—including the future—since before time began.

God's supernatural knowledge of all of time explains his ability to predict the end from the beginning, as he does in the book of Revelation where he merges important prophetic messages throughout the Bible that began in ancient Babylon at the Tower of Babel. Using his supernatural foreknowledge, he graciously reveals to us events of the future, warning and enabling us to prepare for the inevitable.[21]

In fact, God warned humanity in Genesis 11 against ever attempting to create another Babylon—the first world governmental, economic, and religious system. It's one of the central themes in Revelation. Today, a globalist world government, economic system, and religion are being rapidly assembled right before our eyes.

We're Standing on the Very Edge of Eternity

We are standing at the very edge of the end of the age, because the time is coming when this entire planet and the heavens will be burned up, and the new heaven, new earth, and New Jerusalem will exist in a dimension the Bible calls eternity.

When people receive Jesus into their life, they receive the promise of eternal life. So, every person reading this book who has chosen to receive Christ will enter eternity with a brand-new glorified body that is perfect in every way. Your new body will be an eternal body given to you to live in an eternal world, where you will live forever and never age.

You will rule and reign with Christ, the King of kings and Lord of lords, as a joint heir in heaven, which will be so mind-blowing and incredible that no one can possibly explain it. So, now each one of us is standing before a great doorway into another dimension beyond space and time.

A Titanic Prophecy Shift Is Upon Us

Today, we are standing at the door of a titanic prophetic shift into what theologians call the conclusion of the "Seventy Weeks of Daniel." This is the chronological key to Bible prophecy that culminates with the seven-year Tribulation period, the latter half of which will involve the greatest suffering the world has ever known.

We are about to discuss things of such intensity that they may put some readers into psychological overload. Before we do, I want to give you some assurance. While none of us is remotely capable of dealing with what's coming, we must remember that we are not alone. The whole message of the Bible is that we need a savior because we can't save our-selves. Jesus can help you if you will only ask. He will carry your burdens. Jesus said in Matthew 11:30 (NIV), "For my yoke is easy and my burden is light." You were not created to be a beast of burden. Jesus will lift that burden off you right now if you will allow him to. He's sitting on a daz-zling, multicolored throne in heaven, and in a nanosecond, he'll answer your request. Just lift it up and believe like a little child.

Learn to Walk with God During the Countdown to Armageddon

Things are going to get intense for a while, but as you learn to walk with God, your fears of the future will fade very quickly.

Unfortunately, millions of people have forgotten about God, ignored his message of salvation, or have never heard it. God's love for us is so intense that he is going to allow things to be shaken up a bit to command the atten-tion of mankind. Remember, Jesus came and died on a cross to remove everyone's sin if they will just put their faith in the gospel he preached. God has been very patient for over two thousand years, but before humanity chooses to completely self-destruct, Jesus is going to intervene and grab every person who is willing to receive his salvation, which means he prom-ises to deliver "us from the wrath to come" (1 Thess. 1:10 KJV).

The world is now in the countdown to Armageddon, a time when many nations are amassing and threatening the use of weapons of mass destruction. Military tensions are building between nations such as America, North Korea, Russia, China, Iran, and Syria, and there is a very real possibility that terrorist groups now have "dirty nukes" and EMP weapons that can potentially crash the entire U.S. electrical grid. This would mean that most cars would not start; water would stop running because it's run by electrical pumps; and computers, laptops, smartphones, cell phones, and traffic lights would stop working. In short order, grocery stores would run out of food, pharmacies would run out of medications, and society could descend into chaos. And it could take months or years to reboot America's massive electrical grid.

In addition, prophecy experts believe a major war is on the horizon—the "War of Gog and Magog" predicted in Ezekiel 38–39—involving Russia and a coalition of militant Islamic nations that invade Jerusalem either before or at the beginning of the Tribulation.

The Showdown Between Satan and Jesus Christ

We've arrived at a time like no other in human history when we are hurling at hyper speed toward the Apocalypse, along with the potential for an end-times awakening in which millions of Americans will begin to turn to Jesus, making America the launching pad for a last-days worldwide revival.

Although most people on earth sense that some massive events are about to happen, many don't know that we are in the greatest spiritual battle in the history of mankind, involving the final showdown between Satan and Jesus.

Lucifer, who has been leading a rebellion against God, has enlisted one-third of the angels, along with the occult globalist elite of mankind who have pledged a dark Satanic oath to worship and follow him.

Yet, Jesus is the only true God who proved his divinity by resurrecting from the dead. Jesus along with two-thirds of the angels and countless millions of people who have accepted God's free offer of salvation are now part of the supernatural Body of Christ on earth. Jesus has given the Body of Christ not only the keys to his kingdom but also the authority to "tread on serpents and scorpions, and over all the power of the enemy: and nothing shall by any means hurt you" (Luke 10:19 KJV).

This means God's people are to take authority over the demonic powers here on earth. If members of the supernatural Body of Christ accept their various assignments in partnership with God, then we could see the prophetic destiny of America fulfilled. Jesus, who is seated upon the throne as the King of kings and Lord of lords in heaven, has called each of us to "Occupy till I come" (Luke 19:13 KJV), which means that we are to spiritually occupy America through intercessory prayer, fasting, evangelism, and actively participating in the political process of our nation.

Is Trump a Sign of a Divine "Reprieve" for America?

Many Christians and Christian leaders believe that Trump's election represents a divine reprieve or extension of time for God's people to fulfill America's destiny in the last days. In short, they don't view Trump as a kind of messiah but rather as a unique man God raised up in answer to years of prayer from Christians who were deeply concerned about America's accelerating anti-Christian direction.

Many of these leaders have said that Hillary Clinton's election would have meant increased persecution of Christians. One well-known Bible prophecy teacher commented that Trump's election had thrown a wrench into the plans of the globalists seeking to destroy the United States and merge it into a world government.

Learning Your God-Ordained Destiny

A significant percentage of churches rarely or never teach on Bible prophecy. As you'll discover here in our final message, "A Christian Manifesto II," it's vitally important to diligently study the entire Bible, because the "truth will set you free" (John 8:32 NIV).

God wants to reach out and save, deliver, and guide both nations and individuals through the wisdom of his Word. However, if they choose to reject his Word, they open themselves up to powerful spiritual deceptions. Since Lucifer deceived Adam and Eve in the Garden of Eden and became the temporary god of this world, he's expanded his control and power by convincing people to believe in ideas that will ultimately destroy them.

Yet knowledge and wisdom give you power, because when you understand things that are of critical importance to you and your loved ones, you can avoid or be set free from the devil's deceptive traps. We've collectively spent several decades researching and studying the most important truths every person must know to be victorious in Christ in the last days.

Remember, God knew you before the foundations of the world and called you to be here "for such a time as this" (Esther 4:14 NIV). Before you were conceived in your mother's womb, God knew that he would equip you with certain unique gifts and talents so that you could fulfill the important destiny he has for your life. But unless you pursue wisdom, knowledge, and truth, and seek the face of God, you may never know why God created you or learn his incredible destiny for your life. It's a great tragedy that most people, including many Christians, have no idea what their destiny is. This is even a greater tragedy today as we watch the world and the church fall for the devil's greatest deception.

The Communist and Humanist Manifestos

Since ancient Babylon, Lucifer and his minions have employed a well-planned and highly organized strategy to create an all-powerful state ruled by the elite. In recent centuries, some historic manifestos have provided the basic framework for these plans.

The Communist Manifesto by Karl Marx and Friedrich Engels develops the theory that all of mankind's problems can be reduced to a class struggle within capitalist society and that all capitalist societies will eventually become socialist.

The 1848 document called for a violent revolution by workers, the complete redistribution of wealth, the abolition of all private property, and an all-powerful totalitarian state. *The Communist Manifesto* is specifically anti-Christian in its intent, and its goal is to destroy Christianity.

Communism and the communist revolutions ignited by *The Communist Manifesto* were financed by extremely wealthy capitalists and international banking families in America, Great Britain, and other nations. The brutal secret of these regimes that killed tens of millions of people is that communism could not exist except for its ultra-wealthy capitalist backers. Further, communism was first developed by the Illuminati as a strategic way to gain total control over humanity. At the very top levels of this invisible hierarchy are some of the wealthiest and most powerful people in the world who are Luciferians.

While communism promises wealth redistribution and social justice, almost all the wealth goes to the secret elite behind the communists and the upper-level communist leaders, who live in great luxury. Communism succeeds through the ignorance of the people it enslaves.

The Communist Manifesto was followed by the *Humanist Manifesto I* in 1933, the *Humanist Manifesto II* in 1973, and the *Humanist Manifesto III* in 2003. All three are evolving documents that reject the God of the Bible and the Creation account. They promote Darwinian evolution, total sexual freedom, anti-nationalism, and a one-world socialist government. Although the language and ideas are phrased somewhat differently, the *Humanist Manifestos* mirror much of the thinking in the UN Universal Declaration of Human Rights and the EU Charter of Fundamental Rights. Collectively, they represent the plans of some very famous humanist thinkers, writers, and planners of the New World Order based on humanism.

A Christian Manifesto

The only Christian who attempted to combat the negative impact of *The Communist Manifesto* and the *Humanist Manifestos* was Presbyterian pastor Francis A. Schaeffer, who wrote *A Christian Manifesto* in 1981.

In the book, Schaeffer, one of the greatest evangelical theologians and philosophers of the past century, revealed why morality and freedom had crumbled in society. Schaeffer, who with his wife, Edith, founded the L'Abri Fellowship student commune in the Swiss Alps, called for a "massive movement—in government, law, and all of life—to reestablish our Judeo-Christian foundation and turn the tide of moral decadence and loss of freedom."

During his years in ministry, Schaeffer "reshaped American evangelicalism." "Perhaps no intellectual save C. S. Lewis affected the thinking of evangelicals more profoundly; perhaps no leader of the period save Billy Graham left a deeper stamp on the movement as a whole," Michael Hamilton wrote in a *Christianity Today* article. "Together the Schaeffers gave currency to the idea of intentional Christian community, prodded evangelicals out of their cultural ghetto, inspired an army of evangelicals to become serious scholars, encouraged women who chose roles as mothers and homemakers, mentored the leaders of the New Christian Right, and solidified popular evangelical opposition to abortion. The Schaeffers left an imprint on the wildly diverse careers of Jesus People organizer Jack Sparks; musicians Larry Norman and Mark Heard; political figures Jerry Falwell, Pat Robertson, Jack Kemp, Chuck Colson, Randall Terry, C. Everett Koop, Cal Thomas, and Tim and Beverly LaHaye; and scholars Harold O. J. Brown, Os Guinness, Thomas Morris, Clark Pinnock, and Ronald Wells."[22]

Schaeffer believed that evangelical Christians in America are predominately interested in worshipping the false gods of "personal peace" and "prosperity"—meaning many Christians pretend to worship and serve Jesus, but every decision and choice is based on how this will enable them to maintain their personal peace and prosperity.

Schaeffer called this the great sin of the evangelical church and an accommodation to the world spirit of this age. For a church today, this might mean preaching a watered-down gospel and never teaching Bible prophecy because it might offend some people.

Schaeffer often taught about what he termed "true spirituality." True spirituality was a biblically authentic spirituality that incorporated a solid biblical worldview regarding salvation, marriage, sexuality, economics, science, government, politics, art, culture, law, government, and every part of life—all areas the Bible deals with from Genesis to Revelation.

Schaeffer revealed that non-biblical spirituality was accepted, taught, and practiced in most evangelical churches. Non-biblical spirituality is that which confines Christian spirituality exclusively to a world of personal prayer, Bible study, church attendance, evangelism, and worship. Schaeffer taught that this form of spirituality is not the "true spirituality" that the Pilgrims, Puritans, and other great Christians practiced.

Schaeffer delivered this message based on *A Christian Manifesto* in a 1982 sermon at the Coral Ridge Presbyterian Church in Fort Lauderdale, Florida: "I want to say to you, those of you who are Christians or even if you are not a Christian and you are troubled about the direction that our society is going in, that we must not concentrate merely on the bits and pieces. But we must understand that all of these dilemmas come on the basis of moving from the Judeo-Christian worldview—that the final reality is an infinite creator God—over (against) this other reality which is that the final reality is only energy or material in some mixture or form which has existed forever and which has taken its present shape by pure chance."[23]

What Schaeffer meant is that Christians wouldn't be able to change the direction of our nation and world without a complete understanding of the various philosophical, political, economic, and supernatural forces operating within a wide historical spectrum. This would include the powerful secret societies at work behind the scenes, such as the Illuminati and Freemasonic influences behind the French Revolution, that led to the communist revolutions and the elite globalist revolution of our time.

Schaeffer strongly criticized the evangelical Christian movement for its anti-intellectualism, anti-art, anti-philosophy, and anti-cultural stance. He believed this seriously weakened evangelical Christianity's ability to engage a militantly humanistic culture on a higher level because it hadn't paid the price. Christianity had neither preserved a biblical theology that refuses to accommodate the pervasive secular culture nor engaged in the intense education needed to reveal exactly what Christians are fighting spiritually now and have fought throughout history.

It may be difficult for some to accept the claims we've made about the Illuminati and the globalist elite. Sadly, over the years, we've encountered too many Christians and Christian leaders who have dismissed these claims simply because they have been programmed by the media and educational systems to reject them as "conspiracy theories."

Each time we've encountered such reactions, they have never been based on actual research. The person who dismisses these subjects by crying "conspiracy theory" or marches out of a conference without checking the facts has embraced the anti-intellectualism that Schaeffer warned the evangelical church to avoid.

Trump Has a Surprisingly Deep Biblical Worldview

Trump, in many ways, has a surprisingly deep biblical worldview, and he understands how it relates to the importance of America as an independent sovereign nation. He understands the threat of globalism and the danger of NATO, trade and climate change treaties, and the UN.

Sadly, most Christians leaders, professors at Christian colleges, and Christian youth have little understanding of how important these things are. In Genesis 11, God specifically endorsed the independent nation-state. Yet, your average Christian is taught a socialist worldview by Christian educators who endorse globalism and are clueless about its dark biblical significance. We are in the greatest spiritual battle in the history of mankind, and countless millions of Christians have never been taught a truly biblical worldview. Thus, they are incapable of winning people to Jesus, making disciples of all nations, and occupying the land until Christ returns.

Earthly military generals will tell you that the primary battlefield is in the minds of men and women, and that is even more true in the great spiritual battle we are now in. In determining whether they should vote for Trump in the 2016 election, many Christians asked the completely wrong questions. They judged the candidates on superficial external measures and on an outward appearance of piety versus true piety.

Many candidates knew how to play the game with Christians to win their vote but deliver nothing. Outwardly, they acted pious and made sure they were not caught saying anything offensive. Absolutely, Trump should have used his words far more wisely; we are not defending everything he has said. But the real issue was, which man or woman would truly be a champion of Christian beliefs and values? Trump has already proven by his actions that this is where his heart is.

Anti-Intellectualism Is Not a Biblical Worldview

Tragically, many evangelical Christians lack any real education concerning the very real and documented role that secret societies play in our world. This lack of education, along with a prevailing anti-intellectualism, has given the church a kind of powerlessness in the real world.

Contrast this with the life of the prophet Daniel, who prophesied and interpreted the vision of Babylonian king Nebuchadnezzar. The king ruled over an extremely powerful occult kingdom, and his inner court was filled with prophets, soothsayers, clairvoyants, magicians, and others who practiced a very real supernatural power. If they couldn't use that power in the service of the king they would be executed.

When the occult prophets failed to interpret the king's dream, all of them were sentenced to death. This event resulted in Daniel's promotion when he supernaturally interpreted the dream, causing Nebuchadnezzar to openly proclaim that Daniel's God was the only true God. Daniel modeled for us exemplary behavior in the middle of great power. He didn't refuse to educate himself as to the occult nature of Babylon's elite hierarchy, nor did he call for their deaths to eradicate their evil influence. Because he understood the great evil he faced and trusted his God, he rose to great power in those pagan kingdoms. Should we be surprised today that behind the seats of great political power and wealth are intense concentrations of supernatural and occult religions? This is simply how it's always been. The Bible reveals this repeatedly.

The New Jesus Revolution

We don't mean to pick on the millennial generation, because in our time we were just as scientifically dumbed down as young people are today. Our generation is known as the hippie generation, and our 1960s and 1970s counterculture was just as programmed as millennials and younger generations are today.

We were programmed with a bunch of words and slogans—"Make love, not war," "Peace," and "Sex, drugs, and rock 'n' roll"—and we really had no idea what we were talking about. Then suddenly millions of us stopped acting like a bunch of programmed robots when what *Time* magazine called "the Jesus Revolution" began in the late 1960s and early 1970s. It originated on the West Coast and spread throughout North America, Europe, and much of the world before subsiding by the late 1980s. Suddenly, long-haired hippies began carrying Bibles and started boldly preaching the gospel and the fact that Jesus Christ was coming soon. Few people in the Jesus movement had any theological training or came from Christian churches. The spirit of the time was something akin to what you read in Acts 2—a spontaneous outpouring of the Holy Spirit that radically changed millions of lives.[24]

"When the Day of Pentecost had fully come, they were all with one accord in one place. And suddenly there came a sound from heaven, as of a rushing mighty wind, and it filled the whole house where they were sitting" (Acts 2:1–2 NKJV).

The disciples were so filled with the power and glory of the Spirit that they were walking around laughing and filled with joy. Peter stood up and explained that they were witnessing the fulfillment of a prophecy from the book of Joel.

"And it shall come to pass in the last days, says God, that I will pour out of My Spirit on all flesh; your sons and your daughters shall prophesy, your young men shall see visions, your old men shall dream dreams. And on My menservants and on My maidservants I will pour out My Spirit in those days; and they shall prophesy. I will show wonders in heaven above and signs in the earth beneath: Blood and fire and vapor of smoke. The sun shall be turned into darkness, and the moon into blood, before the coming of the great and awesome day of the Lord. And it shall come to pass that whoever calls on the name of the Lord shall be saved" (Acts 2:17–21 NKJV).

The Jesus movement exploded right in the middle of the hippie and counterculture movements that were based on sex, drugs, and rock 'n' roll. It was not the result of some human plan of evangelism on how to reach the youth. Most churches didn't want the saved hippies, except for pastors like Chuck Smith at Calvary Chapel Costa Mesa, whose main message was to receive Jesus as your savior because Jesus is coming soon!

God Rocked America with the Outpouring of His Spirit During the Jesus Movement

It was evident that God still had his hand upon America, because in the middle of an immoral, occult-enmeshed, drug-taking, and rock 'n' roll rebellion, God poured out his Spirit on young people outside of the walls of the churches.

God miraculously saved both Troy and me during the Jesus movement. I was raised in an atheist home in New York City, got involved in the New Age movement and radical politics, and began taking psychedelic drugs after reading Aldous Huxley's book *The Doors of Perception and Heaven and Hell*, in which he advocated the use of the drug mescaline. I took a dual major at the University of Missouri in filmmaking and altered states of consciousness. Then, while hitchhiking on the back roads of Missouri in what can only be described as a *Field of Dreams* experience, a series of powerful miracles happened, and I invited Jesus Christ into my life and was born again, which changed my life forever. At age eleven in 1979, Troy met a Jesus movement youth pastor from Southern California who had trained under Hal Lindsey at the J. C. Light and Power Company seminary at UCLA. This youth pastor and his wife, along with a dozen other "Jesus people," moved to Troy's small hometown in Oregon and led him to Jesus. Afterward, Troy spent several years learning more about Bible prophecy from this youth pastor. He began holding prayer meetings and Bible studies telling students about the Second Coming.

If people in America and throughout the world will seek God and pray, repent, and ask God to send a biblical revival, he will do that. It's not complicated on a logical or theological level.

Think Supernaturally and Act Supernaturally

You can change the world and your life. The first thing you must do is to begin to think and act supernaturally.

The number one lesson to be learned from various social movements is that anyone who wants to transform society needs to have a clear vision of what he or she wants to accomplish and how.

The second lesson is that you must totally believe in what you are doing and commit your life to that cause. You must be prepared ahead of time for resistance, setbacks, and even grave disappointments. But if you are truly committed, you will remain in the game no matter what.

You must have a long-term plan—one that lasts decades or longer. You must also reevaluate your plan to make sure that what you are doing is producing the results you want. If not, you must be flexible enough to make any necessary changes.

You must be so committed to your cause that you no longer care about what other people think. You must constantly train yourself and others, which includes a great deal of self-education, so that you are prepared to deal with people who will rise to oppose you. If you really know your stuff, the opposition will fade quickly.

The Great Commission and God's Marching Orders

The number one thing we need to know about God is that God is love. It's the love of God that motivates him to do everything he does, and this includes creation. The very first verses of the Bible tell of God's astounding and infinite creativity, explaining that he is the creator of everything that exists, including all life. Genesis 1:26 tells us that when he created humanity, he did something incredibly special: "And God said, Let us make man in our image, after our likeness" (KJV). Being made in the image of God indicates an incredibly high calling for mankind. We know that each man and woman was created for a unique and special purpose, because each of us is uniquely created as distinct individuals. Everything about us—our fingerprints, eyes, hair, form, and even our DNA—is distinct from all other individuals who ever lived.

Yet many people close their eyes to the clear evidence of God's existence, power, and creativity in order to escape their high destiny and pursue their own sinful ways. But as Romans 1:20 tells us, "The invisible things about Him—His eternal power and deity—have been clearly seen since the creation of the world and are understood by the things that are made, so that they [who suppress the truth about God] are without excuse" (MEV).

This brings us to God's number one priority, which is to reach as many of these deceived men and women as he can. In Mark 16:15, we read our marching orders from Christ himself as he calls us to participate with God in this project: "Go into all the world and preach the gospel to all creation" (NIV).

We're on the Verge of a Supernatural End-Times Awakening

This is it... This is our greatest moment. God specifically planned before the beginning of time for you to be here in America at this particular moment. The same principles apply to people from other nations, but our present focus is on America. Because it has been given so much, so much more is expected.

The 2016 presidential election was a divine act of the grace of God. Almost all of Trump's opponents in his own party, as well as Hillary Clinton, were bought and paid for by powerful multinational corporations, giant banks, big investment companies, and globalists. Their inner character was revealed by what they did and didn't do. It's blatantly apparent that the elite of both political parties and many members of Congress work for the globalists and haven't worked for the American people in many decades.

It was also blatantly obvious to most Americans that some of the best-known politicians on both sides of the fence, including ex-presidents from both parties, work for the same elite globalists. But on the Republican side, we saw ex-presidents who never said one word to promote Trump and rarely said anything supportive of America or the Christianity they pretend to embrace. Many, many things were brought to light in this election—we believe by God. Now we see openly what was once concealed from us, which enables us to understand the deep corruption and spiritual darkness presently waging war against Trump, his family, and his administration.

This is our moment in time, and we must seize it in faithfulness to God. We believe there is a deep connection between the spiritual corruption in the church and the corruption in Washington, DC. As we face this corruption by drawing a line in the sand and obeying the call of God, we must first acknowledge our sin before the Lord.

Today, every man and woman we know who walks with God can sense the great spiritual war we are now in. These people know in their hearts what God is calling us to do. Those who walk in the light have been given spiritual eyes to see clearly the vision Jesus has for our nation, the world, and the future.

This is the time…Recognize it, for it will not come around again. God is calling people to engage in spiritual warfare against spiritual enemies attempting to permanently dominate our nation. The same evil spirits that knocked on the door of Nazi Germany and Russia are now knocking on America's door. There is only one power on earth that can restrain and bind those spirits from coming in, and that is the supernatural Body of Christ on earth, exercising its authority given by the Lord Jesus Christ.

For too long the American church has been playing church. It is way past time to repent of our sins. The Lord God Almighty is calling us to a spiritual battle wielding spiritual weapons that are mighty through God for "pulling down strongholds" (2 Cor. 10:4 NKJV). This spiritual war is peaceful and law abiding, but by no means passive. The time has come to stand and believe God as our spiritual forefathers did. And as we pray and act, it must be in a spirit of peace.

The Lord is speaking loudly and clearly to the believing church. He is not asking. He is commanding, and if you are truly his, you will obey. The spiritual forces of darkness disguise themselves as terrifying mighty giants. But, as in Joshua and Caleb's time, we are the spiritual giants, and when we arise in faith, they will see us as giants and themselves as grasshoppers.

Humble yourselves therefore under the mighty hand of God and commit to him your ways. Fall on your face before him, and believe that he will clothe you with power from on high. Let the Lord anoint his people for battle, and let his enemies begin to flee.

Arise in faith and receive his boldness, and your enemy, who is a coward, will run and hide. The Lord will send revival like you have never seen before. Prepare yourselves with expectation, because the power of God will begin to flood our nation, and the power released will overturn the works of darkness and drive out the enemy by force.

For the Lord has heard your prayers and he has issued his decree; it is time to preach the gospel and set the captives free.

"And Jesus came and spoke to them, saying, 'All authority has been given to Me in heaven and on earth. Go therefore and make disciples of all the nations, baptizing them in the name of the Father and of the Son and of the Holy Spirit, teaching them to observe all things that I have commanded you; and lo, I am with you always, even to the end of the age.' Amen" (Matt. 28:18–20 NKJV).

Acknowledgments

Shortly after the astonishing election of Donald Trump as president of the United States, Paul McGuire called me (Troy) with the idea that ultimately became *Trumpocalypse*. McGuire said, "God has given us a spiritual nuclear weapon."

While perhaps we'll never know what role our bestselling globalism exposé *The Babylon Code* played in Trump's campaign and election, we do know that nine months following the book's release, Trump announced what the *Washington Post* described as the central strategy of his campaign for president: "Americanism, not globalism, will be our credo."

The day after McGuire called me, we spoke to Kevin Jessip, founder of the Global Strategic Alliance and a descendant of John Robinson, pastor of the "Pilgrim Fathers," about his plan for a National Day of Repentance. "The gist of the National Day of Repentance is a platform that the president can pivot to when he's ready to pivot to it," Jessip told us. "We haven't had one since 1863 when Abraham Lincoln was president, and it's time for the nation, facing all the ills we have; we need restoration, and national restoration only comes through national repentance. We don't need a glorified prayer meeting. We need the leader of the free world to call a nation to bend its knee before a holy God and pray for mercy in the face of judgment."

Believing God placed this concept on our hearts, we spoke to our agent Bryan Norman at the Alive Literary Agency a few days later. During the call, Norman said Trump's election seemed like "almost a countermove against globalization." Keying in on a meme spreading quickly in the media, Norman proposed calling the book *Trumpocalypse*, and asked us to write a book proposal. After we sent it to him in early January 2017, he e-mailed us, saying, "I couldn't believe my eyes when I opened up the document—to make (the Introduction) so compelling and so clear at the onset. My jaw dropped. I was taking it around the office and reading paragraphs to people because you just hit the nail on the head."

Thus began the journey to write *Trumpocalypse*—our second investigative book exploring the nexus between current events, secret societies, and end-times biblical predictions. While the preliminary research and interviews for what would later become *Trumpocalypse* started shortly after we finished *The Babylon Code* in early 2015, I (Troy), from late 2016 through the summer of 2017, interviewed over fifty of the world's most respected geopolitical, economic, and military affairs experts; faith leaders; and biblical scholars for this book—one that McGuire believes could "change the history of America and the world. God has given this nation [President] Trump. If we allow him to fail because we did not back him, God will hold all of us accountable for the nightmare that will follow."

We believe God called us to write *Trumpocalypse* to reach millions of people with its urgent message to support and pray for President Trump, stand up to the globalist elite, and help America fulfill its prophetic destiny that began with the Pilgrims to take the good news to all the world.

As with *The Babylon Code*, many people played significant parts in the development of *Trumpocalypse*.

I (Paul) dedicate this book to my third-grade teacher, whose knowledge and wisdom enabled me to believe and achieve the impossible. I want to thank all those teachers and people of other professions who chose not to always follow the "official program" or say, "I am just doing my job," but dared to help others become what they were created to be, and who chose to serve and not be served. I publicly honor you before the large numbers of people who will read this book here in America and around the world. You are by far among the most valued! I'd also like to honor some of my mentors and friends who inspired me over the years, including Dr. Francis Schaeffer, Pastor Jack Hayford, Bill Bright, Israeli general Shimon Erem, David Hocking, Dr. D. James Kennedy, Pastor Chuck Smith, American novelist Thomas Pynchon, and all the people at Paradise Mountain Church International.

I (Troy) dedicate this book to my beautiful, full of life, and angel-hearted wife, Irene. Like a heavenly blue sapphire—the holy stone of royalty and wisdom, of prophecy and divine favor—I believe God chose her as the gem of gems to help us fulfill his often mystifying but always intriguing calling on our lives. I also dedicate this book to our lovely, charming, and brilliant daughters, Marlee and Ashley. In addition, I'd like to honor Irene's sister, Maggie, who listened to God's voice and played an instrumental role in the creation of *Trumpocalypse*.

Further, I'd like to thank my childhood youth pastor Richard Wheeler, who studied Bible prophecy at the J. C. Light and Power Company seminary at UCLA under Hal Lindsey, author of the bestselling nonfiction book of the 1970s *The Late Great Planet Earth*. One of about a dozen "Jesus People" from Southern California who showed up in their VW buses in my small hometown in Oregon in the late 1970s, he led me to the Lord at age eleven and instilled in me a great appreciation for the Bible and its prophecies.

I'd also like to honor my grandmother Trella Schiller who encouraged me to become a writer and follow in the footsteps of my great-grandfather-plus, famed poet and playwright Friedrich von Schiller. He wrote the poem "Ode to Joy" that Ludwig van Beethoven set to music in the *Ninth Symphony*, along with the plays *Maria Stuart* (the story of the last days of Mary, Queen of Scots), *Wilhelm Tell* (the inspiration for the theme song to *The Lone Ranger*), *The Maid of Orleans* (the tale of Joan of Arc), and *Don Carlos* (an inspiration for George Lucas's *Star Wars*). Interestingly, President Abraham Lincoln was a fan of Schiller's works and often quoted him in his campaign for president. About 250,000 German Americans, including several generals, many inspired by Schiller's play *Wilhelm Tell*, fought on Lincoln's side, helping win the Civil War and free African American slaves. It was during the midst of the Civil War that Lincoln called for a National Day of Humiliation, Fasting, and Prayer.

I'd further like to thank the founder of *Charisma* magazine, Steve Strang, who hired me as the managing editor, and later promoted me to executive editor of *Charisma* and Charisma Media, while I was writing *The Babylon Code*. After Paul and I completed the book, Strang and I flew to the United Nations in New York in the spring of 2015, where he delivered a speech about the persecution of Christians in the Middle East. At dinner that night, Hubie Synn, who is known for his prophetic gift and has seen the miraculous take place in the lives of those he's ministered to, including Jonathan Cahn, the *New York Times* bestselling author of *The Harbinger*, tapped me on the shoulder to give me a message. "God wants to show you that it's not going to be routine in your life. It's going to be supernatural in your life, kind of like you see it in other people... It's only the beginning of what he wants to do with you... You have a lot of gifts inside of you, and he's going to start bringing them out like revelation, insight; you've got discernment, you just know something is coming..." Afterward, my wife, Irene, suggested I keep a journal of things in our lives that seem supernatural. Since then, I've recorded over one hundred events that seem miraculous in nature. It's been a big faith builder, and I'd like to thank Synn.

During the research, interviewing, and writing process, our Bible study group in Irvine, California, led by Sam and Ming and David and Esther, played a key role—encouraging us in our work and praying for the Lord's guidance and spiritual covering. During this time, Mariners

Church pastor of prayer Collin Cumbee prayed with us on several occasions about both *Trumpocalypse* and *The Babylon Code* feature films/ television series projects, likening *The Babylon Code* to a "three-stage rocket" waiting for someone to launch it into the sky to impact millions of people worldwide. As we were writing the acknowledgments, our agent informed us that a major Hollywood producer is very interested in turning *The Babylon Code* and *Trumpocalypse* into films and television series. We anticipate making an announcement soon regarding these projects. I'd also like to thank Saddleback Church pastor Rick Warren. While I was serving as executive editor of *Charisma*, Warren was instrumental in setting up an interview with Mark Burnett and Roma Downey, producers of *The Bible* and the *A.D. The Bible Continues* television series. My wife and I were honored to meet and interview them at their home in Malibu, California, for the "Jesus Goes to Hollywood" cover story in the April 2015 issue of *Charisma*. Burnett told us that he's fascinated by Bible prophecy and Downey said she loves my ancestor Friedrich von Schiller's play *The Maid of Orleans* about Joan of Arc. In addition, I'd like to thank my brother Dempsey Anderson, who played an instrumental role in my faith journey and remarked upon hearing the description of *Trumpocalypse*, "That sounds like a made-for-film book." I'd also like to thank John DeSimone, an author and ghostwriter and former director of the Orange County Christian Writers Conference, who has been a mentor and good friend.

We'd especially like to thank everyone who took the time to do interviews, including Billy Graham, Anne Graham Lotz, Dr. Tim LaHaye, Jerry B. Jenkins, David Horowitz, Patrick Buchanan, Sid Roth, Rabbi Jonathan Bernis, S. Douglas Woodward, Jan Markell, Pastor Rodney Howard-Browne, Pastor Jim Garlow, Thomas R. Horn, Kevin Jessip, Derek P. Gilbert, Pastor Billy Crone, Frank von Hippel, Seth Baum, John Hogue, Jim Marrs, Daniel Estulin, Pastor Michael Youssef, Ron Rhodes, Dr. Peter Vincent Pry, Dr. Rivkah Lambert Adler, Adam

Eliyahu Berkowitz, Chuck Missler, Rev. William "Bill" Schnoebelen, Pastor Jack Graham, Joseph E. Uscinski, John Fonte, Michael Snyder, Constance Cumbey, Carolyn Hamlett, Larry White, Peter Schiff, Danielle DiMartino Booth, Bob Cornuke, retired U.S. Army Brigadier General Norman H. Andersson, Lieutenant General William G. "Jerry" Boykin, and many others.

In addition, we'd like to give a special thanks to the Alive Literary Agency—the "nation's largest, most influential literary agency for faith-based and inspirational authors," whose authors have written over a dozen number one *New York Times* bestsellers, including the Left Behind series by Dr. Tim LaHaye and Jerry B. Jenkins, and *Heaven Is for Real* and *Same Kind of Different As Me*—all of which have been turned into movies in recent years. We'd especially like to thank our incredible agent, Bryan Norman, who Alive founder and chief executive officer Rick Christian promoted to president in 2016.

We'd like to give special thanks and honor to our editing and publicity team at FaithWords/Hachette Book Group, including editorial assistant Hannah Yancey Phillips, publicist Sarah Falter, associate online marketing director Katie Connors, marketing executive Sara Beth Haring, vice president of CBA sales and marketing Gary Davidson, vice president of marketing/publicity Patsy S. Jones, and senior vice president and publisher Rolf Zettersten.

Further, we'd like to honor Joey Paul, our editor at FaithWords/Hachette. Paul, a brilliant and superbly talented editor who has worked with numerous authors over many decades such as Billy Graham, Pat Robertson, Frank Peretti, Chuck Swindoll, Philip Yancey, David Jeremiah, Ravi Zacharias, Robert A. Schuller, and Dr. James Dobson, asked us to write *Trumpocalypse* and retired as we were writing the book. This is a portion of the letter we wrote to him upon his retirement: "You're an incredibly wise and courageous editor and we hold you in the highest regard…We believe God brought us together, and that through your assistance, this new book will help change the nation and reach countless souls around the world...As with *The Babylon Code*, we've experienced many 'coincidences' in putting together this 'five thousand-piece puzzle.'"

Upon his retirement, Paul recommended an outstanding editor, Thomas Williams, who has written and collaborated on many bestselling books, including *New York Times* bestsellers. He did a remarkable, first-class job editing *Trumpocalypse*. "The book is fascinating, extremely well researched and well written," he told us. "I can't put it down."

Appendix A

Prayer of Salvation

It's no accident that you're reading this page now. From the foundations of the world, the Lord Jesus Christ knew that you would read it. As the authors, we want you to know that no matter what you've done, Jesus is willing to forgive you if you respond to the call of his Holy Spirit upon your life now. First, ask Jesus Christ to give you the supernatural power to renounce Satan and any oath you ever made with him (if you ever did). You will sense the most intense spiritual battle in your life, but God will give you his power to overcome the powers of darkness. Simply ask Jesus to give you his power. As God's power begins to come upon you, ask Jesus to forgive you of all your sins and to cleanse you of those sins with his blood. Then ask Jesus to come into your life, to make you "born again," and to save you. The Bible teaches us that the blood of Jesus cleanses us of all sin, which means there is nothing that you may have done that will not be forgiven if your repentance is sincere.

Every person who has chosen to ignore or reject God's free offer of salvation in Jesus Christ has, in effect, made the decision to serve Lucifer. If you want to be saved and receive the gift of eternal life with God in heaven, you must pray this prayer to be saved. If you didn't make a ritualistic or blood oath to Satan, you are not required to renounce something that you did not do. Simply pray the prayer below. We rejoice with you that we will have the privilege of meeting you in eternity in a place called heaven at the Marriage Supper of the Lamb.

How to Pray a Simple Prayer of Salvation in Order to Be Saved:

1. If you truly want to be saved from your sins and experience eternal life in heaven with Jesus Christ, know that when you pray this prayer you will receive God's free offer of salvation in Jesus Christ. You are not saved by some list of good things you have done in life.
2. Pray this simple prayer aloud by faith, but only pray it if you really want to be saved. If you are sincere when you pray, Jesus Christ will save you at that very moment, whether you feel anything or not.

Lord Jesus Christ, I come to you now and ask you to forgive me of my sins. Jesus Christ, I invite you to come into my life and make me born again. Lord, I ask you to cleanse me of all my sins. Lord, I thank you for cleansing me of all my sins and coming into my life and making me born again. Amen.

No matter what sins you have committed, the Lord has forgiven you of all your sins. Also, your simple willingness to ask Jesus Christ to forgive you and make you born again by faith is all that is needed to be saved. If you prayed the above prayer, you are now saved and born again. Some people experience, to various degrees, the sense of God's presence—sometimes even in an overwhelming way. Some people seem to feel nothing initially, but as the days and weeks go by, they begin to experience the reality of God in their lives in ways they never dreamed possible.

We want to personally welcome you into the family of God!

Appendix B

The Trump Presidency Quotes

It is hard to find words to capture the fact that humans are facing the most important question in their history—whether organized human life will survive in anything like the form we know—and are answering it by accelerating the race to disaster. Similar observations held for the other huge issue concerning human survival; the threat of nuclear destruction, which has been looming over our heads for seventy years and is now increasing.

—NOAM CHOMSKY, PROFESSOR EMERITUS AT
THE MASSACHUSETTS INSTITUTE OF TECHNOLOGY

It's hard to [estimate the probability], but let's just say over the next ten years, I would say—if I check my gut—there is maybe a chance of a third [33 percent] of us blowing up the world. It's much too high.

—FRANK VON HIPPEL, A NUCLEAR PHYSICIST AND
PROFESSOR OF PUBLIC AND INTERNATIONAL AFFAIRS
EMERITUS AT PRINCETON UNIVERSITY AND
A MEMBER OF THE BULLETIN OF ATOMIC
SCIENTISTS—KEEPER OF THE DOOMSDAY CLOCK

[Super-EMP weapons] are the most dangerous weapons known to man. A single Super-EMP warhead detonated over North America could permanently black out the U.S. and Canada and kill up to 90 percent of the population through starvation and societal collapse.

—FORMER CIA DIRECTOR R. JAMES WOOLSEY AND
PETER VINCENT PRY, A FORMER CIA
MILITARY ANALYST AND CHIEF OF STAFF
AT THE CONGRESSIONAL EMP COMMISSION

I think people feel like something has got to come to a climax. There seems to be an underlying climax that is on the horizon. For me, as a Christian, I believe that is going to be a massive war, what the Bible calls Armageddon. The end of days. If things continue as they are going, something has got to give. I believe a lot of people are nervous about the long-term future...Something is going to snap. Something is going to break. I believe that could be the start of the end times for us.

—WILL GRAHAM, AN EVANGELIST AND THE GRANDSON OF
WORLD-RENOWNED EVANGELIST BILLY GRAHAM

It is without a doubt the most momentous election of my lifetime, and one that will substantially, and perhaps irrevocably, set a path for generations to come. I cannot remember a more critical juncture in the history of our nation. The next president will appoint anywhere from two to four justices to the Supreme Court. If the appointees continue the shift to a liberal, progressive ideology, the high court will quickly and aggressively abandon the conservative moral principles that have guided this nation for hundreds of years.

—FRANKLIN GRAHAM, PRESIDENT OF THE
BILLY GRAHAM EVANGELISTIC ASSOCIATION

From my perspective, there is a Cyrus anointing on Trump. He is, as my friend Kim Clement said three years ago, "God's trumpet." I predicted his nomination, and I believe he is the chaos candidate set apart to navigate us through the chaos that is coming to America. I think America is due for a shaking regardless of who is in office. I believe the forty-fifth president is meant to be an Isaiah 45 Cyrus.

—LANCE WALLNAU, BUSINESS CONSULTANT AND
AUTHOR OF *GOD'S CHAOS CANDIDATE*

It's true that an eight-year national nightmare is ending. It's been a time when Christians have been targeted, America has declined, lawlessness has abounded, corruption has been the norm, and aberrations have been celebrated. It would be difficult to explain to a Martian why putting children at risk in transgender bathrooms is cool. So, millions of righteously indignant Americans got fed up with heavy-handed government telling them how to behave, what to believe, and what light bulbs to buy. They were sickened that the values of Jay-Z, Beyoncé, Katy Perry, and Madonna were not just celebrated but pushed on the average American. They went at the future for their children and grandchildren and went to the polls to bring sanity back.

—JAN MARKELL, HOST OF THE *UNDERSTANDING
THE TIMES* SYNDICATED RADIO SHOW

We have a movement. It's a movement like the world has never seen before. It's a movement that a lot of people didn't expect. And even the polls, although some of them did get it right, but many of them didn't.

—DONALD TRUMP, PRESIDENT OF THE UNITED STATES

People are so shocked when they find…out I am Protestant. I am Presbyterian. And I go to church, and I love God, and I love my church.

—DONALD TRUMP, PRESIDENT OF THE UNITED STATES

I'm a true believer. And you're many true believers—I hope all—is everybody a true believer in this room? I think so. But Christianity is under tremendous siege.

—DONALD TRUMP, PRESIDENT OF THE UNITED STATES

I am very, very proud to say that I am pro-life.

—DONALD TRUMP, PRESIDENT OF THE UNITED STATES

It is time to remember that old wisdom our soldiers will never forget: that whether we are black or brown or white, we all bleed the same red blood of patriots, we all enjoy the same glorious freedoms, and we all salute the same great American flag.

—DONALD TRUMP, PRESIDENT OF THE UNITED STATES

I think Ronald Reagan was one of the great presidents, period, not just recently. I thought he had the demeanor. I thought he had the bearing. I thought he had the thought process.

—DONALD TRUMP, PRESIDENT OF THE UNITED STATES

I think the big problem this country has is being politically correct. I've been challenged by so many people, and I don't frankly have time for total political correctness. And to be honest with you, this country doesn't have time either.

—DONALD TRUMP, PRESIDENT OF THE UNITED STATES

The forgotten men and women of our country will be forgotten no longer.

DONALD TRUMP, PRESIDENT OF THE UNITED STATES

We will no longer surrender this country or its people to the false song of globalism.

—DONALD TRUMP, PRESIDENT OF THE UNITED STATES

The Deep State and media elite see Trump as an interloper, a threat to their agenda, and [an] illegitimate president, and are determined to bring him down the way they brought down Nixon and sought to bring down Reagan in Iran-Contra. Absent some deus ex machina, President Trump faces four years of this.

—PAT BUCHANAN, WHITE HOUSE COMMUNICATIONS DIRECTOR
UNDER REAGAN, FORMER PRESIDENTIAL CANDIDATE, AND
SYNDICATED COLUMNIST

[The world is] definitely moving toward global Marxism. Remember that Karl Marx said, "My objective is to dethrone God and destroy capitalism," and he also went on to say that "religion is the opiate of the masses." He was a staunch atheist. Now look at everything that is happening today with globalization, but also right here in our own country in terms of the steps being taken to move us to Marxism. People say, "Why are we doing this?" It's because we're moving to Marxism, and under Marxism you cannot have a reliance upon unalienable rights. You need to be totally dependent upon the government. I believe very much that is in some way part of the end-times strategy of the enemy.

—LIEUTENANT GENERAL WILLIAM G. "JERRY" BOYKIN, EXECUTIVE
VICE PRESIDENT OF THE FAMILY RESEARCH COUNCIL AND FORMER
U.S. DEPUTY UNDERSECRETARY OF DEFENSE

For myself, I was praying that God would put his choice in office and so when Donald Trump won I believe also that was an answer to prayer—that God has put him in office. So then, what's he put him in office for? And then only God really knows what the purpose is. And I would pray that it would bring us to a point as a nation that we would repent of our sins and return to God. So, other than that I pray for him, I pray for the people he's put around him, pray for his decisions. We've living in a very dangerous time. I do believe that it could be a time of setting up the world stage for the return of Jesus so the fact that he's in that office, and we know from Scripture that God puts people in office—he removes some and he exalts others— so I believe God certainly had a hand in it, but for what purpose I think time will tell.

—ANNE GRAHAM LOTZ, FOUNDER OF ANGEL MINISTRIES AND
DAUGHTER OF BILLY GRAHAM

Notes

▬▬▬▬

Introduction: The God Factor

1. Franklin Graham, Facebook post, November 16, 2016.
2. C. J. Polychroniou, "Trump in the White House: An Interview with Noam Chomsky," *Truthout*, November 14, 2016, http://www.truth-out.org/opinion/item/38360-trump-in-the-white-house-an-interview-with-noam-chomsky.
3. William Steakin, "Religious Activist Claims Donald Trump Is 'God's Chaos Candidate,'" AOL, October 31, 2016, http://www.aol.com/article/news/2016/10/31/religious-activist-says-donald-trump-is-gods-chaos-candidate/21594990.
4. Dr. Thomas R. Horn, *Revelation in the News*, December 2, 2016, https://www.youtube.com/watch?v=pp7OBPYwLWs&feature=em-share_video_user.
5. Dr. Thomas R. Horn, interview on *The Jim Bakker Show* as shown on *Revelation in the News*, December 2, 2016, https://www.youtube.com/watch?v=pp7OBPYwLWs.
6. Jeffrey Rodack, "Did Nostradamus Foresee Trump's Big Win?," *Newsmax*, November 12, 2016, http://www.newsmax.com/Headline/nostradamus-trump-foresee/2016/11/12/id/758564; *Nostradamus: Election 2016*, History Channel, http://www.history.com/specials/nostradamus-election-2016; Lance Wallnau, "Why I Believe Trump Is the Prophesied President, Charisma News, October 5, 2016, http://www.charismanews.com/politics/opinion/60378-why-i-believe-trump-is-the-prophesied-president; Paul Steller, "End Times President," the *Huffington Post*, April 21, 2017, http://www.huffingtonpost.com/entry/end-times-president_us_58f9639ce4b0f02c3870e88c.
7. "The World in 2017," *Economist*, December 2016.
8. S. Douglas Woodward, "A Stunner! Ben Baruch Interprets 2017 Economist Tarot Card Predictions," Doomsday Doug, December 4, 2016, http://faith-happens.com/a-stunner-ben-baruch-interprets-2017-economist-tarot-card-predictions.
9. Edwin Vieira, Jr., "A Monetary Litmus Test for Mr. Trump," News with Views, January 10, 2017, https://www.newswithviews.com/Vieira/edwin296.htm.
10. Stephen Stromberg, "The Horsemen of the Trumpocalypse," *Washington Post*, March 16, 2016, https://www.washingtonpost.com/blogs/post-partisan/wp/2016/03/15/the-horsemen-of-the-trumpocalypse/?utm_term=.4564049252c5; Mike DeBonis and Kelsey Snell, "Trump's Victory Heralds a Golden Age for Republicans on Capitol Hill," *Washington Post*, November 9, 2016, https://www.washingtonpost.com/news/powerpost/wp/2016/11/09/trumps-victory-heralds-a-golden-age-for-republicans-on-capitol

-hill; Jessilyn Justice, "Trump's Fulfilled Prophecies Prove How Close We Are to the End," Charisma News, November 14, 2016, http://www.charismanews.com/opinion/ 61246-trump-s-fulfilled-prophecies-prove-how-close-we-are-to-the-end; Doug Stringer, "Are We Living in a Nineveh Moment?," September 15, 2015, DougStringer.com, http://www.dougstringer.com/2015/09/15/are-living-in-a-nineveh-moment.

11. "Trumpocalypse," *Urban Dictionary*, http://www.urbandictionary.com/define .php?term=trumpocalypse; Michael Barbarono and Matt Flegenheimer, "Donald Trump Is Elected President in Stunning Repudiation of the Establishment," *New York Times*, November 9, 2016, http://www.nytimes.com/2016/11/09/us/politics/ hillary-clinton-donald-trump-president.html?_r=0.

12. Stromberg, "The Horsemen of the Trumpocalypse"; Dugald McConnell and Brian Todd, "Wherever Trump Goes, Nuclear 'Football' to Follow," CNN Politics, November 18, 2016, http://www.cnn.com/2016/11/17/politics/donald-trump-nuclear-codes.

13. Polychroniou, "Trump in the White House."

14. Frank von Hippel, telephone interview with Troy Anderson for *Trumpocalypse*, December 1, 2016.

15. John Mecklin, "It Is Two and a Half Minutes to Midnight," Bulletin of the Atomic Scientists, January 26, 2017, http://thebulletin.org/sites/default/files/Final%20 2017%20Clock%20Statement.pdf.

16. Owen Cotton-Barratt, Sebastian Farquhar, John Halstead, Stefan Schubert, and Andrew Snyder-Beattie, "Global Catastrophic Risks 2016," Global Challenges Foundation and the Future of Humanity Institute, University of Oxford, April 28, 2016, http://globalprioritiesproject.org/wp-content/uploads/2016/04/Global -Catastrophic-Risk-Annual-Report-2016-FINAL.pdf.

17. Adam Edelman, "North Korea Threatens 'Super-Mighty Preemptive Strike' on U. S.," *New York Daily News*, April 20, 2017, http://www.nydailynews.com/news/world/ north-korea-threatens-super-mighty-preemptive-strike-u-s-article-1.3080815; "Trump at UN: US May Have to 'Totally Destroy' North Korea," *Newsmax*, September 19, 2017, http://www.newsmax.com/Politics/trump-united-nations-speech/2017/09/19/ id/814408/?ns_mail_uid=26940664&ns_mail_job=1754297_09192017&s=al&dkt _nbr=010502rx06rf.

18. Jessilyn Justice, "Trump's Fulfilled Prophecies Prove How Close We Are to the End," Charisma News, November 14, 2016, http://www.charismanews.com/ opinion/61246-trump-s-fulfilled-prophecies-prove-how-close-we-are-to-the-end; Jonathan Cahn, "The Harbinger of Baal, Donald Trump, and Where We Are Now," *Prophecy in the News* magazine, January 2017, 26–29.

19. Franklin Graham, Facebook post, November 10, 2016.

20. Maureen Dowd, "Election Therapy from My Basket of Deplorables," *New York Times*, November 26, 2016, http://www.nytimes.com/2016/11/26/opinion/sunday/ election-therapy-from-my-basket-of-deplorables.html.

21. DeBonis and Snell, "Trump's Victory Heralds a Golden Age"; Joel Rosenberg, "She. Has. Been. Stopped," *Joel C. Rosenberg's Blog*, November 9, 2016, https:// flashtrafficblog.wordpress.com/2016/11/09/she-has-been-stopped-a-stunning -and-historic-night-braceforimpact; Amy Brittain and Sari Horwitz, "Justice Sca- lia Spent His Last Hours with Members of This Secretive Society of Elite Hunt- ers," *Washington Post*, February 24, 2016, https://www.washingtonpost.com/

world/national-security/justice-scalia-spent-his-last-hours-with-members-of-this
-secretive-society-of-elite-hunters/2016/02/24/1d77af38-db20-11e5-891a
-4ed04f4213e8_story.html?utm_term=.8932c95ab2c1.

22. Michael Snyder, "12 Signs of Extreme Optimism in America Now That Donald Trump Has Been Elected," Charisma News, November 30, 2016, http://www .charismanews.com/opinion/61535-12-signs-of-extreme-optimism-in-america-now -that-donald-trump-has-been-elected; Luke Kawa and Julie Verhage, "Soaring Consumer Confidence: Are Americans Happy It's Trump, or Just Happy It's Over?" Bloomberg, November 23, 2016, https://www.bloomberg.com/news/ articles/2016-11-23/soaring-consumer-confidence-are-americans-happy-it-s -trump-or-just-happy-it-s-over.

23. Jan Markell, "So Is the Rapture Now on Hold?," Olive Tree Ministries, November 21, 2016, https://www.olivetreeviews.org/news/headlines/item/11678-so-is-the-rapture -now-on-hold-jan-markell.

24. Tom Petruno, "Another Financial Crisis? Soaring Global Debt Since 2008 Raises Risk As World Economy Sputters," Los Angeles Times, July 9, 2016, http:// www.latimes.com/business/la-fi-investing-quarterly-debt-20160710-snap-story .html; Dion Rabouin, "Total Global Debt Tops 325 Pct of GDP As Government Debt Jumps," Reuters, January 4, 2017, http://www.reuters.com/article/ us-global-debt-iif-idUSKBN14O1PQ.

25. George Soros, "Open Society Needs Defending," Project Syndicate, December 28, 2016, https://www.project-syndicate.org/onpoint/open-society-needs-defending-by -george-soros-2016-12.

26. Eric Levenson, "In R-Rated Anti-Trump Rant, Madonna Muses About 'Blowing Up White House,'" CNN Politics, January 21, 2017, http://www.cnn.com/2017/ 01/21/politics/madonna-speech-march.

27. Sid Roth, telephone interview with Troy Anderson for Trumpocalypse, January 30, 2017.

28. William Tobey, telephone interview with Troy Anderson for Trumpocalypse, April 24, 2017; Andrew Arenge, Hannah Hartig, and Stephanie Perry, "NBC News Poll: American Fears of War Grow," NBC News, July 18, 2017, http://www.nbcnews .com/politics/national-security/nbc-news-poll-american-fears-war-grow-n783801.

29. Evan Osnos, "Doomsday Prep for the Super-Rich," New Yorker, January 30, 2017, http:// www.newyorker.com/magazine/2017/01/30/doomsday-prep-for-the-super-rich.

30. Jim Carlton, "Earthquakes: Reckoning with 'the Big One' in California—and It Just Got Bigger," Wall Street Journal, November 20, 2016, http://www.wsj.com/ articles/earthquakes-reckoning-with-the-big-one-in-californiaand-it-just-got -bigger-1479643228; "Volcanic Activity Strengthening Around the World," Costa Rica News, December 28, 2016, http://thecostaricanews.com/volcano-activity -strengthening-around-world; Becky Oskin, "What Would Happen If Yellowstone's Supervolcano Erupted?" Live Science, May 2, 2016, https://www.livescience.com/ 20714-yellowstone-supervolcano-eruption.html.

31. Elliott Abrams, "President Trump and the Art of the 'Ultimate' Israel-Palestine Peace Deal," Foreign Policy, December 4, 2006, http://foreignpolicy.com/2016/12/04/ president-trump-and-the-art-of-the-ultimate-israel-palestine-peace-deal; "Trump Suggests Son-in-Law Kushner Could Help Broker Peace," Times of Israel, November

23, 2016, http://www.timesofisrael.com/trump-would-love-to-broker-peace-between
-palestinians-israel/#; Adam Eliyahu Berkowitz, "BIN Exclusive: Sanhedrin Asks
Putin and Trump to Build Third Temple," Breaking Israel News, November 10,
2016, https://www.breakingisraelnews.com/78372/bin-exclusive-sanhedrin-asks
-putin-trump-build-third-temple-jerusalem; 1 Thessalonians 5:3, New International
Version; Aaron Blake, "Henry Kissinger's Lukewarm Non-Endorsement of Jared
Kushner Is Even More Damning Than It Seems," *Washington Post*, April 20, 2017,
https://www.washingtonpost.com/news/the-fix/wp/2017/04/20/henry-kissingers
-lukewarm-non-endorsement-of-jared-kushner/?utm_term=.27c40fc0ac59.

32. "18 Revelations from WikiLeaks' Hacked Clinton Emails," BBC News, October
27, 2016, http://www.bbc.com/news/world-us-canada-37639370; Lee Stranahan,
"WikiLeaks Reveals Long List of Media Canoodling with Hillary Clinton," Breitbart,
October 14, 2016, http://www.breitbart.com/wikileaks/2016/10/14/wikileaks-reveals-
long-list-clinton-media-canoodling.

33. Craig Timberg, "Russian Propaganda Effort Helped Spread 'Fake News' During Election, Experts Say," *Washington Post*, November 24, 2016, https://www.washingtonpost
.com/business/economy/russian-propaganda-effort-helped-spread-fake-news-during
-election-experts-say/2016/11/24/793903b6-8a40-4ca9-b712-716af66098fe_story
.html?utm_term=.49ae0ea7962a; Greg Gilman, "Researchers Identify 200 Websites That 'Reliably Echo Russian Propaganda' to Millions of Americans," the Wrap,
November 25, 2016, http://www.thewrap.com/russian-propaganda-us-election-donald
-trump-hillary-clinton-wikileaks-drudge-report-info-wars.

34. Art Swift, "Americans' Trust in Mass Media Sinks to New Low," Gallup, September
14, 2016, http://www.gallup.com/poll/195542/americans-trust-mass-media-sinks
-new-low.aspx; American Press Institute, "A New Understanding: What Makes
People Trust and Rely on News," April 17, 2016, https://www.americanpressinsti
tute.org/publications/reports/survey-research/trust-news; Matea Gold and Jenna
Johnson, "Trump Calls the Media 'the Enemy of the American People,'" *Washington Post*, February 17, 2017, https://www.washingtonpost.com/news/post-politics/
wp/2017/02/17/trump-calls-the-media-the-enemy-of-the-american-people/?utm
_term=.c4b00d1b0638.

35. S. Douglas Woodward, telephone interview with Troy Anderson for *Trumpocalypse*,
December 9, 2016.

36. "New Poll Shows More Americans Trust the White House Than the Media," Fox
News Insider, July 5, 2017, http://insider.foxnews.com/2017/07/05/poll-more
-americans-trust-trump-white-house-media-journalists-press?nmsrc=email&utm
_source=newsletter&utm_campaign=scoop&utm_medium=email.

37. David Deming, "Hate Speech Hysteria at the University of Oklahoma," American
Thinker, December 17, 2016, http://www.americanthinker.com/articles/2016/12/
hate_speech_hysteria_at_the_university_of_oklahoma.html.

38. Donald Trump, "Transcript: Donald Trump's Speech Responding to Assault Allegations," NPR, October 13, 2016, http://www.npr.org/2016/10/13/497857068/
transcript-donald-trumps-speech-responding-to-assault-accusations.

39. Tyrel Linkhorn, "Decades on, NAFTA Still Political Flash Point," *The Blade*,
March 13, 2016, http://www.toledoblade.com/business/2016/03/13/Decades-on
-NAFTA-still-political-flash-point.html.

40. Paul Blumenthal, "No, Donald Trump Isn't Self-Funding His Campaign," *Huffington Post*, October 11, 2016, http://www.huffingtonpost.com/entry/donald-trump-self-fund_us_57fd4556e4b00c1fb2b023e0.

41. Linda J. Bilmes, "The Financial Legacy of Iraq and Afghanistan: How Wartime Spending Decisions Will Constrain Future National Security Budgets," Harvard University John F. Kennedy School of Government, March 2013.

42. Franklin Graham, "Franklin Graham: We Need a Christian Revolution in America," Billy Graham Evangelistic Association, November 2, 2016.

43. Michael Snyder, "Donald Trump Was Born Exactly 700 Days Before Israel Became a Nation," *The Economic Collapse Blog*, January 3, 2017, http://theeconomiccollapseblog.com/archives/donald-trump-was-born-exactly-700-days-before-israel-became-a-nation.

44. Michael Snyder, "A Major Prophetic Sign Appeared the Moment Donald Trump Stepped to the Inauguration Platform," Charisma News, January 23, 2017, http://www.charismanews.com/politics/opinion/62574-a-major-prophetic-sign-appeared-the-moment-donald-trump-stepped-to-the-inauguration-platform.

45. Michael Gryboski, "Franklin Graham at Rainy Trump Inauguration: 'Rain Is a Sign of God's Blessing,'" *The Christian Post*, January 20, 2017, http://www.christianpost.com/news/franklin-graham-trump-inauguration-rain-sign-gods-blessing-173271/#I2upc6FTjP8qRP30.99.

46. Jim Garlow, telephone interview with Troy Anderson for *Trumpocalypse*, July 7, 2017.

47. Lance Wallnau, *God's Chaos Candidate: Donald J. Trump and the American Unraveling* (Keller, TX: Killer Sheep Media, Inc., 2016), 15; Jonathan Cahn, "Jonathan Cahn's Last Words to Obama and Charge to President Trump," Charisma News, January 26, 2017, http://www.charismanews.com/opinion/watchman-on-the-wall/62623-jonathan-cahn-s-last-words-to-obama-and-charge-to-president-trump.

48. Mary Colbert and Mark Taylor, *The Trump Prophecies: The Astonishing True Story of the Man Who Saw Tomorrow…and What He Says Is Coming Next* (Crane, MO: Defender, 2017), 110.

49. Colbert and Taylor, *The Trump Prophecies*, 123.

Chapter One: Trumpocalypse Now

1. Donald Trump, "Inaugural Speech," January 20, 2017; Shane Dixon Kavanaugh, "Liberal Preppers Stock Up on Guns, Food As Trumpocalypse Looms," Vocativ, http://www.vocativ.com/390175/liberal-preppers-stock-up-on-guns-food.

2. Corey Charlton, "War Footing: Nuclear War with Russia Is Less Likely Under Donald Trump 'Because Hillary Clinton Was More Likely to Use NATO to Threaten Russia,'" *Sun*, January 18, 2017, https://www.thesun.co.uk/news/2642378/nuclear-war-with-russia-is-less-likely-under-donald-trump-because-hillary-clinton-was-more-likely-to-use-nato-to-threaten-russia; Damien Sharkov, "Russia Ups Nuclear Missile Troop Drills by 50 Percent," *Newsweek*, January 10, 2017, http://www.newsweek.com/russia-ups-nuclear-able-missile-troop-drills-50-percent-540919.

3. Dugald McConnell and Brian Todd, "Wherever Trump Goes, Nuclear 'Football' to Follow," CNN Politics, November 18, 2016, http://edition.cnn.com/2016/11/17/politics/donald-trump-nuclear-codes.

Notes

4. Sharkov, "Russia Ups Nuclear Missile Troop Drills"; Loren Thompson, "Modernizing the U.S. Army Could Make Nuclear War with Russia Less Likely," *Forbes*, January 3, 2017, http://www.forbes.com/sites/lorenthompson/2017/01/03/how-modernizing -the-u-s-army-can-make-nuclear-war-less-likely/#7fa798926974.

5. "George Bush Defines the New World Order," C-SPAN, September 11, 1990, https://www.c-span.org/video/?c4528359/george-bush-defines-new-world -order; Daniel Trotta, "Reagan Diaries Reveal President's Private Musings," Reuters, May 1, 2007, http://www.reuters.com/article/us-reagan-idUSN012308352007042; Paul McGuire, "Ronald Reagan and the Secret Occult Destiny of America," News with Views, January 12, 2014, http://www.newswithviews.com/McGuire/paul199 .htm.

6. Frank von Hippel, telephone interview with Troy Anderson for *Trumpocalypse*, December 1, 2016.

7. Seth Baum, telephone interview with Troy Anderson for *Trumpocalypse*, April 21, 2017; Baum, "What Trump Means for Global Catastrophic Risk," Bulletin of the Atomic Scientists, December 9, 2016, http://thebulletin.org/what-trump -means-global-catastrophic-risk10266.

8. Tessa Stuart, "Jennifer Lawrence: A Trump Presidency Would Be the 'End of the World,'" *Rolling Stone*, November 13, 2015, http://www.rollingstone.com/politics/ news/jennifer-lawrence-a-trump-presidency-would-be-the-end-of-the-world -20151113.

9. David Horowitz, telephone interview with Troy Anderson for *Trumpocalypse*, January 23, 2017.

10. Dan Nowicki, "'Daisy Girl' Political Ad Still Haunting 50 Years Later," *Arizona Republic*, September 7, 2014, http://www.usatoday.com/story/news/politics/ 2014/09/07/daisy-girl-political-ad-still-haunting-50-years-later/15246667; Horowitz, telephone interview with Troy Anderson for *Trumpocalypse*, January 23, 2017.

11. John Hogue, telephone interview with Troy Anderson for *Trumpocalypse*, February 24, 2017.

12. Charlie Cooper, "ISIS Nuclear Bomb Is a Serious Threat, Warns Barack Obama," *Independent*, April 1, 2016, http://www.independent.co.uk/news/world/politics/isis -nuclear-bomb-is-a-serious-threat-warns-barack-obama-a6964621.html; Dr. Michael Youssef, telephone interview by Troy Anderson for *Trumpocalypse*, January 24, 2017.

13. "Just 8 Men Own Same Wealth As Half the World," Oxfam, January 15, 2017, https:// www.oxfamamerica.org/press/just-8-men-own-same-wealth-as-half-the-world.

14. Sarah Knapton, "Human Race Is Doomed If We Do Not Colonise the Moon and Mars, Says Stephen Hawking," *Telegraph*, June 20, 2017, http://www.telegraph .co.uk/science/2017/06/20/human-race-doomed-do-not-colonise-moon-mars -says-stephen-hawking.

15. Jeffrey M. Jones, "Record-High 77% of Americans Perceive Nation As Divided," Gallup, November 21, 2016, http://www.gallup.com/poll/197828/record-high -americans-perceive-nation-divided.aspx6; "Global Unemployment Projected to Rise in Both 2016 and 2017," International Labour Organization, January 19, 2016, http://www.ilo.org/global/about-the-ilo/newsroom/news/WCMS_443500/lang --en/index.htm; Ashley Cullins, "Kathy Griffin Says She's Gotten Death Threats,

Contacted by Secret Service over Trump Stunt," *Hollywood Reporter*, June 2, 2017, http://www.hollywoodreporter.com/thr-esq/kathy-griffin-says-shes-gotten-death -threats-contacted-by-secret-service-1009761; Rachel Elbaum, "Johnny Depp Raises 'Last Time an Actor Assassinated a President,'" NBC News, June 23, 2017, http:// www.nbcnews.com/pop-culture/pop-culture-news/johnny-depp-when-was-last -time-actor-assassinated-president-n775881.

16. "2017 State of the Bible Report Offers New Insights into Bible Engagement in America," American Bible Society, April 12, 2017, http://news.americanbible.org/ blog/entry/corporate-blog/2017-State-of-the-Bible-Report-Offers-New-Insights -into-Bible-Engagement.

17. Samuel Smith, "79 Percent of Evangelicals See Violence in Middle East as Sign End Times Are Near," *Christian Post*, December 5, 2015, http://www.christianpost .com/news/79-percent-of-evangelicas-see-violence-in-middle-east-as-sign-end -times-are-near-151702/#SY5KEmF9tKcYMz5m.99; Shibley Telhami, "American Attitudes Toward the Middle East and Israel," Brookings Institution, December 5, 2015, https://www.brookings.edu/wp-content/uploads/2016/07/2015-Poll -Key-Findings-Final-1.pdf.

18. Tim LaHaye, e-mail interview with Troy Anderson for "The End Is Really Near" in the September 2015 issue of *Charisma* magazine, May 27, 2015; Jeremy Weber, "Died: Tim LaHaye, Author Who 'Left Behind' a Long Legacy," *Christianity Today*, July 25, 2016, http://www.christianitytoday.com/gleanings/2016/july/tim-lahaye -dies-left-behind-coauthor-stroke.html.

19. Ron Rhodes, telephone interview with Troy Anderson for "The Great Convergence" in the September 2015 issue of *Charisma* magazine, January 28, 2015.

20. Jonathan Bernis, telephone interview with Troy Anderson for *Trumpocalypse*, February 3, 2017.

21. Lindsay Kimble, "Meet JFK's Alleged Mistresses—and How Some Met Mysterious Ends," *People*, December 1, 2016, http://people.com/politics/john-f-kennedys -mistresses; "JFK Took Many Drugs for Secret Health Problems," ABC News, November 18, 2002, http://abcnews.go.com/GMA/story?id=125593&page=1.

22. "Sally Hemings," History.com, http://www.history.com/topics/sally-hemings; Charles Lachman, "Grover Cleveland's Sex Scandal: The Most Despicable in American Political History," the Daily Beast, May 23, 2011, http://www.thedailybeast .com/grover-clevelands-sex-scandal-the-most-despicable-in-american-political -history; "Andrew Johnson," Biography.com, https://www.biography.com/people/ andrew-johnson-9355722; Joshua Wolf Shenk, "Lincoln's Great Depression," *Atlantic*, October 2005, https://www.theatlantic.com/magazine/archive/2005/10/ lincolns-great-depression/304247; Nicole L. Anslover, *Harry S. Truman: The Coming of the Cold War* (New York: Routledge Historical Americans, 2013), 34; "Lucy Mercer," *Time*, http://content.time.com/time/specials/packages/arti cle/0,28804,1908008_1908007_1907977,00.html; Eric Bradner, "Bill Clinton's Alleged Sexual Misconduct: Who You Need to Know," CNN, October 9, 2016, http://www.cnn.com/2016/01/07/politics/bill-clinton-history-2016-election/ index.html.

23. Jonathan Cahn, "Jonathan Cahn's Last Words to Obama and Charge to President Trump," Charisma News, January 26, 2017, http://www.charismanews.com/

opinion/watchman-on-the-wall/62623-jonathan-cahn-s-last-words-to-obama -and-charge-to-president-trump.

24. Cahn, "Jonathan Cahn's Last Words"; David Horowitz, *Big Agenda: President Trump's Plan to Save America* (West Palm Beach, FL: Humanix Books, 2017), 1.

25. Joey Millar, "Kim Jong-un Threatens 'Merciless' Attack on America in Retaliation for South Korea Drills," *Express*, March 14, 2017, http://www.express.co.uk/ news/world/778963/kim-jong-un-north-korea-attack-usa-war-south-korea; David E. Sanger, "Rex Tillerson Rejects Talks with North Korea on Nuclear Program," *New York Times*, March 17, 2017, https://www.nytimes.com/2017/03/17/world/ asia/rex-tillerson-north-korea-nuclear.html; Jon Lockett, "Korea Suicide: Donald Trump Set to Send B-52 Nuclear Bombers to South Korea After North Fires Missiles at Japan and U.S. Warns of 'Overwhelming' Response," *Sun*, March 9, 2017, https://www.thesun.co.uk/news/3049573/donald-trump-sends-b-52-nuclear -bombers-to-south-korea-after-north-fires-missiles-at-japan-and-us-warns -of-overwhelming-response; James Pearson, "U.S. Deploys Attack Drones to South Korea amid Tension with North," Reuters, March 13, 2017, http://www.reuters .com/article/us-southkorea-usa-drones-idUSKBN16K0VB; Jason Devaney, "Navy SEAL Team Six Practicing N. Korean Decapitation Strike," *Newsmax*, March 13, 2017, http://www.newsmax.com/Newsfront/Navy-SEAL-Team-Six-decapitation -military/2017/03/13/id/778504; Tom Michael, "Kim Jong-un Vows to Reduce the U.S. 'to Ashes' with Nuke Strikes If Donald Trump Fires 'Even a Single Bullet' at North Korea," *Sun*, March 20, 2017, https://www.thesun.co.uk/news/3131278/ kim-jong-un-nuclear-weapons-donald-trump-north-korea; Paul Joseph Watson, "Google Searches for 'World War 3' Hit Highest Ever Peak," Infowars, April 12, 2017, https://www.infowars.com/google-searches-for-world-war-3-hit-highest-ever -peak; Barbara Demick, "Escalating Tension Has Experts Simulating a New Korean War, and the Scenarios Are Sobering," *Los Angeles Times*, September 25, 2017, http://www.latimes.com/world/la-fg-korean-war-20170925-story.html; S. Douglas Woodward, "Decision Time for Trump: Will North Korea Evade Another President's Threats?" *Prophecy in the News*, October 2017, http://faith-happens .com/decision-time-for-trump-will-north-korea-evade-another-presidents-threats.

26. Youssef El-Gingihy, "World War 3 Is Coming…," *Independent*, March 10, 2017, http://www.independent.co.uk/news/long_reads/world-war-3-is-coming-a7622 296.html; Peter Vincent Pry, "Nuclear Missile Surprises," *Washington Times*, March 14, 2017, http://www.washingtontimes.com/news/2017/mar/14/nuclear-missile -programs-in-north-korea-iran-need; Sue-Lin Won, "North Korea State Media Warns of Nuclear Strike If Provoked As U.S. Warships Approach," Reuters, April 11, 2017, http://www.reuters.com/article/us-northkorea-nuclear-idUSKBN17D0A4; Ariel Conn, "Forget the Cold War—Experts Say Nuclear Weapons Are a Bigger Risk Today," Future of Life Institute, May 10, 2017, https://futureoflife .org/2017/05/10/forget-cold-war-experts-say-nuclear-weapons-bigger-risk-today.

27. Jamie Micklethwaite, "Shock Claims Russia Backing North Korea's Nuclear Weapons Programme," *Daily Star*, April 27, 2017, http://www.dailystar.co.uk/ news/world-news/609206/North-Korea-world-war-3-Russia-world-war-3-United -States-Donald-Trump-Vladimir-Putin-Japan.

28. Bernis, telephone interview with Troy Anderson for *Trumpocalypse*, February 3, 2017.

29. Katie Mansfield, "End of the World Prophecy: Pastor Says Bible Hints at Devastating US-North Korea Nuke War," *Express*, May 16, 2017, http://www.express .co.uk/news/weird/805461/north-korea-united-states-nuclear-ww3-donald -trump-bible-prophecy-end-times-apocalypse.

30. Hogue, telephone interview with Troy Anderson for *Trumpocalypse*, February 24, 2017; Hogue, "Is War with Iran Imminent?" Hogue Prophecy Bulletin, February 12, 2017, http://www.hogueprophecy.com/2017/02/war-with-iran-imminent.

Chapter Two: Nostradamus, Nuclear "Football," and Bible Codes

1. Nostradamus, *The Prophecies*, Century III, Quatrain 81.

2. U.S. Air Force Major Harold L. Hering, who was discharged from the Air Force in 1973.

3. Michael Dobbs, "The Real Story of the 'Football' That Follows the President Everywhere," *Smithsonian* magazine, October 2014, http://www.smithsonianmag .com/history/real-story-football-follows-president-everywhere-180952779.

4. Mallory Shelbourne, "Mar-a-Lago Guest Takes Picture with Nuclear 'Football' Briefcase," the Hill, February 13, 2017, http://thehill.com/homenews/administration/ 319211-mar-a-lago-guest-posts-pics-with-nuclear-football-carrier.

5. Ron Rosenbaum, "An Unsung Hero of the Nuclear Age," *Slate*, February 28, 2011, http://www.slate.com/articles/life/the_spectator/2011/02/an_unsung_hero_of _the_nuclear_age.html.

6. Melissa Chan, "Here's What Donald Trump Has Said About Nuclear Weapons," *Time*, August 3, 2016, http://time.com/4437089/donald-trump-nuclear-weapons-nukes.

7. Ed Hindson and Tim LaHaye, *The Popular Encyclopedia of Bible Prophecy* (Eugene, OR: Harvest House Publishers, 2004), 304–305.

8. Sean Martin, "Nostradamus Predicted 'Audacious' Trump's Victory—and Now World Could End," *Express*, November 10, 2016, http://www.express.co.uk/news/ weird/730526/donald-trump-nostradamus-end-of-the-world-hillary-clinton.

9. *Encyclopaedia Britannica*, s.v., "Nostradamus," https://www.britannica.com/biogra phy/Nostradamus; "Nostradamus," History.com, http://www.history.com/topics/ nostradamus.

10. John Hogue, *A New Cold War: The Prophecies of Nostradamus, Stormberger, and Edgar Cayce* (Langley, WA: Hogue Prophecy Publishing, 2014), 4–5.

11. Hogue, *A New Cold War*, 13.

12. Hogue, telephone interview with Troy Anderson for *Trumpocalypse*, February 24, 2017.

13. Hogue, *A New Cold War*, 32.

14. Mario Reading, *Nostradamus: The Complete Prophecies of the Future* (London, England: Watkins Media Limited, 2006, 2010, 2015), 2–4.

15. *Nostradamus: Election 2016*, History Channel, http://www.history.com/specials/ nostradamus-election-2016/fullspecial.

16. Hogue, telephone interview with Troy Anderson for *Trumpocalypse*, February 24, 2017; Hogue, e-mail interview with Troy Anderson for *Trumpocalypse*, February 23, 2017.

17. Hogue, "Did Nostradamus Foresee Donald Trump?" Hogue Prophecy Bulletin, December 6, 2016, http://www.hogueprophecy.com/2016/12/hogue-predicts-jill -stein-recount.

18. Hogue, *Trump for President: Astrological Predictions* (Langley, WA: Hogue Prophecy Publishing, 2015), 1.

19. Neil Howe, "Where Did Steve Bannon Get His Worldview? From My Book," *Washington Post*, February 24, 2017, https://www.washingtonpost.com/ entertainment/books/where-did-steve-bannon-get-his-worldview-from -my-book/2017/02/24/16937f38-f84a-11e6-9845-576c69081518_story .html?utm_term=.1af83171a2a1; David Kaiser, "Donald Trump, Stephen Bannon and the Coming Crisis in American National Life," *Time*, November 18, 2016, http://time.com/4575780/stephen-bannon-fourth-turning; Neil Howe and William Strauss, *The Fourth Turning: An American Prophecy* (New York: Broadway Books, 1997), 6.

20. Hogue, *Nostradamus: The Complete Prophecies* (Boston, MA: Element Books, Inc., 1997), 11, 27.

21. "Divination and Magic," *Holman Illustrated Bible Dictionary* (Nashville, TN: Holman Bible Publishers, 2003), 433–434.

22. Hogue, "Nostradamus, a New Cold War, Russia Bashing and the Media's NFL Referee Syndrome," Hogue Prophecy Bulletin, September 6, 2014, http://www .hogueprophecy.com/2014/09/ceasefire-in-ukraine-while-nato-rattles-spearhead -did-russia-really-invade-nostradamus-a-new-cold-war-russia-bashing-and-the -medias-nfl-referee-syndrome-comments-about-hogue-on-coast-to; Hogue, *A New Cold War*, 18.

23. Hogue, *A New Cold War*, 15.

24. Hogue, "A Resurrection of the Ukrainian Civil War: A Nuclear War Threat and a Geopolitical Chess Game," Hogue Prophecy Bulletin, February 12, 2017, http://www.hogueprophecy.com/2017/02/war-with-iran-imminent; Hogue, "Hogue Remains 13 and 0 Predicting Presidents by Popular Vote," Hogue Prophecy Bulletin, November 16, 2016, http://www.hogueprophecy.com/2016/11/hogue-remains -13-and-0.

25. Hogue, "Did Nostradamus Foresee Donald Trump?"; Hogue, "Trump Apology. One Step Closer to World War III—U.S. Suspends Talks with Russia of Syria," Hogue Prophecy Bulletin, October 11, 2016, http://www.hogueprophecy .com/2016/10/trump-apology-1.

26. Hogue, *Nostradamus: The Complete Prophecies*, 219.

27. Hogue, *Nostradamus: The Complete Prophecies*, 423.

28. Hogue, "Gorbachev at Berlin Wall Sees a New Cold War Coming," Hogue Prophecy Bulletin, November 8, 2014, http://www.hogueprophecy.com/2014/11/midterm -election-prophecy-assessed-gorbachev-at-berlin-wall-sees-a-new-cold-war-coming -was-hogue-foreseen-as-the-american-nostradamus-music-as-a-prophecy-tool.

29. Hogue, *Nostradamus: The Complete Prophecies*, 377.

30. Hogue, "Nostradamus, the 'Barbare' (Libyans), the Source of World War III?" Hogue Prophecy Bulletin, March 30, 2011, http://www.hogueprophecy.com/2011/03/nostra damus-the-barbare-libyans-the-source-of-world-war-iii.

31. Hogue, "Is Osama or Saddam Nostradamus' Third Antichrist?" Hogue Prophecy Bulletin, May 13, 2011, http://www.hogueprophecy.com/2011/05/is-osama-or-saddam-nostradamus-third-antichrist.
32. Hogue, telephone interview with Troy Anderson for *Trumpocalypse*, February 24, 2017.
33. Eric Sapp, "Trump Isn't the Antichrist but He Is Anti-Christ," *Christian Post*, February 10, 2017, http://www.christianpost.com/news/trump-isnt-the-antichrist-but-he-is-anti-christ-174617.
34. Jerry B. Jenkins, e-mail interview with Troy Anderson for *Trumpocalypse*, May 3, 2017.
35. Gabriel Campanario, "Donald Trump, the Herald of Evangelicals' End Times," *Seattle Times*, September 30, 2016, http://www.seattletimes.com/opinion/donald-trump-the-herald-of-evangelicals-end-times.
36. Hogue, "Nostradamus and the Antichrist: Code Named Mabus," Hogue Prophecy Bulletin, September 22, 2008, http://www.hogueprophecy.com/mabus.
37. Hogue, *Nostradamus: The Complete Prophecies*, 798–800.
38. Hogue, "Is Donald Trump Nostradamus' Third Antichrist: Mabus?" Hogue Prophecy Bulletin, December 5, 2016, http://www.hogueprophecy.com/2016/12/hogue-predicts-jill-stein-recount.
39. Hogue, *A New Cold War*, 110.
40. Hogue, *Nostradamus: The Complete Prophecies*, 201.
41. Hogue, "Nostradamus and the Antichrist: Code Named Mabus."
42. Dr. Rivkah Lambert, "Bible Codes Predict Trump Win," Breaking Israel News, November 1, 2016, https://www.breakingisraelnews.com/77884/bible-codes-predict-trump-win/#ve74j2Zsufac62dj.97; Derek P. Gilbert, *The Great Inception: Satan's Psyops from Eden to Armageddon* (Crane, MO: Defender, 2017),xiii.
43. "Rabbi Sees Donald Trump Ascendancy in Bible Codes," World Net Daily, November 3, 2016, http://mobile.wnd.com/2016/11/rabbi-sees-donald-trump-ascendancy-in-bible-codes.
44. Adam Eliyahu Berkowitz, "Biblical Numerology Predicts Trump Will Usher in Messiah," Breaking Israel News, May 16, 2016, https://www.breakingisraelnews.com/67748/biblical-numerology-predicts-trump-will-usher-messiah/#QbVvxePIkxrk2uC5.97.
45. J. Daniel Hays and J. Scott Duvall, *The Baker Illustrated Bible Handbook* (Grand Rapids, MI: Baker Publishing Group, 2011), 1127–1133.
46. Jim Marrs, *Rule by Secrecy: The Hidden History That Connects the Trilateral Commission, the Freemasons, and the Great Pyramids* (New York: Perennial, 2000), 357–358; Edith Starr Miller, *Occult Theocrasy, Volume 1* (TheResistanceManifesto.com, 1933), 26, 77.
47. Thomas R. Horn, interview on *The Jim Bakker Show* as shown on *Revelation in the News*, December 2, 2016, https://www.youtube.com/watch?v=pp7OBPYwLWs.
48. Horn, interview on *The Jim Bakker Show*.
49. Hindson and LaHaye, *The Popular Encyclopedia of Bible Prophecy*, 24.
50. Hindson and LaHaye, *The Popular Encyclopedia of Bible Prophecy*, 371–374.
51. Hindson and LaHaye, *The Popular Encyclopedia of Bible Prophecy*, 119–122.

52. Adam Eliyahu Berkowitz, "The Mystical Gog and Magog Connection Between North Korea and Iran," Breaking Israel News, April 24, 2017, https://www.breaking israelnews.com/87017/one-rabbi-predicted-22-years-ago-koreas-role-end-days -will-shock/#69PXc6wYEBFhzTob.97.

53. Adam Eliyahu Berkowitz, telephone interview with Troy Anderson for *Trumpocalypse*, May 3, 2017.

54. Lucas Tomlinson and Jennifer Griffin, "Pentagon Eyes Iran-North Korea Military Connection," Fox News, May 5, 2017, http://www.foxnews.com/politics/ 2017/05/05/pentagon-eyes-iran-north-korea-military-connection.html.

55. Laura Sigal, "North Korea Threatens Israel with 'Merciless, Thousand-Fold Punishment,'" *Jerusalem Post*, April 29, 2017, http://www.jpost.com/Israel-News/North -Korea-threatens-Israel-with-merciless-thousand-fold-punishment-489316.

Chapter Three: Super-EMP Threat and "Daughter of Babylon"

1. Rabbi Yosef Berger as quoted by Adam Eliyahu Berkowitz, "Prophecy Deciphered After 1,500 Years Reveals North Korean Conflict Precedes Messiah," Breaking Israel News, April 26, 2017, https://www.breakingisraelnews.com/87149/1500 -year-old-hidden-prophecy-finally-revealed-chilling-warning-north-korea/ #ulEPgCevZSYg8VIS.97.

2. Eliezer Danzinger, "Who Are the 36 Hidden Tzadikim?" Chabad.org, http://www .chabad.org/library/article_cdo/aid/837699/jewish/Who-Are-the-36-Hidden -Tzadikim.htm?gclid=Cj0KEQjwi7vIBRDpo9W8y7Ct6ZcBEiQA1CwV2HbaJ lS95yW8aECkz-C6j_zcpqEY7CMJzDT6P4O-U04aAszD8P8HAQ; Adam Eliyahu Berkowitz, telephone interview with Troy Anderson for *Trumpocalypse*, May 3, 2017.

3. Berkowitz, "Prophecy Deciphered After 1,500 Years."

4. Berkowitz, telephone interview with Troy Anderson for *Trumpocalypse*, May 3, 2017; *Nevu'at ha-Yeled*, Jewish Virtual Library, http://www.jewishvirtuallibrary .org/nevu-at-ha-yeled.

5. Berkowitz, telephone interview with Troy Anderson for *Trumpocalypse*, May 3, 2017.

6. *Encyclopaedia Britannica*, s.v., "Ten Lost Tribes of Israel," https://www.britannica .com/topic/Ten-Lost-Tribes-of-Israel; Jonathan Bernis, "Lost No More," *Charisma* magazine, October 2015; Berkowitz, "Prophecy Deciphered After 1,500 Years."

7. Dr. Rivkah Lambert Adler, telephone interview with Troy Anderson for *Trumpocalypse*, May 8, 2017.

8. Peter Vincent Pry, telephone interview with Troy Anderson for *Trumpocalypse*, March 9, 2017; Peter Vincent Pry, *The Long Sunday: Nuclear EMP Attack Scenarios* (Washington, D.C.: Center for Security Policy, 2016), 11; "High and Extra High Voltage Transformers—the Most Critical U.S. Electrical Infrastructure Component—Risk and Impact of Solar Storms & EMP Attacks—U.S. Market, Installed Base and Suppliers 2015–2020 Analysis and Forecasts," Amadee and Company, October 11, 2016, http://www.prnewswire.com/news-releases/ high-and-extra-high-voltage-transformers-the-most-critical-us-electrical -infrastructure-component-risk-and-impact-of-solar-storms--emp-attacksus-market -installed-base-and-suppliers-2015-2020-analysis-and-forecasts-300343119.html.

9. Peter Vincent Pry, "*Popular Mechanics* Publishes 'Fake News' on North Korean Nuclear Threat," letter to the editor, *Popular Mechanics*, April 2017.

10. R. James Woolsey and Peter Vincent Pry, "Don't Underestimate North Korea's Nuclear Arsenal," *Wall Street Journal*, February 27, 2017, https://www.wsj.com/articles/dont-underestimate-north-koreas-nuclear-arsenal-1488239693.

11. Eric Talmadge, "North Korean Official: Ready for War If Trump Wants It," *Newsmax*, April 14, 2017 http://www.newsmax.com/Headline/north-korea-trump-war-vicious/2017/04/14/id/784433/?ns_mail_uid=26940664&ns_mail_job=1725481_04142017&s=al&dkt_nbr=z5y2cbo6; William M. Arkin, "U.S. May Launch Strike If North Korea Reaches for Nuclear Trigger," NBC News, April 14, 2017, http://www.nbcnews.com/news/world/u-s-may-launch-strike-if-north-korea-reaches-nuclear-n746366; Tom Rogan, "The Day the U.S. Strikes North Korea," the Daily Beast, April 13, 2017, http://www.thedailybeast.com/articles/2017/04/14/the-day-the-u-s-strikes-north-korea.html.

12. William Tobey, Harvard University's Belfer Center for Science and International Affairs "Lurking Crises, Hidden Opportunities" Conference, December 16, 2016, http://www.belfercenter.org/event/lurking-crises-hidden-opportunities-2017-national-security-reality-check.

13. Jessica Brown, "Barack Obama Flies to Island in French Polynesia to Relax at Luxury Resort 'the Brando,'" *Telegraph,* March 16, 2017, http://www.telegraph.co.uk/news/2017/03/16/barack-obama-flies-island-french-polynesia-relax-luxury-resort.

14. Thomas E. Ricks, "Elevator Pitches to Trump by the Blob, aka the Foreign Policy Establishment," *Foreign Policy*, December 19, 2016, http://foreignpolicy.com/2016/12/19/elevator-pitches-to-trump-by-the-blob-aka-the-foreign-policy-establishment.

15. Melissa Chan, "Here's What Donald Trump Has Said About Nuclear Weapons," *Time*, August 3, 2016, http://time.com/4437089/donald-trump-nuclear-weapons-nukes.

16. "Critical Infrastructure Protection Act (CIPA) Passage Out of Homeland Security Committee Is Decisive Step to Protect the Nation," House Committee on Homeland Security, June 25, 2015, https://homeland.house.gov/press/critical-infrastructure-protection-act-cipa-passage-out-homeland-security-committee.

17. Pry, *The Long Sunday*, 4–5.

18. Pry, "Is the U.S. Prepared for a Nuclear EMP to Shut Down New York City?," the Hill, May 15, 2017, http://thehill.com/blogs/pundits-blog/defense/333377-is-the-us-prepared-for-a-nuclear-emp-to-shut-down-new-york-city.

19. Alix Culbertson, "'Number One Threat' Russia Is a Danger to America's Existence, Top Military Officials Warn," *Daily Express*, December 5, 2016, http://www.express.co.uk/news/world/740009/Russia-biggest-threat-United-States-Nato.

20. Anton Barbashin and Hannah Thoburn, "Putin's Brain," *Foreign Affairs*, March 31, 2014, https://www.foreignaffairs.com/articles/russia-fsu/2014-03-31/putins-brain; James D. Heiser, *The American Empire Should Be Destroyed: Aleksandr Dugin and the Perils of Immanentized Eschatology* (Malone, TX: Repristination Press, 2014), 9, 13, back cover; Robert Zubrin, "Dugin's Evil Theology," *National Review*, June 18, 2014, http://www.nationalreview.com/article/380614/dugins-evil-theology-robert-zubrin; Onur Ant and Henry Meyer, "Alexander Dugin—the One Russian Linking Donald Trump, Vladimir Putin and Recep Tayyip

Erdogan," *Independent,* February 3, 2017, http://www.independent.co.uk/news/world/americas/alexander-dugin-russian-academic-linking-us-president-donald-trump-vladimir-putin-turkey-president-a7560611.html.

21. Benjamin Baruch and J. R. Nyquist, *The New Tactics of Global War: Reflections on the Changing Balance of Power in the Final Days of Peace* (Coeur d' Alene, ID: Scribe Publications, 2015), 8.

22. Patrick Reevell, "Russian Television Warns of Nuclear War amid US Tensions," ABC News, October 14, 2016, http://abcnews.go.com/International/russian-television-warns-nuclear-war-amid-us-tensions/story?id=42773541; Will Worley, "Russia Has Hidden Nuclear Bombs Ready to Detonate Along US Coastline, Says Former Kremlin Spokesman," *Independent,* May 2, 2017, http://www.independent.co.uk/news/world/europe/russia-nuclear-weapons-seeding-us-coastline-kremlin-defence-spokesman-putin-donald-trump-missiles-a7713061.html; "Russia 'Can Launch Tsunami Against U.S. with Nuclear Bombs Buried in Ocean,'" *Telegraph,* May 2, 2017, http://www.telegraph.co.uk/news/2017/05/01/russia-can-launch-tsunami-against-us-nuclear-bombs-buried-ocean; "Russia Conducts Largest Number of Defense Drills Since the Cold War," *New York Post,* November 1, 2016, http://nypost.com/2016/11/01/russia-conducts-largest-number-of-defense-drills-since-the-cold-war; Sebastian Shukla and Laura Smith-Spark, "Russia Unveils 'Satan 2' Missile, Could Wipe Out France or Texas, Report Says," CNN, October 27, 2016, http://www.cnn.com/2016/10/26/europe/russia-nuclear-missile-satan-2; Charlie Bayliss, "Vladimir Putin's Nuclear Weapons 'Could Wipe Out All of America's East Coast in One Swipe,'" *Daily Express,* October 24, 2016, http://www.express.co.uk/news/world/724410/Vladimir-Putin-Russia-east-coast-satan-nuclear-weapon-Hiroshima-Nagasaki-world-war-3.

23. Max Tegmark, "Why 3,000 Scientists Think Nuclear Arsenals Make Us Less Safe," *Scientific American,* May 26, 2017, https://blogs.scientificamerican.com/observations/why-3-000-scientists-think-nuclear-arsenals-make-us-less-safe.

24. "Billy Graham Named on 'Most Admired' List for Six Decades," Billy Graham Evangelistic Association, December 28, 2016, https://billygraham.org/story/billy-graham-named-on-most-admired-list-for-six-decades; Billy Graham, e-mail interview by Troy Anderson for a seven-part World Net Daily series and www.tothesource.org story about the My Hope America with Billy Graham evangelistic outreach, August 20, 2013; Samuel Smith, "Billy Graham's Daughter: God Keeping My Father Alive Might Have Something to Do with the 'Return of Jesus,'" *Christian Post,* May 26, 2016, http://www.christianpost.com/news/billy-grahams-daughter-god-keeping-father-alive-return-of-jesus-164541.

25. Douglas W. Krieger, Dene McGriff, and S. Douglas Woodward, *The Final Babylon: America and the Coming of Antichrist* (Oklahoma City, OK: Faith Happens, 2013), 3–4.

26. Mark Corner, "Towards a Global Sharing of Sovereignty," Federal Trust for Education & Research, August 2008, http://fedtrust.co.uk/wp-content/uploads/2014/12/Essay44_Corner.pdf.

27. Chuck Missler, telephone interview with Troy Anderson for *Trumpocalypse* and "The End Is Really Near" in the September 2015 issue of *Charisma* magazine, June 24, 2015.

28. Baruch and Nyquist, *The New Tactics of Global War*, 8.
29. S. Douglas Woodward, *Is Russia Destined to Nuke the U.S.?* (Oklahoma City, OK: Faith-Happens, 2015), 31; Woodward, telephone interview with Troy Anderson for *Trumpocalypse*, December 9, 2016.
30. David Wilkerson, "In One Hour Everything Is Going to Change," World Challenge, September 3, 2007, https://worldchallenge.org/newsletter/one-hour-everything -going-change.

Chapter Four: Deep State Coup and Occult Explosion

1. Lieutenant Colonel Bob Maginnis as quoted by Michael W. Chapman, "FRC's Lt. Col. Maginnis: There's 'a Lot of Witchcraft' in Washington, D.C.," CNSNews .com, April 24, 2017, http://www.cnsnews.com/blog/michael-w-chapman/lt-col -maginnis-theres-lot-witchcraft-washington-dc.
2. S. Douglas Woodward, "The Devil You Say? And Satanic Ritual Abuse?" Doomsday Doug, November 4, 2016, http://faith-happens.com/the-devil-you-say-and -satanic-ritual-abuse.
3. Angie Drobnic Holan, "What Ben Carson Said About Hillary Clinton, Saul Alinsky and Lucifer," Politifact, July 20, 2016, http://www.politifact.com/ truth-o-meter/article/2016/jul/20/what-ben-carson-said-about-hillary-clinton -saul-al; Gideon Resnick, "The Devil Is a Woman," the Daily Beast, July 19, 2016, http://www.thedailybeast.com/articles/2016/07/20/ben-carson-ties-hillary -clinton-to-lucifer-as-gop-swaps-campaign-for-witch-trial; Abby Ohlheiser, "No, John Podesta Didn't Drink Bodily Fluids at a Secret Satanist Dinner," *Washington Post*, November 4, 2016, https://www.washingtonpost.com/news/the-intersect/ wp/2016/11/04/no-john-podesta-didnt-drink-bodily-fluids-at-a-secret-satanist -dinner/?utm_term=.11f2c046d488.
4. Amy Goodman and Glenn Greenwald, "Greenwald: Empowering the 'Deep State' to Undermine Trump Is Prescription for Destroying Democracy," Democracy Now, February 16, 2017, https://www.democracynow.org/2017/2/16/greenwald _empowering_the_deep_state_to.
5. Goodman and Greenwald, "Greenwald: Empowering the 'Deep State.'"
6. Robert Costa, Ashley Parker, and Philip Rucker, "Inside Trump's Fury: The President Rages at Leaks, Setbacks and Accusations," *Washington Post*, March 5, 2017, https://www.washingtonpost.com/politics/inside-trumps-fury-the-president -rages-at-leaks-setbacks-and-accusations/2017/03/05/40713af4-01df-11e7-ad5b -d22680e18d10_story.html?utm_term=.e3d5402e26f0; Paul Sperry, "How Obama Is Scheming to Sabotage Trump's Presidency," *New York Post*, February 11, 2017, http://nypost.com/2017/02/11/how-obama-is-scheming-to-sabotage-trumps -presidency.
7. Brian Bennett and Noah Bierman, "Trump Lashes Out, Calls Russia Investigation a 'Witch Hunt,'" *Los Angeles Times*, May 18, 2017, http://www.latimes.com/poli- tics/la-na-pol-trump-special-counsel-20170518-story.html.
8. Adam Credo, "Investigation: Trump Admin Hit with at Least One National Secu- rity Leak a Day, Threatening U.S. Operations," *Washington Free Beacon*, July 6, 2017,

http://freebeacon.com/national-security/investigation-trump-admin-hit-least -one-national-security-leak-day-threatening-u-s-operations-2.

9. Dan Lyman, "Buchanan: DC Elite Trying to Overturn Election of 'Courageous Trump,'" InfoWars, May 12, 2017, https://www.infowars.com/buchanan-dc-elite -trying-to-overturn-election-of-courageous-trump.

10. Michael Snyder, "The 'Arch of Baal' Was on Display for the Third Time in Honor of the 'World Government Summit,'" Charisma News, February 17, 2017, http://www.charismanews.com/opinion/63105-the-arch-of-baal-was-displayed -for-the-third-time-in-honor-of-the-world-government-summit; Thomas Horn and Josh Peck, *Abaddon Ascending: The Ancient Conspiracy at the Center of CERN's Most Secretive Mission* (Crane, MO: Defender, 2016), back cover; Chelsea Schilling, "What the Devil? Scientists Tap Power of 'Lucifer,'" World Net Daily, January 20, 2013, http://www.wnd.com/2013/01/what-the-devil-scientists-tap-power -of-lucifer/#uddlebZI5GOdktYw.99; Rebecca Boyle, "Lucifer Instrument Helps Astronomers See Through Darkness to Most Distant Observable Objects," *Popular Mechanics*, April 23, 2010, http://www.popsci.com/science/article/2010-04/ devil-named-telescope-helps-astronomers-see-through-darkness; "Wicca: What's the Fascination?," CBN, http://www1.cbn.com/books/wicca%3A-what%27s-the -fascination%3F; Rachel Ray, "Leading US Exorcists Explain Huge Increase in Demand for the Rite—and Priests to Carry Them Out," *Telegraph*, September 26, 2016, http://www.telegraph.co.uk/news/2016/09/26/leading-us-exorcists-explain -huge-increase-in-demand-for-the-rit.

11. William "Bill" Schnoebelen, telephone interview with Troy Anderson for *Trumpocalypse*, November 11, 2016.

12. Lily Rothman, "The Evolution of Modern Satanism in the United States," *Time*, July 27, 2015; Hal Lindsey, "Satan Is Still Alive and Well on Planet Earth," World Net Daily, January 23, 2002, http://www.wnd.com/2002/01/12488; Hal Lindsey with C. C. Carlson, *Satan Is Alive and Well on Planet Earth* (Grand Rapids, MI: Zondervan Publishing House, 1972), 11, 17.

13. Johann Grolle, "Antimatter: Next Holy Grail for Physics," ABC News, July 15, 2012, http://abcnews.go.com/Technology/antimatter-holy-grail-physics/story?id =16765682; Adam Eliyahu Berkowitz, "'Portal-Like Clouds' Form Above Massive Experiment Physicists Say Could Destroy the World," Breaking Israel News, July 7, 2016, https://www.breakingisraelnews.com/71404/physics-experiment-geneva -destroy-universe-one-physicist-says-yes/#joSDKhdkfg0KIlcU.97; Kelly Dickerson, "Stephen Hawking Says 'God Particle' Could Wipe Out the Universe," Live Science, September 8, 2014, http://www.livescience.com/47737-stephen-hawking -higgs-boson-universe-doomsday.html; Horn and Peck, *Abaddon Ascending* (Crane, MO: Defender, 2016), 45–49; "New Portal to Unveil the Dark Sector of the Universe," Science Daily, March 23, 2017, https://www.sciencedaily.com/releases/ 2017/03/170323083904.htm.

14. Snyder, "The 'Arch of Baal' Was on Display."

15. Sean Teehan, "Satanic Temple Headquarters to Open Quietly in Salem," *Boston Globe*, September 20, 2016, https://www.bostonglobe.com/metro/regionals/ north/2016/09/20/satanic-headquarters-hopes-for-quiet-opening-salem/GcS

4kooiHUCdDGdRHVq9xK/story.html; "Satanic Temple to Establish HQ in Historic Home Town of Salem Witch Trials," RT.com, September 20, 2016, https://www.rt.com/usa/3600000-satanic-temple-salem-headquarters; "The Satanic Temple Leverages Religious Freedom Laws to Put After School Clubs in Elementary Schools Nationwide," the Satanic Temple press release, https://afterschoolsa tan.com/press-releases; Travis Weber, "How to Respond to the 'After School Satan Clubs,'" Family Research Council, August 10, 2016, http://www.frcblog .com/2016/08/how-respond-after-school-satan-clubs; "Satanic Temple Cleared to Install Monument for the First Time in Minnesota Park," Fox News, May 8, 2017, http://www.foxnews.com/us/2017/05/08/satanic-temple-cleared-to-install -monument-for-first-time-in-minnesota-park.html.

16. Rachel Ray, "Leading U.S. Exorcists Explain Huge Increase in Demand for the Rite—and Priests to Carry Them Out," *Telegraph*, September 16, 2016, http://www.telegraph.co.uk/news/2016/09/26/leading-us-exorcists-explain-huge -increase-in-demand-for-the-rit.

17. "Witches Cast Mass Spell with Hopes of Removing Trump from Office," Fox News Insider, February 25, 2017, http://insider.foxnews.com/2017/02/25/witches-cast -spell-donald-trump-crescent-moon-removal-office; Chris Spargo, "Double, Double, Donald's in Trouble: Witches Including Lana Del Rey will gather at Midnight to Cast a Spell on President Trump and His Supporters in Hopes of Banishing Him from Office," *Daily Mail*, February 24, 2017, http://www.dailymail.co.uk/news/ article-4257216/Witches-gather-midnight-cast-spell-Donald-Trump.html#ixzz 4hPI72Xmg; Diana Wagman, "I Put a Spell on You, Mr. President," *Los Angeles Times*, May 23, 2017, http://www.latimes.com/opinion/op-ed/la-oe-wagman -put-a-spell-on-donald-trump-20170523-story.html.

18. Anne Graham Lotz, telephone interview with Troy Anderson for *Trumpocalypse*, June 6, 2017.

19. Dr. Jack Graham, telephone interview with Troy Anderson for "The End Is Really Near" in the September 2015 issue of *Charisma* magazine, May 27, 2015.

20. Lance deHaven-Smith, *Conspiracy Theories in America* (Austin: University of Texas Press, 2013), 7, 21.

21. Liam Stack, "Globalism: A Far-Right Conspiracy Theory Buoyed by Trump," *New York Times*, November 14, 2016, https://www.nytimes.com/2016/11/15/us/ politics/globalism-right-trump.html?_r=0.

22. Joseph E. Uscinski, telephone interview with Troy Anderson for *Trumpocalypse*, February 10, 2017.

23. Mark Hitchcock, *The End* (Carol Stream, IL: Tyndale House Publishers, Inc., 2012), 361.

24. Jim Garlow, "If You're on the Fence About Your Vote, This Pastor Clarifies How the Very Future of America Is at Stake," Charisma News, August 11, 2016, http:// www.charismanews.com/politics/opinion/59206-if-you-re-on-the-fence-about -your-vote-this-pastor-clarifies-how-the-very-future-of-america-is-at-stake.

25. Charles P. Blair and Rebecca L. Earnhardt, "Has the Deep State Hoodwinked Trump?" Bulletin of the Atomic Scientists, May 2, 2017, http://thebulletin.org/ has-deep-state-hoodwinked-trump10730; Rosa Brooks, "3 Ways to Get Rid of

President Trump Before 2020," *Foreign Affairs*, January 30, 2017, http://foreign
policy.com/2017/01/30/3-ways-to-get-rid-of-president-trump-before-2020
-impeach-25th-amendment-coup.

26. Jim Marrs, *Our Occulted History: Do the Global Elite Conceal Ancient Aliens?* (New
York: William Morrow, 2013), 54, 134, 154–157; "The Illuminati," *The Media
Source Presents Secret Societies: The Truth Revealed*, 2013; Dr. I. D. E. Thomas, *The
Omega Conspiracy: Satan's Last Assault on God's Kingdom* (Crane, MO: Anomalos
Publishing House, 2008), 23–24.

27. *Encyclopaedia Britannica*, s.v., "Tower of Babel"; Ed Hindson and Tim LaHaye,
The Popular Encyclopedia of Bible Prophecy (Eugene, OR: Harvest House Publishers, 2004), 42–44.

28. Gary Stearman, "Revisiting the Tower of Babel," *Prophecy Watchers*, August 2016.

29. Paul McGuire, "Overlords of Chaos: Illuminati Plan for WW III, Stargate Technology, and the End of the Age," News with Views, April 14, 2014, http://www
.newswithviews.com/McGuire/paul208.htm.

30. "Illuminati: Eye of Power," *Secret Societies: Unlocking the Mysteries of Inner Circles
and Cults Through the Ages*, 2015; "Secret Societies: Infiltrating the Inner Circle,"
Newsweek, 2015; Jim Marrs, *The Illuminati: The Secret Society That Hijacked the
World* (Detroit, MI: Visible Ink Press, 2017), 336.

31. Marrs, *The Illuminati*, 86–92.

32. Marrs, *The Illuminati*, xiii–xiv.

33. Barna Group, "Competing Worldviews Influence Today's Christians," May 9,
2017, https://www.barna.com/research/competing-worldviews-influence-todays
-christians.

34. Paul McGuire, "Babylon-A-Go-Go: The UN, the Pope & World Government," Paul McGuire Report, September 21, 2015, http://www.paulmcguire.us/
nwv092815.html; Patrick M. Wood, *Technocracy Rising: The Trojan Horse of Global
Transformation* (Mesa, AZ: Coherent Publishing, 2015), 14.

35. Brent Jessop, "The Mass Media Division of UNESCO," Global Research Cen-
tre for Research on Globalization, August 14, 2008, http://www.globalresearch
.ca/the-mass-media-division-of-unesco/9830.

36. Aldous Huxley, *Brave New World Revisited*, 1958, https://www.huxley.net/bnw
-revisited.

37. Arthur C. Clarke, "Magic's just science that we don't understand yet," Goodreads,
https://www.goodreads.com/quotes/547452-magic-s-just-science-that-we-don
-t-understand-yet.

38. Christen Nichols, "The Rothschild Family's Net Worth Is $400 Billion," Bankrate
.com, April 21, 2017, http://www.bankrate.com/lifestyle/celebrity-money/rothschild
-family-net-worth; "The World's Richest Families Revealed," MSN.com, April
11, 2016, https://www.msn.com/en-in/money/photos/the-world%E2%80%99s
-richest-families-revealed/ss-BBmRgsr#image=32; Richard Kersley and Markus
Stierli, "Global Wealth in 2015: Underlying Trends Remain Positive," Credit
Suisse Research Institute, January 10, 2015, https://www.credit-suisse.com/us/
en/about-us/research/research-institute/news-and-videos/articles/news-and
-expertise/2015/10/en/global-wealth-in-2015-underlying-trends-remain-positive
.html.

39. John Coleman, *The Conspirators' Hierarchy: The Committee of 300* (Las Vegas, NV: World Int. Review, 2010), ii, iii, 163, 302–303; "History," Lucis Trust, https://www.lucistrust.org/about_us/history.

40. Edward L. Bernays, "The conscious and intelligent manipulation of the organized habits and opinions of the masses is an important element in democratic society. Those who manipulate this unseen mechanism of society constitute an invisible government which is the true ruling power of our country...We are governed, our minds are molded, our tastes formed, our ideas suggested, largely by men we have never heard of," Goodreads, https://www.goodreads.com/quotes/203430 -the-conscious-and-intelligent-manipulation-of-the-organized-habits-and.

41. Ian Schwartz, "Kucinich: 'Deep State' Trying to Take Down Trump, 'Our Country Is Under Attack Within,'" RealClearPolitics.com, May 18, 2017, http://www .realclearpolitics.com/video/2017/05/18/kucinich_deep_state_trying_to_take _down_trump_our_country_is_under_attack_within.html.

42. David Remnick, "There Is No Deep State: The Problem in Washington Is Not a Conspiracy Against the President; It's the President Himself," *New Yorker*, March 20, 2017, http://www.newyorker.com/magazine/2017/03/20/there-is-no-deep-state.

43. Marrs, *The Illuminati*, 221.

44. "The Churchill You Didn't Know," *Guardian*, November 27, 2002, https://www .theguardian.com/theguardian/2002/nov/28/features11.g21.

Chapter Five: The Great Mass Deception

1. Bert M. Faris, "The Great Deception in the American Church," Charisma News, May 19, 2014, http://www.charismanews.com/opinion/the-flaming-herald/43894 -the-great-deception-in-the-american-church.

2. Dave Hunt, *Occult Invasion: The Subtle Seduction of the World and Church* (Eugene, OR: Harvest House Publishers, 1998), 568.

3. Bill Schnoebelen, telephone interview with Troy Anderson for *Trumpocalypse*, November 11, 2016.

4. Thomas R. Horn, *Zenith 2016: Did Something Begin in the Year 2012 That Will Reach Its Apex in 2016?* (Crane, MO: Defender, 2013), 54, 80–81.

5. Mark Hitchcock and Jeff Kinley, *The Coming Apostasy: Exposing the Sabotage of Christianity from Within* (Carol Stream, IL: Tyndale Momentum, 2017), vii, 24, 31–32.

6. Derek P. Gilbert, telephone interview with Troy Anderson for *Trumpocalypse*, May 5, 2017; Ed Stetzer, "Barna: How Many Have a Biblical Worldview?" *Christianity Today*, March 9, 2009, http://www.christianitytoday.com/edstetzer/2009/march/ barna-how-many-have-biblical-worldview.html.

7. "100 Million Church Members Don't Understand Bible Prophecy," Olive Tree Ministries, September 5, 2009, https://www.olivetreeviews.org/news/prophecy -watch/item/462-100-million-church-members-dont-understand-bible-prophecy; Billy Crone, telephone interview with Troy Anderson for *Trumpocalypse*, March 7, 2017; Paul McGuire, e-mail interview with Troy Anderson for *Trumpocalypse*, May 26, 2017; Jan Markell, telephone interview with Troy Anderson for *Trumpocalypse*, January 13, 2017.

Notes

8. Hunt, *Occult Invasion*, 313.
9. Crone, telephone interview with Troy Anderson for *Trumpocalypse*, March 7, 2017; Billy Crone, "New Age or New Ager?" *Prophecy in the News*, March 2017; Billy Scher, "The Serious Case for Oprah 2020," Politico, March 1, 2017, http://www.politico.com/magazine/story/2017/03/oprah-winfrey-run-president-2020-reasons-trump-214851.
10. *Encyclopaedia Britannica*, s.v., "New Age Movement," https://www.britannica.com/topic/New-Age-movement.
11. "History," Lucis Trust, https://www.lucistrust.org/about_us/history; Crone, telephone interview with Troy Anderson for *Trumpocalypse*, March 7, 2017.
12. Crone, "New Age or New Ager?"
13. Barna Group, "Competing Worldviews Influence Today's Christians," May 9, 2017, https://www.barna.com/research/competing-worldviews-influence-todays-christians; Albert Mohler, "All Roads Lead to Heaven?—Kathleen Parker Does Theology," May 12, 2010, http://www.albertmohler.com/2010/05/12/all-roads-lead-to-heaven-kathleen-parker-does-theology; Jeff M. Sellers, "The Higher Self Gets Down to Business," *Christianity Today*, February 1, 2003, http://www.christianitytoday.com/ct/2003/february/1.34.html.
14. Linda Goudsmit, "Globalism: Persuading the Individual to Stop Being an Individual," *Canada Free Press*, May 23, 2017, http://canadafreepress.com/article/globalism-persuading-the-individual-to-stop-being-an-individual.
15. Dan Merica and Sophie Tatum, "Clinton Expresses Regret for Saying 'Half' of Trump Supporters Are 'Deplorables,'" CNN, September 12, 2016, http://www.cnn.com/2016/09/09/politics/hillary-clinton-donald-trump-basket-of-deplorables; Paul McGuire, "Born Again Babylon: U.N. Luciferian Global State," News with Views, September 21, 2015, http://www.newswithviews.com/McGuire/paul268.htm.
16. Jim Marrs, *Population Control: How Corporate Owners are Killing Us* (New York: William Morrow, 2015), 1, 5–6.
17. Marrs, *Population Control*, 1–4.
18. Ronald Bailey, "Tom Hanks Endorses 'Malthusian Theory' of Overpopulation," Reason.com, October 26, 2016, http://reason.com/blog/2016/10/26/tom-hanks-endorses-malthusian-theory-o1; Marrs, *Population Control*, 6–7; Prince Philip, "In the event that I am reincarnated, I would like to return as a deadly virus, in order to contribute something to solve overpopulation," Goodreads, https://www.goodreads.com/quotes/6486538-in-the-event-that-i-am-reincarnated-i-would-like; "Population," Accuracy in Media, https://www.aim.org/wls/category/population.
19. Ben Farmer, "Bioterrorism Could Kill More People Than Nuclear War, Bill Gates to Warn World Leaders," *Telegraph*, February 18, 2017, http://www.telegraph.co.uk/news/2017/02/17/biological-terrorism-could-kill-people-nuclear-attacks-bill.
20. *An Evangelical Agenda, 1984 and Beyond: Addresses, Responses, and Scenarios from the Continuing Consultation on Future Evangelical Concerns, Held in Overland Park, Kansas, December 11–14, 1979* (Pasadena, CA: William Carey Library, 1979), 35; Hunt, *Occult Invasion*, 196, 217; Sellers, "The Higher Self Gets Down to Business."

21. Todd Van Luling, "5 Beatles Fan Theories You'll Think Are So Crazy They Might Just Be True," *Huffington Post*, December 3, 2014, http://www.huffingtonpost.com/2014/12/03/the-beatles-fan-theories_n_6258074.html; John Coleman, *The Conspirators' Hierarchy: The Committee of 300* (Las Vegas, NV: World Int. Review, 2010), 77; John Coleman, *Tavistock Institute of Human Relations: Shaping the Moral, Spiritual, Cultural, Political, and Economic Decline of the United States of America* (Carson City, NV: World in Review, 2005), vii.

22. Daniel Estulin, *Tavistock Institute: Social Engineering the Masses* (Walterville, OR: Trine Day LLC, 2015), 1–3.

23. "Karl Marx: From Christian to Satanist," World Net Daily, November 28, 2010, http://www.wnd.com/2010/11/232217; John J. Walters, "Communism Killed 94M in 20th Century, Feels Need to Kill Again," Reason.com, March 13, 2013, http://reason.com/blog/2013/03/13/communism-killed-94m-in-20th-century.

24. David Horowitz, telephone interview with Troy Anderson for *Trumpocalypse*, January 23, 2017.

25. "We Are All Still Children of the Frankfurt School," the Nation, May 23, 2017, http://www.nationmultimedia.com/news/opinion/letter_to_editor/30316005; Clare Ellis, "The Socialist-Capitalist Alliance: the Fabian Society, the Frankfurt School, and Big Business: Part I," Council of European Canadians, June 23, 2014, http://www.eurocanadian.ca/2014/06/socialist-capitalist-alliance-fabian-society-frankfurt-school-and-big-business-part1.html.

26. Bertrand Russell, *Impact of Science on Society* (London: Allen & Unwin, 1952); Bertrand Russell, "The social psychologists of the future will have a number of classes of school children on whom they will try different methods of producing an unshakable conviction that snow is black. Various results will soon be arrived at. First, that the influence of home is obstructive. Second, that not much can be done unless indoctrination begins before the age of ten. Third, that verses set to music and repeatedly intoned are very effective," Wikiquote, https://en.wikiquote.org/wiki/The_Impact_of_Science_on_Society.

27. The Beatles Wiki, "I Am the Walrus," http://beatles.wikia.com/wiki/I_am_the_Walrus.

28. Michael W. Chapman, "Rev. Graham on 'The Great Deception': Hollywood Wants You to Celebrate Sin," CNSNews.com, October 18, 2016, http://www.cnsnews.com/blog/michael-w-chapman/rev-graham-great-deception-hollywood-wants-you-celebrate-sin.

29. Markell, telephone interview with Troy Anderson for *Trumpocalypse*, January 13, 2017.

Chapter Six: The Trump Revolution

1. President Donald J. Trump, Joint Session of Congress Address, February 28, 2017.

2. Jessica Chasmar, "Democrats Abandoned Middle Class in 2016 Election, Joe Biden Says," *Washington Times*, March 31, 2017, http://www.washingtontimes.com/news/2017/mar/31/joe-biden-democrats-abandoned-middle-class-during.

3. Paola Chavez and Veronica Stracqualursi, "From 'Crooked Hillary' to 'Little Marco,' Donald Trump's Many Nicknames," ABC News, May 11, 2016, http://abcnews

.go.com/Politics/crooked-hillary-marco-donald-trumps-nicknames/story?id
=39035114.

4. Ben Jacobs, "Donald Trump Calls Pope Francis 'Disgraceful' for Question-
ing His Faith," *Guardian*, February 18, 2016, https://www.theguardian.com/
us-news/2016/feb/18/donald-trump-pope-francis-christian-wall-mexico-border;
Paola Chavez, Meghan Keneally, and Veronica Stracqualursi, "How the War of
Words Between Trump and Pope Francis Has Evolved," ABC News, May 23, 2017,
http://abcnews.go.com/Politics/war-words-trump-pope-francis-evolved/story
?id=47582353.

5. Joseph Farah, "The Coming Trump Revolution," World Net Daily, February
21, 2017, http://www.wnd.com/2017/02/the-coming-trump-revolution; Jennifer
Harper, "Franklin Graham Asks Nation to Pray for America on Election Day,
Calls for 'Christian Revolution,'" *Washington Times*, November 6, 2016, http://
www.washingtontimes.com/news/2016/nov/6/frankling-graham-asks-nation
-to-pray-on-election-d.

6. Franklin Graham, "Franklin Graham: We Need a Christian Revolution in America,"
Billy Graham Evangelistic Association, November 2, 2016, https://billygraham.org/
story/franklin-graham-we-need-a-christian-revolution-in-america.

7. Franklin Graham, "Franklin Graham: Pray for Our New President," Billy Graham Evangelistic Association, November 21, 2016, https://billygraham.org/
story/franklin-graham-pray-for-our-new-president.

8. Chasmar, "Democrats Abandoned Middle Class in 2016 Election."

9. David A. Fahrenthold, "Trump Recorded Having Extremely Lewd Conversation
About Women in 2005," *Washington Post*, October 8, 2016, https://www.washing
tonpost.com/politics/trump-recorded-having-extremely-lewd-conversation-about
-women-in-2005/2016/10/07/3b9ce776-8cb4-11e6-bf8a-3d26847eeed4_story
.html?utm_term=.2e2d018eb301.

10. S. Douglas Woodward, telephone interview with Troy Anderson for *Trumpocalypse*,
December 9, 2016.

11. Daniel Franklin, "From the Editor," *Economist*, January 2017, http://www
.theworldin.com/edition/2017/article/12575/world-2017.

12. Marc Fisher and Michael Kranish, *Trump Revealed: An American Journey of Ambition, Ego, Money and Power* (London: Simon & Schuster, 2016), 3.

13. Nancy Gibbs, "The Choice," *Time*, December 19, 2016.

14. Aaron Blake, "Donald Trump's Strategy in Three Words: 'Americanism, Not
Globalism,'" *Washington Post*, July 22, 2016, https://www.washingtonpost.com/
news/the-fix/wp/2016/07/22/donald-trump-just-put-his-border-wall-around-the
-entire-united-states/?utm_term=.11c44b32ada4.

15. Donald J. Trump, "Remarks by President Trump at the Faith and Freedom Coalition's Road to Majority Conference," White House, June 8, 2017, https://www
.whitehouse.gov/the-press-office/2017/06/08/remarks-president-trump-faith-and
-freedom-coalitions-road-majority.

16. Sid Roth, telephone interview with Troy Anderson for *Trumpocalypse*, January 30,
2017.

17. "President Trump," *Newsweek* Special Commemorative Edition, November 2016; "Donald Trump," Biography.com, https://www.biography.com/people/donald-trump

-9511238; *Encyclopaedia Britannica*, s.v., "Donald Trump," https://www.britan nica.com/biography/Donald-Trump; Fisher and Kranish, *Trump Revealed: An American Journey*, 22–27; Steve Dougherty, "Hazed and Confused," *Time* Special Edition, November, 2016.

18. Fisher and Kranish, *Trump Revealed: An American Journey*, 35, 37, 41.

19. "In the Beginning," *Newsweek* Special Commemorative Edition, November 2016; Fisher and Kranish, *Trump Revealed: An American Journey*, 81.

20. "The Life of Trump," *Time* Special Edition, November 2016.

21. "Donald Trump," Biography.com, https://www.biography.com/people/donald -trump-9511238.

22. "Donald J. Trump Biography," the Trump Organization, http://www.trump.com/ biography; "Name Brand," *Newsweek* Special Commemorative Edition, November 2016.

23. Fisher and Kranish, *Trump Revealed: An American Journey*, 1; Brandon Rotting-haus and Justin Vaughn, "New Ranking of U.S. Presidents Puts Lincoln at No. 1, Obama at 18; Kennedy Judged Most Overrated," *Washington Post*, February 16, 2015, https://www.washingtonpost.com/news/monkey-cage/wp/2015/02/16/ new-ranking-of-u-s-presidents-puts-lincoln-1-obama-18-kennedy-judged-most -over-rated/?utm_term=.2a9cfce43f87.

24. Donald J. Trump, *Crippled America: How to Make America Great Again* (New York: Threshold Editions, 2015), 1–4.

25. Matthew Nussbaum, "Has Trump Found Religion in the Oval Office?" Politico, April 16, 2017, http://www.politico.com/story/2017/04/has-trump-found-religion -in-the-oval-office-237239.

26. James Dobson, "Dr. James Dobson on Donald Trump's Christian Faith," Dr. James Dobson's Family Talk, http://drjamesdobson.org/news/dr-james-dobson -on-trumps-christian-faith.

27. Jim Garlow, telephone interview with Troy Anderson for *Trumpocalypse*, July 7, 2017.

28. Alex Ross, "The Frankfurt School Knew Trump Was Coming," *New Yorker*, December 6, 2016, http://www.newyorker.com/culture/cultural-comment/the -frankfurt-school-knew-trump-was-coming.

29. Dan P. McAdams, "The Mind of Donald Trump," *Atlantic,* June 2016, https://www .theatlantic.com/magazine/archive/2016/06/the-mind-of-donald-trump/480771.

30. Robert Reich, "Robert Reich: How to Tell Whether Trump Is a Dictator," *News-week*, May 1, 2017, http://www.newsweek.com/robert-reich-how-tell-whether-trump -dictator-592238.

31. Ruth Ben-Ghiat, "Trump Is Following the Authoritarian Playbook," CNN, January 17, 2017, http://www.cnn.com/2017/01/16/opinions/trump-following -authoritarian-playbook-ben-ghiat/index.html.

32. Associated Press and Ariel Zilber, "Obama Has Made Life Worse for Young People: The 'Youth Misery Index' Has Risen by 36% to Its Highest Point in History Since He Entered Office," *Daily Mail*, January 17, 2017, http://www.dailymail.co.uk/ news/article-4128088/Poll-Young-Americans-fear-worse-post-Trump.html;ErikMebust, "The Economic Crisis, Addiction, and Suicide," *Wilson Quarterly*, Summer 2016, https://wilsonquarterly.com/quarterly/the-decline-of-the-american-middle-class/the-economic-crisis-addiction-and-suicide.

33. "Declaration of Independence," USHistory.org, http://www.ushistory.org/declaration/document.

34. Jim Marrs, *The Illuminati: The Secret Society That Hijacked the World* (Detroit, MI: Visible Ink Press, 2017), 227–228, 234.

35. John J. Walters, "Communism Killed 94M in 20th Century, Feels Need to Kill Again," Reason.com, March 13, 2013, http://reason.com/blog/2013/03/13/communism-killed-94m-in-20th-century.

36. Tim LaHaye, e-mail interview with Troy Anderson for "The End Is Really Near" in September 2015 *Charisma* magazine, May 27, 2015.

37. "Democracy on Deadline," PBS, http://www.pbs.org/independentlens/democracyondeadline/mediaownership.html; Michael Carlson, David Rockefeller obituary, *Guardian*, March 26, 2017, https://www.theguardian.com/us-news/2017/mar/26/david-rockefeller-obituary.

Chapter Seven: Battle Against the Globalist Elite

1. Donald J. Trump, campaign speech, June 22, 2016, http://www.breitbart.com/2016-presidential-race/2016/06/22/2016-election-trumps-policy-americanism-vs-clintons-policy-globalism.

2. Matt Drudge, tweet in response to Trump's speech, June 22, 2016, http://www.breitbart.com/2016-presidential-race/2016/06/22/2016-election-trumps-policy-americanism-vs-clintons-policy-globalism.

3. *Encyclopaedia Britannica*, s.v., "Tower of Babel," https://www.britannica.com/topic/Tower-of-Babel.

4. *Secrets: Tower of Babel*, Smithsonian Channel, June 17–18, 2017, https://www.smithsonianchannel.com/shows/secrets/tower-of-babel/1003102/3437403.

5. Adam Eliyahu Berkowitz, "Tower of Babel Discovered? Ancient Tablet Describes Mesopotamian Structure Built By 'Multitudes,'" Breaking Israel News, May 8, 2017, https://www.breakingisraelnews.com/87748/ancient-tablet-proving-existence-tower-babel-deciphered-100-years-video/#voubrLvTYOoWYrEa.97.

6. John Baines, Leonard H. Lusko, Byron E. Shafer, and David P. Silverman, *Ancient Egypt: Gods, Myths, and Personal Practice* (Ithaca, NY: Cornell University Press, 1999), 117; "Nothing New Under Heaven," *Economist*, January 16, 2011, http://www.economist.com/node/18836024; Evelyn S. Shuckburg, *The Histories of Polybius*, vol. 1 (New York: Macmillan and Co., 1889).

7. Dave Hunt, *A Woman Rides the Beast* (Eugene, OR: Harvest House Publishers, 1994), 43, 45.

8. Hunt, *A Woman Rides the Beast*, 52–53.

9. Joel Richardson, *Mystery Babylon: Unlocking the Bible's Greatest Prophetic Mystery* (Washington, D.C.: WND Books, 2017), 42–45; John F. Walvoord, *The Prophecy Knowledge Handbook* (Wheaton, IL: Victor Books, 1990), 604–610.

10. Chuck Missler, telephone interview with Troy Anderson for "The Great Convergence" in the September 2015 issue of *Charisma* magazine, June 24, 2015.

11. "Gallery of World Visionaries," Democratic World Federalists, http://www.dwfed.org/gallery-of-world-visionaries; John Fonte, "The False Utopia of Global Governance," *Charisma* magazine, September 2015.

12. Winston Church, Wikiquote, https://en.wikiquote.org/wiki/Talk:Winston_ Churchill; Albert Einstein, *The Einstein Reader* (New York: Citadel, 2006), 125.
13. Christoph Ash, "Bill Gates: 'We Need a World Government,'" *Huffington Post*, January 27, 2015, http://www.huffingtonpost.de/2015/01/27/bill-gates-wir-brauchen -eine-weltregierung_n_6556658.html?utm_hp_ref=germany.
14. Jim Marrs, *The Illuminati: The Secret Society That Hijacked the World* (Detroit, MI: Visible Ink Press, 2017), 251–252.
15. *Encyclopaedia Britannica*, s.v., "Eugenics," https://www.britannica.com/science/ eugenics-genetics.
16. "Planned Parenthood and Racism," Students for Life, http://studentsforlife.org/ planned-parenthood-and-racism; Becky Yeh, "7 Incredibly Shocking Quotes from Planned Parenthood Founder Margaret Sanger," Life News, February 23, 2015, http://www.lifenews.com/2015/02/23/7-shocking-quotes-from-planned-parent hood-founder-margaret-sanger.
17. Marrs, *The Illuminati*, 76–77, 278–281; Jim Marrs, *The Rise of the Fourth Reich: The Secret Societies That Threaten to Take Over America* (New York: William Morrow, 2008), 19.
18. Mike Rothschild, "Secret Technologies Invented by the Nazis," Ranker.com, http:// www.ranker.com/list/secret-technologies-invented-by-nazis/mike-rothschild; Annie Jacobsen, *Operation Paperclip: The Secret Intelligence Program That Brought Nazi Scientists to America* (New York: Back Bay Books, 2014), xi.
19. Adolf Hitler, *New World Order* (unpublished manuscript, 1928), https://archive .org/stream/pdfy-0IryYbwVIPGFodSS/Hitler%20-%20New%20World%20 Order%20(1928)_djvu.txt; Marrs, *The Illuminati*, 277; Marrs, *The Rise of the Fourth Reich*, 1–16; Mark Hitchcock, *The End of Money: Bible Prophecy and the Coming Economic Collapse* (Eugene, OR: Harvest House Publishers, 2009, 2013), 13–19; Hal Lindsey, *The Late Great Planet Earth* (Grand Rapids, MI: Zondervan, 1970), 99, 103.
20. *Encyclopaedia Britannica*, s.v., "European Union," https://www.britannica.com/ topic/European-Union; Marrs, *The Rise of the Fourth Reich*, 215–216.
21. Ambrose Evans-Pritchard, "The European Union Always Was a CIA Project, As Brexiteers Discover," *Telegraph,* April 27, 2016, http://www.telegraph.co.uk/ business/2016/04/27/the-european-union-always-was-a-cia-project-as-brexiteers -discov; Patrick M. Wood, *Technocracy Rising* (Mesa, AZ: Coherent Publishing, 2015), xii, 60.
22. "The Founding Fathers of the EU," European Union, https://europa.eu/european -union/about-eu/history/founding-fathers_en.
23. Justin Trudeau, "Leaders' Statement on a North American Climate, Clean Energy, and Environment Partnership," Prime Minister of Canada, June 29, 2016, http:// pm.gc.ca/eng/news/2016/06/29/leaders-statement-north-american-climate-clean -energy-and-environment-partnership.
24. Wood, *Technocracy Rising*, 60.
25. *Encyclopaedia Britannica*, s.v., "Lisbon Treaty," https://www.britannica.com/ event/Lisbon-Treaty; "Hungary: Orban Accuses EU of 'Sovietization,' Calls for Stronger Borders," Sputnik International, October 24, 2016, https://sputniknews .com/europe/201610241046673329-hungary-eu-sovietization-europe; Ted Widmer,

"Draining the Swamp," *New Yorker*, January 19, 2017, http://www.newyorker
.com/news/news-desk/draining-the-swamp.

26. Jack Kinsella, "A Woman Rides the Beast," the Omega Letter, June 27, 2005,
http://www.omegaletter.com/articles/articles.asp?ArticleID=5581.

27. Ron Rhodes, telephone interview with Troy Anderson for "The Great Convergence" in the September 2015 issue of *Charisma* magazine, January 28, 2015.

28. Ian Johnson, "Seven in 10 Brits Support 'World Government' to Protect
Humanity from Global Catastrophes," *Independent*, May 23, 2017, http://www
.independent.co.uk/News/uk/home-news/climate-change-global-warming
-nuclear-war-asteroid-pandemic-volcano-global-catastrophe-a7752171.html;
"Global Challenges Foundation Global Risks Survey," ComRes, May 24, 2017, http://
www.comresglobal.com/polls/global-challenges-foundation-global-risks-survey.

29. Meghan Werft, "The State with the Highest Homelessness Rate Could Be First
to Create Universal Basic Income," Global Citizen, June 16, 2017, https://www
.globalcitizen.org/en/content/hawaii-universal-basic-income-bill.

30. Owen Cotton-Barratt, Sebastian Farquhar, John Halstead, Stefan Schubert, and
Andrew Snyder-Beattie, "Global Catastrophic Risks 2016," Global Challenges
Foundation, https://api.globalchallenges.org/static/reports/Global-Catastrophic
-Risk-Annual-Report-2016.pdf.

31. Owen Cotton-Barratt, Haydn Beifield, Sebastian Farquhar, John Halstead, Stefan
Schubert, and Andrew Snyder-Beattie, "Existential Risk: Diplomacy and Governance," Global Priorities Project 2017, February 3, 2017, http://globalprioritiespro
ject.org/2017/02/existential-risk-diplomacy-and-governance.

32. John Fonte, telephone interview with Troy Anderson for "The Great Convergence"
in the September 2015 issue of *Charisma* magazine, June 9, 2015.

33. John Fonte, "The False Utopia of Global Governance," *Charisma* magazine, September 2015.

34. Caryn Carver, "The Who's Who of the 2015 Global Citizen Festival," Global
Citizen, September 21, 2015, https://www.globalcitizen.org/en/content/the-whos
-who-of-the-2015-global-citizen-festival.

35. "BMI Announces Top 100 Songs of the Century," BMI, December 13, 1999, https://
www.bmi.com/news/entry/19991214_bmi_announces_top_100_songs_of_the
_century; "500 Greatest Songs of All Time," *Rolling Stone*, http://www.rollingstone
.com/music/lists/the-500-greatest-songs-of-all-time-20110407/john-lennon
-imagine-20110516; AZLyrics, "John Lennon Lyrics," http://www.azlyrics.com/
lyrics/johnlennon/imagine.html.

36. "Obama's 2008 Berlin Speech vs. Today's, by the Numbers, Words, and Themes,"
Atlantic, June 19, 2013, https://www.theatlantic.com/national/archive/2013/06/
obamas-2008-berlin-speech-vs-2013-brandenburg-gate-speech/314084.

37. Alex Newman, "UN Agenda 2030: A Recipe for Global Socialism," *New American*, January 6, 2016, https://www.thenewamerican.com/tech/environment/item/
22267-un-agenda-2030-a-recipe-for-global-socialism.

38. Michael Snyder, "This Happened in September: The UN Launched 'The Global
Goals'—a Blueprint for a United World," *The Economic Collapse Blog*, September 28,
2015, http://theeconomiccollapseblog.com/archives/this-happened-in-september
-the-un-launched-the-global-goals-a-blueprint-for-a-united-world.

39. "Goal 10: Reduce Inequality Within and Among Countries," United Nations, http://www.un.org/sustainabledevelopment/inequality.
40. Newman, "UN Agenda 2030: A Recipe for Global Socialism."
41. "62 People Own Same Wealth as Half the World," press release from Oxfam, January 18, 2016, https://www.oxfamamerica.org/press/62-people-own-same -wealth-as-half-the-world; Robert Gebeloff and Dionne Searcy, "Middle Class Shrinks Further As More Fall Out Instead of Climbing Up," *New York Times*, January 25, 2015, https://www.nytimes.com/2015/01/26/business/economy/middle -class-shrinks-further-as-more-fall-out-instead-of-climbing-up.html?_r=0.
42. Wood, *Technocracy Rising*, 80, 90–91, 97.
43. Jerome R. Corsi, "Author: Vatican Aligns with U.N. on 'World Governance,'" World Net Daily, April 15, 2015, http://www.wnd.com/2015/04/author-vatican -aligns-with-u-n-on-world-governance; John Hooper and Stephanie Kirchgaessner, "Pope Francis Warns of Destruction of Earth's Ecosystem in Leaked Encyclical," *Guardian*, June 16, 2015, https://www.theguardian.com/world/2015/jun/15/pope -francis-destruction-ecosystem-leaked-encyclical.
44. *Encyclopaedia Britannica*, s.v., "Antiglobalization," https://www.britannica.com/ event/antiglobalization.
45. Sarah McCammon, "Make Britain Great Again? Donald Trump's Remarkable Reaction to 'Brexit,'" NPR, June 24, 2016, http://www.npr.org/2016/06/24/483353866/ make-britain-great-again-donald-trumps-remarkable-reaction-to-brexit.
46. Tim Hains, "Trump Accepts Nomination: Americanism, Not Globalism Will Be Our Credo," Real Clear Politics, July 21, 2016, https://www.realclearpolitics .com/video/2016/07/21/trump_nominated_we_will_honor_the_american_people _with_the_truth_and_nothing_else.html.
47. "Lance Wallnau: Why Trump Is 'God's Chaos Candidate' and 'Wrecking Ball,'" CBN News, March 21, 2017, http://www1.cbn.com/cbnnews/us/2017/march/ lance-wallnau-weighs-in-on-gods-chaos-candidate-now-americas-president.
48. Lance Wallnau, *The Jim Bakker Show*, February 3, 2017, https://www.youtube .com/watch?v=JXrl3wE-u94; *Encyclopaedia Britannica,* s.v., "Cyrus the Great," https://www.britannica.com/biography/Cyrus-the-Great.

Chapter Eight: The Illuminati's Secret Plan

1. Manly P. Hall, *The Secret Destiny of America* (New York: Jeremy P. Tarcher/Penguin, 1944), 44.
2. Alice Bailey, *The Externalization of the Hierarchy* (New York: Lucis Trust, 1957), 485–486.
3. Jeremiah 23:24 (NIV).
4. Lucis Trust, "The Esoteric Meaning of Lucifer," https://www.lucistrust.org/ arcane_school/talks_and_articles/the_esoteric_meaning_lucifer.
5. Lucis Trust, "About World Goodwill," https://www.lucistrust.org/world_goodwill/ about_wg; Jim Marrs, *The Illuminati* (Detroit, MI: Visible Ink Press, 2017), 319.
6. Lucis Trust, "Support of the United Nations," https://www.lucistrust.org/about_us/ support_un; Alice Bailey, *The Reappearance of the Christ* (New York: Lucis Trust, 1947), https://www.lucistrust.org/store/item/the_reappearance_the_christ6; Philip H.

Lochhaas, *New Age Movement* (Saint Louis, MO: Concordia Publishing House, 1998), 16.

7. Bailey, *The Externalization of the Hierarchy,* (New York: Lucis Trust, 1957), https://www.lucistrust.org/online_books/the_externalisation_the_hierar chy_obook/section_four_stages_in_the_externalisation_the_hierarchy_part1/ the_return_the_christ_part4.

8. Marrs, *The Illuminati,* 287–309; Devra Newberger Speregen and Debra Mostow Zakarin, *Secret Societies: The Truth Revealed* (Plain City, OH: Media Source, 2013), 10; Carolyn Hamlett, telephone interview with Troy Anderson for *Trumpocalypse,* February 15, 2016.

9. J. R. Church, *Guardians of the Grail* (Oklahoma City, OK: Prophecy Publications, 1989), 169.

10. Thomas R. Horn, "The Mark of the Beast Is Here," NewsWithViews.com, December 7, 2013, http://www.newswithviews.com/Horn/thomas222.htm; Robert Carver, "Did Hitler's Obsession with the Occult Lose Him the War?" *The Spectator,* June 17, 2017, https://www.spectator.co.uk/2017/06/did-hitlers-obsession-with-the-occult -lose-him-the-war/#; Marrs, *The Illuminati,* 278.

11. Constance Cumbey, *The Hidden Dangers of the Rainbow: The New Age Movement and Our Coming Age of Barbarism* (Shreveport, LA: Huntingon House, Inc., 1983), 24–25, 54.

12. Cumbey, *The Hidden Dangers of the Rainbow,* 39.

13. Cumbey, "Yes, There Will Be Global Warming—but Not for the Reasons Many Think," My Perspective—What Constance Thinks, June 6, 2017, http://cumbey .blogspot.com; Cumbey, "Obama, Hillary, Al Gore, et al Firmly Intend to imple-ment Agenda 21—What It Really Was About," My Perspective—What Constance Thinks, October 15, 2016, http://cumbey.blogspot.com/2016/10.

14. Dennis L. Cuddy, "The Plan Proceeds on Schedule," NewsWithViews.com, December 14, 2015, http://www.newswithviews.com/Cuddy/dennis322.htm.

15. *Encyclopaedia Britannica,* s.v., "United Nations," https://www.britannica.com/ topic/United-Nations.

16. Paul McGuire, "Born Again Babylon: U.N. Plan to Bring in Luciferian Global State," NewsWithViews.com, September 21, 2015, http://www.newswithviews .com/McGuire/paul268.htm; Alex Newman, "UN, Obama, and Gates Are Global-izing Education via Common Core," *The New American,* March 26, 2014, https:// www.thenewamerican.com/culture/education/item/17925-un-obama-and-gates -are-globalizing-education-via-common-core; Lucis Trust, "About Alice Bailey," https://www.lucistrust.org/books/about_alice_a_bailey; Lucis Trust, "The Tibetan Master's Work," https://www.lucistrust.org/arcane_school/introduction/the_tibetan _master_work1; Cumbey, *The Hidden Dangers of the Rainbow,* 193–194.

17. Bill Schnoebelen, telephone interview with Troy Anderson for *Trumpocalypse,* November 11, 2016.

18. Cumbey, *The Hidden Dangers of the Rainbow,* 17, 193–194.

19. Lochhaas, *New Age Movement,* 49.

20. Cumbey, *The Hidden Dangers of the Rainbow,* 49–50.

21. Carolyn Hamlett, telephone interview with Troy Anderson for *Trumpocalypse,* February 15, 2016; All News Pipeline, "Carolyn Hamlett Exposes the Illuminati

Shocking Plan to Kill Christians!" November 24, 2015, http://allnewspipeline
.com/Carolyn_Hamlett_Exposes_The_Illuminati.php.

22. Billy Crone, telephone interview with Troy Anderson for *Trumpocalypse,* March 7, 2017.
23. Alex Newman, "UN Goals for Humanity Target Children as 'Agents of Change,'"
The New American, September 7, 2015, https://www.thenewamerican.com/culture/
education/item/21532-un-goals-for-humanity-target-children-as-agents-of-change.
24. Hilary Weaver, "Oprah Should Reconsider Her Presidential Run, New Poll Shows,"
Vanity Fair, March 16, 2017, http://www.vanityfair.com/style/2017/03/oprah
-winfrey-presidential-poll.
25. Public Policy Polling, "Only 24% of Voters Support GOP Health Care Plan," March
14, 2017, http://www.publicpolicypolling.com/pdf/2017/PPP_Release_National
_31517.pdf.
26. William F. Jasper, *The United Nations Exposed* (Appleton, WI: John Birch Society,
2001), 145.
27. "WikiLeaks Goes After Hyper-Secret Euro-American Trade Pact," WikiLeaks,
August 11, 2015, https://wikileaks.org/WikiLeaks-goes-after-hyper-secret.html; Jeff
Sessions, "Sessions on TPP: 'My Fears Confirmed'; Shut Down Fast-Track Now,"
November 5, 2015, http://www.sessions.senate.gov/public/index.cfm/news-releases
?ID=711D14A5-8B65-4E4B-AAE1-7DCAA93EE60B; Jeff Sessions, "Sessions: Fast-
Track Guarantees Three Mammoth Global Pacts Encompassing up to 90% of
World GDP," June 17, 2015, http://www.sessions.senate.gov/public/index.cfm/news
-releases?ID=5D45FE75-3EEB-46B1-AF2E-CB2466162A0F; Deutsche Welle,
"Angela Merkel Welcomes US Offer to Resume TTIP Talks," June 27, 2017, http://
www.dw.com/en/angela-merkel-welcomes-us-offer-to-resume-ttip-talks/
a-39446579.
28. "WikiLeaks Goes After Hyper-Secret Euro-American Trade Pact."
29. Newman, "Chinese Tyrant Seeks Global Control After Obama Gave Up Internet," *The New American,* November 16, 2016, https://www.thenewamerican.com/
tech/computers/item/24648-chinese-tyrant-seeks-global-control-after-obama
-gave-up-internet; Judson Phillips, "Obama Gives Away the Internet and, with It,
Our Liberty," *Washington Times,* September 13, 2016, http://www.washingtontimes
.com/news/2016/sep/13/obama-gives-away-internet-and-it-our-liberty.
30. *Encyclopaedia Britannica,* s.v., "Bilderberg Conference," https://www.britannica
.com/event/Bilderberg-Conference; Bilderberg Meetings, "Bilderberg Meeting
2017," May 31, 2017, http://www.bilderbergmeetings.org/press-release.html.
31. Marrs, telephone interview with Troy Anderson for *The Babylon Code,* February
28, 2014.
32. Daniel Estulin, telephone interview with Troy Anderson for *The Babylon Code,*
May 27, 2014.
33. "Bilderberg Meeting 2017," Bilderberg Meetings, May 31, 2017, http://www
.bilderbergmeetings.org/press-release.html.
34. "Trust in Government," Gallup, http://www.gallup.com/poll/5392/trust-govern
ment.aspx; "The Leader's Report," the Government & Public Sector Practice,
January 2017.
35. J. D. Heyes, "Government Claims Americans Have 'No Reasonable Expectation of
Privacy' with Cell Phone Usage," Natural News, October 15, 2012.

36. Marrs, *The Illuminati,* 310–314; Antony Sutton, *America's Secret Establishment: An Introduction to the Order of Skull & Bones* (Walterville, OR: Trine Day, 2002), 5.

37. Sutton, *America's Secret Establishment,* 212–214; Buster Brown, "Skull & Bones: It's Not Just for White Dudes Anymore," *The Atlantic,* February 25, 2013, https://www.theatlantic.com/national/archive2013/02/skull-and-bones-its-not-just-for-white-dudes-anymore/273463.

38. M. J. Stephey, "A Brief History of the Skull & Bones Society," *Time,* February 23, 2009, http://content.time.com/time/nation/article/0,8599,1881172,00.html.

39. Marrs, *The Illuminati,* 310–314; Brown, "Skull & Bones."

40. Speregen and Zakarin, *Secret Societies,* 42–47.

41. Marrs, *The Illuminati,* 310–314; Paul McGuire, "Illuminati & New World Order: Star Trek, America, Syria, Russia and the Race to Armageddon," NewsWithViews.com, September 17, 2013, http://www.newswithviews.com/McGuire/paul186.htm; Sutton, *America's Secret Establishment.*

42. Tom Hayden, "When Bonesmen Fight," *Politic,* May 17, 2004, http://www.alternet.org/story/18726/when_bonesmen_fight.

43. Marrs, *The Illuminati,* 344–345.

44. Jim Marrs, *The Rise of the Fourth Reich* (New York: William Morrow, 2008), 4.

45. Marrs, *The Rise of the Fourth Reich,* 4–16.

46. North Atlantic Treaty Organization, "Relations with the European Union," June 23, 2017, http://www.nato.int/cps/in/natohq/topics_49217.htm.

47. Hal Lindsey, *The Late Great Planet Earth* (Grand Rapids, MI: Zondervan, 1970), 97.

48. Dave Boyer, "More Funds Expected to Flow to NATO After Trump's Blunt Rebuke to Allied Leaders," *Washington Times,* May 25, 2017, http://www.washingtontimes.com/news/2017/may/25/donald-trump-blasts-nato-leaders-anti-terror-immig; Glenn Kessler, "Trump's Claim that the U.S. Pays the 'Lion's Share' for NATO," *Washington Post,* March 30, 2016, https://www.washingtonpost.com/news/fact-checker/wp/2016/03/30/trumps-claim-that-the-u-s-pays-the-lions-share-for-nato/?utm_term=.ca8b4d72ae6d; Brett D. Schaefer, "America, We Pay Way Too Much for the United Nations," Fox News, June 16, 2015, http://www.foxnews.com/opinion/2015/06/16/america-pay-way-too-much-for-united-nations.html.

49. Edwin Vieira, Jr., "A Monetary Litmus Test for Mr. Trump," NewsWithViews.com, January 10, 2017, http://www.newswithviews.com/Vieira/edwin296.htm.

50. Crone, telephone interview with Troy Anderson for *Trumpocalypse,* March 7, 2017.

51. Marrs, *The Illuminati,* 292–298; Speregen and Zakarin, *Secret Societies,* 37; "Svali," Project Camelot, http://projectcamelot.org/svali.html.

52. David Nova, "Uncovering The Trump-Freemason Connection," Deus Nexus, February 1, 2017, https://deusnexus.wordpress.com/2017/02/01/trump-freemason-connection; Walter Benjamin, "Election Mirrors War between Masonic Factions," HenryMakow.com, October 30, 2016, https://www.henrymakow.com/2016/10/election-mirrors-war.html.

53. Scottish Rite of Freemasonry, "Temple Architects Hall of Honor," https://scottishrite.org/headquarters/virtual-tour/temple-architects-hall-of-honor; Michael Kranish and Marc Fisher, *Trump Revealed* (London: Simon & Schuster, 2016), 81; Gwenda Blair, "How Norman Vincent Peale Taught Donald Trump to Worship Himself,"

Politico, October 6, 2015, http://www.politico.com/magazine/story/2015/10/donald-trump-2016-norman-vincent-peale-213220.

54. Marrs, *The Illuminati,* 182.

55. Schnoebelen, telephone interview with Troy Anderson for *Trumpocalypse,* November 11, 2016.

56. Paul Joseph Watson, "Gingrich: Establishment Scared of Trump Because He 'Didn't Belong to the Secret Society,'" InfoWars.com, March 4, 2016, https://www.infowars.com/gingrich-establishment-scared-of-trump-because-he-didnt-belong-to-secret-society; *Encyclopaedia Britannica,* s.v., "The Bohemian Club," https://www.britannica.com/topic/The-Bohemian-Club.

Chapter Nine: The Economic Reset

1. "An Insight, An Idea with Christine Lagarde," Bloomberg, January 31, 2014, https://www.bloomberg.com/news/videos/b/85e29297-56a2-45a9-b825-b924b861067a.

2. Nathan Meyer Rothschild, "Who controls the issuance of money controls the government!" Brainy Quotes, https://www.brainyquote.com/quotes/quotes/n/nathanmeye502389.html.

3. "An Insight, An Idea with Christine Lagarde."

4. Christine Lagarde, "National Press Club Luncheon with Christine Lagarde," National Press Club, January 15, 2014, https://www.imf.org/external/np/tr/2014/tr011514.pdf.

5. Jake Arnott, "Aleister Crowley's Lives," *Telegraph,* May 30, 2009, http://www.telegraph.co.uk/culture/books/5407318/Aleister-Crowleys-lives.html.

6. Tony Koretz, "Donald Trump, the Presidency and Christine Lagarde's Occult IMF Speech," a Minute to Midnite, November 2016, https://aminutetomidnite.com/nwo-news/donald-trump-the-presidency-and-christine-lagardes-occult-imf-speech.

7. Alex Spence, "Agnellis, Rothschilds Close in on Economist," *Economist,* August 11, 2015, http://www.politico.eu/article/agnellis-rothschilds-close-in-on-economist-magazine-sale-pearson.

8. Jim Marrs, *The Illuminati* (Detroit, MI: Visible Ink Press, 2017), 200; Robert Hieronimus with Laura Cortner, *Founding Fathers, Secret Societies: Freemasons, Illuminati, Rosicrucians, and Decoding of the Great Seal* (Rochester, VT: Destiny Books, 1989, 2006), 103–116.

9. Reddit.com, "1988 Economist Cover Predicting a World Currency by 2018," https://www.reddit.com/r/Bitcoin/comments/4nag4b/1988_economist_cover_predicting_a_world_currency.

10. Jim Marrs, *Our Occulted History: Do the Global Elite Conceal Ancient Aliens?* (New York: William Morrow, 2013), 213–214; *Encyclopaedia Britannica,* s.v., "Money," https://www.britannica.com/topic/money; *Encyclopaedia Britannica,* s.v., "Banking," https://www.britannica.com/topic/bank#ref383544.

11. David A. Patten, "The Crusade to Make America a Cashless Society," *Newsmax,* April 2017.

12. "Art Swift and Steve Ander," Gallup, July 15, 2016, http://www.gallup.com/poll/193706/americans-foresee-death-cash-lifetime.aspx.

13. Larry White, telephone interview with Troy Anderson for *Trumpocalypse*, April 19, 2017.

14. John Morgan, "Harvard Economists to IMF: Global Government Debt Is the Worst in 200 Years," *Newsmax*, January 3, 2014, http://www.newsmax.com/t/finance/article/545071; Carmen M. Reinhart and Kenneth S. Rogoff, "Financial and Sovereign Debt Crises: Some Lessons Learned and Those Forgotten," International Monetary Fund, December 2013.

15. "Emerging Market Borrowing Spree Lifts Global Debt to Record $217 Trillion," Reuters, June 28, 2017.

16. Chuck Missler, telephone interview with Troy Anderson for "The End Is Really Near" in the September 2015 issue of *Charisma* magazine, June 24, 2015.

17. Jim Marrs, *Rule by Secrecy* (New York: Perennial, 2000), 64–78.

18. Michael Snyder, "Guess How Many Nations in the World Do Not Have a Central Bank?" *The Economic Collapse Blog*, June 8, 2015, http://theeconomiccollapseblog.com/archives/guess-how-many-nations-in-the-world-do-not-have-a-central-bank.

19. Jim Marrs, *The Trillion-Dollar Conspiracy: How the New World Order, Man-Made Diseases, and Zombie Banks Are Destroying America* (New York: Harper, 2010) 57–69; Federal Reserve History, "Federal Reserve Act Signed by President Wilson," https://www.federalreservehistory.org/essays/federal_reserve_act_signed; Charles A. Lindbergh Sr., "This [Federal Reserve Act] establishes the most gigantic trust on earth. When the President [Woodrow Wilson] signs this bill, the invisible government of the monetary power will be legalized . . . the worst legislative crime of the ages is perpetrated by this banking and currency bill," Goodreads.com, https://www.goodreads.com/quotes/161870-this-federal-reserve-act-establishes-the-most-gigantic-trust-on.

20. Craig Wilson, "Jim Rickards: Debt, the Death of Money and Gold," the Daily Reckoning, April 3, 2017, https://dailyreckoning.com/jim-rickards-debt-death-of-money-gold; James Rickards, "7 Things You Need to Know: 'New World Money' Goes Live Tomorrow," the Daily Reckoning, September 29, 2016, https://dailyreckoning.com/7-things-need-know-new-world-money-goes-live-tomorrow; Ralph Benko, "James Rickards, 'Dr. Tail Risk,' Takes Us on a Tour of 'the Road to Ruin,'" *Forbes*, March 30, 2017, https://www.forbes.com/sites/ralphbenko/2017/03/30/james-rickards-dr-tail-risk-takes-us-on-a-tour-of-the-road-to-ruin/#7d145c5a3510.

21. Peter Schiff, telephone interview with Troy Anderson for "The End Is Really Near" in the September 2015 issue of *Charisma* magazine, June 12, 2015.

22. Preston Pysh, "An Interview with Jim Rogers—Of Course We Are in a Stock Market Bubble," *Forbes*, June 21, 2017, https://www.forbes.com/sites/prestonpysh/2017/06/21/an-interview-with-jim-rogers-of-course-we-are-in-a-stock-market-bubble/#635f00166394; Kara Chin and Jacqui Frank, "Jim Rogers: The Worst Crash in Our Lifetime Is Coming," Business Insider, June 9, 2017, http://www.businessinsider.com/jim-rogers-worst-crash-lifetime-coming-2017-6.

23. Michael Snyder, "The Federal Reserve Must Go," *The Economic Collapse Blog*, May 14, 2017, http://theeconomiccollapseblog.com/archives/the-federal-reserve-must-go.

24. Danielle DiMartino Booth, *Fed Up: An Insider's Take on Why the Federal Reserve Is Bad for America* (New York: Portfolio Penguin, 2017), 1–10.

25. Todd M. Johnson, "The Case for Higher Numbers of Christian Martyrs," Gordon-Conwell Theological Seminary, http://www.gordonconwell.edu/resources/documents/csgc_Christian_martyrs.pdf.
26. William F. Jasper, "Insider: EU-U.S. Must Take More Refugees, Get Rid of Sovereignty," *New American*, October 10, 2015, https://www.thenewamerican.com/world-news/item/21730-insider-eu-u-s-must-take-more-refugees-get-rid-of-sovereignty; Rowan Scarborough, "Hillary Clinton Embraces George Soros' 'Radical' Vision of Open-Border World," *Washington Times*, October 20, 2016, http://www.washington times.com/news/2016/oct/20/hillary-clinton-embraces-george-soros-radical-vis.
27. Tim LaHaye, e-mail interview with Troy Anderson for "The End Is Really Near" in the September 2015 issue of *Charisma* magazine, May 27, 2015.
28. Associated Press, "Would You Let Your Employer Implant an ID chip in Your Arm? 150 Employees at Swedish Startup Get Microchipped," *Daily Mail*, April 3, 2017, http://www.dailymail.co.uk/sciencetech/article-4375730/Cyborgs-work-employees-getting-implanted-microchips.html#ixzz4mSCi9QyV.
29. Emma Reynolds, "Australians Embracing Super-Human Microchip Technology," News.com.au, August 15, 2016, http://www.news.com.au/technology/gadgets/wearables/australians-embracing-superhuman-microchip-technology/news-story/536a08003cb07cba23336f83278a5003; Jade Scipioni, "Wisconsin Company to Implant Microchips in Its Employees in August," Fox Business, July 24, 2017, http://www.foxbusiness.com/features/2017/07/24/wisconsin-company-to-implant-microchips-in-its-employees-in-august.html.
30. Mark Ellis, "Mark of the Beast May Be Here: Elon Musk's Brain Computers to Prevent 'Summoning Demons,'" Charisma News, February 16, 2017, http://www.charismanews.com/world/63092-mark-of-the-beast-may-be-here-elon-musk-s-brain-computers-to-prevent-summoning-demons.
31. "Transhumanism Just Another 'Religion' in Which Man Seeks to Become God," World Net Daily, July 1, 2017, http://www.wnd.com/2017/07/tranhumanism-just-another-religion-in-which-man-seeks-to-become-god/#Z0BvMdMDmMXhfpyD.99; Jillian Eugenios, "Ray Kurzweil: Humans Will Be Hybrids by 2030," CNN Tech, June 4, 2015, http://money.cnn.com/2015/06/03/technology/ray-kurzweil-predictions.
32. Marg Prigg, "US Military Reveals $65m Funding for 'Matrix' Projects to Plug Human Brains Directly into a Computer," *Daily Mail*, July 10, 2017, http://www.dailymail.co.uk/sciencetech/article-4683264/US-military-reveals-funding-Matrix-projects.html.
33. Carole Smith, "Intrusive Brain Reading Surveillance Technology: Hacking the Mind," Global Research Center for Research on Globalization, December 13, 2007, http://www.globalresearch.ca/intrusive-brain-reading-surveillance-technology-hacking-the-mind/7606; Keith Veronese, "The Scientist Who Controlled People with Brain Implants," Io9 (Gizmodo), December 28, 2011, http://io9.gizmodo.com/5871598/the-scientist-who-controlled-peoples-minds-with-fm-radio-frequencies.
34. Paul McGuire, "All Americans to Receive Microchip Soon," News with Views, July 12, 2012, http://www.newswithviews.com/McGuire/paul136.htm.
35. Paul Joseph Watson, "Google Exec Behind Ingestible ID Chips to Attend Bilderberg 2015," InfoWars, June 8, 2015, https://www.infowars.com/google-exec-behind-ingestible-id-chips-to-attend-bilderberg-2015.

36. Matt Kessler, "The Logo That Took Down a DARPA Surveillance Project," *Atlantic*, December 22, 2015, https://www.theatlantic.com/technology/archive/2015/12/darpa-logos-information-awareness-office/421635.

37. Marrs, *The Illuminati*, 174–175.

Chapter Ten: King Cyrus and the Third Temple

1. Donald J. Trump, "Remarks by President Trump at the Israel Museum," White House, May 23, 2017, https://www.whitehouse.gov/the-press-office/2017/05/23/remarks-president-trump-israel-museum.

2. Adam Eliyahu Berkowitz, "Sanhedrin Asks Putin and Trump to Build Third Temple in Jerusalem," Breaking Israel News, November 10, 2016, https://www.break ingisraelnews.com/78372/bin-exclusive-sanhedrin-asks-putin-trump-build-third -temple-jerusalem.

3. Bob Cornuke, "Temple," Bible Archaeology, Research and Exploration Institute, http://www.baseinstitute.org/pages/temple/22.

4. Bob Cornuke, telephone interview with Troy Anderson for *Trumpocalypse*, June 2, 2017.

5. Henry H. Haley, *Halley's Bible Handbook* (Grand Rapids, MI: Zondervan, 2000, 2007), 58.

6. *Encyclopaedia Britannica*, s.v., "Temple of Jerusalem," https://www.britannica .com/topic/Temple-of-Jerusalem; Haley, *Halley's Bible Handbook*, 60–61.

7. Norman H. Andersson, telephone interview with Troy Anderson for *Trumpocalypse*, June 7, 2017.

8. Robert Knight, "Was the Temple Mount Not the Site of Solomon's Temple?" Townhall, July 31, 2014, https://townhall.com/columnists/robertknight/2014/07/31/was-the-temple-mount-not-the-site-of-solomons-temple-n1872583.

9. Cornuke, "Temple"; Haley, *Halley's Bible Handbook*, 58.

10. Cornuke, "Temple."

11. Haley, *Halley's Bible Handbook*, 937–954.

12. Leo Hohmann, "Prayers to God in Wrong Spot?" World Net Daily, February 22, 2015, http://www.wnd.com/2015/02/are-jews-praying-in-wrong-spot.

13. Joshua Wander, "Massive Infrastructure to Transport Millions of Pilgrims to Third Temple Underway," Breaking Israel News, June 27, 2017, https://www .breakingisraelnews.com/90393/infrastructure-bring-millions-pilgrims-temple -mount-quietly-constructed/#BBsierLjKiWoJ1dI.97; Chris Mitchell, "'The Temple Mount Is in Our Hands!' Hope Reborn for the Third Temple," CBN News, May 30, 2017, http://www1.cbn.com/cbnnews/israel/2017/may/six-day-war-victory -rekindled-hope-for-the-third-temple.

14. Jake Wallis Simons, "The Rabbi, the Lost Ark and the Future of Temple Mount," *Telegraph*, September 12, 2013, http://www.telegraph.co.uk/news/world news/10287615/The-rabbi-the-lost-ark-and-the-future-of-Temple-Mount.html.

15. Mike Mitchell, *Holman Illustrated Bible Dictionary* (Nashville, TN: Holman Bible Publishers, 2003), 377–378.

16. Flavius Josephus, *The Antiquities of the Jews*, Book 11, Chapter 1, http://www.ccel .org/j/josephus/works/ant-11.htm.

17. Josephus, *The Antiquities of the Jews*, Book 11, Chapter 1.

18. Jona Lendering, "Messianism, Roots 4: Josiah and Cyrus," Livius.org, http://www .livius.org/articles/religion/messiah/messiah-roots-4-josiah-and-cyrus.

19. Benjamin Glatt, "Is Trump a False Cyrus?" *Jerusalem Post*, May 20, 2017, http:// www.jpost.com/Christian-News/Comment-Is-Trump-a-false-Cyrus-492307.

20. Lachlan Markay, "Defense Department Classifies Catholics, Evangelicals as Extremists," *Washington Times*, April 5, 2013, http://www.washingtontimes.com/ news/2013/apr/5/dod-presentation-classifies-catholics-evangelicals; Shawn Thew, "Donald Trump and the FEMA Camps Crowd," *Newsweek*, August 19, 2016, http://www.newsweek.com/donald-trump-fema-camps-crowd-491841.

21. Paul Revoir, "John and Yoko Were Saved from Heroin Addiction by Greedy Drug Dealer," *Daily Mail*, June 11, 2007, http://www.dailymail.co.uk/news/ article-461071/John-Yoko-saved-heroin-addiction-greedy-drug-dealer .html#ixzz4nPbWOYtH.

22. Steve Turner, "John Lennon's Born-Again Phase," *Christianity Today*, January 3, 2007, http://www.christianitytoday.com/ct/2007/januaryweb-only/001-22.0.html ?start=1; Tony Rennell, "Was John Lennon's Murderer Mark Chapman a CIA Hitman? Thirty Years On, There's an Extraordinary New Theory," *Daily Mail*, December 3, 2010, http://www.dailymail.co.uk/news/article-1335479/Was-John -Lennons-murderer-Mark-Chapman-CIA-hitman-Thirty-years-theres -extraordinary-new-theory.html#ixzz4nQCl6KBh; Dominic Sandbrook, "A Cruel, Greedy, Selfish Monster: A Peace-Loving Visionary? No, Argues a Blistering Book. John Lennon Was a Nasty Piece of Work Who Epitomised Our Age of Self-Obsession," *Daily Mail*, October 2, 2015, http://www.dailymail.co.uk/news/article -3258235/A-cruel-greedy-selfish-monster-peace-loving-visionary-No-argues -blistering-book-John-Lennon-nasty-piece-work-epitomised-age-self -obsession.html#ixzz4nQIowi; "John Lennon Net Worth," Celebrity Net Worth, https://www.celebritynetworth.com/richest-celebrities/rock-stars/john-lennon-net -worth.

23. Todd Van Luling, "5 Beatles Fan Theories You'll Think Are So Crazy They Might Just Be True," *Huffington Post*, December 3, 2014, http://www.huffingtonpost .com/2014/12/03/the-beatles-fan-theories_n_6258074.html.

24. Jonathan Bernis, telephone interview with Troy Anderson for *Trumpocalypse*, February 3, 2017.

25. Lauretta Brown, "Pence: 'Day Will Come' When Trump Delivers on Promise to Move U.S. Embassy to Jerusalem," Townhall, July 18, 2017, https://town hall.com/tipsheet/laurettabrown/2017/07/18/pence-says-trump-will-deliver -on-promise-to-move-us-embassy-to-jerusalem-not-a-question-of-if-it-is-only -when-n2356561.

26. Brown, "Pence: 'Day Will Come' When Trump Delivers."

27. Sid Roth, telephone interview with Troy Anderson for *Trumpocalypse*, January 30, 2017.

28. David Martosko, "Trump Unloads on United Nations Members After Stunning Anti-Israel Vote As He Says 'They Cause Problems' and Are 'Not Living Up' to Potential," *Daily Mail*, December 28, 2016, http://www.dailymail.co.uk/news/ article-4071954/Trump-unloads-United-Nations-following-controversial-anti -Israel-vote-says-cause-problems-not-living-potential.html#ixzz4nV5eRF5P.

29. Michael Youssef, telephone interview with Troy Anderson for *Trumpocalypse*, January 24, 2017.
30. *Encyclopaedia Britannica*, s.v., "Asherah," https://www.britannica.com/topic/Asherah -Semitic-goddess.
31. "Bio-electromagnetic Weapons: The Ultimate Weapon," Global Research Center for Research on Globalization, May 29, 2007, http://www.globalresearch.ca/bio -electromagnetic-weapons-the-ultimate-weapon/5797; Derek Murdock, "Trump Haters Call for Presidential Assassination," *National Review*, March 25, 2017, http://www.nationalreview.com/article/446110/trump-assassination-threats -investigate-prosecute; Marrs, *The Illuminati*, 247; Michael Snyder, "Debt-Free United States Notes Were Once Issued Under JFK and the U.S. Government Still Has the Power to Issue Debt-Free Money," *The Economic Collapse Blog*, December 19, 2011, http://theeconomiccollapseblog.com/archives/debt-free-united-states-notes -were-once-issued-under-jfk-and-the-u-s-government-still-has-the-power-to-issue -debt-free-money.
32. Dean Henderson, "The Federal Reserve Cartel: Freemasons and the House of Rothschild," Global Research Center for Research on Globalization, June 8, 2011, http://www.globalresearch.ca/the-federal-reserve-cartel-freemasons-and-the -house-of-rothschild/25179; "John Wilkes Booth," Biography.com, https://www .biography.com/people/john-wilkes-booth-9219681; Marrs, *The Illuminati*, 246, 269.
33. Adam Eliyahu Berkowitz, "Sanhedrin Calls for Trump to Fulfill King Solomon's Mandate by Praying on Temple Mount," Breaking Israel News, May 15, 2017, https://www.breakingisraelnews.com/88117/sanhedrin-calls-trump-fulfill-king -solomons-mandate-praying-temple-mount/#txhrZCuHHkdywAyV.97.

Conclusion: Last Trump or Nineveh Moment?

1. Mike Pence, "Remarks by the Vice President to the Faith and Freedom Coalition," White House, June 10, 2017, https://www.whitehouse.gov/the-press-office/2017/ 06/10/remarks-vice-president-faith-and-freedom-coalition.
2. Billy Graham, e-mail interview with Troy Anderson for a seven-part World Net Daily series and www.tothesource.org story about the My Hope America with Billy Graham evangelistic outreach, August 20, 2013.
3. "Billy Graham Named on 'Most Admired' List for Six Decades," Billy Graham Evangelistic Association, December 28, 2016, https://billygraham.org/story/ billy-graham-named-on-most-admired-list-for-six-decades.
4. Billy Graham, "Billy Graham: 'My Heart Aches for America,'" Billy Graham Evangelistic Association, July 19, 2012, https://billygraham.org/story/billy-graham-my -heart-aches-for-america.
5. Billy Graham, e-mail interview with Troy Anderson for a seven-part World Net Daily series and www.tothesource.org story about the My Hope America with Billy Graham evangelistic outreach, August 20, 2013.
6. Anne Graham Lotz, telephone interview with Troy Anderson for *Trumpocalypse*, June 6, 2017.
7. "American Heritage of Fasting, Prayer and Humiliation," National Day of Repentance, http://ndor.wpengine.com/?page_id=826.

8. Kevin Jessip, telephone interview with Troy Anderson for *Trumpocalypse*, July 22, 2017.

9. Jim Garlow, telephone interview with Troy Anderson for *Trumpocalypse*, July 7, 2017.

10. Jonathan Bernis, telephone interview with Troy Anderson for *Trumpocalypse*, February 3, 2017.

11. Brandon Showwalter, "YWAM Founder: 'Spiritual Awakening' Is Coming; by 2033 Bible Will Be in Every Language," *Christian Post,* April 10, 2017, http://www .christianpost.com/news/ywam-founder-spiritual-awakening-is-coming-by-2033 -bible-will-be-in-every-language-179830.

12. Graham Lotz, telephone interview with Troy Anderson for *Trumpocalypse*, June 6, 2017.

13. Troy Anderson and Sandra Chambers, " 'Supernatural' Prophetic Voice Points Toward End-Time Revival," Charisma News, June 18, 2015, http://www.charismanews .com/world/50129-supernatural-prophetic-voice-points-toward-end-time-revival.

14. Sid Roth, telephone interview with Troy Anderson for *Trumpocalypse,* January 30, 2017.

15. Tim LaHaye, e-mail interview with Troy Anderson for "The End Is Really Near" in the September 2015 issue of *Charisma* magazine, May 27, 2015.

16. "The Future of World Religions: Population Growth Projections, 2010–2050," Pew Research Center on Religion & Public Life, April 2, 2015, http://www.pewforum .org/2015/04/02/religious-projections-2010-2050; Michael Lipka, "A Closer Look at America's Rapidly Growing Religious 'Nones,' " Pew Research Center, May 15, 2015, http://www.pewresearch.org/fact-tank/2015/05/13/a-closer-look-at -americas-rapidly-growing-religious-nones.

17. Tom Phillips, "China on Course to Become 'World's Most Christian Nation' Within 15 Years," *Telegraph*, April 19, 2014, http://www.telegraph.co.uk/news/ worldnews/asia/china/10776023/China-on-course-to-become-worlds-most -Christian-nation-within-15-years.html.

18. Thomas R. Horn, Donna Howell, and Larry Spargimino, *Final Fire: Is the Next Great Awakening Right Around the Corner?* (Crane, MO: Defender, 2016), 26.

19. Thomas R. Horn, "Tom Horn: The Final Fire," *Prophecy Watchers*, December 29, 2016, https://www.youtube.com/watch?v=ebmO9DlTKXY.

20. C. I. Scofield, *The New Scofield Reference Bible* (New York: Oxford University Press, 1967), 1351.

21. Bodie Hodge, "Was the Dispersion at Babel a Real Event," Answers in Genesis, August 19, 2010, https://answersingenesis.org/tower-of-babel/was-the-dispersion -at-babel-a-real-event.

22. Michael S. Hamilton, "The Dissatisfaction of Francis Schaeffer," *Christianity Today*, March 3, 1997, http://www.christianitytoday.com/ct/1997/march3/7t322a .html?order=&start=1.

23. Francis A. Schaeffer, address delivered in 1982 at the Coral Ridge Presbyterian Church in Fort Lauderdale, Florida, http://www.peopleforlife.org/francis.html.

24. "The Jesus Revolution," *Time*, June 21, 1971, http://content.time.com/time/ covers/0,16641,19710621,00.html.

About the Authors

Paul McGuire is an internationally recognized prophecy expert; Fox News, History Channel, and Discovery Channel commentator; and host of GOD TV's *Apocalypse and the End Times*. He's the bestselling author of *The Babylon Code* (FaithWords/Hachette Book Group), *A Prophecy of the Future of America: 2016–17*, and *The Day the Dollar Died*, and has written extensively about Bible prophecy. He's a professor of eschatology at Dr. Jack Hayford's The King's University and a Hollywood filmmaker. He appeared on two of the History Channel's highest-rated specials, *7 Signs of the Apocalypse* and *Countdown to Apocalypse: Four Horsemen*.

For a decade, McGuire was the nationally syndicated radio talk show host of the *Paul McGuire Show*, which aired out of Los Angeles for three hours during driving time Monday through Friday. On the program, he interviewed numerous world leaders, presidents, and prime ministers, including former president Jimmy Carter, U.S. senator John McCain, former White House press secretary Tony Snow, Israeli prime minister Ehud Olmert, Oliver North, Pastor Rick Warren, Joel Rosenberg, Dr. Tim LaHaye, Dr. James Dobson, and Ann Coulter. He also interviewed secretaries of state, generals, and high-ranking members of the Pentagon and Palestine Liberation Organization, along with Israeli Defense Forces generals. He's debated many of the nation's leading economists on *Fox News*. The late Israeli general Shimon Erem said, "Paul McGuire is a Watchman on the Walls of Jerusalem, one of the best." Each year,

McGuire speaks to tens of thousands of people at Bible prophecy conferences.

McGuire grew up in New York City. A former atheist and countercultural radical, he demonstrated with activist Abbie Hoffman, was made an honorary member of the Black Panther Party, and was recruited by the Weather Underground. He studied film and Altered States of Consciousness at the University of Missouri. He lives in the Los Angeles area.

www.paulmcguire.us

https://www.facebook.com/pages/Paul-McGuire/143707940365

https://www.facebook.com/paul.mcguire.7798?fref=ts

https://twitter.com/radiomcguire

Troy Anderson is a Pulitzer Prize–nominated investigative journalist, bestselling author, former executive editor of *Charisma* magazine and Charisma Media, speaker, and television and radio commentator. He spent two decades working as a reporter, bureau chief, and editorial writer at the *Los Angeles Daily News*, *The Press-Enterprise*, and other newspapers. He writes for *Reuters*, *The Huffington Post*, *Newsmax*, *Christianity Today*, *National Wildlife*, *Charisma*, *Human Events*, *Outreach*, and other media outlets. He's interviewed many prominent national figures, including Billy Graham, Franklin Graham, Anne Graham Lotz, Pastor Rick Warren, Dr. Tim LaHaye, Hal Lindsey, Noam Chomsky, David Horowitz, Patrick Buchanan, Dinesh D'Souza, Pastor Greg Laurie, Joel Rosenberg, Rabbi Jonathan Cahn, Sid Roth, Rabbi Jonathan Bernis, Pastor Mark Hitchcock, Nick Vujicic, Lee Strobel, Pat Boone, and Kirk Cameron.

During his career, Anderson has received numerous journalistic accolades: more than two dozen local, state, and national writing awards; 2011 and 2012 Eddie Awards (*Folio*: magazine's prestigious journalism awards); two 2015 Charlie Awards (Florida Magazine Association's top award); and a Pulitzer Prize nomination. He's a member of the American Society of Journalists and Authors, the nation's premier association of writers of nonfiction who have met ASJA's exacting standards of professional achievement. He's also a member of the Association of Ghostwriters and a graduate of the Act One screenwriting program.

Anderson graduated from the University of Oregon in 1991 with a bachelor's degree in news-editorial journalism and a minor in political science. He's coauthor of the bestseller *The Babylon Code* (FaithWords/Hachette Book Group), which is in development as a feature film/TV series, and *Trumpocalypse* (FaithWords/Hachette). He lives with his family in Irvine, California.

www.troyanderson.us

www.troyandersonwriter.com

https://www.mediabistro.com/freelance-marketplace-profiles/
    troyanderson

https://www.facebook.com/troy.anderson.16144

https://www.facebook.com/troyandersonwriter

https://twitter.com/TroyMAnderson

https://www.linkedin.com/in/troyandersonwriter

http://www.christianspeaker.net/speaker.php?mid=182